THE GREAT WAR AND THE BRITISH PEOPLE

J.M. Winter

MACMILLAN

First published 1986
Reprinted 1987

Published by
MACMILLAN EDUCATION LTD
Houndmills, Basingstoke, Hampshire RG21 2XS
and London
Companies and representatives
throughout the world

Printed in Hong Kong

British Library Cataloguing in Publication Data
Winter, J. M.
The Great War and the British people.
1. World War, 1914–1918—Social aspects—
Great Britain   2. Great Britain—Social
conditions—20th century
I. Title
941.083   HN385
ISBN 0–333–26582–3
ISBN 0–333–26583–1 Pbk

Contents

v

List of Tables and Figures

Tables

Appendix Tables

Figures

Acknowledgments

Over the years that this book has been written, many people have given freely of their time and advice. It would be impossible to list them all by name, but special thanks are due to Fritz Stern, who started it all. Let me also warmly acknowledge the help of the following friends and colleagues: Volker Berghahn, Michael Teitelbaum, Tony Wrigley, Bob Dare, Peter Simkins, Fiona Caldicott, Mary Bernard, Heather Glen, Howard Erskine-Hill, Avner Offer, and Naomi Eilan. I am particularly indebted to Noelle Whiteside, Antonia Ineson, and Bill Nasson, who acted as research associates on various aspects of this study. Literally hundreds of students in Jerusalem, Warwick and Cambridge have also helped unwittingly by casting doubts on many of the propositions advanced in this study; they have done more than they will ever know to make it a better book.

Grants from the Social Science Research Council, the Wellcome Trust, and the Ellen MacArthur Fund of the University of Cambridge helped to extend research and defray typing costs.

Permission to cite from unpublished sources has been granted by the following: from HM Crown Copyright, for manuscripts deposited in the Public Record Office, Kew; from the British Medical Association, for BMA records; from the British Library of Political and Economic Science, for a reference to the Dalton papers; and from the Imperial War Museum and David M. Griffiths, for citations from their manuscript collection. Permission to use material from previously published articles has been given by the editors of *Population Studies*, the *Economic History Review*, the *Journal of European Economic History*, and the *Journal of Contemporary History*.

Introduction

In the aftermath of the First World War, the Carnegie Endowment for International Peace commissioned hundreds of scholars and civil servants in all combatant countries to chronicle the social and economic history of the conflict. In the British case 31 volumes appeared which covered virtually every area of public life. The one part of the British story which remained untold was that of the effects of war on civilian health and population trends. Two books on the subject were begun, but apparently never completed.[1] In the 60 years which have elapsed since the Armistice, no attempt has been made to remedy this omission. This is all the more surprising, given the two impressive studies produced in the early 1930s on the subject of French and German population history during the war.[2] One of the aims of this book is to fill in this gap in our knowledge of the history of the Great War.

A social and demographic history of Britain during the 1914–18 war can also contribute to the more general historiography of the conflict in another way. It can help bridge two divides: the first is the separation of the history of the Home Front from the history of the Frontline; the second is the methodological divide between literary and quantitative approaches to the history of the war.

As to the first divide: the gap in experience between soldiers and civilians was, of course, fundamental, as many contemporaries stated at the time.[3] But there is no reason to perpetuate it in the way we write the history of the war. Although stimulating and provocative books have appeared in recent years on the subject of the impact of trench warfare on the men who fought, even the best of them leave civilian life largely in the shadows.[4] Similarly, accounts of industrial militancy or political developments after 1914 at times neglect even to mention that there was a war on or to give full weight to the fact that what happened on the Western Front was of paramount importance to the men and women whose

1

fathers, brothers, husbands, sons, and friends were in or near the line of fire.[5] At the same time we must steer clear of the absurdity of the view, announced in the calm and authoritative pages of the Census of England and Wales of 1921, that soldiers who died abroad would be treated as permanent émigrés, and therefore were no concern of Census enumerators.[6]

But perhaps most importantly for our purposes, such splitting of the war experience into Home-Front and Frontline compartments precludes treating one of the most intriguing contrasts between the civilian and military aspects of the conflict. For the war, with all the suffering it caused, was the occasion of a completely unanticipated improvement in the life expectancy of the civilian population. This paradox is the core of this book.

To approach the history of the war from the viewpoint of the social and demographic historian may also help to bridge the second, methodological, divide which separates much writing on the history of the period. The study of population inevitably involves quantification, which is an effective antidote to the vagueness of many impressionistic studies of the impact of war. In addition, using the quantitative procedures of demographic history permits us to enter into one of the most difficult, and yet most important, areas which confront the historian of war. Such methods provide a strict framework for asking counter-factual questions about what would have happened had there been no war. The use of counter-factual arguments in history is highly controversial. However, population historians who approach such counter-factual questions do not suffer from the maddening difficulties facing economic historians who engage in such exercises as constructing a counter-factual railway-free economy in order to estimate the contribution of railways to national income.[7] Fortunately demographic historians can construct realistic counter-factual models without entering such realms of historical fantasy, and they are therefore able to distinguish between the effects of war and the passage of time, a problem bedevilling all historians concerned with armed conflict in the past.[8] Why this is so will be discussed in chapter 3.

While this study explores ways of using quantitative evidence to unravel the problem of the impact of the war on British society, it is not exclusively a work in quantitative history. The reason for exploring sources that exist in both numerical and literary forms is a simple one. For any demographic historian of the war period, quantifying the effects of the world conflict is essential. But it is also misleading if it is the sole means of examining the effects of war. Firstly, since attitudes affect behaviour, fully examining the demographic aspects of the war means studying contemporary responses to war losses, attitudes to the age of marriage, the health of mothers and children, and so forth. The value of thus extending the domain of demography from the biological to the social is demonstrated by the most sophisticated and pioneering study in historical demography to appear in many years, Wrigley and Schofield's *Population History of England 1541–1871*, which ends with the recognition that some of the most important demographic issues are not quantitative at all, but involve questions of mentality, attitudes, and beliefs.[9] As I shall argue below in chapter 9, this point holds even more strongly in the study of war and its aftermath.

As it is only by entering the world of contemporary ideas and imagination that we can identify the social context in which statistical trends take on their full meaning, methods other than quantitative are needed to give the whole story. For this reason, the organization of this book does not follow the classic demographer's map tracing the route from birth rates to marriage rates, with alternative paths for migration, and finally to death rates. We shall deal with many of these questions in chapter 8, but they are the material out of which an interpretation of aspects of the impact of the war must be fashioned, and do not furnish explanations of their own. This is why this study of the social and demographic history of the Great War begins with a discussion of popular beliefs about social class, poverty, and military power in pre-war Britain and ends with an analysis of some literary reconstructions of the war experience.

If this book has succeeded in persuading readers to set aside the two futile distinctions between historians who know how to count and historians who know how to read, and between military history in one compartment and social-demographic history in another, then it has achieved part of its aim.

The argument of this study is implicit in its structure. It is that the social and demographic impact of the war was the product of two distinctive processes: (i) the unprecedented recruitment and attrition of British manpower in uniform, discussed in chapters 2 and 3; and (ii) the mobilization of a civilian war economy, the unintended and fortuitous benefits of which were the source of the disturbing paradox that the Great War was both an event of unparalleled carnage and suffering and the occasion of a significant improvement in the life expectancy of the civilian population, and especially of the worst-off sections of British society. Chapter 4 explores the evidence pointing to this unanticipated and important aspect of the history of the war. The possible causes of the decline in civilian mortality are examined in chapters 5–7. It is argued that neither an improvement in medical care (which did not take place) nor an extension of public health services (which, to a certain extent, did take place) were primarily responsible for the decline in mortality rates in wartime. The fundamental cause of this phenomenon was an improved standard of living, and in particular, improved standards of nutrition among the urban and rural working class. Here is the key to the striking contrast between the demographic gains of the civilian population and the demographic losses of the generation that went off to war.

This paradox is an important part of any history of British society in the period of the Great War. But as the discussion of the aftermath of war in chapters 8 and 9 suggests, the phenomenon of improvements in public health during the Great War was eclipsed (and inevitably so) by the shadow of the 'Lost Generation'. Since it was in literary form that much contemporary comment on war losses was expressed, we turn in conclusion to the fictional and poetic reconstruction of this side of the war. Our hope is to go beyond the statistical record of the war years to the memory of war which was probably its most lasting legacy.

It is necessary to emphasize strongly that the social and demographic impact of war must be separated from its causes or justification. Whatever the gains, nothing could compensate for the suffering of those who fought and of those whom the dead left behind. The evidence of demographic gains in wartime is an indictment of a society that tolerated conditions of deprivation in peacetime but that found the means to alter them in wartime. It also points to the social and economic benefits of a 'command economy' for the working population, and especially for the most vulnerable parts of it. But it is not and never can be an excuse for failing to remind generations born long after 1914 of the cruelty and carnage of the war.[10] Anyone who reads the evidence of the slaughter presented in chapter 3 can begin to see the outline of the faces behind the statistics, the profiles of the men we have come to call the 'Lost Generation'. It is their presence which continues to haunt this writer many years after this study was begun.

The story of their lives and the society for which they fought is intrinsically important to tell. But there is another level on which the experience of the war has been perceived by later generations. For the men who died in the Great War have come to represent not only a particular generation facing a particular war; they also stand as the first in a long line of casualties extending through the barbaric and bloody military conflicts which have occurred since 1918. In later years most soldiers certainly did not see themselves in this way, and we must guard against reading back into the 1914–18 war the tragedies that were to come. But in a sense, the Great War was the opening of an era, which, in time, may come to be called the second Thirty Years' War. Hardly anyone, even in his wildest nightmares, knew this at the time, but the mountains of corpses which were deposited at Verdun or on the Somme announced an even more terrible age. To return to its beginning is to begin to understand some disturbing truths about the world in which we live.

1. Strategic Demography: Population, Poverty, and Military Power in Pre-1914 Britain

IN Europe between 1870 and 1940 it was a common phenomenon for public figures to seek in the demographic sphere the causes of and antidotes to perceived shortcomings in political and military affairs. It should cause little surprise, therefore, that in the aftermath of the Boer War, in which a handful of South African settlers managed for a considerable period to keep the British army at bay, many concerned individuals responded to the military shortcomings of the campaign by calling for an enquiry not only into prevailing notions of command or logistics, but also into the health of the population.

Military incompetence precipitated in Edwardian Britain a surge of interest in what may be called 'strategic demography', or the investigation of the military and political implications of population movements. This was already a subject of heated discussion particularly in France but also elsewhere on the continent in the late nineteenth century. What the British debate shows is that the character of such exercises in strategic demography depended in large part on the organization of military service itself. In France, conscription helped concentrate attention on questions of quantity and the need to increase the birth rate to cope with the German threat. In pre-1914 Britain, a voluntary system of military enlistment gave precedence to questions of 'quality' and the need to improve the fitness of the strata within the working class from which recruits came forth. A brief discussion of French problems and perceptions may help to illuminate the distinctiveness of

6

British responses to the question of how their demographic development affected their military strength.

I THE FRENCH CONNECTION

German manpower was the spectre haunting all strategic-demographic discourse in France after the terrible defeat of 1870–1. In 1906, for example, approximately 1,200,000 men were called up for military service in Germany – over 500,000 at age 20 and 670,000 men who had been deferred in previous years. In contrast, the French, with a much smaller birth cohort in the late 1880s, could muster twenty years later only 368,000 recruits, of whom 318,000 were 20-year-olds, and 40,000 were previously deferred men. The Germans, having more than three times the number of men from whom to choose frontline soldiers, could actually afford to send home over 55 per cent of the men called up, on the grounds that their families needed them as wage-earners. Another 16 per cent went into the reserves. Of these, about half went to the *Ersatzreserv*, which consisted of men who could be useful in some capacity in the army. The other half went to the *Landsturm*, or Civil Guard. These men did have something seriously wrong with them physically, such as blindness in one eye, heart disease, partial deafness, or deformities. But, on the principle that anyone who could follow an active life as a civilian could also do so in uniform, they were not rejected outright, but placed in a class to be called up only if the nation were in danger. Only 3 per cent of all those conscripted were rejected on medical or moral (that is, criminal) grounds. After all this sifting, only 26 per cent of all recruits, or approximately 278,000 men, were conscripted into the regular German Army in that one year.[1]

It was entirely different for France. In order to match the German army in the field, the French had to take two-thirds of their conscripts directly into the regular army. Whereas the Germans placed men with disabilities in their reserve units, the French had to take them in for active service, and budgeted for an 8 per cent drop-out rate of men invalided soon after enlistment. The luxury of returning hundreds of thousands of recruits to their civilian jobs and families was simply out of the question. By separating men from their wives and by making it necessary for many marriages to be deferred, conscription actually increased the likelihood of a further decline in the birth rate, which was the source of the military problem in the first place.[2] The military meaning of population stagnation was, therefore, apparent to all but the most blinkered observers of continental affairs.

These statistics were the reality out of which grew the French fear of population decline in the years prior to the First World War. Given the fact that German and French crude death rates were roughly equivalent, but that the German birth rate was considerably higher than the French, it was natural that particular emphasis should have been placed on fertility rather than on mortality. Throughout the decades prior to the 1914–18 conflict cries of alarm emanated from many individuals and political groups who shared virtually nothing other than the belief that an increase in the birth rate was essential for national survival itself. We can savour some of the special flavour of French attitudes to the question in the popular literature of the day. This is particularly true in the case of the novelist Emile Zola. In the midst of the Dreyfus affair, in the later stages of which he played a prominent part, Zola fled to London and wrote there a long melodramatic novel entitled *Fécondité*. It was a baroque history of two families, each of which demonstrated the virtues of procreation and the vices of contraception. Hundreds of similar statements can be found among men of the French political right. But it is when we find men like Zola – Zola, the scourge of army corruption and injustice during the Dreyfus affair as well as the chronicler of the sufferings of the downtrodden and exploited – joining in the pro-natalist chorus, and doing so deliberately at a time of national crisis, that we can appreciate the extent to which demographic, political, and military concerns suffused French opinion prior to 1914.[3]

II THE BRITISH CONNECTION

There is nothing quite like *Fécondité* in English literature or journalism, because there has never been anything in Britain like the overwhelming consensus in France that the birth rate had to rise for the nation to retain its place in international affairs. While pro-natalist sentiment was widespread in Britain,[4] the absence of a system of military conscription, combined with a belief in the invincibility of the Royal Navy, gave precedence to a discussion not of the numbers of recruits, but of their physical 'quality'.

This provided the essential link between military questions and the state of the public health. Indeed, the poor physical condition of many men who presented themselves as recruits was taken as but one indication of the legacy of urban poverty in pre-war Britain. Deprivation took its toll from infancy onward, and, if left unremedied, was likely to weaken the nation for generations to come.

Contemporaries referred repeatedly to infant mortality rates (deaths before age 1 per 1,000 live births) as blunt indicators of the extent to which urban squalor shortened or stunted the lives of a substantial part of the British population. The contrasts between the survival chances of infants born to prosperous and to poor families were revealed each year in annual reports of registrars-general. For example, at the turn of the century, approximately 200 per 1,000 infants failed to survive the first year of life in the following English county boroughs: Birmingham, Blackburn, Bootle, Burnley, Dudley, Middlesbrough, Preston, Salford, Sheffield, Stockport, Wakefield, Wolverhampton, and York. The names read as if taken from a Baedeker guide to industrial England. In more prosperous areas the infant mortality rate was well below the national average. In the London metropolitan borough of Hampstead, for example, in 1910, 60 per 1,000 infants died in the first year of life; in England and Wales as a whole, the infant mortality rate was 105. Over the years 1910–12, children of unskilled workers were subject to an infant mortality rate twice that of children of professional men and women.[5] Indeed, no one doubted that a working-class child born in late-Victorian or Edwardian Britain had an uphill struggle for survival, much more hazardous than that faced by its middle-class or upper-class brethren. This was the demographic meaning of social inequality in pre-1914 Britain.

National statistics reflected working-class mortality experience more than that of the better-off simply because of the numerical preponderance of the labouring class, estimated to be roughly 80 per cent of the population in 1900.[6] To set the aggregate demographic position of Edwardian England and Wales in historical perspective, we may note that the reported infant mortality rate in

1911 was twice as high as that reported in Egypt in 1972 or of non-white South Africans in 1975. In the years 1910–12, life expectancy at birth for men in England and Wales was 51.5 years. This figure is slightly higher than that registered for Ecuadorian males in 1961–3, and about the same as that registered for Iraqi males in the more recent period 1970–5.[7] It is therefore not an exaggeration to suggest that in large parts of working-class Britain, though not amongst the middle class, there were before 1914 conditions of poverty and ill-health that today we associate with countries of the third world.

But as all concerned with public health realized, infant mortality statistics did not describe the extent to which poverty crippled as well as killed. For disturbing evidence of the lingering effects of a deprived childhood in late nineteenth and early twentieth century Britain, many doctors, politicians, soldiers, churchmen, and social commentators drew attention to military enlistment statistics. These seemed to provide the essential link between the realm of public health and the health of the realm.

The impact of this debate on British social policy in the Edwardian period has been analysed before.[8] What is perhaps less well known is the extent to which the furore over recruitment precipitated a reappraisal within the medical profession itself and among many others concerned with public health as to the nature of poverty and its medical and possible genetic implications. It is important to note the terms in which the pre-1914 discussion of these matters took place in order to appreciate the extent to which the problem of poverty was transformed by the war experience. For despite all the discussion of the subject in the pre-war period, contemporaries came to no consensus about what effective measures could be taken to relieve the plight of the urban poor – until the First World War did it for them.

A Degeneration: Hereditary or Environmental?

The two forums in which these questions were raised with substantial publicity were the hearings of the Royal Commission on Physical Training in Scotland, which sat between 29 April and 3 October 1902,[9] and the Interdepartmental Committee on Physical Deterioration, which sat between 3 December 1903 and 20 June 1904.[10]

The Scottish inquiry was held at the instigation of the Earl of Meath to explore ways to promote physical training in schools as an antidote to the physical deterioration of the race. The intriguing feature of this Royal Commission is the way it was hijacked, so to speak, by doctors who used it to show the futility of increasing physical exercise for an underfed population of schoolchildren. This surprising outcome was not uncontested, though; thus the hearings of this body display the full spectrum of eugenic and environmentalist opinion about the causes of 'physical deterioration'.

Before describing the debate, it is perhaps useful to dwell a moment on the highly charged concept of deterioration. No two commentators agreed on how to define it, let alone explain it. Most used 'deterioration' as a physical term, roughly the opposite of 'health', but some gave it moral connotations as well, such as laziness, stupidity, and indifference to familial responsibilities. Some measured deterioration relative to a norm of pre-industrial sturdiness. Others used it to describe the pathogenicity of the urban environment against which each new generation of slum dwellers struggled to survive; they found evidence of physical deterioration in the fact that infant mortality rates were higher in the 1890s than in the 1850s. Finally, many commentators used the term in an international context, to compare the decline in Britain's aggregate physical strength or belligerent potential relative to that of other imperial powers. None of these definitions of deterioration was clear or precise, but they all attested to a general unease among middle-class professionals about the future of a nation dominated numerically (if not politically) by the urban working class. This unease surfaced during the Boer War, as we have already noted, when high rejection rates of recruits became known. It also hung like a cloud over the deliberations of learned inquiries and meetings after the turn of the century.

In the hearings of the Scottish Commission on Physical Training, the hereditarian arguments for progressive degeneracy were advanced by a battery of medical witnesses. It is important at the outset to note the limited nature of this hereditarian position, which was rarely free of environmentalist overtones. Most of the men and women who believed that stunted parents produced stunted children still upheld the virtues of discipline and exercise, in the hope that worse dissipation could be avoided thereby. A true hereditarian would have had none of the view that stunted populations could be improved by exercise or any other means. But what these quasi-hereditarians refused to accept was the primary importance of better wages, food and housing in any effort to reverse the supposed deterioration of the physical stock of the nation.

What these views really reflect is a wider anti-industrial bias among many conservative thinkers of the period, both within and outside the ranks of the medical profession. Such people glorified the strengths of a bucolic past, in which work was outdoors, strenuous, and free in childhood of the tedium and sedentary drudgery of compulsory education. Consider these opinions brought before the 1903 Royal Commission. Sir Lauder Brunton, a distinguished heart specialist and physician to St Bartholomew's Hospital, was a firm believer in the hereditary character of deterioration, which he attributed to urbanization and the limitations which education imposed on physical exercise for young people.[11] John Cantlie, surgeon and lecturer in anatomy at Charing Cross Hospital, presented the case he had been building up for over two decades on the subject of urban degeneration, which had reduced previously healthy rural immigrants to propagators of disease and decay.[12] Supporting him was Francis Warner, physician to the London Hospital, who reported a progressive decline in the circumference of children's heads, caused, he believed, by the congestion of urban building.[13] Dr Thomas Savill, founder of the British College of Physical Education, was similarly convinced of the reality of degeneration. He cited the 'fact' that the Boer War had been 'lost' in part because South African snipers had had better vision than the British common soldier.[14]

These were the views the Royal Commission had expected to hear; but these quasi-hereditarian voices were virtually drowned by a chorus of medical environmentalists, who effectively won over the inquiry to their position. The basis of their case was a study of the health and physical condition of schoolchildren in eight Scottish schools, four in Edinburgh and four in Aberdeen. The authors of the report, to which we shall return below, were two physicians prominent in the field of public health, W. Leslie Mackenzie and Matthew Hay. Mackenzie took the lead in the hearings by introducing the concept of 'generational degeneracy'. The medical member of the Royal Commission, Professor Ogsden of Aberdeen, asked Mackenzie to elaborate, since 'our information hitherto has been that degeneration is a process, that entering into a race, lasts, and is handed down to future generations'. Not so, claimed Mackenzie, who argued that degeneration would disappear if conditions of life were substantially improved for slum dwellers and their children.[15] He went even further, to the apparent dismay of some members of the Royal Commission, by dismissing physical drill in schools as either trivial or dangerous in its effect on the undernourished. It was, in his view, also inimical to the cultivation of independence of mind and civilized behaviour among children. After all, he reminded the inquiry, many Christian saints like St Francis of Assisi were not conspicuously hearty chaps; so much for muscular Christianity.[16]

The effect of Mackenzie's testimony was remarkable. Even after Sir William Turner, Professor of Anatomy in the University of Edinburgh and President of the General Medical Council, tried to show that deterioration could be transmitted if it affected the development of 'bodily function',[17] the Commission took the point that the state had to ensure one way or another that children were adequately fed before any system of physical training could have a chance to take effect.

The role played by Mackenzie in the Royal Commission on Physical Training in Scotland was played by a young doctor, Alfred Eichholz, when the Interdepartmental Committee on Physical Deterioration met the following year to investigate English, Welsh, and Irish conditions. Again, before the environmentalists' case was established, the same or similar anti-urban and hereditarian voices were raised. Sir Lauder Brunton, who had been instrumental in the campaign to create the English inquiry, thought working-class children spent too much time in schools.[18] Sir Charles Cameron, Medical Officer of Health to Dublin, trotted out the usual arguments about the hereditary effects of urban conditions,[19] and Dr Arthur Shadwell pointed out that medical improvements were inevitably reversing the tendency for death to eliminate the unfit before they could breed.[20]

But none of the opinions of these and other witnesses[21] had the force of the testimony of Eichholz, then a London medical inspector of schools. He brought before the committee vivid evidence of the effects of malnutrition on children at school just across the Thames from Westminster. A visit by committee members to the

Johanna Street Board School in Lambeth had revealed the startling fact that about 90 per cent of the children were in a physical
condition bad enough to interfere with their ability to pursue their
studies.[22] His case for the medical inspection of the nation's
schoolchildren followed directly and forcefully from this one con-
crete example.

Eichholz had another objective in his testimony. It was to rebut
the hereditarians by arguing his belief that the vast majority of
babies were born perfectly healthy even in the poorest districts.
The clear implication was that post-natal deprivation or neglect,
and not heredity, was at the heart of the problem of physical
deterioration.[23] Edward Malins, Professor of Midwifery in Birmingham University, seconded this opinion.[24] It was also supported by D. J. Cunningham, Professor of Anatomy at Edinburgh,
chairman of the Anthropometric Committee of the British Association, and the author of a textbook of anatomy which was to
become the bible of generations of medical students. To Cunningham, there was 'a mean standard of national physique which is the
inheritance of the people as a whole'; consequently, 'inferior
characteristics resulting from poverty and acquired during the
lifetime of an individual are not hereditary', but evanescent, if the
conditions of life are improved.[25]

This defence of the inherent strengths of the British race was
attractive to complacent patriot and zealous reformer alike. It
effectively maintained that each generation started anew, whatever the material shortcomings of the previous generation. But to
Mackenzie, this view was unsound as science; it did not account
for the implications of poor health and physique of mothers for the
survival chances of their children. Here again we see that some
environmentalist positions had room in them for an hereditarian
element. Mackenzie cited in support of his argument the Scottish
physician Noel Paton's experiments on guinea pigs to try to show,
as against Eichholz, that the embryo did not have a prior claim to
nourishment vis-à-vis the mother, and that therefore 'the better
the nutrition of the maternal tissues, the greater is the growth of
the young in *utero*'.[26] Conversely, maternal deprivation or indeed
female malnutrition from early childhood could in later years
seriously distort foetal growth patterns. Therefore, malnutrition
had to be combated both before and after a child was born.

This issue is still a controversial one among medical nutritionists, and shows the complexities of a purely environmentalist position. Some studies have shown that the foetus does have first claim on calcium in the mother's food intake, but it is still too early to say with complete confidence whether the mother or child has prior claim on other nutrients. It is not surprising, though, that the interdepartmental committee adopted in its official report the more comforting view of Eichholz and Cunningham on the likely immediate benefits of reform.[27]

B Deterioration and the Alien

There were two other subjects related to the 'quality' of the race which were raised repeatedly in the work of these two inquiries. The first was the troubling case of the Jews. The second was the even more disturbing problem of the unskilled working class, the 'residuum' of the labour market, whose peculiarities were scrutinized by many observers in this period.

The search for physical deterioration unintentionally brought about a direct collision between philo-semitism and anti-semitism in the medical profession and elsewhere. At a time of widespread agitation over the perils of alien immigration, it was inevitable that a number of witnesses would make lugubrious noises about the influx of Eastern European Jews to Britain. Mr Gray of the British Association's Anthropometric Committee said that Britain should learn the lesson of Poland which, prior to the mass entry of Jews, was (at some unspecified date) the tallest nation in Europe. Now, he said, the Poles were on average the shortest.[28] And this was not all; since Jews 'have been shown to be an exceedingly degenerate type in Europe', and since 'there is a high percentage of insanity among Jews, much higher than among the surrounding gentile races', the influx of Jews was bound to be a source of both physical and mental degeneration of an hereditary kind.[29] Dr Warner, chairman of the Childhood Society, warned the Scottish commission too that Jews had the highest percentage of 'defective' children in London.[30]

As soon as the subject of child care was raised, though, a series of witnesses had little trouble in dismissing the fantasies of such men. Time and again, medical officers of health or physicians testified as to the low rates of infant mortality among Jews and the sturdiness of Jewish schoolchildren, which they attributed to the high incidence of breast-feeding, the low incidence of female extra-domestic employment, and the non-existence of alcoholism and venereal disease in the Jewish community.[31] In fact, the Interdepartmental Committee's report accepted Jewish family life as an ideal towards which the rest of the nation had to aim if they really meant to improve the health of children.[32]

C   Deterioration and the Underclass

The second area of social analysis which preoccupied these inquiries was that of the nature of what in a European context would have been called a *lumpenproletariat*. The key problem was that unskilled labourers constituted the great majority of army recruits, whose physical and mental 'deficiencies' most witnesses traced back to early childhood deprivation. While the location of degeneracy primarily in one (admittedly ill-defined) social stratum enabled the committees to reject the worst fears of national deterioration, high fertility rates among the worst-off sections of the population seemed to bode ill for the nation's future. Here was an important element in the British discussion of the connections among fertility, mortality, and military power, expressed frequently in doubts as to the vitality of the 'Imperial Race'.

The assertion that the army (in contrast to the navy[33]) contained only the outcasts of British society was never seriously challenged in these inquiries. But one fundamental problem appeared which undercut attempts to use military recruitment statistics as a guide to the physical state of even one section of the working class, let alone that of the nation as a whole. The testimony of recruiting officers showed that the trade cycle changed the social composition of enlistment in such a way as to alter the mean physical characteristics of the cohort who presented themselves. When times were good, only the 'dregs' of society came forward. Their physical characteristics were, as many noted, appallingly substandard. But, when times were bad, the army got better men, who were unable to find work and a steady income in any other way.[34] Recruitment statistics, therefore, could paint a perverse picture of a spurious deterioration in the physique of the unskilled during prosperous times and an equally spurious improvement in times of depression.

For this reason, both committees shifted the angle of their inquiries away from the recruiting statistics to the causes of ill-health among the infants and children of the urban poor from whom the recruits were drawn. By doing so, they had to deal with the sociology of urban poverty – with, in other words, the fundamental distinction within working-class communities between the better-off 'respectable' strata, who did not on the whole tend to join the army, and the worse-off 'rough' strata, who did. Leslie Mackenzie's classic description of the terribly malnourished children of the North Canongate School in Edinburgh contrasted their physical condition with that of children in three other schools in the city.[35] What he showed was the existence within the urban population of an underclass, whose plight was no worse than that of their fathers, but who were relatively more deprived because they had not shared in the gains in real wages and life expectancy made over time by other sections of the population. While the nation as a whole registered improvements in survival chances, this underclass had continued until the early twentieth century on the treadmill of malnutrition, overcrowding, chronic disease, and early death.

The question of what ought to be done about this substratum of the working class was one that troubled many witnesses. Charles Booth, the author of *Life and Labour of the People of London*, pressed the case for emigration to labour colonies.[36] C. S. Loch of the Charity Organization Society expressed his admiration for the way the German police helped control their *lumpenproletariat*, and advocated a militia system for British boys.[37] According to Mr J. Struthers, assistant secretary to the Scottish Education Department, hooliganism was virtually non-existent in Germany because of better policing and universal conscription.[38] And the Scottish report on physical training was actually based on the assumption that military drill was a civilizing and rehabilitating force.

These opinions were voiced long before the Great War showed that better wages would reduce the extent to which this underclass disfigured or disturbed the body politic. We should not be surprised, therefore, that this possibility was raised by only two witnesses to these turn-of-the-century inquiries. The first was Seebohm Rowntree, author of *Poverty. A Study in Town Life*, in which he had popularized the distinction between primary (subsistence) and secondary (near subsistence) poverty. He suggested that the Interdepartmental Committee should seek the reasons for national deterioration in the fact that between 3 and 4 million people in Britain – fully 10 per cent of the population – could not afford to buy enough food to ensure a minimum level of physical efficiency.[39] Additional evidence along these lines was provided by H. J. Wilson, Inspector of Factories and Workshops in Newcastle-upon-Tyne, who pointed out that the substandard heights and weights of children of workers in the jute mills of Dundee were indicators of chronic malnutrition among the low-paid sector of the labouring population.[40]

Of course advocacy of better pay was not the concern of these committees, on which not a single working-class man or woman sat. Such a radical proposal – radical, that is, in terms of pre-war assumptions about the nature of and antidotes to poverty – would have served only to sink their hopes of rallying support for free school meals for the poor and school medical inspection for all, which were at least steps in the right direction.

No one pretended that such measures would solve the problem of the residuum. Indeed many doubted whether a real solution existed at all. Some hoped that the same decline in fertility which had reduced the birth rate among the more prosperous classes would eventually spread to the lowest orders as well. The fact that such was not yet the case was the source of many complaints at this time about the proliferation of the unfit. Sir John Gorst, MP for Cambridge University and champion of state provision for feeding needy schoolchildren, told the Interdepartmental Committee that he was 'impressed with the idea . . . that the race is propagated in greatest proportion by the least fit part of it'.[41] Sir Charles Cameron lent the weight of his Irish experience to the view that the 'dregs' were reproducing at a much greater rate than were the 'superior stocks'.[42] At a Cambridge meeting of the British Association, the purpose of which was to second the call for an anthropometric survey advanced in the Interdepartmental Committee's report, the Prime Minister, Arthur Balfour, added his voice to the eugenic cause. He pointed out that the most enterprising members of the working class who rose through education and effort started immediately to limit their family sizes in a way that their less successful peers avoided. In consequence, the residuum was growing more and more residual. He was led inevitably, he said, to the 'rather melancholy conclusion that everything done towards opening up careers to the lower classes did something towards the degeneration of the race'.[43] Thus rested the hereditarian case – until it was undermined by the experience of the 1914–18 war.

III CONCLUSION

A Strategic Demography before 1914

The fact that the language of class pervaded the discussion of British population issues should occasion as little surprise as the fact that the German threat underlay most French discussions of demography before 1914. But to offer a full account of these pre-war attitudes, it is necessary to try to separate illusion from reality. The politics of revenge were, after all, inevitable in France, as they would have been in any other country which had suffered a defeat as humiliating as that of 1870–1. In the late nineteenth century it was natural for Frenchmen to feel considerably less secure than their grandfathers a century before, when France was the most populous nation in Europe. But, as the 1914–18 war was to demonstrate with a terrible and bloody finality, it was not the weight of numbers alone that yielded victory, but rather the success of the Allies in distributing goods and services effectively as between military and civilian needs. Whatever the size of the German Army, it was the failure of the German war economy which lost Germany the Great War. The connection between demographic and military power was not so simple as many French (and not only French) pre-war observers thought it was, especially in an age of mechanized warfare.

In considering the pre-1914 flurry of interest in Britain in population questions, it is also essential to separate social fears from military realities. It was very tempting for some to see the failures of the Boer War as reflecting the deterioration of the British race, because it provided a way out of more unpalatable diagnoses. Demographic determinism in both France and Britain, as applied to military and strategic questions, was a useful way of simplifying (and oversimplifying) the world.

The commentators whose work we have been examining also provided a poor guide to the internal stresses embedded in Britain's social structure at the turn of the century. Their language and perceptions demonstrate the centrality of class awareness in pre-war Britain, but what no one was prepared to admit was that it was also one of the most stable nations in Europe. The underclass exposed in these quasi-medical reports did live in scandalous conditions, but this class neither wished to nor could upset the social order. Indeed, as enlistment records after August 1914 demonstrate, a strong sense of working-class identity and patriotism were complementary and not antagonistic sentiments in pre-war Britain; and to understand their compatibility is to begin to see why so many men whose lives were stunted and constrained by a system of class subordination chose in 1914–18 to fight in a cause that preserved and perpetuated it, albeit in a modified form (see chapter 2).

Furthermore, the repeated references in these reports to the persistence of high infant mortality rates as a general indicator of physical deterioration since the 1850s shows their misleading nature in another way. Like Malthus, the medical and social authorities who appeared before pre-war state inquiries on public health tried to account for a demographic regime which at that very time was changing in important respects. Just as Malthus posited the impossibility of a sustained rise in the secular growth rate of populations and a concurrent fall in the price of food – a relationship that was largely true for every earlier generation but not his own – so, a century later, these analysts of infant mortality missed what was too close for them to notice: that the major decline in infant mortality in Britain's demographic history had just begun. We should, therefore, see these debates not as a source of information about demographic events or military potential, but as a reflection of the ways social anxieties were expressed in demographic or biological form in the years before the First World War.

B   The Great War and Strategic Demography in Britain

As we shall see in the course of this book, many (but not all) of these middle-class assumptions about the poor were among the casualties of the Great War. It is true that in the interwar years, some eugenicists continued to conjure up the spectre of an underclass subverting by proliferation the nation's strengths and character. But the war experience tended to marginalize these voices in Britain.

This was for two main reasons. The first was that, after all, Britain had won the war. In 1918 it simply made no sense to dwell on the supposedly progressive and hereditary nature of physical deterioration in a population that had managed to play a central role in the defeat of one of the most remarkable military machines of modern times, the Imperial German Army. We have noted above that environmentalist and hereditarian views were never completely distinct before 1914. But the effective wartime mobilization of the nation's male population, which we shall discuss in chapter 2, sent the pendulum of social thought strongly in the environmentalist direction.

Secondly, almost all social observers were struck by the unintended effects of the war economy in levelling up the earnings of the poorest-paid sections of the working class (see chapter 7). By 1918, much of the residuum which had so exercised pre-war politicians, social administrators, and writers had simply ceased to exist. It is not that poverty disappeared, but rather that after 1914 poverty meant deprivation rather than destitution for the working class (and in particular for most unskilled men and their families) and this continued to be true despite the onset of mass unemployment in 1920. One consequence of the wartime decline in the proportion of society living on the margins of subsistence was, therefore, to transform the discussion of strategic demography in Britain.

We should not be surprised that as the nature of poverty changed, so did the language in which the association between social conditions and military power was expressed. Nevertheless, it is true that the war did give a new lease of life to another aspect of hereditarian opinion. If less attention was directed to the very poor, more was given to the dwindling of the numbers of the privileged classes, supposedly the bearers of innate qualities of leadership and creativity. The slaughter on the Western Front reinforced earlier fears, expressed by the 'father' of eugenics, Francis Galton, of the decline of genius in the modern world.[44] After the war, many observers expressed the view that, due to war losses, the European political and cultural world after 1918 was but a shadow of what it once was and what it might have been.[45] There is some truth in this claim, but like all ventures in strategic demography, it tends to neglect the weight of other forces impinging on political or cultural developments. This is not to say that the demographic element in military history or the military element in demographic history can be ignored; on the contrary. It is rather to suggest that the only way to measure the full impact of war is to examine rigorously the demographic realities underlying these perceptions. It is to the first of these realities – that of manpower – that we turn in chapter 2.

PART I THE DEMOGRAPHIC COSTS OF THE GREAT WAR

2. Manpower and Military Service, 1914–1918

THE central problem of organizing Britain's war effort in 1914–18 was how to distribute resources effectively as between civilian and military requirements. This was nowhere more obvious than in the case of manpower. Essentially there were four primary elements in Britain's manpower equation, each of which placed limits on the scale of her military effort. The first was a given fact: the age-structure of the population; the other three were subject to intervention and organization. These were: the propensity of men to come forward as recruits for the army between 1914 and 1916, and as conscripts thereafter; the necessity of balancing the increasing demands of Army Command for more men against the needs of home industry, and in particular, the needs of those sectors engaged in war-related production; and the physical fitness of the men who joined up. In this chapter we shall consider each of these determinants of military participation in wartime.

The main argument of this chapter is that in examining the three central questions about manpower – Who was prepared to enlist? Who could be spared from the labour force? Who was fit enough to fight? – we shall begin to understand why British forces were not a cross-section of British society. Rather, the higher up in the social scale a man was, the greater were the chances that he would serve from early in the war and be fit enough to be placed in a combat unit. While numerically, the British army was preponderantly working-class in character, nevertheless, proportionately, the highest enlistment rates among salaried workers were registered in the commercial and clerical sectors of the labour force. The implications of these aspects of recruitment for the social structure of British casualties will be examined in Chapter 3.

First, some preliminary remarks about available manpower on

the eve of the war. Despite a major wave of out-migration, particularly among young male workers, in the pre-war period, Britain in 1914 contained more men of fighting age than at any previous point in her history. Despite the slowdown in rates of population growth since the 1870s, she could still draw upon over 12 million men aged 15–49 in Great Britain and in Ireland. Of course, at the outbreak of the war, no one dreamed that more than a small fraction of this population would be called upon to serve, but as time wore on, the total began to look relatively small. It was supplemented throughout the conflict by non-British nationals who for a variety of reasons chose to enlist in British forces, but these never amounted to more than a small fraction of the total of men in uniform. The Irish were, as usual, a special case, and their participation in Britain's war effort, while substantial in the first two years of the war, diminished after the Easter uprising of 1916.

The men who served through the bitter battles of 1916 and 1917, though, were recruited in the early years of the conflict. They were drawn from all sections of British society, but not in the same proportions from all social groups. The surge of enlistment in the first months of the war and its fluctuations in 1915 are the subject of the first parts of this chapter.

I THE VOLUNTARY SYSTEM

It may be useful to provide a rough sketch of the organization of Britain's voluntary system of manpower planning in the first years of the war. Until 1916, the War Office and the Admiralty were responsible for the recruitment and processing of volunteers. Given the need to expand land forces rapidly as the initial war of movement in Belgium and France turned into a war of stalemate and attrition, the role of the War Office, and in particular the Minister of War, Lord Kitchener, grew in political importance and administrative complexity in 1914–15. Kitchener delegated much of the day-to-day responsibility for raising the British Expeditionary Force to his Director-General of Recruiting, Lord Derby, a Lancashire magnate who had been a central figure in the recruiting drive in his county early in the war.

As the reality of a protracted war dawned on the government in 1915, a Ministry of Munitions was set up. This became the War

Office's (and through it, the Army General Command's) major competitor for manpower. Numerous conflicts of interest between them were inevitable, which Lloyd George tried to resolve after he became Prime Minister in December 1916, by setting up a Department of the Director-General of National Service, under Neville Chamberlain. However, this new body was a failure, largely because its authority was restricted to civilian labour only, and even there, it was unable to act freely, since its writ did not extend to the Ministry of Munitions. It was only in August 1917, with the creation of a full Ministry of National Service, under Auckland Geddes, that central control for manpower planning was established. Of course, major difficulties continued for the remainder of the war, but at least in 1917–18, some of the chaos of the first three years of the conflict was averted.[1]

In this section, we are concerned solely with the results of the voluntary system of recruiting between August 1914 and January 1916, when the first Military Service Act of 1916 was passed, inaugurating conscription for single men aged 18–41. Let us consider the yield in military manpower in the first 18 months of the war. Approximately 2.4 million men joined the British army of their own volition in this period. This was ten times the regimental strength of the Regular Army in 1914. Despite the fact that the British army suffered roughly 400,000 casualties in this period, the addition of nearly 2 million men over and above this figure, men who went because they wanted to go, transformed both army and society at this time.

Even after the introduction of conscription in 1916, men could still join up voluntarily. Aggregate statistics on volunteers therefore cover the full period until the formation of the new Ministry of National Service in 1917. These figures indicate that roughly one man in four of eligible age volunteered in England and Wales and in Scotland (Tables 2.1 and 2.2). Irish participation was not as extensive, amounting to roughly 11 per cent of the same age group. But in light of the pre-war clash over Home Rule, it is worthy of note that over 100,000 men volunteered in Ireland to serve King and Country. And this is probably an underestimate, since many Irishmen living and working in Britain were probably incorporated in English, Welsh and Scottish enlistment statistics.

It was the hope of pacifists in the pre-war period that military mobilization on such a scale was impossible. They were pro-

TABLE 2.1 RECRUITMENT FOR THE BRITISH ARMY 1914–18

Country	Recruited by War Office 4 Aug. 1914–31 Oct. 1917		Recruited by Ministry of National Service	Total
	Voluntary	Groups and classes	1 Nov. 1917– 11 Nov. 1918	
England	2,092,242	1,478,250	435,666	4,006,158
Wales	145,255	90,236	37,433	272,924
Scotland	320,589	173,055	63,974	557,618
Ireland	117,063	5,004	12,135	134,202
Total	2,675,149	1,746,545	549,208	4,970,902

Regimental strength of British army, 1 July 1914	244,260
Total who served in British army 1914–18	5,215,162

SOURCE: *General Annual Report of the British Army 1913–1919*, P.P. 1921, XX, Cmd 1193.

TABLE 2.2 PROPORTION OF THE MALE POPULATION IN PARTS OF THE UNITED KINGDOM RECRUITED FOR SERVICE IN THE BRITISH ARMY, 1914–18

Country[a]	Men volunteering as percentage of male population aged 15–49 in 1911	Men conscripted as percentage of male population aged 15–49 in 1911	Total
England & Wales	24.2	22.1	46.3
Scotland	26.9	14.6	41.5
Ireland	10.7	1.6	12.3

[a] Designation of country indicates place of enlistment rather than nationality; for example, Scots or Irish enlisting in England are included in English totals.

SOURCE: See Table 2.1

foundly wrong, because they misjudged completely the strength of patriotic sentiment among the population as a whole at the beginning of the war. Military planners, too, had no idea that such an enterprise as the voluntary recruitment of over 2 million men was a feasible proposition. But it was, and with this powerful intrusion of manpower, the General Staff were able to create a mass army to fight the terrible battles of 1916 and 1917, and with the help of over 2 million conscripts, ultimately to win the war.

II FROM 'PALS' BATTALIONS TO CONSCRIPT ARMIES, 1914–16

With this general background in mind, let us consider the motivation and social composition of the volunteer armies. When war was declared in August 1914, British naval power was a much more formidable force than the Regular Army, the regimental strength of which was approximately 244,000.[2] In support were the part-timers of the Territorial Forces, organized like the Regular Army on a regional basis, and with approximately the same number of men. They were, in theory, to act as a Home Guard if the Regular Army was committed to battle abroad. Few saw them as frontline troops.[3]

The war began on 3 August 1914 with the German invasion of Belgium and northern France. This operation was a huge flanking movement through Belgium, in which, according to the Schlieffen plan, the sleeve of the last German soldier was intended to brush the English Channel. The Germans then would enfold the French and Allied forces around Paris in the same iron grip that had produced their decisive victory in the Franco-Prussian war of 1870–1. This plan failed by a whisker, and the stalemate which ensued opened a new phase in the history of the British army, and indeed, in the history of warfare itself.

Of this last and sombre fact the British and Irishmen who volunteered in 1914 were blissfully unaware. Thousands joined up in a holiday spirit, and with an entirely unfounded conviction that the war would end by Christmas. Some of their leaders were equally wedded to a preposterous idea of how easy victory would be. One characteristic view was expressed by H. A. Gascoyne, the editor of the *Morning Post*. He wrote on 24 September 1914 to Lord Kitchener, who had been appointed Minister of War in the first week of the conflict, that it would be far wiser for Britain to fight the war with a small efficient army than a large inefficient one. The Regulars and Territorials could do the job, with the help of perhaps 50,000 additional men for the 'advance into Germany'.[4] Fortunately, Kitchener knew otherwise. His forecast that the war would last several years brought some glimmer of reality into manpower planning in 1914–15.

But the men who presented themselves for military service in 1914 knew little of these matters of grand strategy. Approximately 300,000 enlisted in August 1914, and a further 700,000 by the end of the year. At the outset of the war, recruits came from every walk of life. But after the first few hectic months of recruiting, the rate of enlistment declined. Partly this was a sign of greater caution on the part of potential recruits; in part, it merely reflected the fact that the early wave of enlistment, which had overwhelmed the War Office, could not possibly continue unabated. In some areas, the supply of potential recruits simply ran out.[5]

A 'Pals' and Others

There were probably as many reasons for volunteering as there were volunteers. But one of the most striking features of enlistment in the first year of the war was the extent to which the recruiting drive tapped powerful sentiments of loyalty felt by men, whatever their occupation, to town, county, or community. This is best seen in the formation of 'Pals' battalions, locally-raised units of men who knew each other at work or in their communities. One of the leaders of the movement to form such units was Lord Derby. Derby wrote to Kitchener in November 1914 about his efforts in forming several Liverpool detachments. He noted that 'certainly in the first battalion they are all middle class men and there are scores of them who from a social point of view would be perfectly fit for commissions'.[6] We shall return to the question of the social selection of the officer corps. But in this context, we should note that many 'Pals' battalions were composed of middle-class men who served as private soldiers. Only later were many of them drawn off to train as officers for other units.

The diary of one man who volunteered in Birmingham gives something of the flavour of the early recruiting campaign and the motives of the men who responded to it. H. V. Drinkwater, who lived in Stratford-upon-Avon, tried once unsuccessfully to enlist in Birmingham. He was too short and not fit enough for the medical board examining him. Another recruiting office took a more lenient line, and he was enlisted in the 2nd Battalion, City of Birmingham, of the Royal Warwickshire Regiment. His recollection was that

Birmingham, in concert with the mayors [sic] of other large towns, first started to raise these battalions. They had in mind the fact that there would be many thousands of fellows in the country not desirous of or willing to wait for a commission, but providing they could join the ranks with their friends and remain with them were keen to become private soldiers . . . [They were] an extraordinary collection of fellows; later on I found out that the fellow next to me in the ranks had never done a day's work in his life, had had something in the nature of a valet to do it for him; he was barely 17. There were barristers, solicitors, bank clerks, qualified engineers, and men and boys who by their looks at least required some good square meals before they would be able to stand the conditions which we were beginning to understand existed in France.

Most of Drinkwater's fellow volunteers applied for a commission when they came to see that the war would last for years, not months.[7]

The training many of these men went through at first varied from the cursory to the derisory. Everything they really needed – including both officers and non-commissioned officers with military experience – was in very short supply. Much marching to and fro went on. One Public School Battalion spent a great deal of time practising the quickest way to get into and out of a train.[8] One of the Liverpool Pals has left a splendid description of 'the curious effect caused by hundreds of chaps using newspapers as rain shields and putting them over head and shoulders' on the march.[9] Newcomers to the 12th (Service) Battalion Gloucesters had to cope with children throwing bricks at sentries and snowballs at men in training.[10] Since whatever khaki available went to the Regular Army, blue serge was the colour of the Kitchener men (as volunteers were called), but this degree of uniformity did not describe other aspects of their provisions. Those who could afford it put their own kits in order; others simply had to wait, and made up in enthusiasm what they lacked in equipment. But all began to learn the essential lessons of military inefficiency and the importance in the life of the soldier of waiting around with nothing to do.

While a number of 'Pals' battalions were composed mainly or exclusively of middle-class men, like the Public Schools Battalions of the Middlesex Regiment and the Royal Fusiliers,[11] or the

'Grimsby chums' formed by a number of old boys at Wintringham Secondary School,[12] as many or more were made up in part or exclusively of working men. One such volunteer to a working-class 'Pals' battalion was T. A. (Tommy) Jennings, aged 20 on the outbreak of war. He was a metalworker in the Birmingham jewellery trade, whose brother had joined up in the first days of the war. At first turned down as undersized, he was given the opportunity a year later to join what was known as a 'Bantam' battalion of men of less than 5 ft 3 inches in height. He saw service with the Gloucestershire Regiment, and was taken prisoner on the Somme. He recalled that 'Bantams' were frequently made up of miners from Yorkshire and County Durham, men who were, according to many accounts, some of the toughest soldiers in the army. Four Bantam battalions were raised in Wales, eight more in the rest of Britain.[13]

Many other units were formed among men with common experiences and loyalties. Some arose out of work, such as the North Eastern Railway Pioneers, more formally known as the Pioneer 17th (Service) Battalion of the Northumberland Fusiliers.[14] This was raised by the company, and in many similar cases, private individuals or groups undertook to clothe, house, and feed these volunteers until the army had the facilities to take over their training and equipment.

The formation of 'Pals' battalions provided a perfect occasion for the public expression of civic culture. Municipalities competed with each other (and with private firms) in the lavishness of their guarantees for the costs of raising 'Kitchener's Armies'. The Citizens' Recruiting Committee of Bristol were early off the mark, and formed a battalion of 'mercantile and professional men' for the Gloucestershire Regiment in late August 1914.[15] In Birmingham, as Lieut Drinkwater remarked, the Lord Mayor and City Council paid for the creation of three city battalions to supplement the Royal Warwickshire Regiment.[16] In Manchester, a number of cotton firms offered £500 to £1000 each to help raise 'Pals' battalions, but the Municipal Gas Company outbid them all, giving £7,000 'out of a special reserve fund in their control'.[17]

Employers did much to help spur on the recruitment drive by promising men that they would not lose earnings or indeed their jobs if they enlisted. On 24 August 1914, the Home Trade Association of Manchester urged employers to provide volunteers with four weeks' full wages, half pay for married men, to be given to their wives, some (unspecified) help for single men with dependants, and a guarantee of re-engagement at work. Names of volunteers were forwarded to recruiting offices by employers, thus ensuring the local character of these units. There is little evidence of coercion here. This practice probably reflects the extent to which all classes shared the patriotic fervour of the early days of the war.[18]

Even though illusions of a short war prevailed at this time, it is still astonishing how many men were willing to go off to war without clear statutory arrangements for the upkeep of their families. And despite the introduction of meagre separation allowances, the financial security of soldiers' families was never completely assured. There can be little doubt, then, that popular sentiment rather than pecuniary considerations lay behind enlistment in the first phase of the 1914–18 war.

B   Occupation and Enlistment

Initially, the recruitment drive drew men into the Forces from all sectors of the labour force. As time went on, though, occupational variations in propensity to enlist emerged. The relevant distinction here is between self-employed professionals and white-collar workers, on the one hand, and manual workers on the other. Roughly twice as many of the first category enlisted as did men in the second category (Table 2.3).

In 1914–15, regional differences in enlistment rates among all occupied workers were slight, but the lowest rates were registered in the East Midlands and Yorkshire as a whole, and among textile and clothing workers in particular.[19] Uncertainty about the state of the textile trade, in which large numbers of married women were employed, probably convinced many that enlistment would mean economic hardship for their families. But, as Dr Dewey has suggested, it is also likely that these figures reflect an important aspect of the social structure of enlistment – the extent to which occupations that traditionally had a comparatively 'old' labour force naturally provided fewer recruits for the army. For instance, the part of the labour force aged 20–44 in textiles was significantly

TABLE 2.3 DISTRIBUTION BY SECTOR OF EMPLOYMENT OF MEN WHO SERVED IN
THE BRITISH ARMY, AUGUST 1914 – FEBRUARY 1916

Occupational sector	Men employed July 1914 (000s)	Men who joined Forces (000s)	Percentage of pre-war labour force volunteering 1914–16
I. Industry	6,165	1,743	28.3
Of which mines and quarries	1,266	313	24.7
II. Agriculture	920	259	28.2
III. Transport	1,041	233	22.4
IV. Finance and commerce	1,249	501	40.1
V. Professions	144	60	41.7
VI. Entertainment	177	74	41.8
VII. Central government	311	85	27.3
VIII. Local government	477	126	26.4
All occupations	10,484	3,081	29.4

SOURCE: PRO RECO 1/832, April 1916.

smaller than the same age group in mining or metalwork, on the
one hand, and in commercial occupations, on the other.[20]

The same considerations probably applied in some parts of the
agricultural sector, the age structure of which was relatively 'old'.
However, in time, military recruitment from rural society reached
or surpassed the national level. By February 1915, 15.6 per cent of
the workforce on the land had joined up, compared to 15.2 per
cent among all industrial workers. Particularly high figures were
registered among permanent as opposed to casual labour in general, and in the South Western labour exchange district, in
particular, 'since considerable numbers have been attracted in
Wiltshire to the various military camps in Salisbury Plain'.[21] By
February 1916, 28 per cent of the rural labour force had enlisted,
which is very near the national average for all occupied men. By
then, the prospect of a scarcity of agricultural labour, drawn into
better-paid urban employment, helped persuade the War Office to
try to restrict recruitment from this sector of the labour force.

But setting aside the questions of the age structure of occupations, we can see two clear features of enlistment in 1914–15:
firstly, the early rush to enlist from most well-paid manual occupa-

tions; and, secondly, the even higher levels of recruitment of non-manual workers. In the first case, much evidence exists as to the success of the recruiting campaign in mining communities, which, it was claimed, provided 'a larger proportion' of volunteers 'than any other industry'. One commentator remarked that miners, who were relatively well-paid workers, 'seem to have been moved to remarkable enthusiasm for the war and they enlisted by the thousands after hearing stories of the British fighting and the destruction of Belgian towns'. As a result, 'in the first days of enlistment, in several streets of miners' houses in the towns of Tyldesley and Atherton only one or two young men were left'.[22] According to one survey, 115,000 members of the Miners' Federation of Great Britain volunteered at the outbreak of the war.[23] This represented 15 per cent of the membership of the Union,[24] and compared favourably with Board of Trade estimates that a little over 10 per cent of the industrial workforce joined up during the first eight weeks of war.[25] By mid-1915, over 230,000 miners – approximately one-quarter of the workforce – had enlisted. The highest rates were in Glamorgan, Durham and Northumberland, and in some Scottish coalfields, areas in which pre-war industrial militancy had been pronounced. The compatibility of class consciousness and patriotism could have no better illustration. Of course, we should never completely discount the desire of some miners to do anything to get out of the mines, but sentiments about nation and empire, rather than discontent, were behind mass enlistment in this industry.[26]

There is considerable evidence that the miners' response was matched throughout most of British industry and commerce. Indeed, one of the striking features of the early phase of enlistment was the high rates of recruitment, not from among workers in precarious trades who had little or nothing to lose by joining up, but rather from among skilled workers in trades that were not threatened by unemployment. By February 1915, 15 per cent of the industrial workforce were in uniform, and particularly high enlistment rates were registered in engineering, chemicals, and iron and steel.[27] Once again, the textile and clothing trades – by now booming with government orders for the new armies – lagged slightly behind. In contrast, 16 per cent of iron and steel workers, 18 per cent of cycle and motor workers, and over 19 per cent of electrical engineering workers had left employment for military service during the first six months of the war.[28] Some unemployed workers had an economic motive for enlistment, but most men volunteered out of conviction and not out of necessity.

Finding replacements early in the war was apparently not a particularly difficult problem in heavy industry. The Board of Trade found very little difference in enlistment rates between large and small firms, but larger firms had less trouble in making up the deficit, at the expense of the smaller. 'One of the tendencies of the war' concluded a Board of Trade report in December 1914, 'is clearly to transfer a more than normal proportion of the nation's business to large concerns'.[29] It is apparent that employers in small firms had a very good reason to persuade their remaining workers to resist any temptation to join up.

Elsewhere an anti-enlistment policy was in operation. With the full consent of the War Office, railway companies tried to keep enough men back to ensure unbroken lines of supply within the country. Nevertheless, 10 per cent of the workforce still left work for the army in the early months of the war, and, as we have noted above, even here, the industry was not prepared to do without its own 'Pals' battalion, the North Eastern Railway Pioneers.[30] By 1915, the enlistment figure had risen to 17 per cent, but this was still much less than the rate for all industrial workers.[31]

In contrast, the highest enlistment rates among employees in the early months of the conflict were registered by men in commercial and clerical occupations. This trend continued throughout 1915 and early 1916, and is illustrated in Table 2.3. Whereas 28 per cent of industrial workers had volunteered by February 1916, a volunteer rate of 40 per cent was registered among men employed in banking, finance, or commerce; in the professions, accountants, architects, solicitors, advertising agents, estate agents; and among men at work in the entertainment trades – in hotels, pubs, theatres, music halls, cinemas, and restaurants. The Ministry of Reconstruction, set up in 1916 to help prepare for the post-war world, suggested that this surplus enlistment was related to the greater flexibility of distributive or service trades as compared with industrial trades. It was argued that the former could manage with fewer workers, and that it was easier to put a woman teller in a bank than to introduce a woman metalworker to the assembly line of a factory. Again the age structure of the labour force in different occupations had a bearing on enlistment rates. Food, drink, and tobacco, for example, had a relatively 'young' labour force, and labour turnover in this sector was high in the pre-war period.[32]

The age factor probably accounted in part for the relatively low enlistment rates among employers. The Ministry of Reconstruction committee dealing with enlistment noted that 'owing to age distribution and business responsibility', employers in all trades did not enlist in large numbers.[33] Instead they joined unofficial Volunteer Battalions for overage and unfit men. Sir William Lever, soon to be ennobled as Lord Leverhulme, was one such man, who joined the 2nd Volunteer Battalion of the Birkenhead and District Volunteer Training Corps, and 'was content to drill as a ranker with other recruits from the Port Sunlight works and officers in a company commanded by his own son'.[34] Lever was much too old to join up, but especially in smaller firms, younger men in management probably held back in order to keep their businesses going, even when short of staff.

Among employees, though, it is clear that men engaged in commercial or distributive trades were in uniform and at risk for longer periods and in relatively larger numbers than were industrial workers, transport workers, and agricultural workers (Table 2.3). Conscription did not alter this pattern. By July 1917, 58 per cent of all men employed in commerce, 57 per cent of those in the entertainment trades, and 53 per cent of those in banking and commerce were in uniform. In no other occupational group did such a large proportion of men go off to war. The proportion of professional self-employed men enlisting in this period was just as high: 56.5 per cent.[35]

We can conclude therefore that enlistment in British forces had a definite social structure. First there were higher enlistment rates among non-manual workers and professional men than among manual workers. Second, recruitment was bound to be greater in those occupations with a 'younger' age structure, compared to other trades with a comparatively 'older' age structure. Third, well-paid workers were conspicuous among working-class volunteers. Men in less well-paid jobs may have hesitated before joining up, but their enlistment rates were not far short of the national average in most cases. And fourth, employers in both large and small firms tended to stay at home with greater frequency than did the men they employed.

C   The End of the Voluntary System

So far we have presented the results of military recruitment by persuasion rather than by the force of law. But despite the fact that 2 million men enlisted between August 1914 and September 1915,[36] the demands made by the War Office for additional manpower continued to rise. Calls for conscription had been made by some of the more militant members of the Conservative Party from the outset of the war, but many Liberal and Labour MPs were dead set against it. Kitchener was reluctant to divide the country over the issue, but was persuaded to sanction the registration of all men by occupation as well as an attestation scheme to identify all men, married as well as single, who were prepared to enlist when needed. Should sufficient signatures be collected, in particular among single men, conscription could be postponed. It is important to bear in mind that many married men who attested under what was known as the 'Derby scheme' did so in order to stay out of the army – that is, to keep the voluntary system alive and to ward off the threat of conscription. Hence it is difficult to use the outcome of the exercise as an indicator of how many men were indeed willing to serve. Still, the attestation statistics did reveal much about how far military mobilization had gone in Britain, and about how much further it could go on the voluntary basis.

This exercise showed the geographical distribution both of men engaged in war-related work, whose registration cards were 'starred' to indicate their special status as men needed in agriculture or on the production line, and of men who were deemed by the War Office to be eligible for military service. Of the 5 million men in the relevant age group 18–41, over 1.2 million men were in the 'starred' category, and with 400,000 unfit or otherwise exempted men, constituted fully one-third of the male population aged 18–41 unavailable for military service. Therefore the exercise showed that there were millions of presumably able-bodied men who were unprepared to step forward and which the voluntary system had no way of tapping for the army.

Not surprisingly, the mining and agricultural regions of Wales, the West Country, and the West Riding of Yorkshire had a higher proportion of 'starred' than of attested men among their populations, whereas in the South and East of England, proportionately fewer men were exempted from military service. By and large, this simply describes the location of mining, agricultural, and other war-related production in the north and west of England, and the concentration of much of the commercial and service sector in the south and east. But more alarmingly, the percentage 'starred' was greatest at ages 18–24, when presumably men were at the peak of their fitness for military service.[37]

If it was Lord Derby's intention to prove that the voluntary system had outlived its usefulness,[38] this exercise presented him with abundant evidence that that indeed was the case. The most damning result was that only 37 per cent of the 'unstarred' men, that is, those who were eligible to go, had attested their willingness to join the Forces. Over 40 per cent of married 'unstarred' men had done so, but only 31 per cent of single 'unstarred' men had signed up under the Derby scheme.

The simple calculation that followed this exercise made conscription inevitable. Of nearly 5 million men canvassed, one-third, or 1.6 million, were unavailable for military service. Of the remaining 3.2 million, only 1.2 million, or roughly 24 per cent of the total male population at home, were prepared to go.[39] And as we have already remarked, some of the married men among them signed attestation forms in order to support the voluntary system rather than to indicate their willingness to go. It is almost certainly the case, therefore, that considerably less then one-quarter of the male population were able and willing to enlist voluntarily (Table 2.4).

As Army Command were committed to a 'big push' in 1916, the government had no choice but to introduce the Military Service Acts of 1916, under which first all single men aged 18–41 and later all single and married men in that age group were deemed to have enlisted. These measures ended the first phase of manpower planning in Britain.

III   MILITARY VERSUS INDUSTRIAL MANPOWER, 1916–18

There is a striking contrast between British manpower planning in the two world wars. In the 1939–45 war, which was fought entirely by conscription, setting the labour requirements of the war economy came first; fixing the manpower targets of military planners

TABLE 2.4 ATTESTATIONS UNDER THE DERBY SCHEME, 1915–16

Age	Total single men in class	Percentage unavailable	Percentage available	Attested as percentage of available single men	Total married men in class	Percentage unavailable	Percentage available	Attested as percentage of available married men
18–24	1,078,983	37.2	62.8	33.4	175,559	44.3	55.7	46.0
25–29	464,561	33.0	67.0	31.7	587,724	37.0	63.0	44.4
30–34	287,362	27.8	72.2	29.7	781,233	35.0	65.0	45.8
35–40	261,325	25.1	74.9	27.1	1,143,138	30.4	69.6	36.9
Total	2,092,231	33.5	66.5	31.6	2,687,654	34.1	65.9	41.5

Summary: Grand total enumerated: 4,779,885   Or: 100.00

of which: 1,616,629 were unavailable for military service   −33.82

3,163,256 were available for military service   66.18

of which: 1,988,017 did not attest   −41.59

1,175,239 attested   24.59 of all men enumerated

SOURCE: PRO, Ministry of National Service Papers, NATS 1/400.

came next.[40] The result was not only a much more efficient system of domestic production than had been in effect in the First World War, but also a reduction of the terrible casualties of the Great War. Anyone who has visited British war cemeteries in France will have seen visual evidence of the enormous difference in scale of war losses in the two conflicts, a point to which we shall return in chapter 3.

One reason for the success of the manpower system of the Second World War was that everyone had in mind the mistakes and lessons of the 1914–18 war. Consequently in the Second World War, military plans were tailored to suit the design of the Home Front, thereby reducing the likelihood of a second slaughter on the 1914–18 scale.

Precisely the opposite was true in the period 1916–18. The establishment of conscription provided the War Cabinet, first under Asquith, and after December 1916 under Lloyd George, with the power to distribute the nation's manpower at will. But even though both leaders were reluctant to accept the demand for more men depressingly made month after weary month, they nevertheless felt they had to do so, *faute de mieux*.[41] This inevitably meant that war production at home would have to tolerate repeated drains on manpower, a problem which made it increasingly difficult to supply the men being sent into battle. It is probably idle to speculate on what would have happened had the war continued in 1919–20, but there is considerable evidence that by 1918 manpower resources in Britain had been stretched to the limit, as in other countries.

The manpower crisis of 1917–18 had ramifications for the social structure of British forces in the Great War. One of the ironies of the introduction of conscription was that it probably made it more difficult to transfer labour from industry to the army. This was in part due to the stubborn opposition of the Labour movement to anything that even hinted at or resembled industrial conscription.[42] But it was also a reflection of the slow but real recognition that the outcome of the war depended as much on the economic strength of the nation as on its ability to provide new drafts for the army.

The man who did most to ensure that manpower planning would be based on this assumption was Auckland Geddes. He was appointed Minister of National Service in late 1917, and replaced the relatively ineffectual Neville Chamberlain, who had had responsibility for manpower over the previous year. Geddes brought a powerful mind and talent for organization to his task, both of which were necessary for the formulation and implementation of a comprehensive manpower policy. It was largely due to his efforts that limits were placed on the drain on men from war-related industry in the last year of the war. While some groups of civilian workers lost their exemptions in this period, others were removed from the army to replace them. Consequently, conscription hit workers in heavy industry and agriculture less severely than it did those in commercial and other sectors of non-manual employment, thereby perpetuating in the last years of the war the occupational structure of enlistment that had emerged in 1914–15.

The first task Geddes set himself in his new office in July 1917 was to establish principles of manpower planning on which to base the work of his ministry. In place of what he called the 'clean out by age' approach of earlier years, he advanced an 'occupation-group theory of recruitment', whereby a full manpower budget would be drawn up according to the nation's industrial structure. Utility at home would determine whether a man would be called, for the simple reason that

> The Nation at War requires to maintain a balance in the distribution of its mental and physical vigour between its armed forces and the civil services, and industries which directly and indirectly support these forces.

The government had to operate, and be seen to operate, a scheme whereby occupation rather than age determined exemption or conscription. Of course, most exemptions were already linked to service in war-related production, but so many irregularities and loopholes existed, that there were indeed grounds for criticism of the way the Military Service Acts were applied. Without a change in policy, Geddes argued, support for the war might fade rapidly. Indeed, he urged his Cabinet colleagues, signs of this alarming development had already appeared.

> The nation is rattled; partly, by the excitement of the Russian Revolution; partly by the price of food; partly by casualties, by the sight of widows and of the broken men returning; but largely, because it does not understand the greatest of all our

problems, the problem of Man-Power, upon which all else depends.[43]

This argument was sufficient to persuade the War Cabinet to give Geddes final say over all manpower questions. It took until November 1917 for the full transfer of responsibility for recruiting to Geddes' ministry. But even before, he provided an answer to the protracted and at times bitter argument between Army Command and the Ministry of Munitions over how far conscription ought to go. This is not to say that Geddes had an easy ride as Minister; on the contrary, but at least by the last year of the war, responsibility for labour supply was in the hands of a man who had a clear idea of how to provide men for the army without crippling home production.

Geddes' full manpower budget was presented to the War Cabinet on 13 October 1917. In it he summarized the then-current distribution of the labour force. Of the approximately 13 million men aged 16–60 in the United Kingdom, 8 million were still in civilian life. Nearly 0.8 million were in the 18–25 year age group, but because of earlier enlistment of fit men, perhaps 270,000 of these were in Grade A physical condition, that is, fit enough for combat. Of these fit men, over 90,000 were in the mines, and another 100,000 were in munitions factories. Clearly not all could go, but Geddes estimated that older or less fit replacements could be found for approximately 200,000 of them. Considering the older age group, 25–41: of the 2.8 million men still at home, perhaps 700,000 were Grade A men. But since many of these older men were needed to release the 18–25 year-olds, only 150,000 could be spared without crippling war-related industry. If we add the approximately 100,000 18-year-olds, soon to become eligible for military service, we reach the absolute limit of manpower available for the army: 450,000 men.[44]

By October 1917, Geddes had concluded, this 'civil reservoir' was drying up. Not only was the proportion of Grade 'A' men among recruits not as high as he had hoped, but military requirements had grown. In Table 2.5 we can see in stark terms the difficulty he (and the nation) faced at this time. On the credit side, the army could count on an additional half-million men already in uniform on home duty, and roughly 350,000 men who were recovering satisfactorily from sickness or wounds. But the debit side was larger still. Not

TABLE 2.5 BRITISH MANPOWER BUDGET, OCTOBER 1917

Credit		Debit	
1. Strength of army at home	527,765	1. Existing deficiencies in average regimental strength	134,600
2. Sick and wounded able to return to units	356,000	2. Required for new units	110,000
		3. Estimated wastage abroad in 1918	800,000
		4. Estimated wastage at home in 1918	20,000
		5. Estimated requirement for Home Forces in 1918	24,000
		6. Estimated minimum strength of reserves	82,000
Total credit	883,765	Total required	1,170,600
		Deficit	286,835

Sources of additional manpower

A. Men 18–24	800,000	With allowance for wastage in training	300,000
of which, in Grade A fitness:	270,000		
of which, can be spared	150,000		
B. Men 25–41:	2,800,000		
of which, in Grade A fitness:	700,000	Deficit still remaining	
of which, can be spared	120,000		30,000
C. Men turning age 18 in Grade A fitness	100,000		
D. Irish	150,000		
E. Men 42–51, if age limit were raised	150,000		

SOURCE: CAB 24/28, GT 2295, 13 Oct. 1917.

only were there already deficiencies of 134,000 in existing units, but 110,000 more men were required for new units. In the terrible euphemism of military thinking, 'wastage' was estimated at 820,000 in the coming year. Once they added to that the approximately 100,000 needed as absolutely minimal reserves, they arrived at the total of nearly 1.2 million men to be found in the coming year. Subtracting the 880,000 on the credit side yields a shortage of 320,000 men. While just about this number was available on the Home Front, and could be removed, albeit with difficulty, it would still mean that virtually no manpower would be available if fighting intensified in 1918, as indeed it did.[45]

In order to find the men the Forces would need in the coming months, a Cabinet Committee on Manpower was set up in December 1917. It had to choose among three unpalatable alternatives. The first was to abolish the existing two months' period of grace granted to anyone whose exemption certificate had been withdrawn, and to review all previous exemptions. The second was to extend the age limit for conscription from 41 to 51; the third was to apply conscription in Ireland. Each of the latter two steps would release 150,000 additional men for the Forces. Geddes favoured the Irish option. Fortunately, wiser counsel prevailed, and the first two proposals became law in the two Military Service Acts of January and March 1918.[46]

These measures probably would have sufficed had not the Germans launched their March offensive of 1918. This presented a challenge which if successful could have forced a negotiated settlement, since the threatened breakthrough would have preceded the arrival of large drafts of American troops.

The War Cabinet asked Geddes to think again about manpower, especially in light of Army Command criticism that his Ministry was preventing the Forces from getting the men they needed. In reply, Geddes presented a detailed manpower budget on 22 May 1918. In it he divided the nation's male population of military age into three groups: those in the Forces or working directly to provision them; those engaged in essential occupations: agriculture, coalmining, dock labour, or railways; and all others unfit or holding exemptions for other war-related work. This total was virtually identical to the entire male population of military age in 1914, plus those who in intervening years had reached the age of 18.

Geddes' conclusion was that recruits could only be found 'at the expense of war industries'.[47] He described the distribution of essential labour among government departments, and defied anyone to find additional sources of manpower for the army. He would make every effort to meet military requirements, but no one could create men, especially fit men, out of thin air. Fortunately for the Allies, the German offensive was checked, and by the summer of 1918 the manpower crisis had abated. In fact, it was over, although no one knew it at the time.

Geddes' manpower budgets and other contemporary estimates show the extent to which manual labour was protected from conscription even in the last year of the war. In the estimate submitted to the Cabinet on 22 May 1918, the Minister provided a comprehensive outline of employment of men in military ages in firms engaged in war-related work. As we can see in Table 2.6, nearly 1 million men were in Admiralty work; nearly 300,000 in Royal Air Force work, and over 1.2 million in Ministry of Munitions or War Office work. When we take into account 450,000 men accounted for by other government departments, and 260,000 engaged in work for other Allied governments, we reach a total of nearly 3.3 million men. The largest contingents were in metalwork and in mining. Here again, it is apparent that however severe the pressure on manpower in the last year of the war, a substantial part of the manual labour force was excluded from the armed forces. The same was true in parts of agriculture, but not in most non-industrial trades.[48]

When we survey patterns of labour substitution by women during the war, we also find that the greatest influx of female labour was into white-collar work in the commercial sector of the economy. By April 1916, the female labour force had grown by 600,000; fully 30 per cent of this growth was in commerce, and over half was in non-industrial occupations. Put in another way, about 50 per cent of all women 'substituting' at work for men in uniform did so in the world of commerce.[49] The same pattern can be detected at the end of the war. In 1918, there were more women replacing males at work in banking, finance, and commerce than in the metal and chemical trades put together.[50] The significance of women's work in heavy industry is not at issue here, but concentration on their part in shell production should not obscure the key role they played in freeing white-collar workers for military service. Here is another reason for the fact that,

TABLE 2.6 OCCUPATIONAL DISTRIBUTION OF LABOUR FORCE IN WAR-RELATED INDUSTRY IN 1918

Trade Group	Admiralty work	RAF work	Ministry of Munitions and War Office work	Other government work	Work for Allied governments	Total labour force directly employed by the state
1. Building	22,000	24,700	70,500	61,000	2,100	180,300
2. Coal mining	121,000	21,000	76,000	23,000	133,000	374,000
3. Other mines and quarries	6,100	2,000	47,400	9,900	100	65,500
4. Metal trades	653,500	198,700	636,600	93,300	66,300	1,648,400
5. Chemical trades	12,800	5,200	89,700	10,200	9,700	127,600
6. Clothing trades	3,400	1,100	35,500	4,300	3,900	48,200
7. Food trades	500	800	15,700	15,300	300	32,600
8. Paper and printing	3,500	1,100	9,300	16,400	700	31,000
9. Wood trades	11,800	12,900	37,500	28,300	500	91,000
10. Other industrial trades	13,200	13,300	82,300	30,300	4,500	143,600
11. Govt establishment dockyards and ordnance factories	84,300	–	155,000	–	15,000	254,300
12. Civil service	4,000	–	11,000	121,000	–	136,000
Total[a]	936,100	280,800	1,266,500	413,000	236,100	3,132,500

[a] The totals in the original document are incorrect; we have corrected them here.
SOURCE: CAB 24/20, GT 4618.

throughout the 1914–18 war, non-manual workers provided a disproportionately high share of the nation's soldiers, sailors and airmen.

Demobilization returns compiled after the Armistice provide similar indications of the social structure of British forces. These tables recorded pre-war occupations, or in the case of very young men, intentions to pursue such occupations. These data are incomplete, since they refer only to the army and the RAF. Furthermore, the occupational categories used are not the same as those in other wartime surveys of the labour force. And obviously, they do not describe the occupational distribution of casualties, a point to which we shall return in chapter 3. But whatever their shortcomings, these figures still show the same contrast between levels of military participation among manual and non-manual workers which we have noted using other sources. When compared to data on the sectoral distribution of the pre-war labour force, they show again that the proportion of the non-industrial workforce which served during the war was substantially greater than the proportion of industrial workers in uniform.

Finally, it may be useful to summarize the degree to which the occupational distribution of the Forces differed from that of the occupied male population. Approximately 6 million men were employed in industrial occupations in 1914. We know that enlistment rates among them were roughly 10 per cent lower than those of non-manual workers. It follows that had white-collar enlistment rates applied to blue-collar workers, another 600,000 working-class men would have been in uniform in the First World War. It was probably by approximately this number that the population of potential recruits was reduced as a result of differential enlistment of manual and non-manual workers.

IV   MEDICAL FITNESS AND MILITARY SERVICE

So far we have shown that the social structure of British forces in the Great War reflected differential enlistment rates as between manual and non-manual workers. But there is another important reason why, relatively speaking, industrial workers were in the Forces for a shorter period of time than were white-collar workers and other middle-class men. It is, ironically, the appallingly low standards of health in many urban working-class districts. Their poor physical state probably saved the lives of many industrial workers who simply did not reach the minimum physical standard for military service, let alone for combat duty. Bank clerks or estate agents, not to mention the wealthy, were better-fed, healthier, and by and large more able to stand the rigours of army life. Their physical condition made them good candidates for combat duty and meant that their chances of survival were smaller than were those of their less privileged contemporaries. The exceptions were miners and agricultural workers, whose regular work involved physical exertion as demanding as that required of soldiers during the war, and who therefore were prime physical candidates for recruitment.

The reports of the medical men who examined recruits for the British army in the Great War provide abundant evidence of the validity of the concern widely expressed in the pre-war period about the military implications of poverty, which we have discussed in chapter 1. They demonstrate graphically the social selection of recruits and the extent to which pre-war deprivation cut into the total manpower available for military service in the 1914–18 war.

The medical examination of recruits was an essential part of the attempt by all combatant nations to find and to train millions of men of sufficient physical fitness to sustain their battle plans. On the Western Front in particular, the problem of endurance was crucial under conditions wherein defensive forces had gained the ascendancy. By the end of the war, the question had arisen in acute form as to how to distinguish between men who were fit enough to fight and men whose presence in uniform or at the Front would do them and their comrades no good at all.

But during the war no adequate medical answer to this problem was found. Consequently, the British military effort was impaired in two ways. On the one hand, medical examinations revealed that a significant proportion of the British working class had grown up and had lived in conditions which made them unable to fight under any definition of fitness. Even the most threadbare net could not fail to catch the disabilities of tens of thousands of men who presented themselves for military service. But, on the other hand, military and medical definitions of fitness were sufficiently imprecise as to ensure that many British men wound up in the army who should never have been there in the first place. As the records of the Ministry of Pensions illustrate, disability due to disease and complications of wounds was in some important respects a function of faulty recruiting standards.

The third key determinant of military manpower – fitness for military service – was, therefore, ambiguous in the extreme. Partly this uncertainty was due to the state of diagnostic medicine at the time; partly, to the pressure of work in processing millions of recruits in a short span of time. But it was also due to the difficulty of having to establish for the first time a medically-defensible standard of military fitness (as opposed to overall state of health) which would give the army the men it needed. The hesitant and only partially successful steps taken in this direction are described in the remainder of this chapter.

A The Medical Examination of Recruits, 1914–17

Before the outbreak of war in 1914, the British army accepted as volunteers only those men between the ages of 18 and 30 who were of good physique and free from all physical defects. Medical officers conducted examinations on the basis of a straightforward list of disabilities which they could identify in a careful and unhurried examination. After 5 August 1914 the quiet days were over. The rush to the colours meant that regimental medical officers were forced to inspect over 200 men per day. None had any illusions as to the adequacy of these examinations. In addition, as the medical officer of the 6th City of London Regiment recalled, examiners were paid one shilling for every man they passed, and nothing for the men they rejected. Not surprisingly, some passed everyone in sight.[51] In 1915, when the Derby scheme was introduced, another deluge of recruits had to be examined, again in such numbers per doctor per day as to ensure a cursory inspection and thousands of mistakes, which army doctors at training camps or in the field had to sort out on top of everything else they had to do.

By the time conscription came into effect in 1916, the War Office had issued standard instructions about medical examinations, to be conducted on an A–B–C system of fitness for military service. 'A' meant fit for general service. 'B' meant fit for service abroad in a support capacity, and 'C' meant fit for service at home only. There were three gradations of 'B' and 'C' fitness, which related to the recruits' aptitude for specific types of work in the army, as well as two categories of unfitness – temporary and permanent. Individual army medical officers therefore had to examine each recruit from head to toe and to make two different decisions: first as to his general fitness, which was primarily a medical question; secondly, as to where he might best serve in the army, which was primarily an administrative question.

Over 2.6 million such examinations were conducted between August 1916 and June 1917 under the aegis of the War Office Department of Recruiting. In this time, its officials slowly but surely came to see the impossibility of the task they had set their doctors. In November 1916, Sir James Galloway, who before 1914 had been senior physician at Charing Cross Hospital, was brought back from army work in France in order to become Inspector of Recruiting Medical Boards. He soon found ample evidence of the deficiencies of the work of these boards and of growing public criticism of them. The matter was serious enough to justify the establishment of a parliamentary select committee in July 1917 to consider the entire question of the medical examination of recruits.[52]

The public hearings of this committee under the chairmanship of Mr Edward Shortt created a major political storm. The story of medical and administrative chaos told by witness after witness was so striking as to ensure the end of the old system of examination of recruits. The first witness was Auckland Geddes. The second was Surgeon-General Sir Alfred Keogh, Director-General of the Army Medical Service. Together they established that neither was responsible for the work of the War Office medical boards, which existed in a curious state of bureaucratic limbo.

But, from the military standpoint, worse was yet to come. The committee received information from a parade of surgeons-general of each Home Command. These were the men to whom medical officers were responsible. Each witness added increasingly damning evidence about the strange workings of these boards. The most spectacular of these unintentionally self-destructive military presentations was that of Surgeon-General Bedford, Deputy Director of Medical Services, Northern Command, who had been a career soldier for 36 years, but who had never practised in civilian life. He told the committee that the boards were made up of recently mobilized doctors. They conducted the examinations, but the president of each board, who classified each recruit whatever the opinion of his junior medical colleagues, was a military man and had to be a military man. 'The reason is this – that the civilian practitioner, all his life has been trained not to look farther than the individual himself, and he has never raised his eyes to the horizon of his country's needs.'[53] Since there were civilian doctors on the committee hearing this evidence, this statement was bound to lead to further trouble for the army.

That trouble came almost immediately, as General Bedford was forced to admit that it was army policy to suppress the judgments of examining doctors who were in favour of exempting a high proportion of recruits on medical grounds. The witness told of a secret meeting which took place in London on or about 15 September 1916, while the Battle of the Somme was still raging. In attendance were Keogh and all surgeons-general of Home Commands. Apparently, by consensus, it was agreed that the rejection rate of recruits was unacceptably high. The remedy was to circulate a letter to the military men who were presidents of medical boards instructing them to reject fewer men, whatever examiners might say. As a result, the rejection rate of 28.9 per cent in 1–15 September 1916 was brought down to 6.5 per cent two months later and to about 3 per cent in the first months of 1917. At the same time, the proportion placed in Grade 'A' suddenly soared from approximately 25 per cent in September 1916 to 50 per cent by the turn of the new year.[54]

Even General Bedford came to see that this instruction was bound to increase dramatically the number of unfit men who joined the army. In June 1917, together with the General Officer Commanding of Northern Command, he inspected a large contingent of Labour Battalion or 'C-3' men near York, and was shocked by their physical condition. Immediately thereafter he issued a second instruction to his medical boards telling them to stop passing the lame, the halt, and the blind, examples of each of which he had just seen in uniform. Under close questioning, Bedford tried to play down the force of his second instruction, which so clearly demonstrated the absurdity of the first. He said he had been temporarily depressed by the sight of disabled men in uniform, and as a result, his response had been too extreme.[55]

It did not take long for members of the select committee to present additional cases of disastrous, and in some instances fatal, misdiagnoses of recruits. Many of the mistakes derived from the fact that the army worked on the assumption that whatever his disability, if a man was fit enough to be in regular employment, he was fit enough to be in the army.[56] Another source of error was that some medical boards classified a man not according to his fitness at the time of the examination, but rather according to what they believed his fitness would be after three or four months of wholesome army life. In the opinion of some medical men, the army was just the right treatment for tubercular or syphilitic men.[57] It is not surprising that there were many complaints about this procedure from recruits, from recently commissioned doctors, and from civilian doctors whose letters certifying a man's disability were, on occasion, torn up.[58]

By July 1917 the case for a radical change drawn from the damaging testimony of the leadership of the Army Medical Corps was so overwhelming that the committee, while still in session, passed a resolution urging the immediate transfer of responsibility for medical examinations from the War Office to the Local Government Board. Lord Derby himself took the unusual step of appearing before the committee five days later to urge them to go even further and support the removal from the military of all responsibility for recruiting. As we have noted above, this was part of the overall review of manpower policy which led to the creation of the revamped Ministry of National Service, under Auckland Geddes.

The new scheme of medical examinations had two important political advantages over the old system. Firstly, the summer of 1917 was a time of growing unrest in the Labour movement. By making medical inspection for military service a civilian affair, the government hoped both to quiet fears about the militarization of British society and to reduce the suspicion and hostility some conscripts were bound to feel towards army doctors. Second, the reorganized Ministry was in a position to assert full control over the mobilization of the medical profession, which prior to 1917 had been in the hands of professional committees. We shall return to this story in chapter 5.

But the most important aim of the reform was to improve the standard of the inspection of recruits. Whether it did so or not is a question we shall address below. Let us summarize the structure of the new scheme. The chief administrator of the new system was Sir

James Galloway, now designated Chief Commissioner of Medical
Services. The country was divided into eight regions, each run by a
full-time regional commissioner. Each region was divided into
areas, in which medical boards were set up, presided over by a
civilian physician and staffed by a rota of civilian doctors, who
were not even employees of the Ministry. They were ordinary GPs
(general practitioners) who worked as consultants part of the week
for a flat fee, usually five guineas per session plus expenses. Only
in London did some doctors do this work full time. Elsewhere, the
work was periodic, after which doctors returned to their practices.[59]

The work of examining recruits was divided among four physicians. The first was to take the man's standard measurements and
distinguishing features. The second was to assess his general
condition and physique and to identify any deformities such as flat
feet. The third was to test vision, hearing, nerve reflexes and to
examine eyes, ears, teeth, throat and thyroid. The fourth was to
inspect the recruit's chest and abdomen, to inquire as to previous
medical history, and to form some judgment as to the man's
'mental condition'. Some doctors interpreted this to mean a question or two about previous incarceration in an asylum; others
asked the men to do simple sums. This fourth doctor was also
required to take urine specimens for analysis when necessary, such
as in cases of suspected diabetes. All this work was done at the rate
of twelve men per hour in two two-and-a-half hour sessions per
day. In other words, each doctor had on average five minutes with
each man. After all the tests had been completed, the doctors
discussed each case under the chairmanship of the president of the
board and reached a collective decision as to his classification.[60]

The Ministry's medical advisory committee devised a new I–IV
scale of fitness for military service. The old class 'A' became Grade
I in the new scheme. Grade II absorbed the old designations 'B-1'
and 'C-1', which consisted of men who had some disability but
sufficient fitness for garrison service abroad or at home. Such men
were supposed to be able to march six miles 'with ease', although
how doctors were able to judge this is unclear. Grade III was
drawn from the rest of the 'B' and 'C' categories. They were unfit
in varying degrees and ways but still could serve in the following
capacities: first, as auxiliary troops: 'sanitary inspectors, batmen,
cooks, storekeepers, butchers, clerks', or in non-combatant duties, such as those of grooms, drivers, and orderlies; secondly, as
labour battalion men, for the 'less mentally alert or older men',

such as bricklayers, carpenters, joiners, navvies, and masons; or thirdly, as men employed in sedentary work, if they were unable, in doctors' opinion, to walk five miles. Every individual of a lower degree of fitness was to be placed in Grade IV and rejected.[61]

Fig. 2.1, which is the frontispiece of the parliamentary paper produced on the medical service board examinations, presents graphic evidence of the contrasts in physique of the men placed in each of the four grades. Symptoms of respiratory tuberculosis, epilepsy, severe spinal curvature, and acute valvular diseases of the heart were deemed to be grounds for placing men in Grade IV. Flat feet, defective vision, rotten teeth, and 'poor physique' would keep most men out of Grade I, but whether they would be placed in Grades II–IV varied according to the temperament or experience of the men examining them.[62] All doctors (and recruits) knew, though, that to place a man in Grade III or IV was to ensure that he would not get into the firing line.

This was the scheme through which over 2.5 million examinations of recruits were carried out between November 1917 and the end of the war. Frequently the conditions under which the doctors worked were difficult, with inadequate light or heating in the masonic hall or redecorated public baths made available to them. In addition, the quota of 60 men per day was frequently exceeded. Even when it was not, the pressure of work was such as to ensure fatigue in the doctors and variations in the quality of their judgment. Provision was made for some diagnostic tests, but on the whole the team of doctors who staffed the boards made their own judgments and did so at a very rapid pace.[63]

They managed to examine and grade a huge population, a feat of medical stamina all the more remarkable in that relatively few doctors were available for this work. The roughly 2,500 men involved were thus responsible for about 1,000 decisions each.[64] In some areas particularly hard hit by medical enlistment, the pace of work was very hectic. The sheer volume of work inevitably meant that the decisions the doctors made, by and large in good faith, were bound to be faulty in a substantial number of cases.

B   Medical Judgments and Medical Misjudgments

The results of these examinations are presented in Tables 2.7 and 2.8. In the nation as a whole, over 41 per cent of recruits were placed in Grades III or IV, that is, outside the ranks of those who

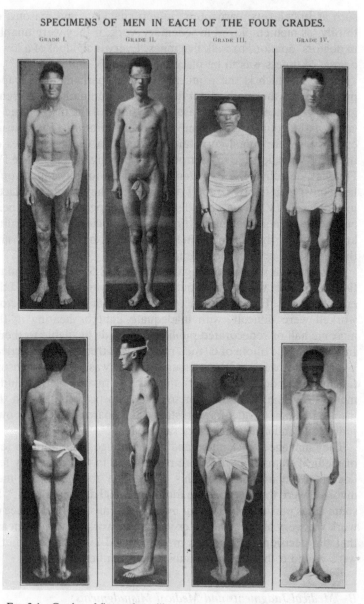

FIG. 2.1 Grades of fitness for military service in the British Army, 1917–18
SOURCE: PP(1919), vol. xvi, Cmd 504

TABLE 2.7 PERCENTAGE DISTRIBUTION OF MEN EXAMINED BY NATIONAL SERVICE MEDICAL BOARDS, IN FOUR GRADES OF FITNESS FOR MILITARY SERVICE, 1917–18

Region	Countries comprising	Grade I	Grade II	Grade III	Grade IV
1. London and south-eastern	London, Kent, Surrey, Hampshire, Sussex	28.2	23.2	36.1	12.5
2. North-western	Lancashire and Cheshire	31.0	25.1	32.6	11.3
3. West Midlands	Staffordshire, Warwickshire Worcestershire, Herefordshire, Shropshire	37.1	22.1	31.4	9.4
4. Yorkshire and East Midlands	Yorkshire, Nottinghamshire, Derbyshire, Leicestershire, Northamptonshire, Rutland	40.9	22.4	29.2	7.5
5. Eastern	Norfolk, Suffolk, Essex, Cambridgeshire, Huntingdon, Bedfordshire, Buckinghamshire, Oxfordshire, Berkshire, Hertfordshire	31.8	25.1	31.3	11.8
6. Northern	Northumberland, Durham, Cumberland, Westmorland	43.6	16.8	29.6	10.0
7. South-West	Gloucestershire, Wiltshire, Somersetshire, Dorsetshire, Devonshire, Cornwall	30.8	23.6	31.6	14.0
8. Scotland		44.2	19.3	28.2	8.3
9. Wales		46.0	21.3	25.2	7.6
Britain		36.0	22.5	31.3	10.3

SOURCE: *Report upon the Physical Examination of Men of Military Age by National Service Medical Boards from November 1st 1917 – October 31st 1918*, PP 1919, XXVI, Cmd 504.

TABLE 2.8 DISTRIBUTION OF MEN EXAMINED BY NATIONAL SERVICE MEDICAL BOARDS, IN FOUR GRADES OF FITNESS FOR MILITARY SERVICE, 1917–18

Region	Total examined	Grade I	Grade II	Grade III	Grade IV
1. London and South-Eastern	432,400	123,328	101,304	157,927	54,841
2. North-Western	385,579	119,670	96,638	125,543	43,728
3. West Midlands	231,835	86,073	51,165	72,906	21,691
4. Yorkshire and East Midlands	388,479	158,839	87,181	113,532	28,927
5. Eastern	216,012	68,604	54,360	67,492	25,556
6. Northern	146,324	63,720	24,640	43,383	14,581
7. South-West	188,746	58,057	44,473	59,705	26,511
8. Scotland	258,878	114,459	49,923	73,059[a]	21,437
9. Wales	171,931	79,019	36,592	43,312	13,008
Britain	2,425,184[a]	871,769	546,276	756,859	250,280

[a] There is a typographical error in the Scottish report, on p. 145, which has been corrected here. Relevant totals have also been adjusted.

SOURCE: See Table 2.7.

would be likely to see combat. Over 10 per cent of all men were deemed completely unfit for military service of any kind. Overall, the south and west of England had the highest proportion of men in these two grades; Scotland and Wales had the smallest. We should not make too much of these regional differences, since they were registered after three years of military recruitment, which as we have noted, was uneven in its regional incidence. For example, the lowest rates of Grade IV classification were reported in Yorkshire and the East Midlands, areas in which recruitment early in the war lagged behind the rest of the nation.

In aggregate terms, it is apparent that even on the basis of cursory medical examinations, over 1 million British men were deemed to be unfit for frontline duty in the last year of the Great War. This is an even clearer demonstration of the strategic costs of poverty than that which came out of the uproar over the rejection rate in the Boer War (see chapter 1). But there is considerable evidence that even this huge total of men placed in Grades III and IV actually *understated* the degree to which unfitness hampered Britain's military effort in the 1914–18 conflict.

A searching discussion of this question took place in the House of Commons on 27 June 1918. The matter at issue was the meaning of Grade I classification at ages 42–51, but the debate quickly revealed serious inadequacies in the way the medical boards ignored disabilities in trying to find as many men as possible for the army. Sir Donald MacLean, chairman of the London Appeals Tribunal and the Commons Ways and Means Committee, informed the House that terrible misdiagnoses had occurred in all too many cases. This was of no possible benefit to the army, which had to direct really fit men to look after the unfit. Sir William Collins, a distinguished physician, went even further and said that while the profession was at its best in treating the sick and wounded, it was 'probably seen at its worst' in these examinations.[65] Collins reminded the House that he had spoken a year earlier during the 1917 army estimates debate about this matter:

After all, medicine and surgery, though progressive sciences, were not exact sciences, and that they did not lend themselves very readily to this strict routine method of categorization imposed upon them. I said an impossible task has been imposed upon the medical men who were asked to perform this process and duties of categorization. . . . We are still asking the doctors, who have struggled to do their best under most difficult circumstances, to do the impossible.

He defied anyone to defend the soundness of judgments made as a result of examinations of a few minutes. What was really happening, he concluded, was that 'The impossible had disguised itself as a fact, and it was going through the hollow mockery of taking place'.[66]

Other MPs added their own experiences of medical misjudgment. Sir Herbert Neild, deputy chairman of Middlesex magistrates, raised the cases of men with active tuberculosis, kidney stones, and gall stones, all certified fit by medical boards. He also pointed out the difficulty of trying to hear a heartbeat in a public hall filled with four doctors, several clerks, and dozens of recruits. Another member described a visit to a London board which had convinced him that many unfit men were being passed fit for the army.[67]

On this and other occasions, doubts were expressed publicly about medical examinations, the results of which appeared to be suspect. There was the case of an epileptic who had died in uniform after a fit, despite the fact that he had brought medical certificates as to his condition to the attention of the medical board.[68] There were examples of men suffering from TNT poisoning being placed in Grade II on the grounds that military training was just what they needed.[69] One irate MP brought up the case of a 43-year-old haemophiliac who had presented to a medical board evidence of his condition. Not only did the board somehow reach the conclusion that he should be placed in Grade III, but to add injury to insult, as it were, he almost died of the examination itself.[70] Within the Ministry of National Service itself, there was concern about the complaint of the RAF in 1918 that grossly unfit men were being placed in Grade I.[71]

The initial workings of the Ministry of Pensions also uncovered evidence of underestimation of disability among recruits. Sir Donald MacLean told the House that of 132 applications to the London war pensions committee in the spring of 1918, 87 (or fully two-thirds) were by men the cause of whose discharge was unrelated to their military service.[72] This problem appeared when MPs discussed the hefty sums required for the payment of war pensions. In late 1919, the Member for East Edinburgh, J. M. Hogge, raised the question of the way medical boards let into the army thousands of unfit men. 'I remember them', he said, 'more in sorrow than in anger', since they had made pensioners out of men who should have stayed out of uniform. 'I feel personally', he argued:

> that these medical boards in most cases were a gross scandal, and it is true to say that the National Service Department has contributed more to the necessity for this large sum of money we are voting than any single organization in the country . . . If their abilities to assess a man who is disabled are about as good as their abilities to consider a man's fitness to go into the Army, then I have nothing more or less than the highest contempt for their particular role.[73]

Another MP, who had served on a medical board, believed that mistakes and haste were 'part of the cause of our heavy pension list'. He knew that under pressure a medical board simply took a man's statement, looked him over, and simply guessed as to his fitness for the army.[74]

Most of these critics recognized that the army had to have some criteria of fitness to bear arms in order to keep up regimental strength during the war. But they never provided a workable alternative, and hence the War Office and the later Ministry of National Service schemes triumphed by default. Today it is difficult enough to diagnose many of the ailments catalogued and counted in the National Service reports. How much more difficult it must have been then for physicians to have identified with any degree of precision the extent to which recruits were suffering from chronic or acute diseases.

Of course, mistakes were made in the opposite direction: some fit men were certainly excluded from the army. One distant reminder of this was the notice in *The Times* of 29 June 1982 that 'Mr Arthur Wood, who was rejected by the Army 60 years ago because of a weak heart, died in an old people's home at Kettering, Northamptonshire, yesterday at the age of 106'. But the balance of misjudgment probably tilted the other way, towards missing conditions which reduced the military usefulness of many recruits to the vanishing point and indeed which made their presence in uniform a positive liability. We must conclude, therefore, that a not insignificant part of the 60 per cent of recruits placed in Grades I–II in 1917 were unfit for combat even before they had begun their training. It is probably futile to put a precise figure on the total number of misclassified men, but since 40 per cent were placed in Grades III and IV, it is probably safe to assume that over half the male population conscripted in 1916–18 were physically unfit for front-line duty.

This was certainly true of industrial areas, in which the proportions in Grades III and IV were considerably higher than in the total population. In Leeds, 'seven out of ten are *hors de combat* before they even shoulder a musket'.[75] In Stockport, the medical boards reported that 'the average man here is, for military purposes, an old man before he reaches the age of forty'.[76] The figures for Leicester told the same story.[77] Consider the 210 18-year-olds from Lancashire and Cheshire who were placed in Grade IV. Their *average* measurements were: height, 4 ft 9 in; weight, 84 lbs; chest girth, 30 in.[78] London and Leeds, areas in which there were concentrations of immigrants as well as poorly-paid, semi-skilled or unskilled native workers, showed the worst fitness record in Britain.[79]

The report of the Ministry of National Service Medical Boards offered a number of explanations of the poor showing of certain occupational groups. The metalworker was unhealthy 'doubtless because he works in a superheated atmosphere and has to stand for long hours upon hot surfaces. These men often age prematurely. . . .'[80] Men in the textile trades showed the effects of cramped and poorly ventilated workshop conditions.[81] In the Scottish report, the 'housing, feeding and social surroundings' in which working-class children had grown up were regarded as the real source of the infirmities illustrated in these medical examinations.[82]

The major exception to this pattern of low standards of working-class health were the miners. They 'produced an excellent type of recruit, hard, well-developed, and muscular . . . . Though rather undersized and apt to be anaemic, he makes rapid improvement under the favourable conditions of training, feeding, and fresh air provided in the Army.'[83] Among Welsh miners, those of the western region were the healthiest. In the eastern region, where conditions were not as good as in the western seams, the record was less impressive. The reason was that good wages in the eastern pits attracted manual workers from Bristol and other towns. Such men showed the characteristically urban lower physical profile.[84]

There are difficulties in handling some of the evidence in this report, related to the preconceptions of some of its authors.[85] But its basic conclusion was sound. Clearly Britain's war effort was hampered significantly by the 'conditions of life created by our industrial development'.[86]

For our purposes, such conditions meant that the majority of working-class men were, by the medical standards of the day, unfit to shoulder the burdens of trench warfare. Given the fact that roughly four-fifths of the population was working-class, it is probably a conservative estimate to suggest that 200,000 of the 250,000 men placed in Class IV in 1917–18 were working-class. The same number may well have been turned down in the first three years of the war on the same grounds. Some of them were probably kept in the industrial labour force both because they were unfit and because they were needed at home. But if I am right in suggesting that the medical examination of recruits understated disability, in particular among working men, then the total of 400,000 men saved by their infirmities from the trenches may not be far off the truth. We have already noted that the number of potential working-class recruits was approximately 600,000 less than it would have been had manual workers' and non-manual workers' enlistment rates been the same. It is possible to suggest, therefore, that British Forces in the Great War would have constituted a cross-section of British society had they contained roughly 1 million more working-class men.

For this reason, despite heavy enlistment among all sections of society early in the war, casualty rates among manual workers were bound to be lower than among middle-class men or social elites. We have seen how the proportion of men enlisting in the first two years of the war varied from around 30 per cent for manual workers to over 40 per cent for non-manual workers. No similar figures exist for the upper or upper-middle class, but there is every indication that rates of enlistment and of satisfactory physical fitness among young men in these more privileged groups were higher still. We may conclude, therefore, that a man's occupational position had a direct bearing on the length of time he spent in the armed forces and on whether he was likely to see combat. Higher social status carried with it increased risks of becoming a casualty during the Great War.

3. The Lost Generation

THIS chapter constitutes the first full account of the social distribution of British casualties in the Great War. One reason why such a study has not been carried out before is that we have not had reliable estimates of war losses for the nation as a whole. It is a remarkable fact that the most fundamental question about the effect of the war – the number and ages of those who died in it – has never been rigorously examined. Instead, wildly varying estimates have been presented, differing by up to 100 per cent, of the total killed.

It is against this hazy background of conjecture masquerading as fact that all discussions of Britain's war losses have been conducted, including the persistent claim that Britain lost an entire generation of young poets, philosophers, and politicians in the war. It is clear that before we can assess the validity of this enduring belief, we must try to establish a reliable answer to these baffling simple questions: how many men were killed or died on active military service, and what was the age distribution of Britain's war losses? In the first two parts of this chapter, we present the general data on the dimensions and age-structure of British war losses against which the idea that there was a 'Lost Generation' of the privileged will be tested.

In the third and fourth parts of this chapter, we examine the available evidence concerning the social structure of British war losses. In chapter 2 we have examined the statistics relating to enlistment and conscription, which show that rates of military participation varied by occupation so that, the higher up in the social scale a man was, the greater were the chances that he would serve from early in the war and that he would do so in a combat unit. But there are two other important reasons why casualties were unevenly distributed in the British population in a way that was unfavourable to the well-to-do and the highly educated. They are that casualty rates among officers were substantially higher than among men in the ranks, and that the most dangerous rank in the army – the subaltern – was recruited throughout much of the war from current pupils or old boys of the public schools and ancient universities: the finishing schools of the propertied classes. Thus the disproportionate share of casualties suffered by the middle and upper classes was in part a direct consequence of the social selection of the officer corps. The military statistics on casualties by rank and the war service records of the public schools and universities have been used to examine these questions.

I   WAR LOSSES AMONG BRITISH FORCES IN THE 1914–18 WAR

In the two generations that have followed the Armistice, literally thousands of books have been published on the British war effort. One feature they all share is consistent imprecision over war casualties.[1] Most of the writers who addressed the seemingly simple question as to how many British and Irish men died on active service in the First World War wandered into a statistical maze, escape from which apparently was beyond them. Journalists, statisticians, demographers, politicians, and historians have all tried their hand at getting a complete picture of aggregate war losses. Some may have felt that accuracy was pointless when the toll reached hitherto inconceivable dimensions. However, another important reason for such variance in estimates of casualties is the intractability of the sources from which they were drawn. This explanation for wide divergences must remain a conjecture, since most authorities neither cited the sources they used nor explained the methods adopted to interpret them.

Behind all of this there are, however, two objective and connected problems. The first is that there are no straightforward data we can rely on, and therefore the second problem is to devise methods to make up for this lack of recorded evidence. In the past the two main types of sources used to provide an estimate of war losses have been (i) the decennial data in the census and the annual data in registrar-general's reports, and (ii), military reports. Each has its peculiar problems.

Let us deal with each in turn. It was the policy of registrars-general to treat men who died abroad as permanent émigrés, who ceased to be part of the population for census purposes when they left the country.[2] Non-civilians who died in Britain were their responsibility; however some of them were not British, but had served in Allied forces and had died while being treated for wounds or disease in this country. If we consider the unavoidable degree of error in vital statistics and census data collected in less troubled times,[3] we must conclude that there are bound to be substantial inaccuracies in estimates which rely solely on initially distorted sources. Nevertheless, added to Irish war deaths, British census estimates give a very rough idea of the magnitude of British First World War losses. The total derived from these sources of 772,000 differs from many other published estimates[4] (see Table 3.1).

Our first question at this point is how close is this rough estimate to a total that can be obtained from a careful scrutiny of military records, the second problematic set of sources to which I now turn? Most military and naval reports are also afflicted with substantial inaccuracies. Every combatant nation published several sets of statistics relating to its own war losses and, on occasion, to those of its adversaries. Unfortunately, no two are identical. As von Clausewitz remarked, 'The returns made up on each side of losses in killed and wounded are never exact, seldom truthful, and in most cases, full of intentional misrepresentation.'[5] Considering Germany, Austria-Hungary or Russia, where defeat, revolution, and counter-revolution formed a continuum, this confusion is not unexpected. Neither is it surprising that French and German statistics were revised repeatedly to prove that the other side suffered more in the Great War.[6]

In the British case, the explanation seems to lie in a mixture of secrecy, lack of interest, and the loss of relevant documents. The original War Office and systematic Admiralty casualty reports apparently have not survived. Parliamentary papers were issued shortly after the war on the British air effort[7] and naval effort,[8] but neither provides fully satisfactory figures of totals who served and who were wounded or killed. The official medical history of the war devoted a volume to casualties,[9] but this otherwise invaluable work included with British losses those suffered by Dominion and Indian forces. The same imperial approach mars the official War Office statistics,[10] which appeared only a few months after the

TABLE 3.1 ESTIMATES OF TOTAL BRITISH WAR DEAD, 1914–18

Source	Estimate (000s)	Source	Estimate (000s)
1. 1921 Census of England & Wales: deaths abroad	577	14. The Times Diary and Index	662
2. 1921 Census of England & Wales: soldiers' deaths registered at home	68	15. National Register 1939	700
3. 1921 Census of Scotland: deaths abroad	74	16. War Office Statistics	702
4. Scottish Registrar-Genl Reports: soldiers' deaths registered at home	4	17. Hersch (a)	702
5. Ireland's Memorial Record	49	18. Urlanis	715
Total Britain and Ireland	772	19. Dumas & Vedel-Petersen	724
		20. Dearle	729
6. Round Table	550	21. Renouvin	740
7. Cox	550	22. Hersch (b)	745
8. Decennial Suppt. 1911–20[1]	560	23. Hansard	745
9. Glass and Grebenik[1]	563	24. Marwick	745
10. Bogart	616	25. Cruttwell	745
11. Associations françaises	619	26. Greenwood	772
12. Whitaker's 1919	659	27. Archives	803
13. Stevenson	659	28. Barnes	807
		29. Mitchell and Smith	815
		30. Singer and Small	908
		31. Wright	908
		32. Edmonds	996
		33. Le Drapeau Bleu	1,184

[1] England and Wales only.

SOURCES:
1–2 *Census of England and Wales, 1921. General Report with Appendices.*
3. *Census of Scotland, 1921. Preliminary Report.*
4. *60th–65th Annual Reports of the Registrar-General for Scotland, 1914–1919.*
5. *Ireland's Memorial Record 1914–18* (Dublin, 1923).
6. 'Military effort of the British Empire', *Round Table*, IX (1919).
7. P. R. Cox, *Demography* (Cambridge, 1970).
8. *Decennial Supplement to the Registrar-General's Report for England and Wales, 1911–20*, vol. III (1927).
9. D. V. Glass and E. Grebenik, *The Trend and Pattern of Fertility in Great Britain* (1954).
10. E. L. Bogart, *Direct and Indirect Costs of the Great War* (1920).
11. *Bulletin de l'union des grandes associations françaises contre la propaganda ennemie*, 27 May 1919, as cited in S. Dumas and K. O. Vedel-Petersen, *Losses of Life Caused by War* (Oxford, 1923).
12. *Whitaker's Almanac, 1919.*
13. T. H. C. Stevenson, private communication to Dumas and Vedel-Petersen, in *Losses of Life.*
14. *The Times Diary and Index of the War* (1920).
15. *National Register of the United Kingdom and the Isle of Man. State of Population on 19 September 1939* (1944).
16. *Statistics of the Military Effort of the British Empire during the Great War* (1922).
17. L. Hersch, *La mortalité causée par la guerre mondiale*, *Metron*, V (1925).
18. B. Urlanis, *Wars and Population* (Moscow, 1971).
19. See note 11.
20. N. B. Dearle, *The Labor Cost of the World War to Great Britain 1914–1922* (New Haven, 1940).
21. P. Renouvin, *La crise européenne et la première guerre mondiale* (Paris, 1962).
22. L. Hersch, 'Demographic effects of modern warfare', in *What Would Be the Character of a New War?* (1933).
23. *Hansard's Parliamentary Debates*, 6th ser., CXLI, 4 May 1921, cols 1033–4.
24. A. Marwick, *War and Social Change in the Twentieth Century* (1974).
25. C. M. R. F. Cruttwell, *A History of the Great War, 1914–18* (1936).
26. M. Greenwood, 'British loss of life in the wars of 1794–1815 and 1914–1918', *Journal of the Royal Statistical Society*, CV, 1 (1942).
27. 'Les pertes des nations belligérantes au cours de la grande guerre', *Archives de la grande guerre* (1921).
28. H. E. Barnes, 'The World War of 1914–1918', in W. Waller (ed.), *War in the Twentieth Century* (New York, 1940).
29. T. J. Mitchell and G. M. Smith, *Medical Services: Casualties and Medical Statistics of the Great War* (1931).
30. J. D. Singer and M. Small, *The Wages of War 1815–1965. A Statistical Handbook* (New York, 1972).
31. Q. Wright, *A Study of War* (Chicago, 1942).
32. J. E. Edmonds, *A Short History of the World War* (1951).
33. *Le Drapeau bleu*, 13 December 1919, as cited in Dumas and Vedel-Petersen, *Losses of Life.*

officially definitive (and different) total was inserted in *Hansard's Parliamentary Debates* by Austen Chamberlain, the responsible minister, on 4 May 1921.[11] Despite the obvious conflict with other estimates, the authority of *Hansard* has been accepted uncritically in many war studies.

The only alternative to using these general estimates, whose reliability is questionable, or the ideal source, which would have been War Office, Admiralty and, from mid-1918, Ministry of Air unpublished statistics, is to trace the aggregate war losses of each of the three armed forces. These sources are the only possible means of arriving at a reasonably accurate estimate of British war losses in the First World War, and to my knowledge, they have not been used in this way before.

The first step in our analysis is to arrive at an estimate of war losses on the basis of these sources, and then to compare it to the total of 772,000 which arose from census and vital statistical reports. What we need are sources which distinguish between the military effort of Britain and that of other Allied countries. If they recorded the incidence of casualties over time, and if they distrib-uted British casualties by theatre of operation, by branch of service, and by rank, the reliability of the total can be checked against other records. On all these grounds, the most accurate treatment of British war casualties is the *General Annual Report of the British Army* for the war years.[12] For our purposes, though, there is one minor flaw in the report. It includes about 1,000 casualties suffered during the Allied intervention in Russia, which is (at best) a debatable part of the British war effort. But compared with the other available sources it is a paragon of reliability.

Not as detailed but similarly comprehensive is the volume of the Committee of Imperial Defence *History of the Great War* which deals with naval operations.[13] A similar volume was prepared for the war in the air, but like all other sources related to Royal Flying Corps/Royal Air Force casualties, it does not provide a global figure for the number of men who served. Instead we learn the total strength of these forces at different points in the war.[14] The Royal Flying Corps provided each new recruit with a service number, which ran consecutively from 1 onward, and it is likely that the figure given in the official history for total strength on 1 November 1918 actually reflects the total number of men who served in the various air corps from the beginning of the war.[15]

There are further definitional problems here, concerning double counting of naval and army air personnel in the period prior to the birth of the Royal Air Force. But despite all these difficulties, we are unlikely to find a better estimate of the number of men who served in this branch of service than that which appears in the Committee of Imperial Defence volume on *The War in the Air*.[16]

If we add together the best estimates of war losses among the three service arms, we arrive at a total of 722,785 British servicemen who died in the First World War. While this is not identical to the census-based estimate, it is close to several traditional figures on war losses, the derivation of which is unknown (see Table 3.1). Even this total, though, is bound to contain some ambiguity. First, over 41,000 army officers and men were killed between 1 October 1918 and 30 September 1919, but these deaths, occurring after the Armistice, are still treated as war losses. But if we accept this logic, why should we not include deaths suffered after 1 October 1919? In the annual reports of the Registrar-General for Scotland, for instance, war-related deaths are recorded for every year between 1919 and 1939. Many ex-soldiers suffered long after the Armistice from the effects of war wounds or illness. While it is impossible to claim that the deaths of all of them were war-related, it seems sensible to admit the fallacy of defining war deaths as solely those which occurred before 11 a.m. on 11 November 1918. To use *The General Report of the British Army*, together with the naval and air volumes of the official war history, is therefore a compromise, between a legalistic exclusion of post-Armistice deaths and a perhaps too generous inclusion of all deaths of disabled ex-servicemen in the post-war decades.

Having established an acceptable total for British war losses as a whole, it is now possible to describe casualties as a percentage of the total who served, both for British forces as a whole and for different service arms. The data in Table 3.2 show in approximate fashion the nationality and service arms of the over 6 million British and Irishmen who served in the 1914–18 war and who formed the population at risk. In the Great War (in contrast to the 1939–45 conflict), casualties were mainly confined to members of the armed services. Civilian losses, though, did occur. There were over 15,000 deaths among crews and passengers of merchant or fishing vessels and 1,266 civilian ftalities of air and sea bombardment. It was Britain's singular good fortune that of all European combatants,

TABLE 3.2   DISTRIBUTION OF MEN WHO SERVED IN BRITISH FORCES IN THE FIRST
WORLD WAR, BY COUNTRY OF RECRUITMENT AND BRANCH OF SERVICE

Branch of Service	Country			
	England and Wales[a]	Scotland[b]	Ireland[b]	Total
Regular Army and Territorial Forces	4,485,039	584,098	146,025	5,215,162
Royal Navy and Allied Services	550,604	71,707	17,926	640,237
Royal Flying Corps and Royal Air Force[c]	250,411	32,611	8,153	291,175
All services	5,286,054	688,416	172,104	6,146,574

[a] 86 per cent of all men who served were from England and Wales. Hence 86 per cent of the totals for Territorial Forces, Royal Navy, and Royal Flying Corps/Royal Air Force have been designated as English and Welsh.

[b] The ratio of Scots to Irish recruited into the British army was 4:1. Hence of the 14 per cent from those two countries, 11.2 per cent and 2.8 per cent have been designated as Scots and Irish, respectively.

[c] These totals represent the strength of the RAF in November 1918. No comparable figures of total who served in the RFC/RAF appear to have survived.

SOURCES: *General Annual Report of the British Army 1913–1919*, PP 1921, XX, Cmd 1193; H. Newbolt, *History of the Great War. Naval Operations* (1931), vol. V, Appendix J; H. A. Jones, *History of the Great War. War in the Air* (1937), Appendices 35–6.

only her population was virtually out of the line of fire. If we accept the definition of population at risk as those in uniform, then over 40 per cent of those at risk suffered casualties. One in eight was killed. Over one in four was wounded. As we can see in Table 3.3, casualty rates in the army were much higher than in the navy or RFC/RAF where, respectively, one in sixteen, and one in fifty was killed. The proportion wounded in the army was ten times higher than in either of the other two services. In aggregate, those who served in the army had only a one in two chance of surviving the war without being killed, wounded, or taken prisoner.

These statistics can serve as a basis for putting British war losses into perspective. The same strictures against trusting official statistics of British war losses apply, perhaps with even greater force,

TABLE 3.3 CASUALTIES SUFFERED BY BRITISH FORCES IN THE GREAT WAR

Branch of service	Served	Died or killed	Percentage died or killed	Wounded	Percentage wounded	Prisoners of war	Percentage prisoners of war	Total	All casualties as percentage of total who served
Army	5,215,162	673,375	12.91	1,643,469	31.51	154,308	2.96	2,471,152	47.38
Navy	640,237	43,244	6.75	25,323	3.96	5,722	0.89	74,289	11.60
RFC/RAF	291,175	6,166	2.12	7,245	2.49	3,212	1.10	16,623	5.71
Total	6,146,574	722,785	11.76	1,676,037	27.27	163,242	2.66	2,562,064	41.68

SOURCE: See Table 3.2

when we survey the cases of other combatant nations. But it is still worthwhile to use such sources to provide a rough framework of comparison in which to set British casualty rates. Could we trust these data, we would see that, taking the proportion of men killed as a percentage of men mobilized as a measure, loss of life in British forces appears to have been slightly higher than in the German or Austrian armies, similar to that in the Italian, and lower than that in the French army, where one in six was lost. The British figures, though, are much lower than those for losses suffered by the Romanian army, which lost one in three, and in the Serbian army, in which over 37 per cent of the men mobilized were killed.[17] (See Table 3.4.)

If we adopt as an index men killed as a percentage of the total male population aged 15–49, Serbia and Romania still appear as the countries most severely affected by war losses. France's loss of one in eight in this age group was greater than that suffered by Germany or Austria-Hungary (10 per cent) and nearly twice that of Britain (6.7 per cent).[18]

One further comparison may help to set the British statistics in a comparative framework. During the Second World War, the eminent medical statistician, Major Greenwood, produced a study comparing loss of life in the Revolutionary and Napoleonic Wars with that of the 1914–18 conflict. He concluded that roughly equal proportions of the total populations were killed, and that, therefore, the direct cost in terms of deaths was about the same in the two world conflicts.[19] Of course, the concentration of war-related mortality in 4 years of continuous bloodshed as opposed to 23 years of intermittent fighting makes this comparison somewhat forced. More suggestive is Greenwood's comparison of non-battle to battle casualties in the two war periods, 1794–1815 and 1914–1918. Here he drew on the work of W. B. Hodge, who during the Crimean War also took a backward look to the wars against the French. Hodge showed that for every battle casualty in the British army from 1794–1815, there were eight caused by disease or injury not related to enemy action.[20] One hundred years later, Greenwood noted, thanks to medical improvements on the one hand and the refinements of strategy and weapons on the other, the ratio was almost reversed. For every single non-combat casualty in the British army during the 1914–18 war, 5.3 men were either killed, wounded or missing in action.[21]

TABLE 3.4 SOME ESTIMATES OF MILITARY LOSSES AMONG COMBATANT COUNTRIES IN THE 1914–18 WAR

Country	Total killed or died	Total mobilized	Pre-war male pop. 15–49	Total pre-war population	Total Killed		
					per 1,000 mobilized	per 1,000 males 15–49	per 1,000 people
	(in thousands)						
Britain & Ireland	723	6,147	11,540	45,221	118	63	16
Canada	61	629	2,320	8,100	97	26	8
Australia	60	413	1,370	4,900	145	44	12
New Zealand	16	129	320	1,100	124	50	15
South Africa	7	136	1,700	6,300	51	4	1
India	54	953	82,600	321,800	57	1	0
France	1,327	7,891	9,981	39,600	168	133	34
French colonies	71	449	13,200	52,700	158	5	1
Belgium	38	365	1,924	7,600	104	20	5
Italy	578	5,615	7,767	35,900	103	75	16
Portugal	7	100	1,315	6,100	70	5	1
Greece	26	353	1,235	4,900	73	21	5
Serbia	278	750	1,225	4,900	371	227	57
Rumania	250	1,000	1,900	7,600	250	132	33
Russia	1,811	15,798	40,080	167,000	115	45	11
United States	114	4,273	25,541	98,800	27	4	1
Allied Total	5,421	45,001	204,018	812,521	120	27	7
Germany	2,037	13,200	16,316	67,800	154	125	30
Austria-Hungary	1,100	9,000	12,176	58,600	122	90	19
Turkey	804	2,998	5,425	21,700	268	148	37
Bulgaria	88	400	1,100	4,700	220	80	19
Central Powers' Total	4,029	25,598	35,017	152,800	157	115	26
Grand Total	9,450	70,599	239,035	965,321	134	40	10

SOURCES: B. Urlanis, *Wars and Population*; L. Hersch, 'La mortalité causée par la guerre'; *Statistics of the Military Effort of the British Empire*; and Table 3.3.

This completes the first step in the analysis of British war losses: arriving at a reliable estimate of the total number of deaths. The next step is to attempt an analysis of the age structure of deaths, which entails the use of complicated demographic methods of analysis.

II THE AGE STRUCTURE OF WAR LOSSES

The problem of establishing an age structure of war losses is easy to state but extremely difficult to overcome. The problem is that the only existing age breakdown of deaths during the war years does not differentiate between deaths caused by war and deaths attributable to natural causes. Such information for France and Germany has been available for 50 years,[22] but here again British reports are silent. Very sketchy data on the age distribution of Second World War losses have been published,[23] but similar official statistics for the First World War apparently do not exist.

The imperfect data that we do have are not – as one would expect perhaps – registrar-general's reports, which are useless for our purposes since they do not incorporate military mortality abroad. The only source that includes soldiers' deaths within a general population divided into age groups is a set of life tables for the years 1913 and 1915–17 prepared by the Prudential Assurance Company.[24] These data, by themselves, are far from unproblematic, but properly exploited they can serve as a basis for accurately estimating the age structure of British war losses.

This estimate will emerge from a somewhat complex application of what historians call 'counterfactual' reasoning, but first I shall simply describe the nature of the Prudential evidence, its limitations and utility. By the end of the war, the Prudential Assurance Company had been in the business of providing life insurance for working men for 64 years. From modest beginnings in 1854, its industrial department grew rapidly in the following decades, with much of the work centring in the industrial Midlands, Lancashire, and Yorkshire.[25] In fact, the Prudential was so successful that a Post Office departmental committee was set up in 1907 to discover the causes of the unpopularity of Post Office insurance schemes. Sir Edward Brabrook, former Chief Registrar of Friendly Societies, attributed the Prudential's lion's share of industrial assurance to its good management, its reliability, and its tolerance of brief lapses in the payment of small weekly premiums. Brabrook told the committee that for these reasons the Prudential 'has deservedly got the great position of influence which it has amongst the working classes'.[26] In 1915, there were nearly 21 million Prudential life insurance policies in force, which covered the lives of about 5 million men. The data show the structure of mortality of a mixed military and civilian population, perhaps one-quarter of the over 6 million men in the Forces and about one-half of the men who manned the war economy.[27]

There is no way of knowing how representative of the British working class were the 5 million men who held Prudential policies. On the one hand, some unskilled or casual workers may have been unable to keep up the premiums, no matter how small. They were, in fact, only a penny (1d.) a week. Since their mortality rates were well above the national average (see chapter 4) their absence in the insured population means that some downward distortion is bound to occur in the use of the Prudential data. But on the other hand, there is evidence that about 50 per cent of all miners, or over 400,000 men, held Prudential policies at the end of the century.[28] Despite high risks of mortality due to accident and respiratory diseases, the overall mortality levels of miners were relatively low, which introduces another downward distortion in the data. Nevertheless it may be concluded that the Prudential population was composed of the urban, semi-skilled and skilled working class of the industrial Midlands, the north, and the London area. On the shoulders of these men fell much of the burden of war production, and in chapter 4 we shall use this evidence to throw light on the immediate impact of the First World War on the health of the civilian population.

But our purpose here is to describe mortality patterns among all the men who joined the Forces, and in this respect the class bias of the data does present problems. Firstly, only about 30 per cent of Prudential policyholders joined up, a figure substantially lower than the aggregate enlistment rate. And second, until late in the war very few of the men covered by the Prudential would have received commissions. As we shall note below, we cannot assume that casualty rates among officers and men in the ranks were of the same order of magnitude. Hence some distortion is bound to occur in the use of these data in an attempt to describe the age distribution of aggregate military losses. Still, the fact that 19 out of every 20 men in uniform served in the ranks lends weight to the claims of the Prudential's actuary that the data were (and still are): 'The only published statistics showing the incidence of the War on the mortality of a section of the community sufficiently large to be representative of the whole male population' and that 'They are a fair index of the toll that the War has taken of the manhood of the nation'.[29]

For our purposes, there are two difficulties in using these data to obtain estimates of the age structure of war-related mortality. The first minor one is the omission of data for 1914 and 1918. These gaps can be filled, first by estimating 1914 life table mortality rates by combining data for 1913 and 1915 in roughly two to one proportions, given the fact that war began only in August 1914; and secondly, by assuming, *faute de mieux*, that the 1918 mortality schedule was identical to that for 1917. In this way, we have produced an annual breakdown of life table mortality rates for each one of the war years.

We now reach the major problem: the lack of differentiation between civilian and non-civilian mortality rates. Assuming that the 1913 Prudential life tables describe what may be termed the 'normal' pre-war mortality schedule of the male population, we may project this, with adjustments for the secular trend of mortality decline, onto the following five years (1914–18) and take this projection as a hypothetical estimate of what the pattern of mortality would have been had there been no war. This we call the 'hypothetical peace estimate'. We may compare this counterfactual estimate with the actual total mortality derived from the Prudential life tables for each war year – the 'war estimate' – and take the difference as the best estimate of male deaths caused by the war – 'war-related deaths' (see Appendix).

However, two problems still remain. The first is that it should be remembered that the Prudential life tables give us only an indication of working-class mortality rates. For reasons indicated in chapter 2, the proportion of working-class military participation was less than that of the nation as a whole, which makes it reasonable to assume that the total of war-related mortality based on the Prudential data will be an underestimate. Secondly, working-class mortality rates in the pre-war period were higher than those for the male population as a whole, which means that using the Prudential data will lead to an inflated total of male deaths in the counterfactual estimate of 'normal' mortality. In addition the age structure of working-class mortality is not the same as that of the male population as a whole (see Appendix). While it is important to note these biases, it is likely that the one compensates for the other. We can therefore accept these data as good indicators of the age structure of deaths actually caused by the war.

The results of this exercise are presented in Appendix Tables A-2 and A-3 and in Fig. 3.1, which show clearly the way in which war losses mounted as the war went on.[30] We find, not surprisingly, that war-related mortality was greatest at age 20. Over the period 1914–18, men aged 17–37 show between two and eight times the hypothetical mortality they would have registered had there been no war. Men aged 38–46 registered more modest increases in mortality. Over age 48, the effect of the war appears to have been different. As the war continued, it seems that some men in their late forties and fifties, who were less likely than younger men to see combat, actually had improved chances of survival. This is shown by the negative figures of war-related mortality for later age groups in 1916 and 1917. The implications of this finding will be discussed in chapter 4 (see Fig. 4.1, p. 109).

Table A-2 illustrates the major features of the age structure of war-related mortality. After age 20, the rapid fall in the war estimates confirms the popular view that there was a direct correlation between age and chances of survival in British forces in the First World War. After age 45, the convergence of the 'counterfactual' estimate and the war estimate is apparent. Again we can see that the survival chances of men in their later forties and fifties had improved in 1916–17, in that at those ages the totals of war-related deaths are negative.

Of course, there is no way of proving that the figures for war-related deaths represent exclusively the mortality of men in uniform. It is possible that some of the increased mortality for the war years was due to an increase in civilian death rates. This we shall argue below was not the case, but provisionally we may make do with the intuitively plausible assumption that the vast majority of the increase in deaths at younger ages were war casualties.

So far we have been concerned with using the Prudential data for plotting the age-structure of war-related male mortality. However,

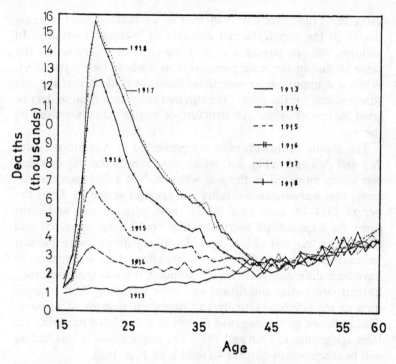

FIG. 3.1 Age-specific male mortality, England and Wales, 1913–18

it is worth noting that if we assume that the 1918 mortality schedule was identical to that of 1917, then the total of war-related deaths in 1914–18 based on the Prudential tables is only 548,749, compared with the total of 722,785 which we have derived from military and naval sources. Since the Prudential estimates were calculated on the basis of the male population of England and Wales only, it is necessary to increase our totals to take account of Scottish and Irish wartime mortality. This was done on the following assumption: since 86 per cent of the men who served came from England and Wales,[31] it is likely that the same proportion of total deaths were also of Englishmen and Welshmen. We have therefore 'inflated' our Prudential estimates of wartime mortality to the total found in Table 3.5. Using the Prudential data, we conclude, therefore, that due to the First World War, mortality levels among British and Irish men rose by over 637,000.

The difference between our estimate of 637,000 excess wartime

TABLE 3.5   TOTAL WAR-RELATED DEATHS IN GREAT BRITAIN AND IRELAND.
1914–18

| Year | War estimate | Hypothetical 'peace' estimate | War-related deaths |
	(1)	(2)	(1)–(2)
1914	121,000	94,000	27,000
1915	162,000	94,000	68,000
1916	215,000	92,000	123,000
1917	258,000	92,000	166,000
1918	256,000	92,000	164,000
1914–18 England and Wales	1,012,000	464,000	548,000
1914–18 Great Britain and Ireland^a	1,177,000	540,000	637,000

a.   Total for England and Wales divided by 0.86.

SOURCE: see text.

deaths and the total derived from military and naval statistics is
partly attributable to the class bias of the Prudential data, which as
we have already noted show the structure of the mortality of only
the working-class population, enlistment rates for which were
lower than those for white-collar workers. An additional relevant

TABLE 3.6   AGE STRUCTURE OF BRITISH WAR LOSSES, 1914–18

Age at death	Percent war deaths in each age group	Total war deaths in each age group
16–19	11.76	85,000
20–24	37.15	268,515
25–29	22.31	161,253
30–34	15.17	109,646
35–39	9.18	66,352
40–44	3.07	22,189
45–49	0.94	6,794
50+	0.42	3,036
Total		722,785

SOURCE: See text.

factor is that civilian health may well have improved in wartime, thereby producing a decline in mortality rates among the population insured by the Prudential. We shall describe in the next chapter how these data may indicate that the life expectation of working-class men who stayed out of the trenches actually rose during the war. Again we may note that projections based on their demographic experience are therefore bound to underestimate total war losses.[32]

It is thus reasonably safe to conclude that the Prudential data show with some precision the age structure of British and Irish war losses. Applying that age structure to the total of 722,785 war deaths yields the results shown in Table 3.6. Finally, we can apply the results of this exercise to describe the depletion of particular cohorts in the 1914–18 war. Of course, these are only approximate figures, since the size of cohorts changed between the 1911 census enumeration and the war period. But as we can see in Table 3.7, which presents data for England and Wales only, men under age

TABLE 3.7. AGE DISTRIBUTION OF MEN FROM ENGLAND AND WALES WHO SERVED
AND WHO DIED IN BRITISH FORCES IN THE FIRST WORLD WAR

Age	1911 census population	Total who served[a]	Total deaths[b]	Deaths as percent of all who served	Deaths as percent of 1911 age group
15–19	1,694,895	494,101	73,100	14.8	4.3
20–24	1,502,652	1,617,202	243,666	15.1	16.2
25–29	1,455,783	1,380,732	144,397	10.5	9.9
30–34	1,375,872	863,883	92,296	10.9	6.9
35–39	1,261,432	539,596	57,063	10.6	4.5
40–44	1,075,076	291,488	14,857	5.1	1.4
45–49	926,102	93,107	8,578	9.2	0.9
Total[c]	9,291,812	5,280,109	633,957	12.0	6.8

[a] Average for 1915–18 'non-civilian' population.
[b] 86.0 per cent of total deaths in Great Britain and Ireland were attributed to men from England and Wales.
[c] Deaths after age 50 have been omitted.

SOURCES: *Census of England and Wales, 1911, Summary Tables*, Table 29; *Decennial Supplement to the Registrar-General's Report for England and Wales 1911–20*, Vol. II, Table 2; Vol. III, Table 1.

25 were most likely to be killed (more than one in seven). At higher ages, the chances of a man in uniform being killed was one in ten at ages 25–40, and about one in twenty after age 40. The staggering burden borne by the men under age 30 is also apparent in these figures. Whereas about 35 per cent of men aged 15–49 in England and Wales in 1911 were under age 30, 70 per cent of all men in uniform and 74 per cent of the men who died were in that age group. Applying this last figure to the total killed, we may conclude that the First World War claimed the lives of over 500,000 men under the age of 30.

III CASUALTIES AND RANK

We are now in a position to be able to describe the incidence of war losses among particular social groups. Here the key argument is that a man's chances of survival in uniform were affected not only by the length of time he served, but perhaps more importantly, by his rank. This proposition can be tested by an analysis of the social composition of the army and RFC/RAF officer corps and of the statistics on casualties suffered by army officers and men in the ranks.

The War Office demobilization statistics make it possible to be fairly precise about the occupational structure of the officer corps. They list occupations previously held or, in the case of very young men, educational status or occupational intentions.[33] Approximately one-third of all officers demobilized from the British army and RFC/RAF were professional men, students or teachers. Of course, this group is but one component of the non-manual labour force; men in commercial or clerical jobs provided an equally significant part of the officer corps. We should note that the significant feature of these data is how high a proportion of middle-class men served as officers, rather than the actual numerical contribution they made. Approximately 44 per cent of all professional men and 38 per cent of all students and teachers who served in the army were officers. Engineering workers, 9 per cent of whom served as officers, provide the sole exception to this pattern of middle-class domination of the officer corps. The same correlation between occupation and rank appears in the RAF demobilization statistics.[34]

We have already noted the intention of Lord Derby to recruit officers from 'socially suitable' middle-class men who joined 'Pals' battalions. As the war went on, many such men were killed, and recruitment from the ranks tended to reduce the social exclusiveness of the officer corps. But the unlikelihood of many working-class men becoming officers, whatever the circumstances, was apparent to many observers at the time. For instance, we can sense this view in the apparently complimentary remark of the Chief Inspector of Mines, R. A. R. Redmayne, that in terms of patriotism, 'no section of the community did better and few as well' as the miners, 'none supplied a better type of soldier and non-commissioned officer'.[35] As we would expect, the class structure of British society was not mirrored primarily in the social composition of the officer corps which did recruit working men to its ranks throughout much of the First World War. Rather it was that most working-class recruits served as private soldiers whereas a far higher proportion of middle- and upper-class men who enlisted served as officers.

If it can be shown that there was a significant difference in casualty rates between officers and men, it will be possible to conclude that the social structure of rank helped determine the social distribution of casualties. How can we break down the army casualty figures? Official documents distribute casualties among service arms and by theatre of operation. Thus, we know that the infantry was by far the largest part of the army and, proportionately, suffered much the heaviest casualties. Whereas roughly two out of every three men in the army served in the infantry, more than four of every five men killed were infantrymen.[36] Of the men who died in the infantry 96 per cent did not have commissions. Even the most elitist observer could not deny the sheer weight of losses among the ranks of infantrymen, 450,000 of whom were killed or died in the war.

We also know that the deadliest theatre of operations was, as expected, France and Flanders, where for every nine men sent out, five were killed, wounded or missing. This figure is well above that for any other combat zone.[37] But what we do not know and cannot determine from the official military statistics are the numbers of corporals, sergeants, lieutenants, etc., and the number of casualties they suffered. The only distinction made is between officers and the rest, which joins together Lord Haig and Robert

Graves, a privilege neither would have appreciated, and justifiably so because it is odd to lump together the chances of survival of the many staff officers based well away from the Front and those of junior officers who manned the trenches.[38] During the First World War, junior officers shared more of the reality of war with NCOs and the men in the ranks than with senior officers, but the statistics have it otherwise.

Still, though we cannot determine the number of junior officers who served and who were killed, we can at least compare the overall figures for officers who served with those who were killed, wounded, or went missing. If it turns out that the percentage of officer deaths exceeds the percentage of officers in the army, we may conclude that officers bore a disproportionate share of war losses.

The hypothesis of 'surplus' officer deaths seems to hold for other armies and during other wars. One scholar, N. N. Golovine, was convinced that whichever of the numerous Russian sources is used, First World War losses among officers exceeded losses among men in the ranks of the Czarist army.[39] Studies of the French army in the 1914–18 war provide similar evidence for every branch of service.[40] The one dissenting voice is that of Alfred Vagts, a student of the military history of the Second World War, who believed that after the first months of open warfare in 1914 'as trench warfare followed, losses became more or less even among officers and the rank and file'.[41] But to Gaston Bodard, author of an historical survey of the human costs of war, the evidence had always pointed the other way. In 1916 he wrote:

> The officers of an army almost always show a much higher percentage of casualties than the men. This is to be explained by the effort to set before his men a good example in cool and courageous conduct. In several armies the relative loss of officers and men has not varied in the course of the wars of the last 150 years; hence the casualty loss of the men can be calculated with reasonable certainty from that of the officers.[42]

One need not go as far as Bodard to see that, when measured against total numbers serving in the First World War, British officers did indeed suffer higher casualties than men in the ranks (see Table 3.8). For example, on 1 October 1914, 33,393 officers were serving in the British army. During the next twelve months, 4,735 officers were killed. These were not the same men as those enumerated on 1 October 1914, since the army grew rapidly in the first year of the war. But the same variations applied to the men in the ranks, and we still find that 14 per cent of the officer corps as against 6 per cent of the rank and file were killed in the first year of the war. These sombre statistics lay behind the claim made by Field-Marshal Sir John French in a preface to a roll of honour of soldiers killed in the first year of the war, that: 'Enormous beyond precedent as these death rolls have been, it is a fact that the proportion of officers to men is in excess of what it has been in any former war.'[43] The surplus of officer deaths continued, although at a slightly lower level, throughout the war. We may note in Table 3.9 that a higher percentage of officers were wounded than were men in the ranks. It is only among missing soldiers that the proportions even out.

Confirmation that a disproportionate share of war casualties was borne by officers may be obtained by examining the military statistics from the angle mentioned earlier. If we take as our base population not the total number who served, but the total who were killed or died, we find that the proportion of officers who were killed or who died was higher than the proportion of officers in the army. As in Table 3.9, for example, from 1 October 1917 to 30 September 1918, 159,113 British soldiers were killed. Among them were 9,880 officers, or 6.2 per cent of all deaths. On 1 October 1917 and again on 1 October 1918, only between 3.6 and 3.8 per cent of the army were officers. The same pattern may be seen in the figures for officers wounded as a proportion of total wounded. And again, a rough parity is reached in terms of men missing and prisoners of war.

These data may be supplemented by figures from those regimental histories and war memoirs which discuss casualties. Despite the variation among units, the overall 'surplus' of officer deaths is common to virtually all of them. These figures are useful to corroborate the results of the analysis of army statistics. But since so many men served in more than one unit, and since the size of units was constantly changing, it is difficult to present precise statistics about the percentage of officers in each unit. Furthermore, the proportion of officers serving in an artillery battery, a tank unit, an infantry battalion, and a casualty clearing station,

TABLE 3.8 ARMY CASUALTIES AS BETWEEN OFFICERS AND OTHER RANKS, 1914-19

Period	Regimental strength at beginning of period		Percentage killed		Percentage wounded		Percentage missing and POWS		Percentage casualties among	
	Officers	Other ranks	Officers	Other ranks	Officers	Other ranks	Officers	Other ranks	Officers	Other ranks
1 Oct. 1914–30 Sept. 1915	33,393	1,293,979	14.2	5.8	24.4	17.4	3.7	2.9	42.3	26.1
1 Oct. 1915–30 Sept. 1916	92,578	2,383,186	8.0	4.9	17.4	14.0	1.3	1.3	26.7	20.2
1 Oct. 1916–30 Sept. 1917	110,786	3,233,011	8.5	4.7	17.6	12.3	1.5	1.1	27.6	18.1
1 Oct. 1917–30 Sept. 1918	143,533	3,739,484	6.9	4.0	17.1	13.9	3.4	3.4	27.4	21.3
1 Oct. 1918–30 Sept. 1919	147,738	3,690,527	1.0	1.1	3.3	2.2	0.1	0.1	4.4	3.4

SOURCE: *General Annual Report of the British Army 1913–1919*, PP 1921, xx, Cmd 1193.

TABLE 3.9. CASUALTIES AMONG ARMY OFFICERS AS A PERCENTAGE OF TOTAL
ARMY CASUALTIES, 1914–18

Period	Percentage of army holding rank of officer at beginning of period	Percentage of officers among		
		Total killed	Total wounded	Total missing or captured	Total casualties
4 Aug. 1914– 30 Sept. 1914	4.4	8.1	7.2	2.4	5.6
1 Oct. 1914– 30 Sept. 1915	2.5	5.9	3.5	3.1	4.0
1 Oct. 1915– 30 Sept. 1916	3.7	5.9	4.6	3.8	4.9
1 Oct. 1916– 30 Sept. 1917	3.3	5.1	4.7	4.4	4.9
1 Oct. 1917– 30 Sept. 1918	3.6	6.2	4.5	3.7	4.7
1 Oct. 1918– 30 Sept. 1919	3.8	3.6	5.6	4.2	4.9

SOURCE: See Table 3.8

was not the same. The different responsibilities of leadership in different units meant different casualty rates for each. In addition, the age structure of units varied. To judge by the lists of medical men trained at Scottish universities who entered the army when aged over 50,[44] the average age of Royal Army Medical Corps officers must have been higher than that of men in other branches of the services. Their mortality rate would certainly reflect this age differential.

The number of officers serving in the British army in August 1914 was 28,060. During the war, combat commissions were granted to 229,316 men. In addition, 5,053 chaplains and 12,692 doctors served as officers. Approximately 22,000 officers relinquished their commissions during the war, but this does not affect the total of 275,121 men who served as army officers during the war.[45] This represents 5.28 per cent of all men who served in the army. This figure seems to be very much in line with that of officers' deaths as a percentage of all army deaths, 5.57 per cent. This similarity is deceptive though, since the monthly accounts of the army's regimental strength show that on average 3.55 per cent of the army were officers.[46]

High losses among junior officers help account for the difference between the average monthly figures of deaths and the proportion of officers in the army. A constant stream of new men replenished the British officer corps. More and more men from the ranks were granted commissions as the carnage continued, which further complicates comparison, but it does not invalidate the claim that there were 'surplus' officer casualties among British forces in the Great War.

The limitations of the statistical record make it just as difficult to prove that within the officer corps, the junior officers bore the heaviest casualties. But, aside from common sense, there are reasons for believing that this must have been true. The 28th Battalion of the London Regiment, the Artists' Rifles, was a unit which specialized in training subalterns, and the men who passed through it suffered higher casualties than those of any other battalion, regiment or division.[47] In a preface to the war memorial book of this unit, Sir John French drew attention to the exceptionally high losses among men who had served in this battalion. He recalled the heavy days of fighting, when

> we had suffered fearful casualties, and the proportion of losses in officers was higher than in any other rank, and it was going on everyday . . . . I may recall at this moment, without frivolity, the fact that these boys, all of them, looked death straight in the face laughing and smiling, and that the Artists earned at that time the sobriquet of 'The Suicide Club'. That perhaps is the highest honour that could be paid to them.[48]

A number of soldier-writers described the fatalism of junior officers aware that their chances of survival were slim indeed. Robert Graves noted almost in passing that 'a man's average expectancy of trench service before getting killed or wounded was twice as long as an officer's'.[49] One of R. H. Mottram's characters in *The Spanish Farm Trilogy* spoke of the philosophical attitude of young infantry officers on the Western Front who knew 'that one had only to go up the Line often enough and death was certain'.[50] Under conditions of trench warfare, junior officers almost always led from the front, whether reconnoitring, raiding, or just holding the line. Few contemporaries had the slightest doubt that they were in a particularly vulnerable and frequently exposed position; hence the high death rates among the subaltern class, and ultimately among the officer class as a whole.

The pattern of higher officer losses is not repeated in the navy, where 8.65 per cent who served were officers, but 6.79 per cent of all sailors who died were officers. The obvious explanation for this discrepancy is that when a ship went down, everyone went down with it. This also helps to account for the fact that more men in the navy were killed than were wounded. In the RFC/RAF, the officer 'surplus mortality' reappears, but here again comparison with other services is difficult, since a large number of machinists and other technicians were needed to service each aircraft. In addition, since most men who actually flew were officers, it is not surprising that three out of four RFC/RAF men killed were commissioned.

Table 3.10 provides data on percentage killed of those who served by branch of service. Of all army officers who served, roughly one in seven was killed (compared to one in eight for the army as a whole), which is lower than the officer death rate in the French army. In the British navy, roughly one officer in twenty was killed, whereas in the RFC/RAF, roughly one in six was killed. Again, mortality rates for army and RFC men in the ranks were lower than for officers. Only in the navy did officers stand a greater chance of survival than the men they led.

The same phenomenon of 'surplus' officer deaths may be noted by briefly examining relevant French military statistics. The French appear to have lost a greater part of their officer corps than the British. Of 195,000 officers mobilized in France, 36,179 or 18.6 per cent were killed, compared to 16.1 per cent of the men who served in the ranks. The French statistics also provide data on death rates in various service arms and in combat and non-combat units. Overall, 29 per cent of all infantry officers were killed, against 23 per cent of infantrymen. All other service arms show the same pattern of 'surplus' officer deaths. In all units engaged in combat, the proportion of officers killed (22.1 per cent) was greater than that of the men they led (17.9 per cent).[51]

One statistician reasoned that 'the proportion of losses among

TABLE 3.10. DISTRIBUTION BETWEEN OFFICERS AND MEN OF BRITISH WAR LOSSES IN THE FIRST WORLD WAR

Branch of Service	Officers			Other ranks			Total		
	Served	Killed	%	Served	Killed	%	Served	Killed	%
Army	247,061	37,484	15.2	4,968,101	635,891	12.8	5,215,162	673,375	12.9
Navy	55,377	2,937	5.3	584,860	40,307	6.9	640,237	43,244	6.8
RFC/RAF	27,333	4,579	16.8	326,842[a]	1,587[a]	0.7	291,175	6,166	2.1
All branches	329,771	45,000	13.6	5,789,803	677,785	11.7	6,146,574	722,785	11.8

[a] Includes cadets in training.

SOURCES: See Table 3.2.

officers is much greater than that of the ranks since leaders in the French army always make it a point of honour to lead by example above and beyond their professional obligations'. The same observer noted that it was the young who suffered most, mainly through 'inexperience, enthusiasm and the impetuousness of youth'.[52] Whether or not he was right, it is apparent that casualties were distributed disproportionately as between officers and men in more than one combatant force during the First World War.

IV   THE SLAUGHTER OF SOCIAL ELITES

So far we have dealt only with the disproportionate burden borne by officers during the war. The final part of our claim that one may discern a social structure in British war losses is that since officers were mainly drawn from the well-educated and well-to-do middle and upper classes, these groups suffered disproportionately heavy losses during the First World War. The best evidence about the war-related losses of social elites is found in the numerous Rolls of Honour published in memory of the educated elite: university graduates and undergraduates and old boys of public schools.

We know that roughly 12 per cent of all men mobilized in Britain during the First World War were killed. If more than 12 per cent of serving members of universities were killed, we may conclude that university men bore a disproportionately heavy burden of war losses. Such a surplus would be accounted for by the fact that, for example, almost all Oxford and Cambridge men recruited received commissions, the great majority as junior officers. Of nearly 1,000 Balliol men who joined up, only 3 per cent served in the ranks.[53]

In Table 3.11 the war records of the universities of Oxford and Cambridge in the First World War are given. The published lists are flawed for our purposes, since they include some men twice, such as Lawrence of Arabia, and they list Australians, New Zealanders, Canadians, South Africans, Indians, Americans, Serbs, French, Italians and Russians (but not Germans or Austrians) who had matriculated and who had fought in the war. In the charged atmosphere of the immediate post-war period, it was not possible for the compilers of the war books of Oxford and Cambridge to admit enemy dead to the lists of the fallen.[54]

TABLE 3.11. MILITARY PARTICIPATION IN BRITISH FORCES OF MEMBERS OF THE
UNIVERSITIES OF OXFORD AND CAMBRIDGE BY YEAR OF MATRICULATION

Year of matriculation	Approx. age in 1914	Oxford			Cambridge		
		Served	Killed	% Killed	Served	Killed	% Killed
1884	50+	490	25	5.1	476	36	7.6
1885–1889	45–49	483	23	4.8	495	38	7.7
1890–1894	40–44	761	73	9.6	860	80	9.3
1895–1899	35–39	1,488	223	15.0	1,520	170	11.2
1900–1904	30–34	1,923	347	18.0	1,926	283	14.7
1905–1909	25–29	2,421	556	23.0	3,151	567	18.0
1910–1914	20–24	3,216	942	29.3	4,358	1,138	26.1
1915–1918	15–19	428	37	8.6	340	52	15.3
1919		1,850					
Not matriculated		343	343				
Total		13,403	2,569	19.2	13,126	2,364	18.0

SOURCES: G. V. Carey (ed.), *The War List of the University of Cambridge*
(Cambridge, 1920); E. S. Craig and W. M. Gibson (eds), *Oxford
University Roll of Service* (Oxford, 1920).

The university war service lists also include those British graduates who found their way into other armies during the war, such as
three Oxford men and three Cambridge men who wound up in the
French Foreign Legion. Because of the variation in casualty rates
in Allied forces, I have presented in Table 3.11 figures that relate
only to university members who served in British forces. The
national average of one man killed for every eight who served was
exceeded among members of every Oxford college but one, and all
Cambridge colleges but one. In some cases, particularly those of
King's, Balliol, New College, University, Oriel, Worcester, Pembroke (Cambridge), and both Corpus Christi, Oxford, and Corpus
Christi, Cambridge, the ratio of those killed to those at risk (in
uniform) was double the national average.

One of the difficulties in interpreting the casualty statistics for
Oxford and Cambridge is that the compilers of their respective war
lists disagreed about who was to be included. The editors of the
Oxford list considered it appropriate to inscribe the names of
ex-soldiers who went up to Oxford after the Armistice. Since many
of those men would have matriculated during the war years, they

were deemed to merit places in the university war list. The compilers of the Cambridge war list thought otherwise. They decided that men who came into residence in 1919–20 were not members of the university during their period of military service, and were therefore not eligible for inclusion in the Cambridge war list. We cannot tell from this source how many Cambridge men who matriculated in 1919 and 1920 served in the war, and consequently a precise comparison of Oxford and Cambridge war losses must adopt the more exclusive Cambridge approach. Of course, removing nearly 2,000 names from the Oxford war list must decrease the number at risk and thereby distort (upwards) the calculation of casualty rates. For purposes of clarity, statistics with and without post-war matriculants are given in Table 3.11. These show that in proportional terms Oxford war losses were only marginally greater than those of Cambridge.

From the data presented in Table 3.12, we can see that this pattern of exceptionally high death rates among university undergraduates and graduates was not repeated uniformly throughout Britain and Ireland. In some provincial universities, such as Liverpool and Birmingham, the ratio of men killed to men serving was much closer to the national average of one in eight. This distinction within the educated population may be explained in part by the fact that a smaller proportion of men from provincial universities served as officers. For example, only 'a majority' of members of Bristol University held commissions, and 60 per cent of the members of Leeds University were officers. In contrast 97 per cent

TABLE 3.12. MILITARY PARTICIPATION OF BRITISH AND IRISH UNIVERSITY GRADUATES AND UNDERGRADUATES IN THE FIRST WORLD WAR

University or college	Total served	Total killed	% killed
1. Aberdeen	2,540	317	12.5
2. Birmingham (to Dec. 1917)	785	115	14.6
3. Bristol (to Nov. 1917)	937	80	8.5
4. Cambridge	13,126	2,364	18.0
5. Durham	2,464	325	13.2
6. Edinburgh	5,828	877	15.0
7. Glasgow	4,300	717	16.7
8. Liverpool	1,505	158	10.5
9. London City and Guilds College	882	184	20.9

TABLE 3.12. *(Continued)*

University or college	Total served	Total killed	% killed
10. Royal School of Mines (London)	161	29	18.0
11. Manchester	2,532	418	16.6
12. National University of Ireland	479	43	9.0
13. Oxford	13,403	2,569	19.2
14. Royal Technical College, Glasgow	3,217	612	19.0
15. St Andrews	900	115	12.8
16. Trinity College Dublin	3,015	454	15.1
17. Wales	1,801	286	15.9
18. Gray's Inn	467	44	9.4
19. Inner Temple (to Dec. 1916)	1,083	146	13.5

SOURCES:

1. M. D. Allardyce (ed.), *University of Aberdeen Roll of Service in the Great War 1914–1919* (Aberdeen, 1920).
2. *The Mermaid Guild of Graduates Supplement, 1917* (Birmingham, 1917).
3. *University of Bristol Annual Report of Council to Court, 1917* (Bristol, 1917).
4. Carey, *Cambridge War List*.
5. *University of Durham Roll of Service* (Durham, 1922).
6. J. E. Mackenzie (ed.), *University of Edinburgh Roll of Honour 1914–1919* (Edinburgh, 1921).
7. *Members of the University of Glasgow and the University Contingent of the Officers' Training Corps who Served in the Forces of the Crown 1914–1919* (Glasgow, 1922).
8. *University of Liverpool Roll of Service in the Great War 1914–1919* (Liverpool, 1921).
9. *Register of the Students of the City and Guilds of London College 1884–1934* (1936).
10. *Register of the Associates and Old Students of the Royal School of Mines* (1935).
11. *Manchester University Roll of Service* (Manchester, 1922).
12. *The National University of Ireland. War List. Roll of Honour* (Dublin, 1919).
13. Craig and Gibson, *Oxford War List*.
14. *The Royal Technical College, Glasgow, Sacrifice and Service in the Great War* (Glasgow, 1921).
15. *University of St Andrews Roll of Honour and Roll of Service 1914–1919 for King and Country* (Edinburgh, 1920).
16. *University of Dublin, Trinity College. War List* (Dublin, 1922).
17. *University of Wales Roll of Service 1914–1918* (Bangor, 1921).
18. *The War Book of Gray's Inn* (1921).
19. C. Darling, *Inner Templars who Volunteered and Served in the Great War* (1924).

of Oxford and Cambridge men were commissioned.[55] This is a striking indication of the extent to which class prejudice informed patterns of recruitment to the officer corps early in the war. Furthermore, many of the men from civic or provincial universities, or from Scottish universities, were trained in science, engineering, or medicine, and served in the Royal Engineers, Royal Artillery, and Royal Army Medical Corps, in some sections of which casualty rates may have been lower than in the infantry, where most Oxford and Cambridge men with classics or literary degrees served.

The claim that more 'humanists' than 'scientists' were killed in the war is true only up to a point. This difficulty is demonstrated in the following comparison of casualties suffered by members of the universities of Liverpool and Birmingham. The percentages killed of Liverpool men who served are, by subject studied: arts – 19 per cent; science – 13 per cent; medicine – 8 per cent; dentistry – 6 per cent; veterinary sciences – 5 per cent; law – 14 per cent; engineering – 12 per cent.[56] Here it was the 'Arts men' whose death rates exceeded the national average of one in eight. But a different pattern appears in the Birmingham data. By subject studied, percentages killed of those who served are: arts – 8 per cent; commerce – 28 per cent; medicine – 11 per cent; science – 18 per cent. Thus in arts and commerce together, one in eight of those who served was killed, whereas in medicine and science, the ratio was one in six.[57] The latter results are consistent with the very high death rates suffered by members of the Imperial College of Science (Royal School of Mines, and City and Guilds College) and of the Royal Technical College, Glasgow.

A more satisfactory explanation of the variation in death rates among university men who served may lie in their length of service. Provincial university men may not have been able for financial reasons, even if they were so inclined, to drop their studies or careers and to join the army. They therefore may have spent less time at risk than did Oxford and Cambridge men, most of whom did not face such difficulties. In addition, many graduates of the ancient universities of England were professional soldiers, who fell in great numbers in the early months of the war, while the New Armies were still in training.[58]

The extent to which Oxford and Cambridge men of all ages suffered casualties well above the national average is shown in

TABLE 3.13. AGE DISTRIBUTION OF BRITISH ARMY AND BRITISH UNIVERSITIES'
WAR LOSSES, 1914–18

		Percentage killed of those who served				
Age in 1914	British army[a]	Oxford[b]	Cambridge	Universities Manchester[b]	Wales	Aberdeen
under 20	16.2	23.7	26.7	13.4	14.1	10.9
20–24	14.9	27.2	21.8	20.2	18.0	18.7
25–29	10.1	20.6	17.6	18.5	15.4	13.9
30–34	10.7	17.9	12.9	12.5	16.5	15.8
35–39	9.8	12.5	10.0	12.9	15.1	5.9
40–44	5.1	8.1	8.8	9.7	10.0	8.0

[a] For university men, age in 1914 determined distribution by cohort. No similar
figures are available for the army as a whole; hence the population of those
at risk was the average ages of all men from England and Wales who served
in British forces during the war.
[b] Excluding 1919–20 matriculants.

SOURCES: See Table 3.12 and *Decennial Supplement to the Registrar-General's
Report for England and Wales, 1911–20*, Vol. III, Table 1.

Table 3.13. For general comparisons, we have grouped the men
who served in five-year age groups, according to their date of
matriculation. But the age structure of war losses is best examined
by taking individual years of matriculation. For instance, Oxford
men who matriculated in 1894 would have been on average aged
38 at the outbreak of the war. Of the 205 men of that year who
served in British forces, 27 or 13.17 per cent were killed. From that
year on, the percentage killed rises until for 1913 matriculants it
reaches the staggering figure of 31 per cent killed of those who
served. The same pattern is repeated in the mortality statistics of
Oxford men who served in other Allied armies. In the case of
Cambridge, the curve is not as steep, but the figures show the same
progression.

We can now use the evidence on the age structure of British war
losses which we have presented above to show that young Oxford
and Cambridge men were more likely to be killed during the war
than were their peers either within the population as a whole or
members of other British universities (see Table 3.13). This concentration of deaths in the two youngest cohorts is not surprising,
but the particular intensity of war losses by age for young Oxford
and Cambridge men accounts for the overall higher casualty rates

of these two universities, compared to other universities or to the army as a whole. For every age group, death rates for Oxford and Cambridge men were well above the national figures. The appalling mortality rate of one in four among men who served and who were under age 25 in 1914 helps to explain why contemporaries wrote repeatedly that a whole generation of the young fell in France and Flanders. H. A. L. Fisher, President of the Board of Education, therefore spoke with some justification when he said in 1917 that 'The chapels of Oxford and Cambridge display long lists of the fallen, and no institutions have suffered greater or more irreparable losses than these ancient shrines of learning and piety'.[59]

Fisher can be forgiven for having overlooked the fact that nearly as high casualty rates were suffered by members of British public schools who served during the war. One commentator pointed out that the large boarding schools contributed more to the war effort than did day schools. With 'greater wealth and influence behind them', members of the former 'could consequently face with the more equanimity the risk to them and theirs in throwing up their posts in civil life . . . .' Furthermore, it was these schools which 'stocked the old Army with most of its Officers'. As a result, 'the death roll of the Public Schools was far heavier in proportion than the general average'.[60] Of course, many names listed therein also appear in the Oxford and Cambridge statistics. But many others by-passed the universities and entered the army directly from school. The 53 schools for which we have been able to collect full data lost about one old boy of every five who served. Thus both public school and university war statistics show mortality rates significantly higher than those of army officers or of the army as a whole. The likely explanation, advanced in R.C. Sherriff's play, *Journey's End*, is that subalterns were drawn throughout most of the war from this section of the educated population. Replying to criticism that his play had 'too much of the English public schools about it', Sherriff wrote that 'almost every young officer was a public schoolboy, and if I had left them out of *Journey's End*, there wouldn't have been a play at all'.[61] The Bishop of Malvern made a similar point when he dedicated the war memorial of Malvern College. The loss of schoolboys in the war, he said, 'can only be described as the wiping out of a generation'.[62]

The war experience of the same social class is described in the service lists of Members of Parliament, peers, and their sons. Of the 22 MPs killed in the war, 13 had been up at Oxford, and 9 at both Oxford and Eton.[63] Some peers were of very advanced age during the war, and like the Royal Family, appear on service lists as a courtesy. But taking only peers and their sons under age 50 in 1914, 18.95 per cent of those serving were killed, a proportion again well above the national average.[64]

C. F. G Masterman, who had been a Liberal MP before the war, pointed out in a book published in 1922 that not since the Wars of the Roses had the English aristocracy suffered such losses as those they had endured during the Great War.[65] The figures provided by Hollingsworth in his more recent study of the ducal peerage for deaths from violence support this argument. Whereas 46 per cent of male members of ducal families born between 1330 and 1479 died violent deaths, 48 per cent of the cohort born between 1880 and 1939 did so.[66] Since casualties in the Second World War were much lower than those of the 1914–18 conflict, these figures provide further substantiation of the claim that war losses were unevenly distributed within the British population in a way that was unfavourable to the well-to-do and the highly educated.

We may therefore conclude that the social structure of British war losses was a function of two separate but overlapping phenomena: first, variation in risk of death by age; and secondly, differential casualties according to rank, which, on account of the social composition of the officer corps, meant that privileged groups bore a disproportionately heavy burden of war losses in the First World War.

PART II   THE PARADOX OF THE GREAT WAR

4. Civilian Health in Wartime Britain

THE unanticipated outcome of the analysis of life insurance statistics conducted in the previous chapter suggested that working-class men lucky enough to stay out of the trenches actually improved their life expectancies during the First World War. After age 40, when there was a substantially reduced chance of military service, the totals of wartime deaths were actually lower than they would have been without the war. This surprising result presented a *prima facie* challenge to the view I shared with other commentators that the war's effect on the health of civilian populations was wholly negative.

There is a substantial body of literature to this effect. In the words of the Swiss demographer Hersch: 'War kills not only directly, . . . but also indirectly by causing an increase of mortality among the civilian population of the belligerent countries and even in many neutral countries.'[1] To the American sociologist Willard Waller, it was clear that: 'War decimates the civilian population, killing many men in battle and a comparable number of civilians by diseases'. Although he was referring directly to the 1939–45 war, he presented data which supported the view that the same applied to the 1914–18 conflict.[2] The distinguished British pediatrician R. W. B. Ellis concurred, stating that 'war must inevitably have an adverse effect on child health'.[3] Similarly, in a discussion of French infant mortality during the two world wars by Ibarolla, we find a similar position:

The struggle against death must be a permanent struggle. When society neglects this combat, because it devotes its principal effort to equipping a war machine with lavish supplies of money and men, the thanatogenic factor, in the phrase of M. Villey,

103

re-asserts its rights and interrupts and at times even temporarily arrests the spectacular progress due to medical treatment.[4]

Other statisticians and demographers have helped propagate the thesis of the negative effects of the war on standards of health in Europe. Many writers have produced estimates of war losses which include figures for 'excess civilian mortality'. Several have settled on the total of 292,000 civilian 'excess deaths' in Britain during the 1914–18 war.[5] A more sophisticated study undertaken by the Office of Population Research at Princeton University for the League of Nations yielded a somewhat higher total. Comparing official figures for the war period with a hypothetical progression of mortality in 1914–18 on the basis of an average of pre-war and post-war data, they concluded that over 400,000 British civilians died as a result of war conditions.[6]

These estimates of the adverse effects of the war on civilian death rates in Britain have never been seriously examined. Neither have the principal assumptions upon which these estimates rest. The first is that deaths due to the influenza pandemic of 1918–19 are attributable to the war. The second is that wartime shortages of food and other commodities impaired the survival chances of substantial sections of the civilian community of all combatant countries in Europe. Consider these statements by authorities on the history of public health. Professor Abel-Smith contended that the 1918 epidemic 'struck hard at a tired and neglected civilian population' which by the end of the war 'began making its own contribution to casualty lists'.[7] And Drummond and Wilbraham, in their study of English nutrition, claimed that:

> There is clear evidence that the general state of health did decline [in wartime]. The most obvious sign was the lowered resistance to infection. The people could not stand up to the terrible pandemic of influenza which swept across Europe in 1918. They died like flies; the mortality in London in some weeks was as high as 2,500. At the time it was thought that the severity of the epidemic was due to a particularly virulent strain of the infective organism. With our modern knowledge of the influence of diet on resistance to infective diseases, we can see that vitamin deficiencies had prepared the way.[8]

There seems, therefore, to be a glaring contradiction between the traditional interpretation of the effect of the Great War on civilian health and the preliminary results of demographic analysis described in chapter 3. This anomalous finding indicated that re-examination of the standard way of looking at the determinants of health in wartime was in order.

The first question to address is how to place the war period within the overall process of mortality decline, which had begun in the 1870s for the population as a whole and after 1900 in the case of infant mortality. As we have noted above, the received interpretation of the impact of war is that it brought about an upward deflection in the trend of mortality rates. This is explained by the suggestion that the working class, which was particularly vulnerable to shortages of goods and services, contributed most to the reversal of the secular downward trend. Our concern in this chapter will be primarily with this second point and other related arguments that it was the least prosperous that suffered most from the war. But first we must note that the background assumption that there was an upward deflection in the general mortality trend is false.

Not only is it the case that life expectancy at birth for men in England and Wales rose from 49 to 56 years and for women, from 53 to 60 years between 1911 and 1921, but these increases were substantially greater than the gains registered either in the first or in the third decade of the twentieth century. It is against such a background that we should place the question of whether the poorer sections of the population continued to play a key role in these declines, for it is this claim, in effect, that the received view contests. Evidence on infant mortality in this period provides dramatic and clear-cut refutation of this view. Throughout Britain, the war period was the occasion of the steepest drop in infant mortality rates in the first 30 years of this century.[9]

The other main way of distinguishing the vulnerable is not by age but by social class and occupation. Here we shall see that one may at least claim that there was no change in the contribution of the working-class population to the overall decline of mortality, and in a number of occupational groups the war period was one of the very rapid improvement in survival rates, compared to the working population as a whole. These issues will be examined in detail in this chapter, but in brief, I shall argue that both for infants and for the poorer sections of British society, it is not true that standards of health deteriorated during the war.

We may also approach the question of wartime health in a more general way by examining the contribution of particular causes of death to overall mortality levels. Here I shall argue that it is not the case that war-related conditions at home led to a recrudescence of some diseases traditionally associated with deprivation, such as diarrhoeal diseases, although other causes of death – respiratory diseases – may have contributed a greater share to the death rate in 1914–18 than they would have done had there been no war. However, the importance of this qualification is limited, for the basic facts to be explained are first that there was no interruption of mortality decline, and second, that working-class standards of health actually improved markedly during the war.

This chapter will therefore be concerned with presenting the evidence against the prevailing view that war conditions impaired the health of the civilian population. Possible explanations of these findings will be offered in chapters 5–7 below.

The structure of this chapter will be as follows. We shall first extend the demographic analysis presented in the previous chapter to the full age group 16–60, which clearly encompassed a population too old to bear arms as well as those eligible for military service. This involves the same comparison between mortality estimates based on pre-war assumptions held constant for the war period and the actual structure of wartime deaths. This provides further confirmation of the hypothesis that civilian mortality levels declined during the First World War.

One of the surprising features of this finding is that it was a working-class population which exhibited rising life expectancies during the war. The next step in our assessment of the received view is to examine the occupational variation of male mortality levels in the war decade. Here too we find a striking decline in the relative disadvantage of particularly poorly paid workers vis-à-vis the occupied and retired population as a whole. That is to say, the lower down the 'pay ladder' you were, the greater were your chances of improving your life expectancy during the war.

So far we have two strong confirmations of the hypothesis of improving survival chances for civilians in wartime. However, one of the problems in the data we have been using is the purely hypothetical nature of the separation of the mortality patterns of civilians and soldiers. Data on the female population present no such problems, and for the purposes of an examination of the civilian population alone, are even more useful than the evidence discussed above. Here we can apply a further criterion for the assessment of the general effect of war on health conditions. By distinguishing among causes of death, we can see to what extent declining mortality reflected a drop in the lethality of traditional 'killer' diseases, many of which were nutrition-related, and which were endemic in the pre-war period.

I MORTALITY DECLINE AMONG CIVILIANS IN WARTIME BRITAIN: WORKING-CLASS MEN, 1914–17

The hypothesis we set out to examine was that in the British case victory in the First World War was not won at the expense of the health of the civilian population. The first part of this exercise involved an extension of the procedure applied in the previous chapter to help determine the age distribution of the 'Lost Generation' (see chapter 3). The Prudential data cover a male population aged 16–60. This permitted a comparison of hypothetical mortality patterns, based on hypothetical 'normal' mortality rates for the years 1914–18, with the actual wartime mortality pattern of men at ages at which we may assume that they were mainly, if not exclusively, civilians.

In Appendix Table A-3, we have listed these estimates of male deaths in 1914–18 at ages 16–60, in quinquennial age groups. The difference between the 'War Estimate' and the 'Hypothetical Estimate' may be viewed as the sum of war-related deaths by age. This table shows that war-related mortality peaked in the early twenties cohort and then declined in intensity until the forties, which is precisely what we would have expected, given the age structure of the army. We have already noted that war-related deaths were as high as seven times 'normal' mortality at ages 20–24, twice as high at ages 35–39, and about the same at age 45. But of greater importance at this point in our study is the fact that after age 49, totals of war-related mortality become negative. In other words, men over the age at which they were likely to see active service had a greater chance of survival than they would have had, had there been no war.

The timing of the wartime diminution of civilian death rates can be located more specifically. Fig. 4.1 shows the annual pattern of war-related deaths at ages 40–60 in 1914–17. Positive totals of war-related deaths show the war's adverse effects; negative totals show wartime improvements in the mortality pattern of the Prudential population. The latter pattern appears after age 50 in both 1916 and 1917. It is unfortunate that no data survive for 1918; we have simply applied 1917 death rates to the 1918 population. Hence there is no certainty that the change for the better at certain ages also occurred in the war's final year. But even with this qualification, the implications of this exercise are obvious. The finding of *negative* war-related mortality throws considerable doubt on the contention that war conditions prejudiced the health of the male civilian population of Britain.

It is essential to note that the hypothetical age structure of male mortality we have constructed over the years 1914–17 suffers from all the limitations of what historians have come to call counterfactual history.[10] We have assumed a steady state of declining mortality rates after 1914, simply because there are no objective constraints that we can apply to any other model. A trial run based on 1913 death rates held constant for the following five years also yielded negative war-related mortality, but to assume no decline at all in death rates is demographically implausible. But in either case, it seems clear that men old enough to avoid military service during the First World War had life expectancies at least as high or perhaps even higher than they would have had, had there been no war.

II   OCCUPATIONAL MORTALITY RATES AMONG MEN IN ENGLAND AND WALES, 1900–23

Thus far we have described the first link in the reappraisal of the effect of the Great War on civilian health in Britain. It showed that the older male working class at home had improved chances of survival. These findings are at variance not only with the prevailing views of historians, as we have already noted, but also with the views of contemporary trade unionists and other figures within the Labour movement, who protested repeatedly at what they saw as a worsening of conditions for working people during the war.[11] It is

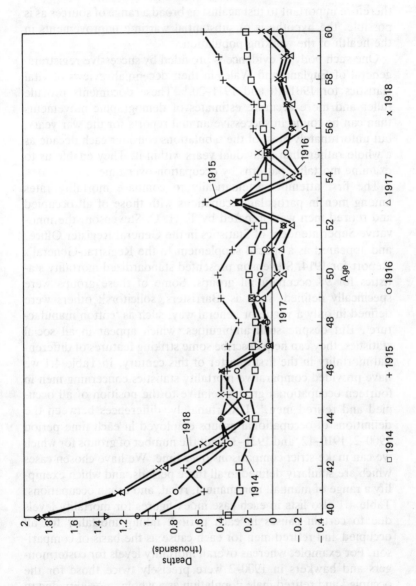

FIG. 4.1. War-related deaths, England and Wales, 1914–18, at ages 40–60
SOURCE: see Appendix

therefore important to test against as broad a range of sources as is possible, the hypothesis of substantial wartime improvements in the health of the working population.

One such body of evidence is provided by successive registrars-general of England and Wales in their decennial reviews of vital statistics for 1901–10 and 1911–20.[12] These documents provide fuller and more accurate estimates of demographic movements than can be found in successive annual reports for the war years, but unfortunately most of the tabulations consider each decade as a whole rather than individual years within it. They enable us to examine mortality patterns by occupation over time.

The first attempt systematically to compare mortality rates among men in particular occupations with those of all occupied and retired men was prepared by T. H. C. Stevenson, the innovative Superintendent of Statistics in the General Register Office, and appeared as a special supplement to the Registrar-General's Report for 1914. Stevenson presented standardized mortality statistics for 98 occupational groups. Some of these groups were specifically defined, such as 'Barristers, solicitors'; others were defined in only a vague or general way, such as 'cotton manufacture'. But despite such ambiguities, which appear in all social statistics, they can help describe some striking features of differential mortality in the first quarter of this century. In Table 4.1 we have provided comparative mortality statistics concerning men in fourteen occupational groups relative to the position of all occupied and retired men.[13] Unfortunately, differences between the definitions of occupational groups employed in each time period 1900–2, 1910–12, and 1921–3 limit the number of groups for which we can make strict comparisons over time. We have chosen cases which are similarly defined in all three periods, and which exemplify a range of manual, non-manual, rural, and urban occupations. Table 4.1 also lists in each case index figures for mortality levels due to certain causes in each period, taking mortality for all occupied and retired men for each cause as the basis of comparison. For example, whereas overall mortality levels for costermongers and hawkers in 1900–2 were precisely twice those for the occupied and retired male population as a whole, mortality due to respiratory tuberculosis in this one occupational group was nearly three times as high as it was in the total male population. We can see, therefore, not only which occupational groups were at a relative advantage or disadvantage vis-à-vis the male population, but also which causes of death contributed most to low or high levels of mortality in particular cases.

The overall pattern described by the turn-of-the-century data is one of extreme variation in the mortality levels of different occupational groups. This is not surprising, given the gap between the poverty of costermongers and street hawkers, at one extreme, and the affluence of barristers and solicitors at the other (see chapter 1). Of course, prosperity had its dangers too: barristers and solicitors suffered twice the level of mortality due to liver diseases as did the male population as a whole. Publicans and innkeepers also had to face such ailments as part of the occupational hazards of their profession. They registered over seven times the aggregate risk of dying from such complaints.

Roughly speaking, five clusters of occupational groups can be discerned in the 1900–2 data: two having relatively high mortality levels; three having average or low mortality levels. The first is that of low-paid, casual workers, or those who worked in difficult or substandard conditions. These men had mortality rates distinctly above those of the population as a whole. For instance, male pottery workers' mortality was roughly 50 per cent higher than the national average. The second group suffering relatively high mortality levels is that of innkeepers, publicans, and general shopkeepers. Such men served what was by definition a transient population, and seem to have been vulnerable to respiratory tuberculosis, easily transmitted to them by their clientele.

Turning to the relatively better placed groups, the first which appear are those manual workers in regular and moderately well-paid occupations, such as metalworkers, coalminers, and railway-engine drivers, whose mortality levels were either at or below those of the general population. Secondly, barristers and solicitors, and commercial and insurance clerks can stand for a number of middle-class occupations, the mortality levels of which were below average. Thirdly, both farmers and agricultural labourers registered mortality levels well below those of all occupied and retired males.

The data in Table 4.1 suggest that in the period 1900–2 to 1910–12, there occurred a narrowing of differential mortality as between occupational groups. But it is clear that this trend was significantly accelerated during the years between 1910–12 and

TABLE 4.1 COMPARATIVE MORTALITY STATISTICS FOR ALL OCCUPIED AND RETIRED MALES, AND FOR SOME OCCUPATIONAL GROUPS, ENGLAND AND WALES IN 1900–2, 1910–12 AND 1921–3 (MORTALITY RATES OF ALL OCCUPIED AND RETIRED MEN = 100)

Occupational group	All causes	Respiratory TB	Bronchitis	Pneumonia	Other respiratory diseases	Digestive diseases	Cirrhosis of the liver	Nephritis
I. 1900–2								
1. Costermongers and hawkers	200	296	284	192	221	126	148	170
2. Inn, hotelkeepers	177	145	90	160	142	167	744	242
3. General shopkeepers	150	189	166	170	174	115	174	156
4. Potters and earthenware workers	149	152	436	114	267	119	78	106
5. Bargemen and watermen	133	90	126	145	115	130	81	110
6. Textile-dyers and bleachers	111	103	140	120	123	126	96	120
7. Tailors	102	133	105	74	89	86	96	119
8. Commercial clerks, insurance service	91	108	59	71	68	100	107	96
9. Engine, machine-fitters, makers, millwrights	91	87	91	89	90	81	78	103
10. Coalminers	88	48	136	93	111	93	63	69
11. Barristers, solicitors	75	49	26	55	47	130	214	90
12. Agricultural labourers, farm servants	62	48	45	59	54	74	30	47
13. Railway engine-drivers, stokers, cleaners	61	35	45	47	47	56	67	67
14. Farmers, graziers	59	41	24	51	43	96	81	81

II. 1910–12

Occupational Group	All Causes	Respiratory TB	Bronchitis	Pneumonia	Other respiratory diseases	Digestive diseases	Cirrhosis of the liver	Nephritis
1. Costermongers and hawkers	191	297	276	212	224	125	138	202
2. Inn, hotelkeepers	160	139	73	155	130	161	769	215
3. Potters and earthenware workers	151	200	454	132	264	143	106	139
4. Bargemen and watermen	139	101	176	157	144	118	106	113
5. Textile-dyers and bleachers	111	103	140	120	123	139	75	131
6. General shopkeepers	104	130	111	96	104	79	131	102
7. Commercial clerks, insurance service	102	122	14	82	79	114	75	111
8. Tailors	101	132	103	82	91	111	100	116
9. Engine, machine-fitters, makers, millwrights	95	93	96	90	105	107	94	108
10. Coalminers	92	53	135	97	110	82	63	71
11. Barristers, solicitors	79	41	19	67	53	157	163	89
12. Railway engine-drivers, stokers, cleaners	68	40	60	46	53	79	63	76
13. Farmers, graziers	63	40	30	64	53	89	88	63
14. Agricultural labourers, farm servants	59	50	38	60	53	68	31	51

TABLE 4.1. (Continued)

Occupational Group	All Causes	Respiratory TB	Bronchitis	Pneumonia	Other respiratory diseases	Digestive diseases	Cirrhosis of the liver	Nephritis
III. 1921–3								
1. Costermongers and hawkers	166	229	269	198	219	127	157	150
2. Inn, hotelkeepers	159	134	86	161	135	345	1155	226
3. Potters and earthenware workers	132	154	304	107	180	100	166	139
4. Bargemen and watermen	129	114	134	121	127	71	64	118
5. Textile-dyers and bleachers	116	111	169	118	131	116	101	143
6. Barristers, solicitors	104	39	18	103	75	310	169	135
7. Coalminers	103	76	149	107	123	86	58	76
8. Tailors	102	142	109	77	89	98	48	105
9. General shopkeepers	100	96	84	93	90	109	163	112
10. Commercial clerks, insurance service	98	110	63	90	83	113	95	80
11. Engine, machine-fitters, makers, millwrights	93	95	68	82	78	96	84	96
12. Railway engine-drivers, stokers, cleaners	79	62	56	76	67	103	31	70
13. Agricultural labourers, farm servants	69	59	49	64	59	67	29	60
14. Farmers, graziers	67	41	23	59	49	99	78	72

SOURCES: *Supplement to the 75th Annual Report of the Registrar-General of England and Wales, Part IV, Mortality of Men in Certain Occupations in the Three Years 1910, 1911 and 1912* (1933), Table V; *Decennial Supplement to the Registrar-General's Report for England and Wales, 1911–20, Part III, Occupational Mortality* (1933), Table D.

1921–3. With some exceptions, the pattern seems to be that the worst-off groups gained most, while those best-off in the pre-war period gained little if anything relative to the population as a whole. It is therefore possible to suggest that in the war decade the demographic distance between the survival chances of different classes and between different strata within classes was reduced.

It is important to note that we are dealing here with relative mortality levels. In absolute terms, all occupational groups registered declining mortality rates in this period, but the pace of decline varied considerably. In addition, we must not lose sight of the fact that the post-war figures are complicated by the return home of over 5 million men, among whom at least 1.6 million had been wounded during the conflict. As we shall see in chapter 8, it was virtually impossible to identify many cases in which wartime stress or injury contributed to the early deaths of ex-soldiers. But given the differential enlistment rates noted in chapter 3, it is likely that some of the decline in the mortality differential by occupation reflects the fact that some trade groups were less likely to serve during the war than other trade groups. Still, such qualifications do not nullify the significance of these findings, which show the striking degree to which the gap between and among occupational groups' mortality levels narrowed in the war decade.

Let us consider three examples to illustrate this process. In 1910–12, mortality levels for potters and earthenware workers were approximately 50 per cent above average. We can attribute this disadvantage confidently to very high levels of respiratory diseases, particularly bronchitis, suffered by this population. By 1921–3, the relative disadvantage of this group was still marked, but it had been reduced to 32 per cent. Similarly, costermongers and hawkers were still a relatively 'unhealthy' group in 1921–3, but not quite to the degree they had been just before the war. Their relative disadvantage in comparative mortality figures had been reduced from 100 to 66 per cent between 1910–12 and 1921–3. In contrast, the relative advantage of barristers and solicitors at the turn of the century (25 per cent below average) was wiped out in the subsequent two decades.

Some working-class occupational groups also lost their relative advantage in the war period. For example, in 1910–12, coalminers were a relatively healthy group which, despite high levels of accident mortality, still registered mortality rates 12 per cent below those of the aggregate population. As we have seen in chapter 2, this phenomenon was noted by medical examiners of recruits during the war. It also appears to have been true of the condition of American miners in the same period.[14] But after the war miners lost their relative advantage and registered comparative mortality figures close to the average for the entire workforce. That is to say, even though miners' death rates declined in this period, those of all occupied and retired males declined faster still. Similarly, textile workers did not improve their relative position in the war decade, and again, a greater than average increase in respiratory diseases appears to have been responsible for their failure to keep up with the overall trend.

Of course, there is no way to be certain that this narrowing of occupational differentials in mortality levels can be confined neatly to the war period. By the time the post-war figures were compiled, the war economy had effectively been wound up, and the interwar depression was well under way. This downturn in trade hit workers in the old staple export trades – mining, textiles, and shipbuilding – with particular severity, and it is conceivable that some of the recrudescence of mortality in the post-1920 period was attributable to the onset of mass unemployment, especially among older 'unemployable' workers. In addition, as we shall note in a moment, the inclusion of data for 1911 in the pre-war statistics may distort the components or indeed the level of mortality for certain occupational groups. Furthermore, some of the post-war mortality reflected in these data may have been due to the after-effects of war service or of exposure to the influenza pandemic of 1918–19. Those who survived both military service and the 'Spanish flu' may have been weakened sufficiently to reduce their survival chances when they contracted 'normal' diseases in later years. But given the unavoidable degree of imprecision in all such data, we may treat these findings as supporting the results of the analysis of life tables for the male working population. Together these studies confirm the contention that over the war period there occurred both an absolute and a relative improvement in the survival chances of manual workers, and in particular of the worst-off groups among them.

III MORTALITY DECLINE AMONG CIVILIANS IN WARTIME BRITAIN: THE FEMALE POPULATION OF ENGLAND AND WALES, 1912–21

We can broaden our discussion of the impact of the First World War on civilian health by considering evidence on mortality decline among the female population. These data are a better guide to demographic trends, since they do not have the drawback of statistics concerning men, which inevitably reflect a highly unusual age structure among non-combatants in wartime. The female population of Britain was more stable and therefore a better subject for analysis over time.

The first way in which such causal analysis can be helpful is in disaggregating the mortality trend into its component parts. Any argument that mortality rates rose during the war must specify the causes responsible. Our claim is to the contrary, and is in fact confirmed by an examination of data on female deaths by cause in the war decade. For almost every category of cause of death, significant declines were registered in these years. Some of these could not have occurred had the population been increasingly malnourished or deprived of other essential goods and services in wartime.

Two exceptions must be noted. The first is a rise in the incidence of certain endemic respiratory diseases. The second is the special case of the 1918–19 influenza pandemic. The first probably can be attributed to the war; the second cannot.

But more importantly, apart from providing additional reasons to discard the view that civilian health deteriorated in wartime Britain, these data also permit us to explore many features of public health in this period. These suggest possible ways in which to account for the unanticipated gains in survival chances registered during the 1914–18 war. In particular, they indicate that an important factor in maintaining and improving public health in wartime was better nutrition. This was particularly important in the case of infants, whose death rates dropped more dramatically than was the case for any other age group in this period.

A Causes of Death and Mortality Decline

Before opening the discussion of the components of mortality decline, it is wise to note the real limitations inherent in the data.

For it is only in recent years that demographers have begun to investigate the cause structure of mortality with the precision already devoted to the age structure of mortality. Inaccuracies in cause-of-death diagnosis and substantial variations in degrees of completeness and in modes of classification undoubtedly exist and ensure that any statistical analysis using cause-of-death data must allow for a wide margin of error. What we must identify is clear and unambiguous evidence concerning specific mortality trends; marginal cases must be discounted due to the high proportion of unspecified causes of death in all official returns.

The most ambitious and searching attempt to overcome these difficulties and to develop a model of causes of mortality is that of Preston, who accumulated and analysed data on mortality in 162 nations over the period 1860 to the present. In work done jointly with Keyfitz and Schoen, he adopted a twelve-part classification of causes of death based on aetiological rather than anatomical criteria and then distributed within this scheme all causes of death enumerated in the successive International Classifications of Causes of Death produced and revised between 1909 and 1955.[15] They then calculated age-specific and cause-specific death rates for each country at decennial or quinquennial intervals. This permitted an analysis of the contribution of different causes of death to overall mortality decline over time, on the assumption that each cause of death was independent of all other causes of death. This premise is questionable, as these authors themselves admitted, since some infectious diseases (such as measles) produce increases in mortality due to their sequelae (such as pneumonia). Some distortion is inevitably introduced, but it is probably small enough to permit us to use this framework for our analysis of British data.

The approach of Preston and his colleagues is of considerable value to the demographic historian. Among the collection of life tables they produced are twelve referring to England and Wales, from 1861 to 1964. One way to begin the analysis of the war decade is to calculate the contribution of specific causes of death to the overall decline of mortality between 1911 and 1921, years for which Preston *et al.* have provided complete statistical tables. Unfortunately, this procedure is positively misleading, for the simple reason that both 1911 and 1921 were years of unusual mortality conditions. The summer of 1911 was particularly hot, and in conjunction with a transport strike ensured perfect conditions for the outbreak of an epidemic of diarrhoeal diseases. A decade later there occurred a severe outbreak of respiratory infections. A comparison of these two years, therefore, will distort the contribution of both gastro-intestinal and respiratory diseases to the process of mortality decline in the war decade.

In the previous section, we had to rely on data for years surrounding census dates. But in this section we can improve on previously published statistics. We have prepared cause-specific and age-specific mortality tables for England and Wales for each year 1912–21, based on the tabulations of deaths by cause and age that appear in the registrar-general's returns. Unfortunately no similar data exist for Scotland, which means that our findings cannot describe this facet of the demographic history of Britain as a whole.

Within the war decade, 1912–14 is identified as pre-war, despite the fact that hostilities began in early August 1914. The first months of the conflict did not involve a major dislocation of the economy, and for this reason we confine the war period to 1915–18. Full decontrol of the war economy came only in 1921; hence the designation of 1919–21 as the post-war period.

Our classification of causes of death differs from Preston, Keyfitz and Schoen's in only one important respect. They chose to limit respiratory tuberculosis to the chronic category, although all registrar-general's reports in this period consider respiratory tuberculosis to encompass both chronic and acute forms of the disease. Since one of Preston's conclusions is that respiratory tuberculosis was relatively unimportant in the process of mortality decline,[16] it seems odd that he chose such a strict definition of the disease. Of course, what matters is the rate of decline rather than the level of any one category; hence his approach would be valid if there were a strict parallelism between the decline of mortality due to chronic and acute forms of respiratory tuberculosis. To avoid such potential difficulties, we have presented data on all forms of respiratory tuberculosis, or phthisis, under one heading in the following tables.

Table 4.2 presents standardized annual death rates for females in twelve categories of causes of death in the period 1912–21. A number of comments are required at this point, concerning the problem of the 'Spanish flu'. Much has been written of this

TABLE 4.2. STANDARDIZED ANNUAL FEMALE DEATH RATES, BY GROUPS OF CAUSES, AT ALL AGES, TO A MILLION LIVING, ENGLAND AND WALES, 1912–21[a]

Cause	1912–14	1915	1916	1917	1918	1919–21
1. All	12,263	13,368	11,999	11,702	15,135	10,992
(without flu epidemic)					11,893	10,694
2. Respiratory tuberculosis	850	864	928	982	1,082	795
3. Other infectious and parasitic infections	1,291	1,525	1,087	1,121	1,402	902
4. Neoplasms	1,027	1,064	1,063	1,039	1,029	1,039
5. Cardiovascular diseases	2,374	2,470	2,338	2,277	2,129	2,084
6. Influenza, bronchitis, and pneumonia	2,006	2,587	2,113	2,092	5,498	2,228
(without flu epidemic)					2,264[b]	1,943[b]
7. Diarrhoeal diseases	519	508	472	367	357	335
8. Certain degenerative diseases[c]	568	567	502	446	405	392
9. Complications of pregnancy	181	174	164	131	125	176
10. Certain diseases of infancy	795	718	719	686	759	788
11. Accidents and violence	308	323	316	312	286	264
12. Other and unknown causes	2,344	2,568	2,297	2,249	2,063	1,989

[a] Crude death rates were standardized by the direct method, using the age structure of the female population of England and Wales in 1901. (Rounding errors account for the difference between the totals and the sum of the 12 categories.)

[b] The average death rate in 1915–17 was used to approximate non-epidemic mortality levels in 1918 and 1919.

[c] Nephritis, Bright's disease, stomach ulcer, diabetes, and cirrhosis of the liver.

SOURCES: Preston, et al., Causes of Death, Table I-2, and p. 242;
Registrar-General's Annual Report, 1912–1919, and Statistical Review, 1920–21.

pandemic which killed perhaps 200,000 people in Britain alone. Ten thousand British soldiers died of the disease.[17] Leaving aside the fact that the pandemic continued after the Armistice, can we attribute these deaths to the war? No one claims that the war somehow generated what Europeans called the 'Spanish flu'. But it was argued that because of the privations of war, civilian populations were much more vulnerable to known strains of influenza and less resistant to the mutant virus of 1918–19 which was transmitted to them by sailors on port call and by soldiers on leave.[18] In other words, the war created conditions suitable to the transformation of an endemic but mainly benign illness to a pandemic killer and also facilitated the international transmission of the disease.

But one of the difficulties inherent in this position is that neutral countries or those whose economies were not adversely affected by the war were hit with as great or even greater severity by the 'Plague of the Spanish Lady' as were Britain, France or Germany. Other features of the epidemic are similarly puzzling. Some of the highest case-fatality and mortality rates attributed to this disease were registered in the United States and in India, rather than in Europe, where the dislocation of the war and the movement of military manpower were most pronounced. These facts, together with the observation of a number of military doctors that stronger and more robust men succumbed to the disease more quickly than weaker men, should make anyone hesitate before reaching the common-sense conclusion that nutritional levels and pandemic mortality were related in any straightforward way. Finally, it was an unmistakable characteristic of the influenza pandemic to attack adults in the prime of life, and to leave virtually untouched more vulnerable groups, such as the elderly.[19] For all these reasons it is probably best to conclude that this modern plague was *sui generis* rather than war-related. In consequence, we have recalculated standardized death rates by cause and age without pandemic influenza mortality in order to trace the underlying mortality pattern of England and Wales in the war period.

Taken together with Table 4.3, these data show the extent and components of female mortality decline in England and Wales in the war decade.[20] First let us deal with variations over time, and then turn to variations by cause of death. Taking standardized annual female death rates in 1912–14 as our basis of comparison,

TABLE 4.3. AN INDEX OF STANDARDIZED ANNUAL FEMALE DEATH RATES, BY GROUPS OF CAUSES, AT ALL AGES, TO A MILLION LIVING, ENGLAND AND WALES, 1912-21[a] (1921-14 = 100)

Cause	1912-14	1915	1916	1917	1918	1919-21
1. All	100	109	98	95	123	90
(without flu epidemic)					97	87
2. Respiratory tuberculosis	100	102	109	116	127	94
3. Other infectious and parasitic infections	100	118	84	87	109	70
4. Neoplasms	100	104	104	101	100	101
5. Cardiovascular diseases	100	104	98	96	90	88
6. Influenza, bronchitis, and pneumonia	100	129	105	104	274	111
(without flu epidemic)					113[b]	97[b]
7. Diarrhoeal diseases	100	98	91	71	69	65
8. Certain degenerative diseases[c]	100	100	88	79	71	69
9. Complications of pregnancy	100	96	91	72	69	97
10. Certain diseases of infancy	100	90	90	86	95	99
11. Accidents and violence	100	105	103	101	93	86
12. Other and unknown causes	100	110	98	96	88	85

[a] Crude death rates were standardized by the direct method, using the age structure of the female population of England and Wales in 1901.

[b] The average death rate in 1915-17 was used to approximate non-epidemic mortality levels in 1918 and 1919.

[c] Nephritis, Bright's disease, stomach ulcer, diabetes, and cirrhosis of the liver.

SOURCES: Preston, et al., Causes of Death, Table 1-2, and p. 242; Registrar-General's Annual Report, 1912-1919, and Statistical Review, 1920-21.

index figures show that 1915 was a year of high mortality due both to influenza, bronchitis, and pneumonia and to the general category of 'other infectious and parasitic diseases', incorporating common diseases of childhood, such as whooping cough, diphtheria, and measles, as well as more general ailments such as non-respiratory tuberculosis and meningitis. Some of this increase was probably due to the normal periodicity of infectious diseases, a point to which we shall return below. After 1915, though, mortality rates for most categories clearly declined.

This is most emphatically the case with diarrhoeal diseases, which afflicted the very young and the very old, and which are a very sensitive indicator of nutritional levels. Death rates due to this one cause declined by 35 per cent between 1912–14 and 1919–21. A similarly impressive decline of over 30 per cent over the war period was also registered by certain degenerative diseases (such as nephritis and cirrhosis of the liver), which kill older people. Between 1912–14 and 1918, mortality due to complications of pregnancy also dropped by 30 per cent, although some of these gains were reversed in the immediate post-war period. This was probably a reflection of the high incidence of influenza among young women in 1918–19, a point to which we shall return below. We shall also refer to some special problems in dealing with this category, which qualify the significance of this finding (see p. 144).

These data also show which diseases did not contribute to the overall pattern of declining mortality in wartime. First, we can detect only minor changes in death rates for neoplasms. Secondly, and more importantly, it is apparent that the only category which moved unambiguously against the general trend was respiratory tuberculosis.

In Table 4.4, which lists index figures of age-specific female death rates, we can see which age groups' death rates declined most sharply during the war. Taking age-specific death rates in 1912–14 as 100, these data show that after 1915, children below the age of 5 and adults between ages 30 and 60 registered clear gains in survival chances. The very elderly and those in the age group 10–30 were not so fortunate, largely because of an increase in their death rates due to respiratory tuberculosis and other infectious diseases. The first conclusion we can draw from this analysis, therefore, is that a number of nutrition-related diseases, affecting

TABLE 4.4   AN INDEX OF AGE-SPECIFIC FEMALE DEATH RATES, ENGLAND AND
WALES, 1912–21
$(1921-14 = 100)^a$

Age	1912–14	1915	1916	1917	1918	1919–21
0–1	100	99	87	85	92	71
1–4	100	122	85	92	103	68
5–9	100	119	99	99	109	81
10–14	100	114	108	109	113	84
15–19	100	113	111	119	125	93
20–24	100	108	107	108	119	94
25–29	100	106	105	101	112	94
30–34	100	103	97	94	84	84
35–39	100	111	105	99	101	83
40–44	100	103	95	93	90	73
45–49	100	105	96	92	90	74
50–54	100	111	101	94	94	76
55–59	100	104	95	92	87	75
60–64	100	108	94	93	88	77
65–69	100	108	103	98	97	82
70–74	100	111	102	95	90	76
75–79	100	115	108	107	101	81
80–84	100	111	106	100	95	75
85+	100	114	111	104	97	68

^{a} Age-specific death rates for pneumonia and influenza in 1915–17 have
been used to approximate non-epidemic mortality trends.

SOURCES: Totals of causes of death were found in the *Registrar-General's
Annual Reports* (later *Statistical Reviews*) *for England and Wales*,
1912–21; age-specific populations were taken from *Decennial
Supplement to the Registrar-General's Report for England and Wales,
1911–20*, (1933) Pt 1, Table 1.

in particular, young children, older adults, and (with some qualifications) women in childbirth, led the overall decline in wartime
mortality rates.

B   The Peculiarities of the English

It may be helpful at this point to return to Preston's studies to
show that the recrudescence of respiratory infection in this period
may have been due as much to the vagaries of the English climate
as to the war. Data presented in Table 4.5 show that high mortality

from certain respiratory infections other than tuberculosis was one of the chief defining features of English and Welsh mortality conditions. Preston and his colleagues produced life tables which show that a woman subject all her life to the set of age-specific and cause-specific death rates for females in England and Wales in 1901 would have approximately a 16 per cent chance of dying of influenza, bronchitis or pneumonia, and could expect to live to approximately 50 years of age. At this level of life expectancy, we find in contrast a predicted probability of 14 per cent of dying from this one cause. In the next 30 years, the gap between predicted and observed probability of dying from this cause grew substantially in this country. For example, English and Welsh males in 1921 had a 60 per cent greater chance of dying of influenza, bronchitis, or pneumonia than would be expected at their level of life expectancy. It is clear that the population of England and Wales achieved an increased life expectancy of 12 years for women and 13 years for men between 1901 and 1931 through a cause-of-death structure unusual in several important respects. The fact that in the war period mortality due to respiratory complaints moved against the general downward trend therefore may have had as much to do with enduring features of British life, such as the climate and the degree of urbanization, as with the special circumstances of war.

We can develop this point further by combining age-specific and cause-specific data. Again, Preston's analysis is of use here.[21] He has divided his national data sets into two groups: those in which life expectancy rose from less than 45 to 70+ years; and those in which life expectancy rose from 45–54 years to 70+. Clearly the latter group is the relevant one for our purposes. Preston then established which two diseases or conditions contributed most to the overall decline in age-specific mortality in his aggregate population. We have repeated the exercise for England and Wales in the period 1912–21. The results may be found in Table 4.6. Preston's data show that in 11 out of 19 age groups, respiratory complaints contributed most to mortality decline. In contrast, in only one age group (30–34) in England and Wales in the war period was a respiratory disease the primary cause of mortality decline among females. Under age 15 there is a strong similarity between the English and Welsh case and Preston's model, but thereafter the most striking feature of the British data is the importance of

TABLE 4.5. PROBABILITY (× 100) THAT A PERSON AGED 0 WILL EVENTUALLY DIE FROM A PARTICULAR CAUSE IN ENGLAND AND WALES, 1901–31, AND IN POPULATIONS AT SIMILAR LEVELS OF LIFE EXPECTANCY AT BIRTH

Life expectancy at birth	(2)	(3)	(4)	(5)	(6)	Cause[a] (7)	(8)	(9)	(10)	(12)	(13)	(14)[b]
Females												
1901	49.93	5.46	7.49	8.26	21.19	16.21	4.84	4.19	1.22	3.92	2.17	26.05	35.22
e_0^c	50.00	6.66	7.07	6.43	18.83	14.27	6.08	4.33	1.24	3.57	1.90	29.63	35.32
1911	53.40	4.54	6.91	9.79	22.43	14.98	5.91	4.66	0.88	3.55	2.14	24.21	33.22
e_0	55.00	5.70	5.59	8.14	23.25	12.28	5.07	4.83	1.04	3.09	2.18	28.83	29.68
1921	59.92	4.44	4.12	12.41	28.06	16.66	2.30	4.09	0.88	2.69	1.99	22.34	28.40
e_0	60.00	4.55	4.16	10.04	29.03	10.41	3.92	5.03	0.80	2.61	2.55	26.90	23.84
1931	62.36	3.63	3.38	13.55	37.02	14.59	0.82	5.19	0.68	2.24	2.67	16.21	18.84
e_0	65.00	3.20	2.77	12.13	36.15	8.65	2.62	4.94	0.52	2.15	3.04	23.83	17.76

Males

1901	45.32	7.74	8.78	5.23	18.15	16.52	5.19	4.83	5.00	4.89	23.65	38.23
e_0	45.00	8.08	8.24	3.92	15.62	15.69	6.21	4.38	4.48	5.78	27.50	38.52
1911	49.38	6.41	7.86	7.45	19.92	15.45	6.38	5.22	4.44	4.72	22.17	36.10
e_0	50.00	6.27	6.65	5.77	19.33	13.33	5.55	5.04	3.91	6.24	26.91	32.80
1921	55.94	5.93	4.95	10.44	25.34	17.40	2.60	4.98	3.45	4.28	20.64	30.88
e_0	55.00	6.15	5.07	8.17	24.66	11.16	4.37	5.30	3.32	6.53	25.27	26.75
1931	58.20	5.17	4.45	12.18	32.96	14.94	0.92	5.87	3.02	4.93	15.56	25.48
1931	58.20	5.17	4.45	12.18	32.96	14.94	0.92	5.87	3.02	4.93	15.56	25.48
e_0	60.00	4.73	3.48	11.12	31.41	9.18	2.98	5.18	2.70	6.63	22.59	30.37

[a] See Table 4.7 for a list of causes: (2) is respiratory tuberculosis; (3) is other infectious diseases; and so on.

[b] This column is the sum of the probability of dying from all infectious diseases, represented in columns (2), (3), (6), (7) and (9). To identify causes (2)–(13) see Tables 4.4–7.

[c] e_0 in model life tables constructed by Preston.

SOURCES: Preston *et al.*, *Causes of Death*, pp. 240–55; Preston, *Mortality Patterns*, p. 53.

TABLE 4.6. CONTRIBUTION OF PARTICULAR DISEASES TO OVERALL MORTALITY DECLINE. ENGLAND AND WALES. 1912–21, AND IN A GENERAL POPULATION

Age group	Proportion of total decline when life expectancy at birth improves from 45–55 to 70+ accounted for by		Proportion of total decline in England and Wales in 1912–21 accounted for by	
	Most important cause	Next most important cause	Most important cause	Next most important cause
0–1	Diarrhoeal diseases (.304)	Certain diseases of infancy (.244)	Diarrhoeal diseases (.262)	Infectious and parasitic diseases (.256)
1–4	Infectious and parasitic diseases (.257)	Diarrhoeal diseases (.253)	Infectious and parasitic diseases (.563)	Diarrhoeal diseases (.251)
5–9	Infectious and parasitic diseases (.373)	Bronchitis, pneumonia, influenza (.147)	Infectious and parasitic diseases (.836)	Violence (.075)
10–14	Infectious and parasitic diseases (.284)	Tuberculosis (.178)	Infectious and parasitic diseases (.680)	Cardiovascular diseases (.320)
15–19	Tuberculosis (.376)	Infectious and parasitic diseases (.187)	Infectious and parasitic diseases (a)	Cardiovascular diseases (a)

Age				
20–24	Tuberculosis (.409)	Infectious and parasitic diseases (.138)	Infectious and parasitic diseases (a)	Cardiovascular diseases (a)
25–29	Tuberculosis (.372)	Infectious and parasitic diseases (.122)	Infectious and parasitic diseases (a)	Certain degenerative diseases (a)
30–34	Tuberculosis (.372)	Infectious and parasitic diseases (.111)	Infectious and parasitic diseases (.282)	Cardiovascular diseases (.213)
35–39	Tuberculosis (.257)	Cardiovascular diseases (.125)	Tuberculosis (.220)	Cardiovascular diseases (.200)
40–44	Tuberculosis (.211)	Cardiovascular diseases (.163)	Cardiovascular diseases (.286)	Tuberculosis (.173)
45–49	Cardiovascular diseases (.216)	Tuberculosis (.176)	Cardiovascular diseases (.299)	Certain degenerative diseases (.180)
50–54	Cardiovascular diseases (.248)	Bronchitis, pneumonia, influenza (.158)	Cardiovascular diseases (.389)	Certain degenerative diseases (.181)

TABLE 4.6 (Continued)

Age group	Proportion of total decline when life expectancy at birth improves from 45–55 to 70+ accounted for by		Proportion of total decline in England and Wales in 1912–21 accounted for by	
	Most important cause	Next most important cause	Most important cause	Next most important cause
55–59	Cardiovascular diseases (.254)	Bronchitis, pneumonia, influenza (.188)	Cardiovascular diseases (.344)	Bronchitis, pneumonia, influenza (.165)
60–64	Cardiovascular diseases (.232)	Bronchitis, pneumonia, influenza (.218)	Cardiovascular diseases (.331)	Bronchitis, pneumonia, influenza (.202)
65–69	Bronchitis, pneumonia, influenza (.236)	Cardiovascular diseases (.195)	Bronchitis, pneumonia, influenza (.208)	Cardiovascular diseases (.204)
70–74	Bronchitis, pneumonia, influenza (.264)	Cardiovascular diseases (.093)	Bronchitis, pneumonia, influenza (.097)	Diarrhoeal diseases (.097)

75–79	Bronchitis, pneumonia, influenza (.284)	Diarrhoeal diseases (.084)	Diarrhoeal diseases (.166)	Bronchitis, pneumonia, influenza (.074)
80–84	Bronchitis, pneumonia, influenza (.296)	Diarrhoeal diseases (.095)	Diarrhoeal diseases (.194)	Certain degenerative diseases (.072)
85+	Bronchitis, pneumonia, influenza (.299)	Diarrhoeal diseases (.137)	Diarrhoeal diseases (b)	Violence (b)

a No percentages are given since the fall in the age-specific death rate was so small as exaggerate minute changes in cause-specific death rates.

b No percentages are given since age-specific death rates rose in the period under review.

SOURCES: S. Preston, *Mortality Patterns*, Table 5.1; Preston et al., *Causes of Death*, pp. 240–55 and data derived from *Annual Reports of the Registrar-General of England and Wales, 1912–21*.

declining death rates due to certain degenerative diseases in the overall process of mortality decline. This is characteristic of countries which have passed through what is commonly termed the 'epidemiological transition' from mortality patterns marked by acute and infectious diseases to those dominated by chronic and degenerative diseases.[22]

The data presented in Table 4.7 summarize these findings. The first column in this table is the result of Preston's analysis of cause-of-death statistics for women in 162 countries between 1861 and 1964, including England and Wales. Columns two and three describe the cause-structure of female mortality decline in England and Wales in the period of the First World War in two forms: with and without epidemic influenza mortality. Both latter columns reflect the special features of mortality decline in this country in the war decade: (i) respiratory diseases played little or no part in mortality decline; (ii) between one-quarter and one-third of the overall decline is attributable to the general class of 'other infectious and parasitic diseases'; (iii) roughly 20 per cent of the decline was due to cardiovascular diseases; and (iv) both diarrhoeal diseases and certain degenerative diseases, such as nephritis, cirrhosis, and diabetes, taken as one class, each contributed between 11 and 14 per cent of total mortality decline.

Once again, we need to note that, in evaluating the findings presented here, we must recognize the limitations of all cause-of-death data. Since roughly 30 per cent of all deaths recorded in these years were due to ill-defined, unknown or obscure causes, we must recognize that medical mistakes or changing fashions in medical diagnosis could have affected these results. But even if this is true, the contrast between the first column in Table 4.7, representing an international cause structure of mortality over the past century, and the other two columns, describing the overall shape of the cause structure of mortality in England and Wales in the war decade, is so great, that we may safely conclude that we are dealing not merely with artifacts of a statistical kind, but with acceptable evidence concerning a real facet of the demographic history of wartime Britain.

C Maternal Mortality in Wartime

In Table 4.3 we noted evidence of a wartime decline of about 30 per cent in the standardized death rate for the category of causes

TABLE 4.7 PERCENTAGE CONTRIBUTION OF CAUSES OF DEATH TO THE DECLINE IN FEMALE MORTALITY IN 162 POPULATIONS AND IN ENGLAND AND WALES, 1912–21

Cause of death	Preston estimates for 162 populations	England and Wales 1912–21	England and Wales 1912–21 (without pandemic influenza)
Respiratory tuberculosis	10.6	4.3	3.5
Other infectious and parasitic diseases	14.0	30.6	24.8
Neoplasms	–	–	–
Cardiovascular diseases	1.8	22.8	18.5
Influenza, bronchitis, pneumonia	24.3	–	4.0
Diarrhoeal diseases	10.4	14.5	11.7
Certain degenerative diseases	1.7	13.8	11.2
Maternity	2.0	0.4	0.3
Certain diseases of infancy	4.2	0.6	0.5
Accidents and violence	0.4	3.5	2.8
Other and unknown	33.1	27.9	22.6

SOURCES: S. Preston, *Mortality Patterns*, Table 2.2; and data derived
from *Registrar-General's Statistical Review of England and Wales,
1921*, Table 5.

associated with complications of pregnancy. The numbers of such deaths was relatively small, but still a drop in mortality rates from 181 per million women in 1914 to 125 per million in 1918 is worthy of note. Maternal mortality rates rose after the Armistice, but this probably reflected a state of reduced resistance to disease among mothers who had contracted influenza. Before the pandemic hit Britain, though, the trend of improvement in maternal health seems clear.

Several important qualifications of this finding must be made. The first is that Preston's approach does not provide an adequate account of this category of death for the simple reason that the total population of women (or the denominator of the death rate) is not the real population at risk. For this reason, most discussions of maternal mortality establish a death rate by dividing maternal deaths by the number of live births in any one year. This is a preferable approach in wartime for the simple reason that the birth rate fluctuated violently in this period. In 1917, for example, 668,346 babies were born, or only 75 per cent of the total registered in the immediate pre-war period. Since there were so many fewer deliveries in 1917, it was inevitable that the number of complications of pregnancy and childbirth (and consequent deaths) would also drop. Dividing such deaths by the number of women in England and Wales must also produce a lower death rate for this category.

The second reason why this category is a difficult one is that problems of diagnosis of the primary cause of death are particularly arbitrary here. We have noted above, for instance, that many women died soon after childbirth in the period of the influenza epidemic of 1918–19. But which was the major cause of death and which a contributory cause? As we can see in Table 4.8, to avoid too narrow a definition of maternal mortality, physicians and social statisticians have formulated a subset of 'deaths of women not classed to pregnancy and child-bearing but returned as associated therewith'. When added to 'total puerperal mortality', this should produce a series of sums which describe in a relatively rigorous way trends in maternal mortality.

What these data show is that the risks of pregnancy and childbirth in the war years were no worse but not much better than in either the pre-war or post-war periods. In 1917, for example, total puerperal mortality rates were almost identical to those registered in 1911; associated mortality rates were also indistinguishable from the 1912 levels. As we shall note below with respect to infant mortality, 1915 was a relatively bad year, but taken as a whole, the pre-war trend was not significantly altered during the war. If anything stands out from the figures presented in Table 4.8, it is that the post-war decade was a period of greater risk for women in childbirth than were the years of the 1914–18 conflict.

One final caveat must be entered before concluding that maternal mortality rates were probably more stable in the war period than cause-of-death data suggested. The history of maternal mortality is a particularly difficult subject, since it contains a hidden agenda: the history of abortion. Where the abortion rate goes up, under conditions of illegality, it is likely that the maternal mortality rate will also rise. For this reason, the only true measure of mortality associated with pregnancy and childbirth must be calculated by dividing the number of women who die as a result of abortion or childbirth by the number of women who become pregnant in any one year. It will surprise no one that such data are simply unavailable for this (or later) periods. And since there is no hard evidence either way about abortion rates during the war, we cannot draw any final conclusions on this aspect of the demographic history of the First World War.

D War Conditions and Mortality Decline

We shall discuss below possible explanations for the fact that the war period was marked by a substantial decline in female death rates due to most infectious diseases. But some preliminary comments may be helpful at this point. First, it is important to note that mortality decline in this period is a complex process, reflecting both what happened to generations who were born and came to maturity long before 1914 (cohort effects) as well as what happened during the war itself (period effects). It would be unwise to ignore such cohort effects or other spontaneous changes in the character of viral and bacterial infections in some of the trends we have described. For instance, there was a major break downward in the trend of mortality due to kidney diseases from 1916. This new more favourable trend was not reversed in the post-war period.[23] We may never know to what extent this change was due to the war, and like all other historians we must avoid the *post hoc propter hoc* fallacy at all costs. Still, it is plausible to view these data as reflections of the parallel decline in mortality rates due to scarlet fever and rheumatic fever after 1915 and 1916 respectively. Since there is reason to believe that the incidence of kidney failure is linked to the trend of these diseases, then here too we can see

136

TABLE 4.8. MATERNAL MORTALITY RATES IN ENGLAND AND WALES, 1911–33

| Year | Live births registered | Deaths of women classed to pregnancy and child-bearing | Rates per 1000 live births registered | | | Deaths of women not classed to pregnancy and child-bearing but returned as associated therewith | |
	No.	No.	Puerperal sepsis	Other puerperal causes	Total puerperal mortality	No.	Rate per 1000 live births registered
1911	881,138	3,413	1.43	2.44	3.87	909	1.04
1912	872,737	3,473	1.39	2.59	3.98	848	0.97
1913	881,890	3,492	1.26	2.70	3.96	803	0.91
1914	879,096	3,667	1.55	2.62	4.17	831	0.95
1915	814,614	3,408	1.47	2.71	4.18	881	1.09
1916	785,520	3,239	1.38	2.74	4.12	739	0.94

Year							
1917	668,346	2,598	1.31	2.58	3.89	638	0.95
1918	662,661	2,509	1.28	2.51	3.79	2,529	3.81
1919	692,438	3,028	1.67	2.70	4.37	1,337	1.93
1920	957,782	4,144	1.81	2.52	4.33	1,086	1.13
1921	848,814	3,322	1.38	2.54	3.92	925	1.09
1922	780,124	2,971	1.39	2.44	3.81	1,051	1.35
1923	758,131	2,892	1.30	2.52	3.82	764	1.01
1924	729,933	2,847	1.39	2.51	3.90	849	1.16
1925	710,582	2,900	1.56	2.52	4.08	759	1.07
1926	694,563	2,860	1.60	2.52	4.12	709	1.02
1927	654,172	2,690	1.57	2.54	4.11	861	1.32
1928	660,267	2,920	1.79	2.63	4.42	790	1.20
1929	643,673	2,787	1.80	2.53	4.33	960	1.49
1930	648,811	2,854	1.92	2.48	4.40	774	1.19
1931	632,081	2,601	1.66	2.45	4.11	911	1.44
1932	613,972	2,587	1.61	2.60	4.21	713	1.16
1933	580,413	2,618	1.83	2.68	4.51	828	1.43

SOURCE: J. Campbell, *Maternity Services* (1935), p. 8.

traces of the overall improvement in resistance to infectious diseases during the war.[24]

In other cases, the link between mortality decline by cause and war conditions seems fairly direct. Shortages of sugar helped precipitate a decline in diabetes mortality, and restrictions on the consumption of alcohol caused a drop in the incidence of fatalities due to cirrhosis of the liver.[25]

The material we have presented above does suggest other ways in which the 1914–18 war effort set in motion contradictory forces affecting the health and survival chances of the civilian population. The war economy created some conditions which helped reduce mortality rates. Indeed, the substantial fall in deaths due to diarrhoeal disease and to complications of pregnancy and childbirth would not have been possible had there been a major deterioration in levels of nutrition during the war. The same is true in the case of common infectious diseases, as well as in diseases of maternity and early childhood. We shall present below (see chapter 7) substantial evidence as to the unintentional effects of the war in raising family incomes and thereby nutritional levels especially among the worst-off sections of the community. Despite (or as we shall argue, because of) the fact that a sizeable number of married women joined the workforce during the war, mortality rates among women during childbirth and among their offspring dropped substantially. This was in flat contradiction of the views of many who argued before 1914 that high female workforce participation rates were responsible for high infant and maternal mortality.[26] We shall also return (see chapter 5) to the fact that these gains were registered while more than half the medical profession was in the army and therefore unable to care for the civilian population. Of course, the wartime decline in the birth rate meant that fewer women were pregnant and therefore in need of medical or para-medical assistance at this time, but we shall defer consideration of this question to a later chapter.

The evidence concerning respiratory diseases seems to point in the opposite direction and suggests countervailing aspects of the impact of war. The Registrar-General of England and Wales, in the Decennial Supplement for 1911–20, concluded that undernutrition was responsible for the increase in tuberculosis mortality during the war.[27] Other scholars have followed this lead.[28] But it is surprising that relatively little attention has been directed to two other aspects of the war experience which may account for the recrudescence of respiratory tuberculosis and other respiratory diseases during and after the war. The first is the transfer of large populations, many from rural or suburban areas, to urban centres of war production and their concentration in munitions factories. The second is the deterioration in housing conditions and the postponement of necessary demolition and sanitary work by local authorities during the war. Together these adverse effects of the war probably provided ideal conditions for the spread of respiratory infections, and helped tip the balance between latent and active cases of tuberculosis.[29] The stress of overwork and anxiety over the fate of family and friends in the army may also have undermined the resistance of those (especially among the elderly) suffering from this and other diseases. It is important to note that similar, if not worse, housing conditions during the 1939–45 war produced very similar results. There was a recrudescence of tuberculosis mortality in 1940–2 which paralleled that of 1914–16, and in Hitler's war it was clear that nutritional levels had improved.[30]

It is always dangerous to isolate any one environmental variable and to declare that it was the key element influencing trends in vital statistics. This is why regression analysis is not the most subtle of tools in historical demography. But the link between tuberculosis and other respiratory diseases on the one hand and inadequate housing on the other is well enough established[31] to permit us to advance an argument about the likely effects of this aspect of war conditions on public health.

The view that working and housing conditions rather than increasingly inadequate levels of nutrition were responsible for the rise in tuberculosis death rates in wartime is reinforced by a glance at the post-war history of the cohort which evidenced the most substantial increase in tuberculosis death rates – young people aged 10–25. Had this cohort suffered undernutrition at a critical period of their development, we would expect to see higher than normal death rates among this group ten years later, that is, at ages 20–35 in 1925–28, or 20 years later, at ages 30–34 in 1935–8. But such was not the case.[32] The most likely reason is that most recruits to munitions production returned home after the war, and that by the mid-1920s and certainly by the end of the 1930s, deferred housing improvements had finally been carried out.

E   Conclusion

The overall interpretation that emerges from this analysis of female mortality rates is that the war period was one of major gains in the survival chances of the civilian population. Again we find substantial corroboration for the results of our analyses of life tables and occupational mortality statistics. It is important to note, though, that some causes of death (especially tuberculosis) did rise, and some age groups (especially the very elderly) did not share in the general improvement.

But the general picture seems clear. The Great War created the conditions which helped eliminate some of the worst features of urban poverty which lay behind the appallingly high death rates of late-Victorian and Edwardian Britain. Long-term trends towards improving life expectancy were no doubt of importance, but special features of the war economy underlay both the increasing survival chances of civilians insured by the Prudential and the narrowing of the gap between the mortality experienced by men in low-paid and in better-paid employment.

In sum the evidence presented in this chapter suggests that one of the most important demographic effects of the First World War in Britain was to compress the class structure in such a way as to reduce the distance between the survival chances of different classes and between different strata within classes. It would have surprised many of those who took the decision to go to war in 1914 to know that they were unleashing forces leading not only to unprecedented slaughter but also to an improvement in the conditions under which large sections of the urban and rural population lived. But unbeknownst to them, that may have been precisely where their action led.

We shall deal with the problem of the standard of living of the civilian population in a later chapter. It may be useful at this point, though, to address the question as to how this country managed to pay for the war and at the same time provide the improved nutritional levels which, we have argued, were an unintended by-product of the conflict. The answer is that Britain lived off her capital stock during the conflict. Some of it was invested in the empire, the true economic value of which was proved during the war. But more of it was invested in the form of bricks and mortar, and it is here that we may find the origins of some of the negative effects of war conditions on civilian health. To keep the war effort going required the maintenance of adequate or improved levels of nutrition among munition workers. But especially under conditions of rent control, it was not possible to avoid a situation where essential repairs and improvements were postponed or abandoned. Given the absence of economic incentives, no one was able to prevent a rundown of the nation's stock of housing during the war. As we shall note below (see chapter 7), public authorities were aware of this, but felt they were powerless to do anything about it. The result was to exacerbate conditions leading to an *increase* in death rates for some causes (notably respiratory diseases) virtually as the price that had to be paid for improving conditions leading to a *decrease* in death rates due to other causes (notably diarrhoeal diseases and diseases of maternity and childhood). Here is the source of some of the paradoxical features of public health in Britain during the First World War.

IV THE DECLINE OF INFANT MORTALITY IN WARTIME BRITAIN

There is nothing paradoxical about the decline of infant mortality rates in wartime Britain. This kind of of demographic evidence presents the most clear-cut indication of the surprisingly favourable

TABLE 4.9. AN INDEX OF INFANT MORTALITY RATES IN ENGLAND AND WALES, 1905–25, AT VARIOUS PERIODS OF THE FIRST YEAR OF LIFE (1911–13 = 100)

Month of death	1905–10	1911–13	1914	1915	1916	1917	1918	1919	1920	1921–25
1st	102	100	97	96	93	95	92	101	89	84
2nd–3rd	110	100	93	91	81	83	81	74	75	61
4th–6th	107	100	90	91	73	77	76	63	60	55
7th–8th	109	100	92	106	72	81	87	67	57	58
10th–12th	107	100	92	116	97	87	96	68	51	62
Total	107	100	95	99	82	87	87	80	72	68

SOURCE: *Registrar-General's Annual Reports for England and Wales,* 1905–25.

effects of war conditions on the survival chances of the civilian population of this country. Sir George Newman, Chief Medical Officer to the Board of Education spoke for virtually every recognized authority when he noted that the infant mortality rate is 'the most sensitive and subtle index of all' measures of social welfare and of sanitary administration, especially under urban conditions.[33] If this assertion is correct, and I believe it is, then the war period must be viewed as one of significant improvements in public health. Indeed, as we shall note in a moment, the war years were for most parts of Britain the period in which the most striking gains in infant survival chances were registered in the first thirty years of this century.

When we survey European trends in these years, we are struck again by the exceptional nature of the British experience of the war. Throughout Europe the wartime birth rate declined drastically. Since fewer babies were born, the number of infant deaths dropped as well. But among the major combatant powers there were significant differences in the war's effects on infant mortality rates. In Germany, infant mortality rates were fairly stable, despite wartime shortages and the Allied blockade which continued long after the Armistice. But there was in Germany 'a break in the pre-war pattern of decline' and in France, Italy, and Austria, a serious deterioration in infant mortality rates at different periods of the war.[34] Of all major European powers, only in Britain were there improvements in infant mortality rates during the 1914–18 war. It might be argued that a drop in the birth rate would mean that newborns would receive relatively more attention and that a greater proportion would survive. But a comparison of European infant mortality rates belies such a direct correlation between the birth rate and the infant mortality rate. Birth deficit is thus not a plausible explanation for the course of infant mortality during the First World War.

Not long after the war, the demographer Liebman Hersch wrote that the 'industrial mobilization of women, their employment en masse in different branches of the economy, as well as the scarcity of certain commodities such as milk, etc. contributed without a doubt to the recrudescence of infant mortality' in central and western Europe.[35] The British case appears yet again to be the exception to the rule. The contribution of women to the war effort was just as widespread and intensive as it was on the Continent.

Infant mortality rates in this country, though, do not bear the traces of maternal exhaustion or neglect. In reference to Britain, the above argument was much closer to the mark when it related infant health to food supply, a subject discussed in detail later.

A The Course of Infant Mortality Decline in Britain, 1900–30

Starting from a level of around 150 deaths per 1,000 live births in England and Wales, and around 115 in Scotland around the turn of the century, infant mortality rates dropped by one-half in England and Wales and by one-quarter in Scotland in three decades. But within these decades, there were clear variations in the pace and incidence of infant mortality decline. The initial drop was greater in the south than in the north, and much greater in England and Wales than in Scotland. Indeed in seven counties of Scotland, there occurred a worsening of infant mortality rates in the first decade of this century. In England and Wales as a whole, both the period after the turn of the century and the war period were the occasions of the steepest decline in infant mortality rates in the first thirty years of this century. Taking 1901–3 as the basis of comparison, infant mortality rates dropped by 17 per cent in both the period up to 1909 and in the war period. In Scotland, there is no doubt that the most striking gains in infant survival rates were registered during the First World War. Between 1902 and 1914 only a 6 per cent drop was registered; by 1921, a further 13 per cent decline occurred. In both Scotland and in England and Wales, the wartime rate of change was greater than in the 1920s.[36]

Let us look more closely at the components of infant mortality: neo-natal (or first month) mortality; and post-neonatal (or months 1–12) mortality. The data in Table 4.9 permit a discussion of wartime changes in both neo-natal and post-neonatal mortality. Detailed figures on infant mortality by age within the first year of life were first published in 1905. They show that during the war the most rapid improvements were registered after the first months of life. The sole exception is for 1915, when mortality rates after age 6 months rose steeply. In every other war year, though, after children were likely to be weaned and had lost the protection of their mothers' antibodies against infectious diseases, post-neonatal mortality rates dropped. In 1914, 1916, 1917, and 1918, infants in Britain showed better resistance to or were less afflicted by endemic infectious diseases, and in particular by gastro-enteritis, a classic affliction of malnourished people or those whose food supply is easily contaminated. In the quinquennium 1911–15, the infant mortality rate attributable to this one case was 19.05 per 1,000 live births. In 1916–20, it had fallen to 9.46. No other single source of infant deaths was checked as suddenly or effectively.[37] Here we find corroboration for our earlier discussion of the cause structure of mortality.

Less startling, but nevertheless important, improvements in rates of neo-natal mortality also took place during the war. This change reflects a steady decline in peri-natal (first week) mortality, the toll of which was lower in every war year than in either the pre-war or the immediate post-war periods. Fig. 4.2 illustrates the pattern of wartime neo-natal mortality within the two decades after 1906, when full data first appeared. The sole exception to the pattern of wartime improvement was that of illegitimate neo-natal mortality, which peaked in 1917, but which dropped in every other war year. It seems likely that conditions of confinement during the war were not worse (and probably were better) than those of the pre-war period. Neither overcrowding in centres of war production nor the absence on military service of over 13,000 doctors adversely affected the life chances of most newborns. Indeed, when the doctors returned in 1919, the neo-natal mortality rate actually rose both for legitimate and illegitimate births. This phenomenon was probably related to the influenza pandemic of 1918–19. Mothers who contracted the disease in 1918 may have been weakened and/or their foetuses damaged sufficiently to diminish the survival chances of children born in the following year.[38]

The year 1915 stands out against the wartime trend of improving annual infant mortality rates. This fact may be attributable to a change in the virulence or to the periodicity of certain viral and bacterial infections. A severe outbreak of spring measles accounted for a rise of 67 per cent over the infant death rate in 1914 due to common infectious diseases. There were also outbreaks of whooping cough and meningitis in England and Wales in 1915, as well as a rise in the incidence of infant deaths due to bronchitis and pneumonia. These respiratory diseases are common complications of viral infections and may be seen as adjuncts of them. There was at the same time a slight drop in deaths due to gastro-enteritis,

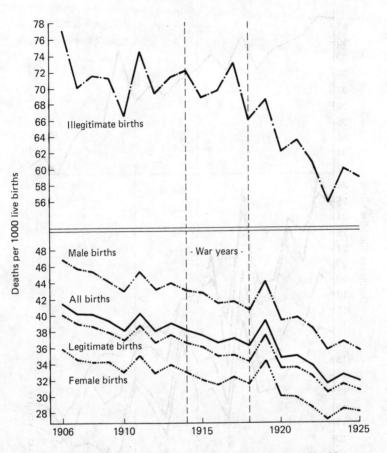

FIG. 4.2. Neo-natal mortality rates, England and Wales, 1096–25
SOURCE: See Fig. 4.1

which may be related to the relatively wet and cool conditions of the summer of 1915.

The data illustrated in Fig 4.3 permit further discussion of the exceptionally high death rates at ages 6–12 months in 1915. The graph shows the overall pattern of decline, which the war did not deflect. Within these decades of improving chances of infant survival, there were four peaks of infant mortality after age 6 months, in 1906, 1911, 1915, and 1918. The downward trend was also checked in 1908 and 1921–2. The 1915 figures therefore may

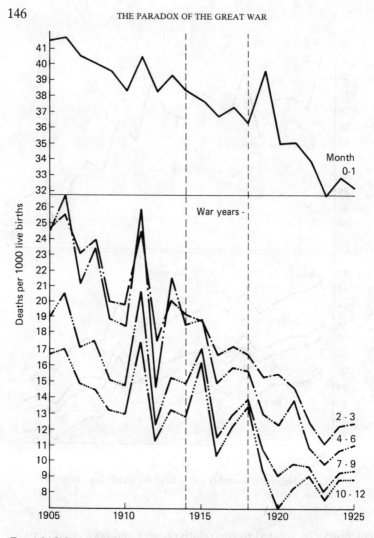

FIG. 4.3. Infant mortality rates, England and Wales, 1905–25, at different periods
of the first year of life
SOURCE: See Fig. 4.1

reflect one of a series of outbreaks of infant disease which occurred
in the early part of this century, at roughly three-year intervals,
and with diminished intensity after 1911.

No one knows precisely why a flare-up of a particular viral
infection occurs, but Scrimshaw, Taylor, and Gordon have shown

that measles and other diseases of infancy occur in three-year cycles. The high mortality of 1915 may be linked to the normal periodicity of such diseases. Therein may lie as well part of the explanation of the sudden disappearance of the same viral infections in 1916 and 1917 both in Scotland and in England and Wales.[39]

Finally, it seems that this general improvement in infant survival rates during the war was not limited to one part of the country. From Table 4.10 it is clear that the outbreak of disease and the resultant infant mortality in 1915 were more severe in the south and in the Midlands than in the north of England or in Wales. But in the following years all regions showed impressive improvements over 1911–13, when regional figures were first published. In 1918, there was a slight increase in infant mortality throughout the country, in all likelihood a reflection of the influenza epidemic. But this setback was not great enough to obscure the real gains in infant health during the war, gains which were maintained in the years after the Armistice.

B The Decline of Infant Mortality in Working-class Communities during the War

The analysis of aggregate data can take us only part of the way towards an understanding of wartime trends in infant mortality. We must also examine evidence on smaller administrative units than counties, which incorporate many diverse social groups. Data on county boroughs in England and Wales, principal burghs in

TABLE 4.10 An Index of Regional Infant Mortality Rates in England and Wales. 1911–25
(England and Wales. 1911–13 = 100)

Region	1911–13	1914	1915	1916	1917	1918	1919	1920	1921–25
North	121	110	112	96	97	102	94	88	82
Midlands	101	86	92	76	77	78	74	64	62
South	93	80	89	71	77	78	68	59	57
Wales	110	99	101	83	85	86	83	77	73
England & Wales	100	95	95	82	87	87	80	72	68

SOURCE: Registrar-General's Annual Reports for England and Wales, 1911–25.

Scotland, and metropolitan districts in London are more indicative of the war's effects on infant mortality among the industrial population. Of course, county borough statistics may also be based on too large a unit of study for some purposes, but in many cases they successfully describe conditions of working-class life for the simple reason that the urban working class was the numerically preponderant part of this population.

Among English and Welsh county boroughs, the most striking gains in infant health were made in urban areas most marked by some of the worst conditions of Victorian and Edwardian poverty. Declines much greater than the average occurred in manufacturing and textile centres like Manchester, Preston and Burnley, in areas of metal manufacture like Birmingham and Sheffield, and in port cities such as Swansea. To take but one example which could be replicated many times, the mixed mining and industrial town of Wigan was, long before George Orwell's famous visit, a district bearing most of the features of nineteenth-century urban poverty. In 1901–3 the infant mortality rate stood at 181 per 1,000 live births. On the eve of the war, the rate was 139, or 23 per cent below the initial figure. After the war, the rate had dropped to 119 or 66 per cent of the turn-of-the-century rate. Thus the rate of decline during the war was nearly twice that of the pre-war period.

Similarly, metropolitan boroughs with distinctly working-class populations played a leading role in the process of infant mortality decline in London. The boroughs registering the greatest gains in infant survival rates during the war were Shoreditch, Bermondsey, Stepney, and Bethnal Green, the heart of 'outcast London'. Again to describe but one of these areas, in Bethnal Green in 1901–3, the average infant mortality rate was 150. By 1914 that figure had been reduced to 119, which constituted a decline of 21 per cent. After the war, the infant mortality rate dipped below the 100 mark for the first time to reach 93. This represented a decline of a further 22 per cent, compared to 18 per cent for London as a whole.

In Scotland, the industrial districts of Coatbridge, Glasgow, Dundee, and Paisley were also well in advance of the Scottish pace of improvement in infant health. The example of the old mining and industrial district of Coatbridge should suffice to illustrate the point. Whereas in Scotland as a whole, there occurred a 13 per cent decline in infant mortality rates over the war period, in this principal burgh, the decline was 19 per cent.

We can illustrate the importance of the war period in the decline of infant mortality in working-class communities in three other ways. The relation between overcrowding, poverty, and women's work on the one hand, and infant mortality on the other, was a subject of wide interest in both the pre-war and war periods. In 1916 Arthur Newsholme presented much important material on these questions in a supplement to the 1916 report of the Local Government Board. A year later, two eminent physicians in the field of public health, E.W. Hope, Medical Officer of Health for Liverpool, and W. Leslie Mackenzie (on whom, see chapter 1) produced substantial volumes under the aegis of the Carnegie UK Trust. Their subject was the health and welfare of mothers and children in Britain.[40]

Newsholme's report ranked administrative areas in terms of how high or low their infant mortality rates were in the period 1911–14 and investigated social conditions in these extreme cases. We have presented in Table 4.11 a list of the eight county boroughs and metropolitan boroughs of highest and lowest infant mortality rates in 1911–14. To these we have added the eight principal burghs registering highest infant mortality rates and the seven registering the lowest infant mortality rates in Scotland. In all three cases, wartime decline was significantly greater in those working-class areas which had high pre-war infant mortality rates. English data show as well that the higher the pre-war infant mortality rate, the greater the wartime rate of decline. In contrast, areas of relatively low pre-war infant mortality rates gained little on average in the war period. These county boroughs of relatively low pre-war infant mortality were all in the south of England, which suggests that the wartime decline was especially marked in the industrial concentrations of the Midlands and the north.

Secondly, data on urban overcrowding collected by Newsholme and Mackenzie point to the conclusion that the greatest wartime gains were registered in areas of inadequate urban housing in the pre-war period. Newsholme ranked county boroughs and metropolitan boroughs according to the percentage of the population living more than two to a room. Mackenzie presented comparable but not identical data on overcrowding in the form of the percentage of families living in two rooms or less in seven Scottish burghs. Table 4.12 shows that the most severely overcrowded areas experienced the greatest wartime improvements in infant

TABLE 4.11. WARTIME INFANT MORTALITY DECLINE IN COUNTY BOROUGHS, METROPOLITAN BOROUGHS, AND PRINCIPAL SCOTTISH BURGHS OF HIGH OR LOW INFANT MORTALITY RATES IN 1911–14

Areas of lowest IMRs in 1911–14	IMR 1911–14	IMR wartime decline	Areas of highest IMRs in 1914	IMR 1911–14	IMR wartime decline
Metropolitan boroughs					
Hampstead	74	8	Shoreditch	148	33
Lewisham	82	12	Finsbury	133	34
Stoke Newington	83	9	Bermondsey	131	29
Chelsea	84	6	Bethnal Green	126	25
Woolwich	84	9	Poplar	123	22
Westminster	92	8	Stepney	122	24
St Pancras	97	10	Southwark	122	21
Wandsworth	94	16	Deptford	112	16
County boroughs					
Bournemouth	77	−1	Burnley	172	31
Eastbourne	77	1	Stoke-on-Trent	161	31
Bath	78	−2	Wigan	159	29
East Ham	82	5	Barnsley	151	19
Oxford	82	21	Preston	149	32
Southend-on-Sea	83	15	Middlesbrough	144	6
Reading	89	14	St Helens	143	26
Coventry	90	8	Blackburn	143	19
Principal burghs					
Falkirk	100	10	Dundee	154	21
Kilmarnock	101	−7	Aberdeen	135	18
Kirkcaldy	104	29	Glasgow	131	19
Motherwell	104	5	Coatbridge	130	27
Perth	105	−6	Ayr	115	24
Clydebank	107	28	Greenock	114	11
Edinburgh	109	4	Hamilton	114	17
			Paisley	114	28

SOURCE: J. M. Winter, *The Impact of the First World War on Infant Mortality in Britain*, SSRC Rept. HR 5091 (1979), Tables 6,9, 15; PP 1917–18, XVI, Cd 8496, pp. 21, 22.

TABLE 4.12. WARTIME INFANT MORTALITY DECLINE AND OVERCROWDING IN HOUSING

Areas of least overcrowding	% over crowded	IMR wartime decline	Areas of greatest overcrowding	% over crowded	IMR wartime decline
Metropolitan boroughs[a]					
Lewisham	4	12	Finsbury	40	34
Hampstead	7	8	Shoreditch	37	33
Woolwich	6	9	Stepney	35	24
Stoke Newington	9	9	Bethnal Green	33	25
Westminster	13	8	Southwark	26	21
Chelsea	15	6	Holborn	26	14
County boroughs[a]					
Bournemouth	2	–1	Gateshead	34	19
Oxford	2	21	Sunderland	33	16
Reading	3	14	St Helens	17	26
Wallasey	3	13	Dudley	15	30
Southport	4	18	Middlesbrough	13	6
Southend-on-Sea	4	18	Wigan	13	29
Croydon	4	13	West Bromwich	12	17
Eastbourne	4	1	Liverpool	10	20
			Principal Burghs[b]		
			Pailsey	65	28
			Dundee	63	21
			Glasgow	62	19
			Greenock	59	11
			Aberdeen	39	18
			Edinburgh	37	4
			Perth	30	26

[a] Percentage of the population living more than two occupants to a room.
[b] Percentage of families living in two rooms or less.

SOURCES: See Table 4.11 and W. Leslie Mackenzie, *Scottish Mothers and Children* (Dunfermline, 1917), ch. X.

mortality rates. Whatever may have been the effects of inadequate housing on the adult population, most infants born in most parts of Britain during the war seem to have been unaffected by them. Again, we must turn to levels of nutrition both of mothers and of weaned infants to account for wartime gains in infant mortality rates (see chapter 7).

Thirdly, we can examine data collected by these men on infant mortality in areas ranked according to the female population in extra-domestic employment. In Table 4.13 we have listed county boroughs and metropolitan boroughs identified by Newsholme on the basis of 1911 census returns as areas of high or low pre-war rates of female employment. To these we have added a second set

TABLE 4.13. WARTIME INFANT MORTALITY DECLINE AND RATES OF
EXTRA-DOMESTIC FEMALE LABOUR

County boroughs of high female employment rates	Total wartime decline in IMRs	County boroughs of low female employment rates	Total wartime decline in IMRs
I. Newsholme Estimates			
Burnley	31	Middlesbrough	6
Wigan	29	St Helens	26
Preston	32	Barnsley	19
Oldham	27	Walsall	22
Salford	21	West Bromwich	17
Manchester	22	Rotherham	29
Blackburn	19	Gateshead	19
Leeds	15	Sheffield	20
II. Hope Estimates			
Blackburn	19	Rotherham	29
Leicester	20	St Helens	26
Nottingham	26	South Shields	8
Preston	32	Newport	27
Oldham	26	Merthyr Tydfil	24
Rochdale	12	Lincoln	12
Stockport	29	Darlington	-9
Blackpool	29	West Hartlepool	9

SOURCES: See Table 4.11 and E. W. Hope, *Report on the Physical Welfare of Mothers and Children*, (Dunfermline, 1917), vol. 1, epitomes of local reports.

of data on rates of employment of married or widowed women in county boroughs in 1916. These figures were estimates reported to Hope by Medical Officers of Health. The reliability of these data is questionable, since they describe guesses by Medical Officers of Health on questions probably beyond their competence. Nevertheless, the fact remains that both sets of data show that wartime infant mortality decline in areas of high levels of female extra-domestic employment was as great or greater than in areas of relatively low levels of female employment. Throughout working-class Britain, therefore, the toll of infant life was reduced substantially in the course of the Great War.

C Conclusion

The above discussion of infant mortality decline in Britain is consistent with the argument advanced in the first three sections of this chapter. The war years were undoubtedly a period of significant gains in civilian health, for the very young as much as (or even more than) for the industrial labour force. There is no basis for the claim that in the short term or in the long term, war conditions were damaging or injurious to the health of men who stayed at home or to their families.

In the case of infant mortality decline in wartime, we may assert with some confidence that in analysing wartime developments, we are dealing more with period effects than with cohort effects, although the latter can never be completely set aside. Maternal health and nutrition well before childbirth have a direct bearing on peri-natal and neo-natal mortality rates. But the importance of the domestic environment to the survival chances of infants especially after they are weaned is a *sine qua non* of social medicine and epidemiology, and what is true in developing countries today was no less true in Britain in 1914.[41] In our case, the period effects point almost entirely in one direction: towards environmental improvements during the war yielding increasing survival chances not only for young children and mothers but also for the bulk of the civilian population. The following three chapters are an attempt to explain why this was so.

5. Medical Care in Wartime

IT is one of the ironies of British history in the Great War that a major increase in life expectancy for civilians occurred while more than half the medical profession had been withdrawn from general or specialist practice to serve in the Forces. As we have seen, death rates due to most infectious diseases declined after 1915, that is, precisely in the years when there was very little medical care to be had at all in many rural and urban areas of Britain. Of course, we must bear in mind that regular medical attendance was the exception rather than the rule for most of the population in the pre-war period; it was only in the last pre-war year that the National Insurance Act, which provided medical care for insured workers, came into force. We must note as well that we are dealing with a period 30 years before the introduction of the powerful antibiotic drugs which have made an enormous difference in the control and eradication of disease. In 1914, most infectious diseases probably took their course, whatever the nature of medical supervision. An extreme example of this was that of the influenza pandemic of 1918–19, which, as we have noted, killed young, healthy adults both in countries depleted of medical care due to military recruitment and in places far removed from the war. In cases requiring surgical intervention, the scarcity of medical personnel was a serious problem during the war, but in less drastic situations, recovery rates were no worse in wartime, and indeed in some cases better than in peacetime.

It would be mistaken, though, to suggest that the medical profession played no part in the successful defence of public health in the 1914–18 war. In Britain the time-honoured association between war and disease was broken during the Great War. And if nutritional improvements rather than medical supervision were at the heart of this change, it is still important to recognize the extent to which the mobilization of mass armies and munitions workers presented real risks of the spread of the diseases which added substantially to the toll of human misery in Central and Eastern Europe at this time. The achievement of the medical community in Britain was basically to prevent worse things from happening.

The fact that there was no crisis in the provision of medical care in wartime Britain was due in part to the vagaries of disease, but it was also a reflection of the efficiency of the medical community's organization for war service. As we shall see below, the history of the medical profession in wartime is largely a history of an exercise in self-government, safe from the interference of the recruiting machine of the War Office and later of the Ministry of National Service. In this isolation from external bureaucracy, the medical profession presents a unique case, and the fact that a squeeze on medical care did not turn into a crisis in part attests to the success of this system.

The way it worked was basically through the drawing up of manpower budgets for the profession. Since they involved only about 25,000 physicians, these budgets were far more detailed and sensitive to local conditions than the similar aggregate estimates upon which overall manpower planning was based. With such complete information on medical personnel, the leadership of the profession in effect operated a form of industrial conscription for doctors in the last two years of the war. The central organizations set up for Ireland, for Scotland, and for England and Wales located every man and woman in Britain licensed to practise medicine, identified those eligible for army service who could be spared, and ensured that their departure did not strip the home population of all medical care. This was no minor operation, but by 1918 it was apparent that the system of letting the medical profession determine the nature and limits of its contribution to the war effort had worked. The army had been given the doctors it had needed, and this had been done without endangering the health of the civilian population. How this was achieved is the subject of this chapter.

I MEDICAL RECRUITMENT AND THE PROBLEM OF CIVILIAN MEDICAL CARE

The flood of enlistment in British forces in the first months of the war brought with it approximately 10 per cent of the country's medical practitioners. Over 2,000 men who had held commissions in the Reserves or Territorial Forces were called up on 2 August, just before hostilities began. Many others with no previous army connection presented themselves and received commissions in the Royal Army Medical Corps (RAMC) as soon as war was declared. In England steps were taken by local practitioners in a number of communities to look after the work and interests of the men who had volunteered.[1] In Scotland, a more collective line was adopted in the first week of the war in order to monitor and counteract any adverse effect of military mobilization on civilian health care. The chairman of the Scottish committee of the British Medical Association (BMA), Dr J. R. Hamilton, called a meeting of representatives of the medical profession in Scotland to consider the war situation. On 12 August 1914, this conference created a 'Scottish Medical Service Emergency Committee' 'for the purpose of assisting to meet the immediate difficulties in regard to medical practice among the civilian population which have arisen or may arise owing to the departure of practitioners summoned to take up military duty'.[2] This body organized local committees to supervise substitution arrangements for doctors who enlisted and to provide free medical attendance for soldiers' families. In one case, the Dundee local medical committee set up 'Emergency Bureaux' at the Royal Infirmary to treat private and insured patients alike.[3]

This corporate response in Scotland to the potential disruption of civilian medical care was well in advance of that south of the border. It was only after about a year of war, long after the hopes of a quick victory had vanished, that a resolution passed at the Representative Meeting of the BMA on 23 July 1915 led to the creation of a group, the stated purposes of which was:

to organize the Medical Profession in England, Wales, and Ireland in such a way as will enable the Government to use every Medical Practitioner fit to serve the country in such a manner as to turn his qualifications to best possible use; to deal with all matters affecting the Medical Profession arising in connection with the War; and to report to the Council.[4]

We must bear in mind that this resolution was passed just after the establishment of the Ministry of Munitions. The creation of a

'Central Medical War Committee' (CMWC) was thus part of the general tendency towards planning for a protracted war.

The committee's membership included most of the major officers of the BMA. Sir Alexander Ogston, BMA president, E. B. Turner, chairman of Representative Meetings, and J. A. MacDonald, Chairman of Council, served ex-officio. Four members were appointed by Council, including Major James Galloway, later to become a key figure in military recruitment. Eight members were appointed by the Representative Meeting of the BMA; among them were the Regius Professors of Medicine at Oxford and Cambridge, Sir William Osler and Sir T. Clifford Albutt. The day-to-day business of the group was placed in the hands of T. Jenner Verrall as chairman and of Alfred Cox, the medical secretary of the BMA. Cox, a general practitioner of working-class origins, who had practised for years in the north-east before entering medical politics, was the central force behind the committee's work. He benefited in particular from a close and longstanding friendship with the previous medical secretary, J. (later Sir James) Smith Whitaker, then a civil servant in the National Health Insurance Commission (NHIC), a body with which, as we shall see, the CMWC had to deal increasingly as the war dragged on.[5]

In the first phase of its work, from July 1915 to June 1917, recruitment for the RAMC was the overriding priority for this body. Its initial business was to draw up a preliminary register of medical men of military age. This survey showed that by July 1915, fully one-quarter of the profession had joined up. This was well above the proportion of the male labour force in uniform (see chapter 2). It was apparent that 'certain areas are already depleted and cannot spare any more men', but in the committee's view, there was still 'a considerable source of men of military age' as yet 'untapped'. Apparently many doctors were still unaware of the gravity of the crisis facing the country.[6] The job of the CMWC was to find such men, and to help free them for military service by arranging for voluntary substitution by older men. To this end local medical war committees were set up throughout the country in areas which corresponded roughly to the local divisions of the BMA. Secretaries of these local committees, who had compiled the war register, continued to inform the CMWC of all local problems.

One week after the first meeting of the CMWC, Sir Alfred Keogh, Director-General of the Army Medical Service, extended both to it and to the Scottish Emergency Medical Committee official recognition as the sole recruiting bodies for the medical profession.[7] The CMWC in turn agreed to launch an enrolment scheme, very similar to the Derby scheme adopted later the same year for the whole male population of military age. Through the CMWC, doctors stated their willingness to serve when called. The procedure for recruitment was, therefore, that the War Office would submit its requirements to the central medical committees, which would in turn ask their local agents to furnish the names of those to go from among those who had already attested. In the latter half of 1915 the system ran smoothly, furnishing approximately 70 doctors per week for the RAMC.[8]

The CMWC and the Scottish committee faced a number of delicate problems virtually from their inception. The first arose from the old antagonism between general practitioners (GPs) and those in the public health service. Some GPs believed that full-time medical officers employed by local authorities were shirking military service. This was not entirely the case, since such men were statutorily obliged to act in a wide variety of ways to defend public health. At no stage of the war did Parliament abrogate or suspend the duties of such doctors employed by the LGB, the Board of Control, the Board of Education, and the Metropolitan Asylums Board, and therefore some doctors simply could not go, even if they had wanted to do so.[9] Not unnaturally, those GPs who prior to 1914 believed that public health physicians posed a threat to their livelihood were loth to volunteer if MOHs and other public health physicians stayed at home. Throughout the war sensitive negotiations on this subject continued between the CMWC and the LGB, in particular through Sir Arthur Newsholme, and with the Board of Education, through Sir George Newman.

The second obstacle to untrammelled medical recruitment was the contractual obligation entered into by over 8,000 physicians to provide medical care for over 12 million insured workers under the National Insurance Act. This constituted three-quarters of the entire working population. As war industries drew into the labour force people who had not worked regularly before 1914, the total number of labourers entitled to benefits rose to approximately 14.2 million in 1918, or 40 per cent of the population.[10] These people had a right to medical care, which the National Health Insurance Commissioners had to provide, whatever the needs of the army. This point was reiterated by the two key civil servants of the NHIC, Sir Robert Morant and J. Smith Whitaker. They successfully defended the panel system under which the insurance scheme operated, but by doing so, they presented the boundary conditions for military recruitment of medical men.

The first real test of the resources of the CMWC was the demand made on 15 October 1915 by the Director-General of Army Medical Services for a total of 2,500 medical men to join the army by January 1916. The committee had been able to provide 550 recruits in its first three months, but the output would have to soar in order to reach the target figure. Cox put it to the committee that they would have to impress a large number of men 'that civil requirements, which have been considered essential to the good of the community in peace time, must give way now to military necessities'. Some public health work for schoolchildren or the tuberculous probably would have to be abandoned, in his view.[11] As we shall see, this position was not shared by many of the doctors in the public health service.

A much more serious obstacle to recruitment arose from the reactions to army service of many men already in uniform. As early as October 1915 reports were filtering back from medical men in the RAMC about the way in which medical manpower was being used. One such letter was presented to General Keogh when he met the CMWC on 18 October 1915. In it an officer who had been a medical registrar in a large hospital before the war claimed that he had little work to do in the army, and the bulk of it was routinely administrative. Keogh was furious. He

protested that the writer had only displayed his total ignorance of military administration; that he had forgotten that the present siege warfare was only temporary; that what was being prepared for was a march on Berlin; and that such letters were impossible to answer.[12]

This outburst was far from the end of the matter, as we shall note below.

Whatever suspicions the CMWC had as to the adequate utilization of medical men in uniform, they had no choice but to try to find the men Keogh wanted. An up-to-date war register identified 5,858 medical men in England and Wales of military age. Of these approximately 1,600 were in the London area. The Army Medical Service anticipated that two out of every five doctors of military age in local areas would come forward under this accounting system. But due to the geographical maldistribution of the medical profession, some areas such as London or Brighton had a surfeit of doctors, while others emphatically did not. The committee therefore had to set different quotas for different areas, and then rely on local committees to identify those who could be spared and to persuade them to go. No other way existed to find recruits without precipitating a deterioration in medical services in areas where shortages were apparent.

This was already the case in a number of centres of munitions production where an influx of labour had occurred. In October 1915, complaints about pressure on medical care reached the CMWC from its local secretaries in Coventry, Preston, and Nottingham. The secretary of the Leicester committee reported that 'local men are working to their utmost capacity'; 68 doctors out of a total of 247 in practice in 1914 had already gone, and 'there is a serious risk of men breaking down under strain if more work is put on them'.[13] The CMWC could not afford to ignore such comments, since it was on the cooperation of their local committees that the success of the recruiting system rested. Consequently the CMWC began to discuss the establishment of a 'Civil Emergency Corps to meet the exigencies of the war conditions in home practice'.[14] This would be a mobile unit prepared to travel at short notice to any part of the country facing a health crisis.

The powerful voice of Sir Robert Morant was added to those who feared, as early as November 1915, that 'the point of dangerous depletion may already have been reached, or will soon be reached, in particular areas', especially in the countryside, but also in some cities. Morant pressed the committee to exempt areas from the need to provide any medical recruits if the ratio of population to GP was over 1,500/1 in rural areas, over 3,000/1 in 'semi-urban' areas, and over 5,000/1 in urban areas. This was the first attempt to define the limits of tolerable depletion of medical services. It was accepted by the CMWC at a joint meeting with Morant and Smith Whitaker on 19 November 1915.

At the same meeting the CMWC decided in which order men

from different branches of the profession should join the services. Their list clearly describes their view of the relative importance of the work of parts of the medical population. The higher up a man was on the following list, the greater the likelihood that he would have to go:

Single or married:	1.	All newly qualified men.
	2.	Junior medical men employed by local authorities.
	3.	Resident medical men at institutions.
	4.	Assistants and partners to general practitioners.
Single:	5.	Chief Tuberculosis Officers if not also Medical Officers of Health.
	6.	Men in single-handed panel practices in cities.
	7.	Men in single-handed private practices in cities.
	8.	Men replacing earlier volunteers.
Married:	9.	Men in single-handed panel practices in cities.
	10.	Men in single-handed private practices in cities.
Rural:	11.	Single men in single-handed private practices in rural areas.
	12.	Married men in single-handed private practices in rural areas.[15]

Note the preference to dispense with public physicians before GPs, and with panel practitioners before private practitioners. A similar ranking system was drafted for consultants and specialists, which again illustrates perceptions of indispensability (or otherwise) among the population working in hospitals. A high place on the list again meant that such men could be spared:

1. Anaesthetists, radiographers.
2. Dentists with medical qualifications.
3. Orthopaedic surgeons.
4. Gynaecologists.
5. Neurologists and alienists.

6. Aurists and ophthalmologists.
7. Physicians.
8. Surgeons.
9. Bacteriologists attached to recognized institutions.[16]

Over the following weeks, both Morant and Newsholme registered strong objections to these orders of recruitment, since they clearly placed the needs of panel patients and others benefiting from public health work on a lower level than the needs of private patients. Morant said that the preference shown for private practice proved that 'the Committee had been thinking entirely about medical interests and not about those of the public'. W. B. Willis of the LGB said that the committee obviously did not realize how depleted the public health services already were. Over one-third of the 237 Tuberculosis Officers in England and Wales had joined up, and to place their class virtually at the top of the list of potential recruits was utterly irresponsible.[17] There was considerable force in these arguments, as the wartime rise in tuberculosis mortality suggests (see chapter 4). The CMWC was forced to give ground, and conducted negotiations throughout the war over virtually every one of the physicians to be called up.

How this worked is easily illustrated. The small Flintshire town of Connah's Quay on the Dee estuary had a population of 5,000. Two doctors looked after this relatively isolated community. When the local medical committee recommended that one should go, the local insurance committee objected, and their case was presented by Morant to the CMWC. It was obviously a mistake to recruit the man in question, since the only other doctor available had been removed from the insurance panel for 'drink'. The upshot was that the nominated man did not go.[18] In other areas secretaries of local committees pleaded the case for special exemption from providing any recruits. The local secretary in Salisbury reported that it was 'absolutely impossible' to lose another doctor.[19] Within London too, overwork was reaching serious levels in the working-class districts of Stepney and Poplar. The local secretary of the Tower Hamlets division echoed earlier suspicions of the RAMC when he wrote that: 'There is very little encouragement to induce more men to go when one finds that men now joining are working four hours a day and having one day off in four. The contrast is too great.'[20]

Specialists and consultants working in hospitals reported the same increase in the pressure of civilian work. For example, William Robinson, chief of the medical board and senior surgeon at the Royal Infirmary and Children's Hospital, Sunderland, wrote to the CMWC about what would be the effect of a further depletion of his staff. His was a hospital of 234 beds, half of which were allocated to wounded soldiers, and half of which served as a surgical centre for a population of approximately 500,000 people engaged in coalmining, shipbuilding and other munitions work. The surgical staff was composed of four surgeons and two assistant surgeons. Two of the senior men had enlisted, leaving four to perform approximately 2,200 operations per year. Of these four, two were of military age. Should either go, the surgical work simply could not be done. Similarly in the children's hospital, there was one temporary physician in charge, replacing his son who had enlisted. If this older man fell ill, there would be no coverage at all.[21] The room for manoeuvre over enlistment was very narrow indeed.

It is likely that these difficulties were responsible for the failure of the committee to come up with Keogh's 2,500 men by January 1916. Only about 500 were passed on to the RAMC as a result of this exercise.[22] The Director-General of Army Medical Services had simply asked for the impossible.

The introduction of compulsory military service in 1916, first for single men aged 18–41, and then in May for all men in that age group, did little to alter the work of medical recruitment. Doctors were still treated as a special case; their age limit was set at 45 for overseas duty and 55 for home duty, although over age 41, compulsion did not apply. The same blend of voluntarism and professional pressure marked medical recruitment in 1916 as it had done before. The one major change, embodied in the Military Service (No. 2) Act of 1916, was that the CMWC, the Scottish Medical Committee, and a Committee of Reference for specialists and consultants were recognized as statutory professional organizations, with powers to act as appeals tribunals for physicians claiming exemption from military service. This time-consuming work was carried on regularly throughout the war, but it still took second place to the overall work of medical manpower planning.

The degree of continuity in recruiting practices is best illustrated by the perpetuation of the CMWC's attestation scheme, even after legal compulsion had come into force. The reason was that the committee believed, with some justification, that a clean sweep of civilian physicians would be disastrous, and they therefore wanted to engage ordinary doctors in a collective effort to balance military and civilian needs. In addition, some physicians over age 45 had attested in 1915, while others below age 45 had not done so. To take only those on the attestation lists might benefit those who had simply kept their heads down, as it were, and had refused to sign anything. Such men were bound to exist, and anticipating professional criticism, the committee decided to draw compulsorily on its attestation lists only when 75 per cent of the profession had signed them.

This figure was reached in June 1916, just in time for the second major call for medical recruits.[23] A few weeks previously, General Keogh had presented to the CMWC a demand for 250 doctors of military age by 7 August, and a further 150 men aged 45–55 by 31 August. The CMWC agreed to bypass rural areas where the population/GP ratio was above 3,000/1 and in urban areas where the ratio was above 4,000/1. The better-endowed local committees were given the job of finding the men to fulfil local quotas drawn up after a scrutiny of local conditions. A total of 112 local committees were instructed to come up with 289 names, of which 113 were to come from the London area alone. Additional names were to be provided by the LGB, the Committee of Reference, Deans of Medical Schools, the Scottish Medical Committee, and the newly-formed Irish Medical War Committee. The result was that 345 physicians were medically examined, and of these men 253 were cleared in time to join the army by 7 August, as instructed.[24]

Even before these men had joined up, the medical committees received the third major call for recruits. By this time, everyone who could read was aware of the terrible casualties of the Battle of the Somme, and it therefore came as no surprise when the CMWC received a supplementary request on 28 July 1916 for 150 more men. This was raised to 180 a few days later, all of whom had to be processed by 18 September. Again the relevant committees found sufficient manpower to meet this demand in the time allowed.[25]

Over the following six weeks the committees sent a steady stream of doctors to the RAMC, but by November 1916 wastage on the army had become so severe that a fourth major call for medical recruits was made. The problem at this point was made worse by contradictory instructions from different officials in the War Office as to precisely how many men were needed. The figures varied from 150 to 400 for those under 45, and between 150 and 500 for those aged 45–55. After some difficulty, the CMWC prised out of the War Office that it wanted 235 men from England and Wales and 60 from Scotland. The remainder of its requirements would be met by men already in uniform on home duty and by 90 American graduates who had volunteered for service in military hospitals in the United Kingdom.[26]

In meeting this fourth call, the CMWC began to question the basis on which War Office demands were being made. Were men needed for new units, to replace casualties, or to replace men whose yearly contract of service had expired, they asked? General Keogh indignantly refused to answer these questions, and preferred to chastise the committee by telling them that their work 'is to provide medical men or to say that they cannot be provided, not to examine the strategical [sic] plans upon which they are founded'.[27] Behind this exchange lay a steady stream of complaints about military inefficiency in handling medical manpower.

Whatever suspicions were harboured by the CMWC, they still made a strenuous effort to find more men. To this end they conducted the first full census of the medical profession in England and Wales, in which every local area was analysed according to the number of physicians practising in it, their ages, and previous history of enlistment. Local committees were asked to name the next man who could be spared, and if well stocked, the next two. A total of 262 names was forwarded, but nearly 100 of these had already been rejected by the army or had been exempted on special grounds. This meant that only 167 men could be found for the fourth call. More alarmingly, it was not clear where more men could be found if there were future heavy demands.[28]

A fifth call for more men came almost immediately, this time for 600 doctors.[29] This was followed by a supplementary call for 500 more in late February 1917, which was adjusted to a grand total of 1,000 to be found by the end of May 1917.[30] We have noted in chapter 2 that this was the period in which full civilian mobilization began for the population as a whole. All previous exemptions were to be reviewed, a step made inevitable by the scale of the slaughter on the Western Front. Army Command was planning a new set of operations in Flanders, and thus required both new drafts to make good the losses on the Somme and fresh men for what came to be known as Third Ypres or the Battle of Passchendaele. British losses in these two operations totalled over 750,000 men. Under these circumstances, a major new draft of medical manpower for the army was essential.

One additional development increased the pressure to enlist more medical men into the army. On 1 February 1917, Germany opened unlimited submarine warfare against the Allies. In March the hospital ships *Asturias* and *Gloucester Castle* were torpedoed and sunk. Four weeks later, two more ships carrying wounded men, the *Donegal* and the *Lanfranc*, were sunk. The War Office decided that in future 'owing to the wholly unforeseen and hitherto unimaginable development of Germany's deliberate policy of torpedoing hospital ships', the wounded would be treated initially in France. Consequently more doctors had to serve abroad,[31] and enlistment notices were sent to every medical man of military age in the country on 21 April 1917.[32]

Even prior to the April call, Morant had warned the War Office that mass conscription of doctors would endanger civilian health so long as no power existed to redistribute medical manpower at home.[33] Now the crisis had come, and still there was no form of compulsion with respect to civilian medical services. It was nearly impossible, therefore, to continue to honour the commitment to provide medical services under the Insurance Act. Additional pressure to withdraw the general call came from the Scottish Medical Committee, which informed Keogh that should a breakdown in medical services occur in Scotland, it was on his head that responsibility would rest. The CMWC even threatened to take no further part in medical recruitment. Not surprisingly, the general mobilization order was withdrawn four days after it had been issued.[34]

Still the medical committees had to find a total of 100 doctors per week for the army until 850 had been nominated. After a thorough review of the medical census it had compiled, the CMWC concluded that the men simply could not be found without 'serious disturbances of medical services for the civil community'. The only alternative was to enforce a system of compulsory substitution of doctors not in uniform or to make reciprocal use of civilian and RAMC men.[35]

This problem was of sufficient importance to engage the attention of the Director-General of Recruiting, Lord Derby. He noted the impossibility of meeting the recruitment quota and asked what was 'the definite date after which you cannot, with due regard to the needs of the civil population, provide further doctors'.[36] The CMWC asked for six weeks to come up with an answer, and concluded that by the end of July 1917 they would have 'released for military service every man who can, with justice to the bare needs of the civilian population, be allowed to leave his practice'.[37] Indeed, precisely on 31 July, Keogh was informed that the country had run out of available medical manpower for the army.[38]

II MANPOWER PLANNING FOR THE MEDICAL PROFESSION, 1917–18

This effectively ended the first phase of the work undertaken by the medical profession to fill the ranks of the RAMC. Between July 1915 and April 1917, it had secured commitments of service voluntarily from 5,235 medical men, and had found 3,399 men for the army. After April 1917, the committee continued to send to the War Office the names of those available for military service, but it increasingly turned its attention to the defence of the medical requirements of the civilian population, whose efforts were essential for the maintenance of munitions production. Here again we see in microcosm the overall pattern of British manpower policy in the last year of the war.

This shift of emphasis occurred against the backdrop firstly, of the overall reorganization of recruitment under the Ministry of National Service; and second, of a review of the organization of the RAMC, about which so many complaints had been lodged. By August 1917, the Army Council had placed the problem of medical recruitment entirely in the hands of Auckland Geddes, Minister of National Service. General Keogh was delighted to lay down this burden, telling Geddes that everyone believes 'that you should take over the question of the supply of doctors'.[39] In addition the Army Command agreed to set up a committee of influential medical men, under the chairmanship of Major General Sir Francis Howard, to investigate the organization of the RAMC and to recommend ways of more efficiently utilizing available manpower.[40] The report of this committee was never made public, but it largely cleared the RAMC of most of the charges of disorganization, while pointing out a number of ways in which medical services could be improved.[41]

The emergence of manpower control through the Ministry of National Service meant that the CMWC would have no further direct contact either with the Army Medical Service or with other government departments. All questions concerning medical personnel would go henceforth to the Minister of National Service, Auckland Geddes, who continued nevertheless to work through the statutory professional committees. This was for four reasons: firstly, his Ministry needed to know what medical opinion was; second, these groups had the confidence of the profession; third, they had the manpower census data essential for the planning of further recruitment; and fourth, their work was the only way to safeguard the professional status and practices of the men in uniform.[42]

Rationalization of administration meant, on occasion, that Geddes had to hear complaints previously directed to the Army Medical Service. For example, at a meeting with the CMWC and the Scottish Medical Committee, Verrall and Cox reported further testimony from doctors about the poor use of medical manpower in the army. Geddes reacted in the same way General Keogh had done a year earlier: he was furious, and said

> I think that a great many of the medical men and others who get their complaints put up for them by outside bodies, Statutory Committees or something of that sort – the medical men who are serving with the forces do not do themselves any good. There never has been an Army that was not full of grouses.

Geddes accepted that there were more soldiers in home hospitals than ever before. This overspill from the front he attributed not only to enemy action but also to the fact that after three years of war 'men are getting "fed up"' and were clogging hospitals. He knew that doctors were overworked at home, but saw no way out of asking them to increase their efforts to free more men for the army. Dr Hallett, chairman of the Committee of Reference, replied that: 'We have got down to the bedrock in the hospitals. We can only say a man may be spared if another man will take his place.' Geddes, who was a physician himself, would have none of this, and countered that they all knew a number of specialists who were not overworked. Sir James Galloway even went further and stated that 'I am quite sure that London wants very drastic combing out'.[43]

The order to 'comb out' doctors throughout the country came within days. Geddes estimated that he would need to call up 40 medical recruits per week throughout 1918. This total of over 2,000 more medical men was more than twice the size of the previous draft of April 1917 which the CMWC did not meet. It was at this point that Morant took the initiative on behalf of the NHIC to declare that the depletion of civilian doctors had gone far enough. He wrote to Geddes on 22 December 1917 that they had done all they could

> in discovering all the doctors under 41 years of age in every nook and cranny throughout England and Wales, whose departure from civil practice to the Army can be effected without involving a real breakdown in the local services, or such a grave diminution of the medical services in the country as to occasion a row in Parliament.

But the new demand of 40 per week was simply unrealistic, and 'any attempt to squeeze anything like such a number as these from the remaining doctors of military age will quite certainly produce such a storm in Parliament that the Government could not possibly stand it'. The strain on those still practising at home was severe, perhaps at breaking point. If they should give way, or if an epidemic should occur, the consequences would be grave.[44] Morant's opinion was seconded by the CMWC in its meeting with Geddes of 29 December 1917.[45]

This convinced him that the matter was one for the War Cabinet to decide. He told his colleagues on 25 February 1918 that current War Office demands for 500 men would reduce civilian medical care sufficiently to trigger off a major protest. The result was a compromise, whereby the Ministry of National Service and the LGB were empowered to work out with the War Office a realistic medical manpower budget. In other words, army requests would have to be tailored to suit the threadbare cloth of the wartime medical profession.[46]

Here again, Morant's intervention was decisive. In consultation with the LGB, he submitted a memorandum to Geddes proving that medical recruitment simply could not be stepped up. On 1 January 1918, 5 million men in uniform were being attended by 12,284 doctors, or 376 soldiers to one medical man. At home 34.5 million people were being looked after by 14,718 doctors, of whom 11,482 were in general practice, or 2,344 civilians to each doctor, and 3,004 civilians to each GP. Thus the army had between six and eight times the number of doctors proportionately available to civilians. Of course, the work of military physicians was very heavy, and crushing on occasion, but so was the work of men in civilian practice, who covered cases (like maternity) unknown in the army, and frequently did not have the advantage of regular group practice or the sharing of work. He pointed out that doctors at home were already working 12–14 hours a day, and queues for surgeries in some munitions areas were seen late into the night. For all these reasons, more doctors could not be spared.[47]

Morant appeared to have demonstrated an inescapable fact, but within days, events had passed him by. On 21 March 1918, the Germans launched a major offensive. Galloway informed the CMWC the next day that all medical reserves had been committed to the Western Front, and consequently civilians would have to take the places of the anticipated 200 casualties among army doctors during the then current fighting.[48] The committee issued an urgent call for volunteers prepared to serve for three months, but only 27 men answered the summons. Clearly more drastic steps were in order.

The first of these was the new Military Service Act of 1918, passed on 18 April. Under it conscription was extended to all men under age 51, but the age limit for doctors was set at 55. In addition, the Military Service (Medical Practitioners) Regulations issued in its wake gave to the CMWC and the Ministry of National Service full power to direct enlisted medical men to practise in parts of the country which were particularly short of doctors. It was apparent that civilian conscription was drawing near.

Every other option had been investigated by the CMWC and the other professional groups long before the crisis of March 1918. Despite protests, Indian, Chinese, Portuguese, and Egyptian doctors filled in for enlisted men in Cardiff, Liverpool and Burnley.[49] Some thought was given to the offer of the Japanese Medical War

Association to provide 2,000 doctors, but language problems were insurmountable.[50] The supply of newly qualified doctors was drying up fast; indeed the CMWC was alarmed lest there be a shortage of men who would have qualified in 1920 and 1921.[51] Dr Jane Walker, President of the Medical Women's Federation, suggested that full-time public health officers of military age could be relieved by female physicians.[52] But little was made of this offer, as 'disciplinary problems' arose in institutions where women medical officers worked alone.[53] Even in wartime, women had to overcome stubborn male resistance to the idea that they were the equals of their male colleagues. The Committee of Reference reported to Geddes that women doctors

> are not suitable for all hospital appointments, nor for all forms of general practice, and of course, are not available for the Navy and Army. It must therefore not be assumed that an increase of women doctors can compensate for a serious shortage of male doctors.[54]

The CMWC preferred to consider forms of collective substitution as a way out of the medical manpower crisis. One such scheme was set up by the Manchester Medical War Committee early in 1916. All panel practitioners agreed to join a rota to cover depleted practices, and to pool their fees in such a way as to provide doctors in uniform with half the sum they had earned in the last full year prior to their having taken up a commission.[55] Elsewhere local practitioners signed a form promising not to accept on their panel lists the patients of doctors in uniform for at least one year after the enlisted men had returned home. This was one of the essential features of the earlier enlistment campaign.[56] As early as 1915 the Glasgow committee proposed the creation of district centres to concentrate panel work.[57] Three years later similar pooling arrangements were set up in Nottingham, Leicester, Birmingham and Hertford.[58] A system grouping London hospitals in fifteen units, thus freeing substantial numbers of surgeons and specialists, was also drawn up in 1918, but not realized.[59]

The collective scheme that came closest to being put into effect was the formation of a Civil Emergency Corps of 200 men who would receive retainers for agreeing to act as a medical flying squad, prepared to meet trouble in industrial areas where insured workers could not be treated due to the enlistment of panel doctors. This idea was the particular work of N. Bishop Harman, a London physician, but it foundered on the questions of selection and payment.[60]

Of greater potential importance and controversy was a compulsory system of medical transfer, whereby civilian physicians would be directed by the CMWC wherever their services could best be employed. Early in 1917 Cox and Verrall worked out the principles of this system, to be financed by the pooled income of practitioners in each area. The idea was that local committees would state a request; the CMWC would direct a doctor from an overstocked area like Bournemouth to a depleted area like Shoreditch. But as Verrall himself was quick to point out, this system was bound to run into serious problems related to the social composition of the medical profession. 'You may shift a doctor from Bournemouth to Shoreditch', he noted, but 'can you make the Bournemouth doctor work against his will in Shoreditch, or can you make the Shoreditchians accept him?'[61] In addition, the scheme was bound to run into the old antagonism between panel and private doctors.[62]

By the summer of 1918, such qualms appeared frivolous. A Treasury guarantee and contract for substitution were agreed with the CMWC. Each substitute would receive an annual salary of £525 plus a percentage share of earnings above this level.[63] In preparation the CMWC wrote to all local committees that they had to face the possibility of several more years of war, during which the reorganization of practices on collective lines was inevitable.[64]

Fortunately, they were wrong, but few realized at the time how close this country had come to the setting up of an embryonic national health service during the First World War. There were four reasons why the difficult course of compulsion was avoided. Firstly, the Americans were coming and in force. Second, the War Office abandoned its policy of maintaining the establishment of the RAMC, and concentrated on securing a steady supply of younger men from medical schools.[65] Third, the Ministry of National Service finally convinced the army that priority had to be given to the 'pressing claims on the part of the civilian community which if unsatisfied would, in many cases, give rise to a serious situation, directly imperilling prosecution of the War'.[66] Fourth, the failure of the last major German offensive in July 1918 opened the way to the final phase of the war, the war of movement leading to the Armistice four months later.

III   THE DEFENCE OF MEDICAL INDEPENDENCE

The men who ran this country's medical war effort were fully prepared to place the services of the profession entirely at the disposal of the state in time of war. But what is equally clear is their vigilance lest the war experience lead to the permanent extension of a salaried full-time state medical service. The majority of the profession firmly believed that this would be detrimental to their interests and independence. It is ironic, therefore, that at the same time as the BMA leadership were scouring the country for men to serve in the army, they were conducting a protracted fight against the spectre of state control and salaried status, which in effect was what an army commission meant. This in part reflected lingering bitterness over the battles recently lost over the panel system set up under the 1911 Insurance Act. But it was also an indication of the worry some doctors felt about the war's effects on the long-term prospects of their profession. These anxieties can be seen in the campaigns waged against the extension of the public health service and against what was known as 'contract practice', whereby a particular occupational group or community employed salaried physicians to provide them with medical care.

A   The Public Health Service

In 1914, six public bodies had responsibility for and made medical appointments related to public health. The Board of Education organized the inspection of schoolchildren. The Board of Control and Lunacy Commission dealt with the treatment of the insane and the mentally deficient. The Home Office had responsibilities under the Inebriates Act and under regulations for the inspection of schools of anatomy. The NHIC provided medical, sickness, and maternity benefit, medical care under the panel system, and sanatorium treatment for tuberculosis. And finally, the LGB supervised medical inspection for Poor Law Unions and oversaw the work of 1,740 Medical Officers of Health.[67]

As we shall see in chapter 6, despite the war emergency, the LGB undertook substantial work to develop its maternal and child welfare services during the war This was done in the face of the concerted hostility of the BMA, which saw in it a threat to the livelihoods of GPs.

The LGB initiative of late July 1914 offering matching grants to local authorities for maternal and child welfare centres was, in the view of the BMA, an unwelcome measure, since it undermined the principle that GPs should be the 'normal means by which the treatment of such classes of persons should be secured'. The expansion of centres for the treatment of mothers and children in which Medical Officers of Health would be in charge meant inevitably that they would usurp 'functions more properly belonging to medical practitioners'. In November 1914, the Medico-Political Committee of the BMA declared that it favoured instead

extending downward the giving of treatment by g.p.s rather than the building up from the first of a system of treatment by salaried whole-time officials – a system which, established as normal for early years, might ultimately be extended in later years in substitution of that now prevailing.[68]

This position was broadcast time and again. Removing maternal and child care from GPs would not only deny them income; it would also alter the relationship of the doctor to his patients by segmenting medical care into parts handled exclusively by specialists.[69] In the past, working-class families did not have a family doctor to consult, but the Insurance Act, Cox argued, had changed that situation. Hence it was wrong to assert that these centres were providing services which most people were denied. GPs could do the job, but if public health centres proliferated, many GPs would lose the experience necessary for successful midwifery, to the detriment both of the profession and the community. But above all, the BMA objected to LGB schemes to expand public health services because 'the history of all such movements shows very clearly that before long this kind of treatment is expected as a right by nearly all persons belonging to the working and lower middle classes'.[70] Thus seemingly innocuous maternity and child welfare centres were transformed into the harbingers of a national health service.

The medico-political committee of the BMA lobbied Members of Parliament against the Notification of Births (Extension) Bill of 1915, making notification of birth without payment mandatory for midwives and GPs. Even after the Act had been passed, the BMA did its best to block the LGB from using this measure to extend child and maternal welfare provision. Cox sent a letter to all clerks and Medical Officers of all sanitary authorities in Britain stating the objection of the BMA to appointments of new health visitors or assistant medical officers of health in this field. The BMA suggested instead the use of a rota of local GPs, if local authorities still pressed ahead with such schemes.[71]

Through this committee the BMA were even prepared to threaten disciplinary action against men or women who accepted posts in these centres. Warning notices appeared in the *British Medical Journal* on occasion. One concerned the desire of Hyde Borough Council to appoint an assistant medical officer of health. The Council were approached by local GPs who wanted to set up a rota system of attendance at the proposed maternity and child welfare centre. The Council wanted to make its own appointment, Dr Helen Lauder of Birmingham. She was notified by the BMA that 'any practitioner taking this post would be received very coldly by the local profession who considered they were quite able and had shown themselves quite willing to undertake the new work the Council were prepared to commence'. Hints were dropped about proceedings for unethical behaviour, for which the BMA could recommend that a practitioner be struck off the Medical Register.[72] But both the Borough Council and Dr Lauder stuck to their guns, and she duly took up her appointment. Similar arguments developed over appointments in Hornsey and Reigate, with the same threats and the same outcome.[73]

The BMA were more successful in thwarting a more unusual foray into maternal and child welfare work. The Mothers' Union had the idea of setting up an 'Infant Consultation Centre for Educated Mothers' in mid-1917. Mrs Maude of this body told the BMA that:

The Centre is intended for mothers whose husbands are in professions, business or trade, or are officers in either Service. It is felt that the mothers and young children of such families have often fewer facilities for medical advice and for the early diagnosis of minor ailments than those who come within the sphere of the Infant Welfare Movement.

To which the BMA replied that they opposed such ventures in general, and in particular they could not accept a scheme providing for a 'class of the community the committee is of opinion are quite able to consult their own family doctor'. That was the end of Mrs Maude's scheme.[74]

A rearguard and ultimately ineffective campaign was launched the same year when the BMA learned of plans to give legislative backing to the expansion of maternity centres. A Maternity and Child Welfare Act was passed in 1918, but before the issue had been settled, Cox wrote to Sir Edwin Cornwall, minister responsible for the NHIC, explaining the emphatic opposition of the profession to such measures. Firstly it would undermine the panel system by taking away from GPs work they had previously done. Second, it would further 'the piecemeal handling of the problem of the provision of medical service which is greatly to be deprecated'. Such measures 'tend to make the general practitioner believe that it is none of his business to keep himself efficient in dealing with tuberculosis, or the emergencies of midwifery, and the diseases of women and young children, because these are the sphere of so-called specialists'. But of greatest importance to the BMA was the potential effect of such measures in 'gradually undermining' private and panel practice 'in favour of a system of whole-time state medical officers'.[75]

A BMA delegation to Lord Rhondda, the new President of the LGB, pressed a similar case. H. B. (later Sir Henry) Brackenbury, a prominent physician and Mayor of Hackney, made the point that child welfare centres were ineffective, because 'the right people were not being attracted to the centre, which, in turn, was due to the fact that the interests and participation of the private practitioners were not encouraged'.[76] What matters more than the outcome of such deputations is the state of mind that lay behind them.

That attitude is reflected in BMA discussions of three other areas of public health work which grew during the 1914–18 war. The first concerned a clause in the Education Act of 1918 to permit the extension of medical inspection of schoolchildren from the ages of 5–14 to the ages 2–18. Again, the BMA suggested that such measures undermined the work of GPs, because there was no effective way of limiting school medical examinations to diagnosis and not to treatment.[77] Efforts to establish a state-aided midwifery service under the Midwives Act of 1916 were also opposed, on the grounds that they would usurp traditional medical functions. Advice by midwives on hygiene was unexceptionable, but medical care was not.[78] Third, the BMA pointed out to Walter Long, when he headed the LGB, that to set up free municipal clinics run by Medical Officers of Health for the treatment of venereal disease, as recommended by a Royal Commission which reported in 1916, would be inimical to the interests of local GPs, who knew more about the disease than public health officials ever would. In this case Long was prepared to instruct local authorities to appoint GPs to committees set up to administer the scheme.[79]

B Contract Practice

Perhaps the clearest example of resistance by the BMA to what they saw as the erosion of the rights of GPs was the conflict over 'contract practice'. This had been a headache for many years before the war.[80] The matter arose out of the arrangement whereby working-class clubs, particularly in South Wales, set up medical aid societies to provide care for their members and then employed doctors as salaried staff. This tended to undercut the practices of some local practitioners, who appealed to the BMA to defend them. This it duly did, and the ensuing struggle is known as the 'war of the clubs'. A truce was arranged in this conflict after the passage of the National Insurance Act of 1911, which recognized the right of Medical Aid Institutions to act as friendly societies empowered to administer funds for medical benefits for insured workers. But the BMA were not satisfied with the truce, and tried throughout the war to prevent any extension of contract practice by placing warning notices in the *British Medical Journal* advising any potential applicant for a job with a medical aid society to contact the BMA before applying.

These contract practice arrangements varied widely. Some were on a firm financial footing and provided good salaries for the men who operated them. The Abertysswg Workmen's Medical Aid

Society paid its medical officer £420 per year to look after 750 insured men, 550 children under age 16, and 1,071 other dependents. The society covered the costs of housing and provided their doctor with a holiday grant.[81] Conditions in Tredegar were even better. A chief surgeon was employed at an annual salary of £1,000 per annum plus a house. His assistants received £450 plus free accommodation. Both there and in Llwynypia, the schemes had the support of colliery officials. In such cases, which were replicated in a number of scattered English towns, 'contract practice' was both popular and represented a clear advance over the patchy or inadequate medical coverage which had previously existed. There were other societies in South Wales and elsewhere with shakier financial foundations, and it was these that the BMA was able to stamp out. The result of their pressure was a compromise, wherein the BMA accepted those institutions which were going concerns in late 1915; in return, the Friendly Society Medical Alliance and the South Wales and Monmouthshire Alliance of Friendly Societies agreed not to organize any further 'contract' schemes.[82]

The BMA clearly had decided to make the best of what it saw as a bad situation. But for our purposes, what this episode illustrates is the persistence and deepening in wartime of the earlier conviction held by medical men in positions of power that salaried work had an 'evil influence' on the 'discipline and status' of their profession. Even under conditions of acute scarcity of physicians in general practice during the war, the BMA was unprepared to countenance the erosion of the GP's prime responsibility for medical care, which they saw as the inevitable outcome of an extension of the public health service.

IV MEDICAL PROVISION AND PUBLIC HEALTH

We have charted the course of medical recruitment during the Great War and the reaction of the profession to developments in public health provision during the conflict. It remains to estimate the extent and effects of the depletion of medical services in particular areas in the 1914–18 period.

Three immediate problems complicate this inquiry. The first is that full statistics on pre-war medical provision simply do not exist.

The National Insurance scheme was still very new at the outbreak of war, and in any event two-thirds of the population were ineligible for its benefits. Second, the ratios calculated during the war to describe depletion of medical care used as their numerator pre-war population totals. These were hopelessly out of date by the time munitions production got under way in 1915. And third, such data as do exist refer to relatively large administrative areas, in which substantial variations in patterns of medical care were bound to exist.

Nevertheless, we can form a rough idea of the extent and incidence of shortages in medical personnel by scrutinizing three sources. Two concern Scotland. The first is a table prepared by the Glasgow Medical War Committee to describe a system of grouping medical care (Table 5.1). The second is a table which records the ratio of population per GP in Scotland as a whole in 1914–18 (Table 5.2). The third is the medical censuses taken by the CMWC at various intervals during the war. These deal with England and Wales. Table 5.3 lists administrative areas in England and Wales which were singled out as particularly depleted in 1918. Table 5.4 lists London Metropolitan Boroughs in rank order of depletion between December 1915 and January 1917.

A glance at Table 5.1 will suffice to show the wide variation in provision of medical care within one major urban centre. In Glasgow as a whole, there was roughly one GP for every 2,500 people. Some districts benefited from proximity to hospital services. Others were less well stocked with medical men. Within less than a year, the population/GP ratio for Glasgow as a whole had doubled, and some districts were above the 5,000/1 mark. There is no doubt that the enlistment of half the medical personnel in Glasgow in the space of ten months meant a major reduction in levels of medical care, both for the insured and the uninsured population. It may be of some help to note that the ratio of population to physician in Guatemala and Mauritius in 1969 were 4,030/1 and 4,500/1 respectively. In Western Europe the ratio has varied between 500/1 and 800/1 in recent years.[83]

Table 5.2 presents similar evidence for Scotland as a whole. The units described are counties, which of course had very different densities and social compositions. In these large units, the ratio of population to GP increased by 35 per cent on average between August 1914 and June 1916. By the end of the war, the ratio was 80

TABLE 5.1 DISTRIBUTION OF MEDICAL SERVICES IN DISTRICTS OF GLASGOW IN 1915

Centre or district	Population	Number on panel lists	Percent on panel lists	Total doctors	Total in army	Total remaining	Population/Doctor in 1914	Population/Doctor in 1915
1. Brown St. Bridgeton	95,670	35,503	37.11	26	13	13	3,680	7,359
2. Whitevale	49,623	20,151	40.61	18	10	8	2,757	6,203
3. Parkhead	33,218	12,094	36.41	10	4	6	3,321	5,536
4. Townhead	97,788	32,233	32.96	27	12	15	3,622	6,519
5. Springburn	47,921	14,645	30.56	10	7	3	4,792	15,974
6. Cowcaddents	34,576	12,526	36.23	12	6	6	2,881	5,763
7. Granville St.	105,072	33,694	32.07	81	40	41	1,297	2,563
8. Eddabank Crescent	63,796	24,309	38.10	36	12	24	1,772	2,658
9. Maryhill	37,476	10,357	27.64	7	3	4	5,354	9,369
10. Temple	5,000	1,952	39.04	1	0	1	5,000	5,000
11. Whiteside	33,930	9,925	29.25	13	4	9	2,610	3,770
12. Partick	50,464	17,906	35.48	25	12	13	2,014	3,882
13. Adelphi House	90,426	43,483	48.09	37	21	16	2,444	5,652
14. Bellahouston	62,233	17,098	27.47	19	9	10	3,275	6,223
15. Govan	96,636	33,630	34.80	33	17	16	2,928	6,040
16. Halfway	2,000	309	15.45	1	1	0	2,000	2,000
17. Pollockshaws	13,621	4,882	35.84	7	3	4	1,946	3,405
18. Cathcart	14,620	3,760	25.72	9	4	5	1,624	2,924
19. Victoria Infirmary	79,591	14,526	18.25	32	21	11	2,487	7,236
20. Shillteston	18,567	6,799	36.62	4	1	3	4,642	6,189
Total	1,032,228	349,782	33.89	408	200	208	2,530	4,963

SOURCE: PRO, NATS1/14/M132, Glasgow Medical Service.

TABLE 5.2. POPULATION PER GENERAL PRACTITIONER IN PRACTICE IN COUNTIES OF SCOTLAND, 1914–18

	1914 1 Aug.	1915 15 May	1915 31 Dec.	1916 7 June	1918 11 Nov.
Aberdeen	2,194	2,803	3,301	3,396	4,009
Argyll	1,364	1,541	1,688	1,688	1,637
Ayr	2,033	2,164	2,333	2,333	3,502
Banff, Elgin and Nairn	1,730	2,003	2,238	2,238	3,111
Caithness and Sutherland	2,007	2,609	2,747	2,899	2,802
Dumbarton	2,570	2,899	3,168	3,168	4,098
Dumfries and Galloway	1,746	2,075	2,310	2,347	2,704
Dundee	2,786	3,391	3,518	3,655	4,645
Edinburgh and Leith	1,728	2,077	2,372	2,330	3,792
Fife	2,704	3,226	3,771	3,771	5,731
Glasgow	2,188	2,606	3,019	3,181	4,476
Inverness	1,713	2,413	2,413	2,528	2,888
Islands	2,679	3,014	2,893	2,893	2,888
Lanark	2,948	3,387	3,915	3,980	5,435
Lothians	2,399	2,741	3,030	3,070	4,529
Orkney	1,295	1,363	1,523	1,523	1,552
Perth	2,391	3,033	3,188	3,272	3,082
Renfrew and Bute	2,154	2,477	2,752	2,831	4,061
Ross and Cromarty	2,307	2,451	2,801	2,801	2,888
South Eastern	2,012	2,483	2,431	2,652	2,937
Stirling	2,170	2,349	2,773	2,852	3,859
Zetland	1,994	1,994	2,791	3,101	2,750
Total	2,192	2,576	2,892	2,959	3,966

SOURCE: Currie, The Mustering of Medical Services in Scotland, p. 193.

TABLE 5.3. ADMINISTRATIVE AREAS WITH POPULATION/GENERAL PRACTITIONER RATIO OF GREATER THAN 5,000/1 IN 1918, IN RANK ORDER OF SCARCITY OF MEDICAL PRACTITIONERS

Administrative area	Region	Ratio	Population in 1911[a]	Practising GPs
1. Sedgely UD	S. Staffs	16,527	16,527	1
2. Lincoln CB	Lincs	11,457	57,285	5
3. Rhymney & Bedwelty UDs	S. Wales	11,332	33,996	3
4. Lowestoft Boro	Suffolk	5,630	33,777	6
5. Brownhills UD	Mid Staffs	8,426	16,852	2
6. Bilston & Coseley UDs	S. Staffs	8,086	48,515	6
7. Ashton-under-Lyne Boro	Lancs	7,623	38,113	5
8. Seeham Harbour UD	Tyneside	7,581	75,807	10
9. Belper & Heage UDs	Derbyshire	7,557	15,114	2
10. Kingswood UD	Bristol	7,545	22,636	3
11. Wombwell, Darfield & Hoyland Nether UDs	Barnsley	7,520	37,601	5
12. Chester-le-Street UD	Durham	7,356	14,712	2
13. Gelligaen UD	S. Wales	7,104	35,521	5
14. E. Deans & United Parishes	Glos	6,651	19,952	3
15. Caerphilly UD	S. Wales	6,569	32,844	5
16. Hemel Hempstead Boro	Herts	6,444	12,888	2
17. Hinckley UD	Leicester	6,419	12,837	2
18. Turton UD	Bolton	6.324	12,648	2
19. Longbeaton & Westslade UDs	Newcastle	6,381	19,142	3
20. Hindley, Ince in Makerfield, Abram & Aspull UDs	Lancs	6,373[b]	61,303	11
21. Smallthorne UD & Norton in the Moors c.p.	N. Staffs	6,319	18,958	3
22. Blaydon & Ryton UDs	Tyneside	6,298	44,087	7
23. Swadlincote UD	Derbs	6,225	18,674	3

TABLE 5.3. *(continued)*

Administrative area	Region	Ratio	Population in 1911[a]	Practising GPS
24. Bedlingtonshire				
UD	Yorks, NR	6,360	25,440	4
25. Kidderminster Boro	Worcs	6,083	24,333	4
26. Skelton &				
Brotton &				
Loftus UDs	Yorks, NR	6,017	24,066	4
27. Chelmsford Boro	Essex	6,003	18,008	3
28. Willenhall &				
Darlaston UDs	S. Staffs	11,984	35,951	3
29. Runcorn UD	Lancs	5,784	17,353	3
30. Llantarnan &				
Llanfranchfa UDs	Monmouth	5,763	11,526	2
31. Stalybridge &				
Dukinfield UDs	Cheshire	5,742	45,935	8
32. Whittington &				
Newbold UDs	Derb	5,738	17,213	3
33. Northampton CB	Northants	5,629	90,064	16
34. Crewe Boro	Cheshire	5,620	44,960	8
35. Hyde Boro	Cheshire	5,573	33,437	6
36. Barnsley CB	Yorks, WR	5,557	94,473	17
37. Stanley, Altofts				
& Normanton				
UDs	Yorks, WR	5,551	33,307	6
38. Jarrow Boro	Durham	5,549	55,489	10
39. W. Bromwich CB	W. Midlands	5,538	199,361	36
40. Gosport,				
Alverston, and				
Farnham UDs	Hampshire	5,372	42,974	8
41. Grimsby CB	Lincs	5,338	96,096	18
42. Widnes	Lancs	5,257	31,541	6
43. Aberavon Boro	S. Wales	5,253	10,505	2
44. Blaenabon &				
Abersyshan UDs	S. Wales	5,238	36,666	7
45. Wallsend Boro	Tyneside	5,183	41,461	8
46. Leicester CB	Leics	5,184	227,222	44
47. Stoke-on-Trent				
CB	Staffs	5,099	234,534	46
48. St Helens CB	Lancs	5,082	96,551	19
49. Heywood Boro &				
Norwood UD	Lancs	5,082	30,494	6
(Rochdale)				

TABLE 5.3. *(continued)*

Administrative area	Region	Ratio	Population in 1911[a]	Practising GPS
50. Todmorden Boro (Rochdale)	Lancs	6,351	25,404	4
51. Morley Boro (Leeds)	Yorks, WR	5,055	35,383	7
52. Chorley Boro (Preston)	Lancs	5,053	30,315	6
53. Middlesbrough CB	Tyneside	5,047	146,352	29
54. Westhoughton UD (Bolton)	Lancs	5,015	15,045	3
Total population in 54 districts			2,571,248	

[a] No corrections made to account for wartime migration
[b] The ratio appears to be incorrect in the document: 61,303 ÷ 11 = 5,573.

SOURCE: British Medical Association Records, Central Medical War Committee Minutes, Report by the Assessment subcommittee and the Executive subcommittee on the Calls made on LMWCs to Meet the Present Demands of the War Office, Jan. 1917; and Minute of January 1918 on Depleted Areas.

per cent above the pre-war level. Some of the worst-hit regions were in rural areas, where a low population was served in normal times by a handful of doctors, but in more crowded southern counties, the pressure on medical care was also severe.

The CMWC medical censuses enable us to locate those areas in England and Wales which were particularly depleted. In January 1918 the CMWC listed 54 areas as dangerously depleted, which it defined as having more than 5,000 people per GP. In these areas, approximately 2.5 million people lived before the war. A reasonable guess as to their wartime population is 3 million. In other words, about 8 per cent of the population of England and Wales were clearly deprived of adequate medical care. Most of these areas were in the Black Country and pottery districts, and in rural areas of the North and Wales. But some were urban centres like Northampton, Leicester, St Helens, and Jarrow, engaged in varying degrees in munitions production.

The CMWC also listed 65 areas that were seriously, but not dangerously depleted, that is, with a population to GP ratio of

TABLE 5.4. LONDON METROPOLITAN BOROUGHS, POPULATION/GENERAL
PRACTITIONER RATIOS, IN RANK ORDER OF SCARCITY OF DOCTORS IN 1915, AND
INDEXED DECLINES IN INFANT MORTALITY RATES BETWEEN 1912–14 AND 1919–21

Metropolitan borough	Pop/GP ratio[a] 18 Dec. 1915	Pop/GP ratio[a] 1 April 1916	Pop/GP ratio[a] 1 Jan. 1917	Wartime decline in IMR
Shoreditch	5,063	5,340	6,188	33
Bethnal Green	4,930	5,127	5,340	25
Poplar	4,641	4,641	5,528[b]	22
Stepney	3,997	4,175	5,528[b]	24
Bermondsey	3,597	3,815	4,663	29
Finsbury	3,517	3,664	4,622	34
Southwark	3,427	3,691	4,463	21
Battersea	3,355	3,289	4,659	18
Woolwich	3,112	3,194	2,858	9
Camberwell	2,780	2,673	3,187	20
Greenwich	2,742	2,742	3,427	16
Islington	2,598	2,598	3,558	19
Hackney	2,445	2,393	3,179	14
Hammersmith	2,295	2,250	2,430	11
Deptford	2,281	2,380	3,532	16
Fulham	2,254	2,322	3,006	18
St Pancras	2,184	2,184	3,033	10
Lambeth	2,000	2,041	2,951	19
Lewisham	1,501	1,546	1,956	12
Wandsworth	1,490	1,462	1,789	16
Chelsea	1,277	1,412	1,747	6
Stoke Newington	1,125	1,055	1,746	9
Holborn	1,122	1,122	1,592	14
Paddington	1,049	1,018	1,697	8
Kensington	753	743	1,038	14
Hampstead	724	673	830	8
Westminster	n.a.	900	1,161	8
St Marylebone	n.a.	664	1,342	13
City	n.a.	634	596	18
London				18

[a] Population in 1911.
[b] Poplar and Stepney were considered as one unit.

SOURCE: BMA Records, CMWC Minutes, 18 Dec. 1915, 1 April 1916, 1 Jan.
1917, and J. M. Winter, 'Infant Mortality', SSRC Report HR 5091,
Table 8.

above 4,000/1 in January 1918. Among these areas were major urban centres of war industry. Birmingham, Coventry, Hull, Wigan, Nottingham, Gateshead, South Shields, Sunderland, Swansea, and Newcastle-upon-Tyne were all in this class. Again an estimate of the total population in wartime is bound to be notional, but it is likely that another 5 million people lived in these depleted areas. This raises the total population without adequate medical coverage to one-fifth of the inhabitants of the country.

Table 5.4 enables us to examine one measurement of the effect of deprivation of medical care. The CMWC collected data on depletion of practitioners within London Metropolitan Boroughs. Of course, the better-off districts like Kensington or Hampstead were well-stocked with physicians during the war, and other districts, like Westminster and St Marylebone, had hospital facilities within their boundaries. It will surprise no one to see the working-class districts of the East End and South London at the top of the list of depleted London boroughs. But when we add a column to describe the degree to which infant mortality had declined in any district during the war period, as a rough indicator both of obstetrical and pediatric care and of overall standards of health, we can see that areas like Shoreditch or Bethnal Green, which were depleted of medical care by anybody's standards, registered striking gains in infant survival chances in these years.

Three qualifications must be made before we conclude that the loss of 14,000 medical practitioners to army service had relatively little effect on the health of the civilian population. The first is that some areas may well have had a surfeit of doctors before 1914. This was the opinion of the Dean of the University College London Medical School, who told the Ministry of National Service that 'the present conditions show that there are in normal times far too many doctors'.[84] In most places this was certainly not the case, but it may have been true for some urban centres. The second is that, without modern antibiotics, the comfort doctors could offer the sick was not very different from that of family and friends. This is not to dismiss their role in the relief of suffering, which is never reflected clearly in mortality statistics, but rather to suggest that a reduction of medical services was compatible in the early years of this century with a fairly stable outlook for public health. The pressure on the tuberculosis services may be an exception, as we have already indicated. The third caveat concerns the difficulty in making comparisons between a pre-war population and one during a war in which 6 million men were absent from their home communities. This must have relieved at least some of the pressure on civilian health care, while increasing it in later years, when the full toll of disablement and disease was apparent. Nevertheless, such indications as we have suggest that a substantial reduction in the extent of medical care in wartime Britain presented no insurmountable obstacle to a major improvement in the life expectancy of the civilian population.

6. Health Administration in Wartime

IN the previous chapter, we have shown the implausibility of arguments which relate the decline in civilian mortality rates in wartime Britain to fuller or more comprehensive levels of medical intervention. It remains to consider the possibility that the public health services and other war-related welfare programmes compensated for the shortage of medical care available to civilians to a degree sufficient to account for the wartime improvement in life expectation among vulnerable sections of the population.

One important area in which this claim has been advanced is that of infant and maternal health.[1] In the first part of this chapter, we evaluate this argument. We first describe the emergence of a wartime consensus on the national – indeed the international – importance of work in this field, and secondly discuss the complex interaction of bureaucratic and local government politics which determined the pace of reform in wartime provision for mothers and children. We conclude that, although there were substantial improvements in public policy on maternal and infant welfare during the war, the major impact of these measures was not immediate, but lay, rather, in the future. Despite the passage of a Maternity and Child Welfare Act in 1918, which consolidated wartime developments, it was still the case at the end of the war that the major forms of state activity in this field were too few, too scattered and too undersubscribed by the working-class population to have had much of an immediate effect on survival rates among mothers or their infants.

Of course, health administration in wartime covered a much broader area than childbirth and early life. In the second part of this chapter, we survey another area of public health policy in wartime – that relating to the health of munitions workers. The

188

major issues here were welfare supervision at work, the extension
of national insurance, and the provision of industrial canteens in
munitions factories. Again our conclusion is similar to that
reached with respect to infant welfare work. While many measures
in these areas were of real importance in the long-term development of the nation's health, it is unrealistic to argue that they were
primarily responsible for the immediate gains in life expectancy
registered among non-combatants in the war period itself. As in
the case of the medical profession during the war, health administration probably prevented worse things from happening. But it
appears that for the true source of wartime improvements in
civilian health, we must look to rising standards of living, especially for the worst-off sections of the population, a subject which
is treated in chapter 7.

I TO SAVE THE NATION'S CHILDREN

A Pro-natalism and Public Health in Wartime

We have noted in chapter 1 the emergence in the years before 1914
of a body of opinion concerned with the political and strategic
ramifications of the secular decline in the European birth rate.
Many of those who felt strongly on this issue were advocates of
large families, but in Britain it was rare for their views to be
expressed with the melodramatic force or apocalyptic imagery
frequently found among French commentators on the subject of
dénatalité, a word which is so alien to English culture that it defies
direct translation.[2] Instead of focusing attention on fertility, the
pre-war British discussion centred more on the question of the
quality of the 'race'. This approach prepared the ground for an
easy acceptance in Britain of the significance of measures directed to preserving child life as part of the overall campaign to
avoid the perils of 'population decline'.[3]

Both before the war and during the 1914–18 conflict, the real
difficulty with much of the agitation about the birth rate was that it
involved the relatively ineffective, if not pointless, exercise of men
telling other men how women ought to behave. This was even
truer of the French obsession with the public virtues of perpetual
pregnancy than of the British debate on the need to save child life

by improved 'Mothercraft'. For in Britain, women health visitors and some women doctors were among the bearers of the message of better child care and better ante-natal and post-natal supervision. Nevertheless, the majority of commentators and administrators who dealt with these questions here were middle-class men, who were bound to approach the problem of maternity from a different perspective from that of the working-class majority of child-bearing women in this country.

Given the different social position of most social reformers in this field and that of most of the women whom they wanted to help, it was perhaps inevitable that such advice about maternity as was proffered in Britain appeared as middle-class male interference in patterns of working-class female life. Even when health visitors and physicians were women whose origins were working-class or lower middle-class, too often they took on the countenance of medical and para-medical missionaries, seeking to remedy maternal ignorance or fecklessness, which was, in the opinion of many of them, the real source of much of the wastage of child life. There were exceptions: some public health workers and organizations such as the Women's Cooperative Guild (WCG) regarded access to a maternal and child welfare centre as a right rather than a privilege for those who did not know enough to keep their children alive on their own.[4] But overall, the 'Lady Bountiful' form of much child welfare work helps explain why the numbers of women who availed themselves of these services were relatively small in these years. It would take another generation before these centres were sufficiently well-integrated within working-class communities to form part of the fabric of the nation's social services, and before a majority of pregnant women visited them early enough in pregnancy to make a substantial difference to their health and that of their children.[5] This, I shall argue, is one of the main reasons why we must look elsewhere for the source of improvements in infant and maternal health in this period.

It would be foolish to claim that public discussion of this issue and developments in public policy had absolutely no effect on the survival chances of mothers and infants. As we shall note below, especially in the first month of life, the quality of the management of delivery does have a bearing on the outcome of pregnancy, and some aspects of maternal and child welfare work did improve conditions of childbirth for some women during the war. But given the fact that the most substantial gains in infant survival rates were registered after the first month of life, we must attend to environmental effects to account for the overall trend of infant mortality. But here too, child and maternal welfare work may have had an indirect role to play, in announcing the benefits of better nutrition for mothers and children and in providing food for them in certain cases. But the catchment area of women who came to these centres was socially very narrow. Indeed, it may be true that the women who attended were precisely those who did not need the help provided. But whoever came, their numbers were simply too small to have made much of a difference to the overall mortality trend.

What we see in wartime is mainly a major advance in the propaganda of infant welfare and a significant bolstering of its institutional structure. In this series of developments, bureaucrats, politicians, physicians and concerned laymen all played a part. Let us consider first the background propaganda which spurred institutional advances. During the conflict, a vast array of *ad hoc* organizations came into being, joined by groups of concerned individuals who spoke fervently on this subject whenever the opportunity arose. It is not difficult to understand why their message appealed at this time. Partly it was because it raised an issue on which people of all political persuasions or viewpoints about the war could agree. Almost everyone shared the conviction that the burden of the war economy must not fall on the frail shoulders of the most vulnerable parts of the population. Secondly, such agitation had a symbolic appeal, in that it demostrated that a nation which demanded the 'supreme sacrifice' at the front demonstrated its true humanity by preserving infant and maternal life at home.

In addition, given the long lists of casualties appearing daily in the national and local press, who could object to the claim that raising the coming generation was a patriotic act? This principle was proclaimed, for instance, in the learned hearings of the appropriately named National Birthrate Commission, a private inquiry which reported initially in 1916. And although the French were well ahead of the British in developing this kind of propaganda, we can find pro-natalist themes illustrated in British pamphlets, cartoons, and in postcards which circulated in wartime.[6] In many of them, infant welfare and fertility were two sides of the same coin of national vitality. Whatever the vagaries of the birth rate, the least the nation could do was to protect its human capital by keeping its infant population alive. In this area, then, collective virtue and national interest clearly coincided.

There is some truth, therefore, in the late Professor Titmuss's claim that part of the power of this message lay in its appeal to the nation to raise the next generation as a healthier generation of future recruits.[7] But we need not adopt a particularly cynical attitude to appreciate the wartime groundswell of public opinion on an issue which really did involve the nation's future and which provided civilians denied the right (by age or sex) to defend their country with an opportunity of showing their patriotic fervour. This was a prime motivation of many behind the campaign to open maternal and child welfare centres throughout urban Britain. As G. F. McCleary, Medical Officer of Health in Battersea, put it, many people saw the establishment of centres for ante-natal and post-natal care as 'a form of war-work that called for the enlistment of many workers'.[8] Sir Arthur Acland, a former president of the Board of Education, helped spread the creed by forming an 'Infant Welfare Propaganda Fund' from which travelling organizers were paid to stimulate interest. Acland claimed a hand in the creation of 200 health centres by his work.[9] Similarly motivated were the 'public-spirited ladies' who in 1917 set up the Children's Jewel Fund with offices in New Bond Street, London. They solicited money, jewels, and other valuables to help finance infant welfare centres. Their slogan was 'a jewel for a baby's life'. Thousands of pounds poured in. One sale of jewels in June 1918 realized £26,000, of which £5,000 was accounted for by the Duchess of Marlborough's pearl necklace. A special performance of *Manfred* in Drury Lane added £500, and a dolls' show raised £4,000.[10] The proceeds went to child welfare associations.

The most spectacular of these demonstrations of support for infant welfare was the convening of a special 'Baby Week' in early June 1917. The week opened with an exhibition at Central Hall, Westminster, attended by the queen. She was received by a guard of honour of 120 mothers and children, who were drawn from 80 maternal and infant welfare centres in London.[11] On the same day, the Bishop of London spoke at a meeting of the Fulham Babies Hospital and Training Centre for Mothers. His address brought out well the mixture of philanthropy and patriotism which lay behind what *The Times* called the growing 'cult of the child'.[12] The bishop told his audience that: 'While nine soldiers died every hour in 1915, twelve babies died every hour, so that it was more dangerous to be a baby than a soldier. The loss of life in this war has made every baby's life doubly precious.'[13] A few weeks earlier, the leader writer of the *Daily Telegraph* had been even more specific about the strategic considerations behind support for infant welfare: 'If we had been more careful for the last fifty years to prevent the unheeded wastage of infant life, we should have had at least half a million more men available for the defence of the country.'[14] One writer in the *Nineteenth Century* called for support for infant welfare in order to help make up 'the huge loss in the man-power of the Empire due to the war'. He complained that 'no benedictions have yet been showered on health visitors and others, who by saving infant lives are doing something to meet our huge war losses'.[15]

We cannot miss the echoes of earlier concern about this aspect of strategic demography.[16] After the Boer War, the same chorus of voices had decried the effects of early childhood deprivation on later recruitment statistics and on the future health of the armed forces (see chapter 1). But the nation's commitment to war and the sheer scale of the slaughter in the 1914–18 conflict were so vast in comparison to anything within living memory that the proponents of public health measures in this field were assured of a measure of public support and a political standing in wartime that they had never previously enjoyed.

B Infant Welfare, Social Policy and Local Politics

We can see clear evidence of the favourable environment for reform in the field of maternal and child welfare by examining the work of the LGB and other government departments during the war. Whatever the need to economize in other areas of public expenditure, the LGB worked virtually without financial constraints and thereby took the lead in promoting the expansion of social provision in this field and in coaxing recalcitrant local authorities to do the same.

This is a good example of the extent to which the war created the political conditions necessary for the implementation of ideas formulated in the pre-1914 period. Just before the outbreak of war, the LGB circularized county councils, county borough councils, metropolitan borough councils, and other sanitary authorities asking that they undertake infant and maternal welfare work and offering to pay fifty per cent of the cost of such work.[17] Their suggestions amounted to a comprehensive system of ante-natal and post-natal care. The LGB was willing to assist in the establishment of ante-natal clinics, in the provision of home visitors for expectant mothers and of hospital space for complicated pregnancies. Support was offered to enable skilled midwives to attend confinements, which could take place in hospital if necessary. In addition, further backing was available to help provide hospital treatment of post-natal complications, for infant and child-care clinics, and for home visitors to families with young children.[18] There was nothing original about these proposals, but what was clear was that by the time they were received by local authorities, the outbreak of war had given them a new and added significance.

The extent to which the environment of war was favourable to these reforms is shown by the fact that two years later the LGB went even further. It offered grants for the salaries and expenses of inspectors of midwives, and for nurses and health visitors engaged in maternity and child welfare work. Money was also allocated for the provision of midwives and doctors for the poor and for understaffed regions, such as the north of England, for the full expenses of ante-natal clinics, and for hospital treatment of some infants.[19]

Parallel developments can be traced elsewhere. In 1915, the Board of Education undertook to set up a network of classes for mothers to help them prevent and treat infant illness more effectively. In the same year, the 1907 Notification of Births Act was extended in two ways: first, to make compulsory rather than optional the notification of birth within 36 hours of delivery to the local MOH; and secondly, to permit the appointment of local committees, with women members, empowered to prepare measures to improve the care of expectant mothers. The first of these new provisions led directly to the second. The 1907 Act was permissive; the 1915, mandatory: it gave the notified MOH the information needed about maternity to enable him to direct health visitors to help protect the life of newborn children. It was obvious that the measure made no sense without local authority expenditure to hire health visitors in order to follow it up. We shall return to this point below.

Other measures reinforced the role of the state in monitoring the management of delivery. In 1916 the Midwives Act of 1902 was amended in order to make midwifery training more rigorous. Under the new Act, midwives had to have six months' training, attendance at 20 cases, and to pass a written examination before qualifying. Since nearly half of the 12,000 midwives who gave notice to practise in 1915 were professionally untrained, and since between 50 and 75 per cent (or more) of all women were delivered by midwives, this change in training standards was bound, in the long run, to be of importance.[20] Many of these initiatives were consolidated and reinforced by the final measure of wartime reform in this field, the Maternity and Child Welfare Act of 1918, which required local authorities to attend to 'the health of expectant mothers and children who have not attained the age of five years and are not being educated in schools recognized by the Board of Education'. To promote and monitor such work, local committees of both sexes were to be set up or extended.

The regulations promulgated under the 1918 Maternity Act illustrate the range of activities for which, in the last months of the war, grants were available from the LGB (and in the immediate post-war period, from the Ministry of Health). They included part or full payment for:

1. the salaries and expenses of inspectors of midwives;
2. the salaries and expenses of health visitors engaged in maternal and child welfare work;
3. the provision of midwives for necessitous women and where there is a shortage of midwives;
4. the provision of doctors for necessitous women ill during pregnancy and for aid during their confinements;
5. the expenses of a centre, providing medical supervision and advice for expectant or nursing mothers and for children under five, and medical treatment at a centre;
6. the arrangements surrounding instruction in the general hygiene of maternity and childhood;
7. the hospital treatment of complicated cases of confinement or those arising after parturition or those in which mothers cannot give birth at home;
8. the hospital treatment of children under age five requiring in-patient care;

9. the cost of food for mothers and children in necessitous cases approved by the MOH;

10. the expenses of creches and day nurseries;

11. the accommodation in convalescent homes for nursing mothers and children under age five;

12. the provision of homes and other arrangements to attend to the health of children under age five whose parents cannot provide a home for them;

13. the cost of experimental work, to be approved by the LGB, on subjects concerning the health of expectant and nursing mothers and young children; and

14. the defraying of contributions by local authorities to voluntary institutions and agencies engaged in maternal and child welfare work.[21]

This set of measures constitutes an impressive achievement. But their contribution to the gains in life expectancy of mothers and children in wartime was qualified, for two reasons. The first is that the full panoply of publicly-funded support for infant and maternal welfare appeared only at the end of the war. The second is that these regulations describe only a set of incentives for local authority action. At the end of the war, it was still open to councillors to refuse to follow the lead of the LGB, or to follow it in only a symbolic way. In the history of social policy, local implementation is frequently more important than bureaucratic formulation; and in this respect, infant and maternal welfare is an excellent case in point. Indeed, one reason why a Maternity and Child Welfare Act was necessary at all was because of the pronounced local variation in the work of voluntary associations and sanitary authorities in this field. We shall consider evidence of both restrictions on the effect of these legislative measures.

In 1916, the Carnegie UK Trust began an enquiry to determine how its resources could be used most effectively to further infant and maternal welfare. The resultant report demonstrated clearly the patchy nature of public and voluntary provision in this field, two years after the LGB had begun its campaign on behalf of maternal and child welfare in wartime. The Carnegie Trust invited MOHs in England and Wales to file reports on health conditions and provisions in their areas of jurisdiction. A similar enquiry was conducted in Scotland. Epitomes of the English and Welsh reports were published in 1917. These provide complete (and probably reliable) data on a range of questions: the number of people employed in infant welfare work; the number of health centres, clinics, or consultations in each district; and the total number of registered midwives as well as (more conjecturally) the proportion of births attended by them.

What these reports show is how embryonic and understaffed were early attempts to provide institutions to which pregnant women or mothers of young children could go for advice before or after childbirth. Two examples should suffice to illustrate this point. The north-eastern industrial town of Middlesbrough had a wartime population of about 125,000 people; approximately 3,600 children were born there in 1915; of these, 548 (or 152 per 1,000) died before reaching the age of one. About half the deliveries were attended by midwives, only 6 of whom were trained. Even if we add the services of the 16 'untrained' midwives who also practised in the city, the pressure on the midwifery service in this one town was clearly substantial. The borough council did not employ a single health visitor to work full-time in this field. Five sanitary inspectors gave part of their time to this work, and probably managed to see about 50 newborns each week. These women also had to attend four ante-natal care clinics or consultations; four other infant welfare centres were run by voluntary associations.[22] It seems that only about 10 per cent of Middlesbrough's babies attended these clinics, which is roughly the same as that for the nation as a whole. If this were the case, then these ventures in health administration could have done very little in the short run to affect the trend of infant mortality decline; and we must look for the main explanation of these improvements elsewhere.[23]

The same point can be made with respect to infant welfare provision in London. The population of the Metropolitan Borough of Wandsworth was over 300,000 in 1915, during the course of which over 6,000 births were registered. Of these 590 (or 92 per 1,000) died in infancy. The same proportion of births were attended by midwives here as in Middlesbrough (50 per cent), but whereas there were only about 20 practising midwives in the northern town, there were 40 practising in this borough, 30 of whom were trained. A more professional midwifery service may have been one (but not the sole) reason why infant mortality rates were lower in London than in the North of England.

But in other respects, Wandsworth's mothers may not have been better provided for than were those in Middlesbrough. Only one full-time and two part-time health visitors were employed by the borough council. This meant that each saw about 50 babies per week in what must have been a very overcrowded schedule of work. The Metropolitan Borough Council of Wandsworth did not support a single municipal ante-natal and child welfare centre at this time, but by 1916 the number of voluntary clinics in the borough had risen to four.[24]

The way one was set up was typical of what was going on in many other parts of wartime Britain. After a public meeting was held on 12 May 1916 to consider opening a school for mothers, funds were gathered enabling a 'Mother's Welcome' to open on the first Tuesday of July at the Anchor Mission. The scene could have been taken directly from Shaw's *Major Barbara*. The mission was situated in a 'thickly populated district which has the highest infant mortality rates of the borough', and 23 mothers attended. They had their babies weighed, consulted a woman doctor, were able to purchase at cost price foods such as a popular brand of dried milk, Glaxo, and they had a cup of tea. Anyone with experience of infant welfare centres today will note that not much has changed in the intervening 70 years. In the course of the year, 35 mothers a session came to the centre, inspiring its sponsors to open a similar centre in Putney the following year. Yearly expenditure in each totalled £160, of which £47 went to the doctor, £28 to the attending nurse, and the bulk of the remainder on food and incidental expenses.[25] As a pointer of things to come, these ventures were admirable, but their presence did more to symbolize philanthropic and public concern about infant and maternal health than to influence it during the war.

No one was more aware both of the limited nature of maternal and child welfare provision in this period and of the bureaucratic impediments to improved legislation than Dr Arthur Newsholme, Chief Medical Officer of the Local Government Board during the war. But between 1914 and 1918 he and his civil servants nonetheless waged an untiring war of attrition against recalcitrant local authorities and physicians who were either complacent or resistant to the idea that state-sponsored provision in this field was essential to the common good.

The modest hopes of LGB officials are clear from their predictions of the likely reception by local authorities of the circular on maternal and child welfare they had sent out on the very eve of the war. On 13 August 1914, Newsholme wrote to Dr Janet Lane-Claypon, who was responsible for inspecting local ventures in this field:

> Although local authorities are not likely at the present time to be willing to pay much attention to the Board's recent circular on Maternal and Child Welfare, certain aspects of this work are particularly appropriate for application in connection with present circumstances, especially in crowded centres of population where employment is or shall be difficult to obtain.[26]

Maternity centres would be the ideal place to give free milk to mothers facing war-related destitution, for such provision could be accompanied by free advice on all aspects of child care. Dr Lane-Claypon concurred, and argued that the best way to promote these centres was as a focus for aid to the wives of the men who had already volunteered for military service. Due to 'shortness of employment' the welfare of their wives and children might be jeopardized, which was a situation which the community would not tolerate:

> It is very desirable that efforts should be made to secure care for these women, and to provide medical supervision both before as well as at the time of and after, their confinement. Further home visitation is desirable with a view to ascertaining the need for, and where required, providing for
>
> (a) the feeding of the mother;
> (b) the clothing of the infant;
> (c) provision for the mother at her confinement;
> (d) adequate home conditions for domiciliary confinement;
> (e) instruction as to care of the infant, especially as to the value of breast-feeding.

'Such measures', she concluded, 'would form the nucleus of maternity centres.'[27]

This indeed was the outcome of their efforts, but their success did not depend on the role maternity centres could play in the relief of wartime distress, which was fortunately less of a problem than it appeared to be in the early days of the war. What helped their campaign along more than anything else was the way it symbolized the nation's commitment to defend life at the very time that the war was claiming its first cluster of victims at the front. The letter sent to the *Westminster Gazette* by the President and Secretary of the Women's Co-operative Guild on 26 August 1914 captured the flavour of this argument. 'We turn just now', Eleanor Barton and Margaret Llewellyn-Davies wrote,

> from the thought of the wreck and waste of young vigorous lives upon the field, with a fresh sense of the value and sanctity of these new lives, and of the imperative need of caring for the mothers and the young children of the race.[28]

Despite the obvious emotive force of this appeal, what is most striking about LGB work in this area is how hard the LGB and sympathetic doctors and councilmen had to work to overcome local resistance to it. This can be shown in three distinct cases, two metropolitan and one provincial. The London Metropolitan Borough of Islington had an active MOH, Dr A. E. Harris, who lost no opportunity to broadcast the national importance of infant welfare work. But his efforts to persuade the public health committee of the borough to spend money in this area were unsuccessful, and Islington consistently refused before the war to adopt the 1907 Notification of Births Act, as indeed it was its right to do. As late as December 1915, the chairman of the borough public health committee was adamant that public funds would be wasted by supporting such efforts, since

> having regard to the moral and economic conditions which lie at the root of infant mortality, the steps proposed to be taken do not provide an effective remedy for the evil, and that the matter is one that can best be dealt with by philanthropic effort rather than by administrative action.[29]

H. O. Stutchbury of the LGB tried to convince the local public health committee that they were mistaken, and after an appeal by the local MOH to do something about the epidemic of measles then spreading through the borough, some progress was made.

The council agreed to hire two health visitors solely for the purpose of dealing with the outbreak of measles, but they were still unwilling to take further steps in this field.

Dr Harris presented a scheme for such work on 29 May 1916, but opponents of the measure succeeded in shelving it. This bit of stalling brought further protests from the LGB. No less a figure than its President, Walter Long, accused the council of 'incurring a grave responsibility in continuing to delay the initiation of this work, particularly at a time when the importance of conserving infant life is paramount'. There was, he suggested, an overwhelming case for the council to appoint five health visitors to supplement the two appointed to look after measles victims.[30] This pressure did no good at all, and may have stiffened the backs of opponents resentful of what they saw as outside interference in their affairs. On 16 July 1916, they voted against appointing any more health visitors, and explained their attitude to the LGB by pointing out that the infant mortality rate had declined over the previous decade when no health visitors were operating in the borough, and it was likely that further progress would be made without them in the future.[31]

Two months later, the LGB renewed its attack, but again failed to breach the ranks of the opposition. Alderman Manchester pointed out that health visitors could not reduce infant mortality, since its source lay elsewhere – in the 'general condition of life of the people, the marriage of the unfit, the incidence of intemperance, disease and immorality'.[32] It was only after the passage of the 1918 Maternity and Child Welfare Act that the borough agreed to provide some very modest support for work in this field.

A similar tale unfolded in the Metropolitan Borough of Camberwell during the war. But here the obstructive personality was that of the MOH himself, Dr Francis Stevens, a man who, according to Newsholme, 'holds peculiar views'. He was against adoption of the 1907 Notification of Births Act, and against the employment of health visitors.[33] The outbreak of war did nothing to change his mind. In 1916 he recommended that the council take no action, and the council concurred. Consequently a deputation of women from the Women's Labour League, the WCG, the Independent Labour party, and the borough Trades and Labour Council approached Stevens to protest. He replied by suggesting that health visitors undermined individual responsibility and withdrew the mother from the care of her local GP. As to the need for a health centre, he believed that such institutions would sound the death knell for voluntary institutions. Such smugness tried the patience of one of Stevens' opponents, Councillor Lucas, to breaking point. 'It was', he said, 'a case of Camberwell against the rest of England . . . . If the Public Health Committee were in France they would be sentenced to death for refusing to do their duty.'[34]

Six months later, Stevens was still not prepared to give in, and Lucas was still fuming. He hoped that the LGB or someone else would 'bomb the public health committee out of their disgust' at their 'colossal stupidity and short-sightedness'. More public meetings and further approaches by the LGB achieved nothing. All that Stevens was prepared to accept was a part subsidy for voluntary work in the area. Consequently, the LGB authorized a one-time payment of £7.2.0 to the borough for its work on behalf of infant and maternal welfare in 1918.[35]

In the case of Cornwall, we find obstruction on grounds of cost rather than principle. Here the county council was equally unwilling to accept the lead of the LGB on this issue. They refused to adopt the 1907 Notification of Births Act before the war, and as Dr Lane-Claypon noted, they would not do so unless compelled. Even when the 1915 Act brought this county in line with the rest of the country, the county council still refused to act. On 4 October 1915, C. Knights of the LGB wrote to J. R. de C. Boscawen, the chairman of the County Sanitary Committee, in emphatic terms. He noted:

> there is obviously very little advantage in requiring the early notification of births unless the information obtained is made the starting point of measures for securing the health of mothers and children: and in bringing the Bill before the House of Commons on Second Reading Mr Long stated that probably at no time in our history was it ever more desirable that we should do everything we could to improve the health of the mothers and infants and to make it more probable that our infants will be able to resist diseases and be so cared for that they will grow to be healthy men and women.

Boscawen's economical reply was that action was postponed due to financial considerations. This elicited the response from the

LGB that this area was precisely the one in which no economies were to be made during the war.[36]

A year later, the county council's stalling tactics were still effective. They said they were prepared to consider a plan for expenditure on infant and maternal welfare, but managed to put off a decision month after month. Finally, they agreed to appoint three health visitors in 1918.[37] By the time the war was over, they had just started to work.

These three cases are extreme examples of obfuscation and obstruction which precluded major progress on infant and maternal welfare during the war. Many MOHs had the full cooperation of their town or borough councils in their efforts to promote infant welfare. Elsewhere, opposition was more sporadic, and less effective. But all over the country, other voices were arrayed in opposition. The Durham MOH had to counter the view that working-class women did not want health visitors in their homes, since they were seen as interfering with 'the liberties of poor people'.[38] Some MOHs shared Stevens' misgivings as to the effectiveness of health visiting and clinic work; others doubted whether anything could be done for working-class children because of the slovenly habits of their parents. The Darlington MOH was of the opinion that 'domestic disorganization' caused high infant mortality, and health visitors or infant and maternal welfare centres would not cure that. The Leeds MOH produced the opposite argument that the infant mortality rate was falling whatever local authorities did; the Southend MOH came up with the ingenious argument that improvements reflected an influx of middle-class people into working-class neighbourhoods. To the Middlesbrough MOH, it seemed that little could be hoped for since the working class of his district were on the whole 'shiftless, careless, and dirty in their habits', while those of West Suffolk were 'exceedingly primitive', in the opinion of the county MOH. Furthermore, we have already noted that the BMA circularized all local authorities advising them against taking action in this field, on the grounds that it would prejudice the interests of GPs (see above, p. 174). Given the nature of such 'advocacy' of infant and maternal welfare work by some physicians, it is not surprising that provision in this area was highly variable.

But even when the local MOH and the LGB saw eye to eye, the obstacles to action were formidable. As we have noted, some confronted opposition on grounds of cost. In many areas, local councillors were reluctant to spend ratepayers' money, whatever the merits of these proposals. The Derby MOH declared that for this reason the war was a setback to health administration. The Tynemouth, Nottingham and Lancashire MOHs reported similar postponements due to the war. In West Hartlepool, Blackpool and Preston child welfare work was handicapped by a shortage of doctors and funds.[39]

It was in part for these very reasons that the Carnegie Trust stepped in to see where its resources could be usefully employed. Their intention was to set up six model health centres in areas where both need and expertise existed. After a thorough survey, in 1918 they chose Edinburgh, Shoreditch, Liverpool, Birmingham, Dublin and the Rhondda. But again, ventures that germinated during the war fully flowered only in later years.[40]

That infant welfare work in Britain expanded during the First World War is not in question. In 1914, there were only 600 full-time health visitors in England and Wales. The number had risen to 1,355 in 1918. LGB grants totalling £22,000 went to 42 voluntary societies and 32 borough or county councils in 1916–17 alone.[41] But it is reasonable to raise doubts about the immediate effects of such provision on infant survival chances. Not only areas where public action was rapid and uncontested, like Liverpool, but also areas which were beset by conflict, like Cornwall or Camberwell, registered major improvements in infant survival rates during the war. This is not to say that public action was meaningless; on the contrary, it almost certainly helped lessen the risks of childbirth and those of the early months of life for a small proportion of the population. In later years, it would do more, but it is best to conclude that the full value of infant welfare work was demonstrated not primarily during the war, but only long after the Armistice.

II TO PROTECT THE NATION'S WORKERS

There was only one set of problems in wartime health administration of even greater immediate importance to politicians than the issue of infant and maternal welfare. That was the question of how to defend and promote the health and efficiency of the industrial labour force. Given the recruitment of married women into the munitions factories, these questions were bound to overlap, but it is still necessary to distinguish between the two facets of health policy during the war: one concerning the future of the race and the welfare of women whether or not they worked outside the home; and the other focusing upon the welfare of the labour force as a whole and how scientific management could contribute to the munitions effort. This section deals with the second issue.

Government policy in this area centred on three problems. The first addressed the question of the health and welfare of munitions workers at work. The second and third were offshoots of the first: they involved the provision of canteens in munitions factories, and the extension of coverage of the National Insurance Act of 1911 to all munitions workers. What separates them from other welfare measures is that they explicitly offered material support to industrial workers and their families. As such they provide the link between health administration and the subject of the following chapter, wartime standards of living.

A   Factory Welfare

The first Minister of Munitions was David Lloyd George. As Chancellor of the Exchequer, he had presided over the introduction of the National Insurance Act of 1911, which provided both sickness insurance and financial support for medical research. It was therefore entirely in character for him to sanction the establishment of a Health of Munitions Workers Committee in September 1915 to advise him on questions concerning 'industrial fatigue, hours of labour, and other matters affecting the personal health and efficiency' of munitions workers.[42] Among those who sat on this committee were Sir George Newman; the Labour MP, J. R. Clynes; E. L. Collis, a medical officer in the Home Office, and several distinguished physicians and physiologists.[43] To give effect to their recommendations, a welfare section of the Ministry of Munitions was set up at the same time. Its first chairman was Seebohm Rowntree, the prominent Quaker industrialist and social investigator, and its first duties were to standardize welfare provision in national factories and controlled establishments and to promote the welfare of workers outside the factories.[44]

This was no easy task, as it involved the supervision and scrutiny

of conditions in a host of workshops doing an astonishing variety
of jobs. By October 1916, over 1.2 million men, 200,000 boys, and
400,000 women and girls were employed in munitions works.[45]
The work on their behalf devolved onto three subcommittees: one
concerned with all workers handling TNT, poisoning by which had
resulted in 52 deaths in 1916 alone[46]; a second concerned with the
health and welfare of women and girls; and a third specializing in
the problems of boy labour. To serve these workers, the Ministry
employed 51 women's welfare inspectors and 16 dealing with boy
workers.

The first subcommittee sought and acted on specialist medical
advice on prevention and cure.[47] The second and third groups
dealt with general problems of welfare under four main heads: (i)
the installation of welfare supervisors in all munitions works
employing women and in those employing 100 or more boys;[48] (ii)
the drawing up of personal records of sickness and injury; (iii) the
establishment of creches and other provisions needed to deal with
maternity problems; (iv) the construction or refurbishing of prem-
ises to provide canteens, cloakrooms, washing accommodation
and other improvements.[49]

The first two tasks were sold to employers as essential to
scientific management. In a description of welfare work at the
Phoenix Dynamo Manufacturing Company, aptly entitled 'Getting
more from workers by giving them more', one welfare supervisor
told the readers of *System. The Magazine of Business* of the utility
of her efforts. Her first job was to select workers and fit them into
their appropriate slots. She had to judge whether or not a woman
worker's previous job prepared her for munitions work. Thus to
note that a woman who had been in a wool-combing factory was
more likely to stand the heat of a forge than an ex-domestic
servant and to distribute labour accordingly was essential to the
efficient working of the factory. In addition, the women's welfare
supervisor worked with the factory medical officer, and oversaw
provision for breaks, refreshment and recreation.[50] A very similar
story was told in the same journal by one of the officials of the
boys' welfare department of the Ministry of Munitions.[51]

The wide range of welfare services performed by Ministry of
Munitions' employees ensured that they would run into trouble
with trade unionists. Officials of the National Federation of
Women Workers (NFWW) believed that such work undermined

the ties women had to their union and served to deepen attitudes of deference and paternalism at work. They therefore persuaded delegates to their annual conference in 1918 to support the abolition of munitions welfare work.[52]

Problems also arose in connection with welfare work for married women with children. Here difficulties arose directly out of the contradiction between the recognized need to recruit married women into war-related industry and the nearly universally held belief that married women ought not work during pregnancy or when their children were very young. The Ministry of Munitions was therefore happy to sponsor the establishment of day nurseries or creches as a temporary, war-related measure. But they were reluctant to establish a precedent since they were convinced that married women with children should not be encouraged to seek industrial work. Mary MacArthur of the NFWW concurred, and added that such welfare might be a cover for the drawing in of cheaper female workers to the labour force.[53]

Similar doubts were expressed by other interested parties. One physician reported to the Ministry of Munitions that the existence of creches encouraged women who would not ordinarily have sought industrial work to go into the factories. This was to be resisted since it discouraged breast-feeding, led to overcrowding and the spread of infection at creches and to a 'slackening' in the mothers' interest in their children.[54] One inspector went even further. After visiting a filling factory in Hayes, he noted that the work was highly responsible. On this premise he constructed an extraordinary syllogism. Responsible women would not put their babies in creches. The existence of factory creches was an invitation to irresponsible women to enter war factories. Hence the creation of day nurseries would undermine munitions production.[55]

The Ministry of Munitions was sensitive to such arguments, but still felt that it had to act to meet 'a possible charge. . . of carelessness with regard to the welfare of children whose mothers are employed in filling factories'.[56] Consequently the Ministry underwrote 50 per cent of the capital and recurrent expenditure for day nurseries for munitions workers. These were on the whole small undertakings, providing, for example, for 50 children in Woolwich or 30 in Newcastle-upon-Tyne. Total expenditure on all 28 creches sponsored by the Ministry in 1917–18 was approximately £11,000.[57] This was not inconsiderable, but the modesty of the state's investment in this kind of welfare was partly a reflection of a general ambivalence about the virtues of encouraging married women with small children to enter the labour force.[58]

B National Insurance

A second area of health administration in wartime which had a direct bearing on the welfare of the industrial labour force concerned the extension of the National Insurance Act of 1911. This measure provided two kinds of benefits. First, workers in seven trade groups – building, construction, shipbuilding, engineering, ironfounding, construction of vehicles and sawmilling – were provided with unemployment insurance on a contributory basis. Secondly, all insured workers were provided with health insurance, conferring five forms of benefit: medical treatment and attendance; treatment in TB sanatoria; 26 weeks of sickness benefit of 10 shillings per week for men and 7 shillings and sixpence for women; and thereafter for incapacitated workers, a further disablement benefit of 5 shillings per week; and a 30-shilling maternity benefit for the wives of insured workers or for insured women workers.[59]

The expansion of the labour force in wartime was bound to throw this measure into disarray, and in consequence a revised unemployment insurance scheme was introduced in 1916. This added seven new trades to the list of insured occupations: ammunition and explosives, chemicals, metal, leather, rubber, building materials and wooden case workers. Although most were clearly involved in munitions production, there was still a considerable overlap with non-military work. Consequently, a series of requests for exclusion were made from different trades on the margins of the war economy, such as glass, hosiery, printing, and food, drink and tobacco. Part of the reason for opting out was that many of these trades had already existing arrangements for part-time work, which the Insurances Act did not cover. In addition, others had evolved benefit schemes more generous than that provided in the 1911 Act, and furthermore, many trade unions resented the lack of consultation prior to the introduction of the 1916 extension and were suspicious of the encroachment of the state in the organization of the labour market. Consequently, as Dr Whiteside has noted, 'by January 1918 only 200,000 of the original 1.5 million destined to be brought under the insurance scheme were, in fact, covered'.[60]

The administration of health insurance was not so controversial, though, because everyone agreed that the welfare of the new recruits to war industry depended upon full medical provision for them where necessary. Furthermore, even though there were over 1 million more women at work than before the war, the number of insured male workers entitled to medical benefit had been reduced enormously by the recruitment of 6 million men for the armed forces.[61]

The one area where additional outlay of public funds appeared to be inevitable, though, was that of maternity benefit. Early in the war, a subcommittee of the National Health Insurance Commissioners considered the likely effects of the war on this form of insurance provision. They estimated that of the roughly 900,000 births that took place each year, only 110,000 were those delivered of women directly insured under the 1911 Act, but another 500,000 were those of the wives of insured workers. Thus the Act provided a benefit for roughly two-thirds of the nation's mothers.[62]

Two years later, that figure had risen to four-fifths of the nation's mothers entitled to maternity benefit under the National Insurance Act. The reasons were clear: a decline in the number of deliveries matched by an increase in the number of married women in the labour force. This led Edwin Cornwall, minister responsible for the National Health Insurance Commission, to argue that all maternity and child welfare work should be handled by his commissioners rather than by the LGB. In this context, he raised the point, which we have noted above, that the LGB scheme depended on local initiatives, which in many cases were simply not forthcoming. But his administrative suggestion was blocked, partly by the same mixed constituency that were resentful of the extension of unemployment provision. Local insurance committees were made up of members of trade unions, friendly societies and insurance companies, and these bodies of what appeared to be 'vested interests' were considered less responsive to public pressure than the LGB (and later the Ministry of Health). Here is a clear example of the way in which popular suspicion of national insurance affected the development of welfare provision in wartime.[63]

C   Industrial Canteens

Another area in which health administration collided with powerful vested interests was that of the control of the drink trade in
wartime. But here the brewing interest had to counter in Lloyd
George a long-time advocate of temperance reform as well as a
powerful consensus that liquor control was essential to the war
effort. As Dr Turner has shown, they did manage to frustrate state
purchase of the trade in all but a handful of areas, but they were
forced to accept restrictions on opening hours and other forms of
regulation which still today are perhaps the most tangible long-
term legacy of the First World War.[64]

In itself, control of the drink trade had a salutary effect on
aspects of the nation's health. That convictions for drunkeness
in wartime should have declined drastically after 1915 is not
surprising,[65] but there were other ways in which a decline in
alcoholism benefited the community. First was the sad case of
'overlaying', a form of infant cot death with an odd periodicity.
Many more such deaths of infants either smothered by blankets or
otherwise unattended were registered on Sundays than on any
other day of the week. The link with excessive Saturday-night
drinking was too obvious to miss, and indeed the daily distribution
of such deaths evened out virtually as soon as drink control was
introduced. But of perhaps even greater importance was that the
restriction of alcoholic consumption in wartime reduced the drain
on working-class budgets which many commentators had lamented
in the pre-war period.[66]

We shall return to this subject in the next chapter, but for our
immediate purposes, what is most revealing in the evolution of
social policy on drink is its linkage with the provision of hot meals
for munitions workers in industrial canteens in wartime. In the
pre-war period, some progressive firms had made arrangements
for hot meals to be served to their workers at midday, but even
after 1914, many employers were slow to see the utility of this
arrangement. Ironically, it was control of the liquor trade from
1915 that changed the situation entirely. The Central Control
Board (Liquor Trade) set up a canteens committee under the
chairmanship of Sir George Newman, which supervised this form
of welfare provision.[67] One contemporary observer brought out
the logic of this exercise. 'It was recognized', Dr Mary Scharlieb

wrote, 'that it is useless to expect sobriety, contentment, and the maximum of work from men and women who are insufficiently fed.'[68] By September 1916, 435 industrial canteens had been opened, serving over 640,000 munitions workers. By the end of the war, this had risen to more than 900 canteens, built at a capital cost to the government of £3.5 million, providing hot meals to over 1 million war workers.[69]

This form of industrial welfare in wartime brings us squarely to the subject of standards of nutrition, which we shall argue, was the fundamental source of improvements in civilian health in wartime. But before turning to that subject, it is important to note that we have been able to survey only a small part of the history of the public health service in the First World War. Important work was done in this period in Poor Law hospitals,[70] in clinics established for the treatment of venereal disease,[17] in various places for the care of the mentally ill,[72] and in nursing, all of which bore directly on the health of the civilian population. But we have not discussed these matters because none can help account for but a tiny fraction of the variation in mortality rates in this period.

One area in which more comment is necessary, though, is on public health policy on a substantial killer in this period, namely, respiratory disease. In this case, it is clear that the state was unable to defend the welfare of the industrial labour force recruited into munitions production. Indeed, the most conspicuous illustration of the limits of health administration in wartime is the fact that nothing could be done to prevent a serious recrudescence of tuberculosis and other respiratory ailments in wartime. Virtually all observers accepted that this was a negative and largely unavoidable consequence of the concentration of large numbers of factory workers working under considerable stress and living in inadequate housing.[73] As one observer put it, TB deaths were a direct outcome of 'overcrowding, overwork, and overstrain', but not of poor nutrition. But we must add to the list of contributory factors the run-down of anti-tuberculosis administration in wartime. There were some exceptions, such as that of Lancashire, which continued to support anti-TB work, but the conscription of MOHs with responsibility in this field and funding restrictions made it difficult for public health physicians to do more than preserve whatever services they could and await the end of the war for more congenial conditions for their work.[74] Physiological and medical research work did continue in wartime,[75] but as in most areas of scientific investigation, benefits could not be expected in the short term. For the more direct sources of both the negative and the positive effects of war on public health, we must turn away from health administration or medical intervention to investigate living standards in wartime.

7. Standards of Living and Standards of Health

In chapter 4 we surveyed the abundant evidence that there was a major decline in civilian mortality rates in wartime Britain. In particular the worst-off sections of the working class, which had registered the highest death rates in the pre-war period, gained the most in terms of life expectancy. We have sought explanations in wartime developments in medical intervention and in health administration, but have found that neither can account for the demographic data we have analysed. This leaves one possible avenue of inquiry: a rise in the standard of living of the working class in general and of the poorest sections within it in particular.

Such an argument has to overcome two kinds of counter-evidence. The first is the persistence of contemporary complaint and protest among working people about what were seen as declining living standards in wartime. The second arises from a glance at aggregate real wage data, which indicate that food prices may have risen more rapidly than wages until 1918. Since the main determinant in the standard of living which bears on health is food consumption, these data suggest that we cannot find the source of the wartime decline in civilian mortality in the standard of living. However, we shall argue that working-class families could afford during the war to maintain and in many cases to improve their food consumption. In order to establish this, we must break down the aggregate data. This breakdown will show first and most importantly that there was a levelling up of wages which benefited most precisely those groups whose mortality declined rapidly during the war. For many poorly-paid occupational groups, wage increases kept pace with or outstripped rising prices. Secondly, with respect to prices, we shall see that the working-class family basket of consumables changed during the war, reflecting the

213

substitution of less expensive, though equally nutritious, foods for more expensive foods. In addition, rent control and control of the liquor trade liberated more family income for food than had been available in 1914. Together, these developments account for the maintenance of living standards during the war period.

There are three additional factors though, which suggest that for a substantial part of the working-class population, standards of living were not only maintained, but rose relative to the pre-war period. First, earnings easily outstripped wages in wartime, due mainly to overtime pay, piece-rate payment, and the eradication of unemployment. Secondly, millions of working-class families were smaller during the war, because the men were in uniform and the birth rate dropped. Consequently there was simply more food to go around in many households. To this we may add a third factor, already mentioned in chapter 6, namely, the material benefits of certain social policies, such as the opening of industrial canteens, the enforcement of closing hours on pubs, as well as the payment of separation allowances to support the families of servicemen.

However, two important qualifications are in order here. The first arises from the fact, presented in chapter 4, that while nutrition-related mortality declined in wartime, respiratory disease mortality rose. The latter is explained by two components of working and living conditions which deteriorated during the war. The first is the run-down in the country's housing stock. The second is an increase in the concentration of workers in factories old and new. Both these developments provided ideal breeding grounds for the spread of respiratory infections.

But as we noted in chapter 4, the increase in respiratory disease mortality was far smaller than the decrease in nutrition-related mortality. We may therefore assume that the maintenance and improvement of food consumption levels during the war offset the detrimental effects to the health of the working population due to worsening housing conditions and to overwork and overcrowding in war factories. Thus we can say that the improvement in the standard of living is the best explanation for the decline in mortality rates among the working population in wartime Britain. This is the main explanation, too, of the central paradox we set out with, that a conflict of unprecedented human costs was also the occasion of an improvement in conditions which made this country a healthier place in which to live.

This chapter therefore presents evidence which permits us to go beyond the aggregate data to assess real purchasing power and consumption patterns in wartime. We begin with an assessment of food prices and patterns of food consumption to establish the real cost-of-living increase. We shall see that despite spiralling food costs, working-class families adjusted their expenditure in such a way as to provide them with at least as good a diet in wartime as they had had before 1914. The question remains as to how they were able to do so. We therefore turn to an examination of wages and earnings in wartime, and show both a levelling up of low wages and a considerable rise in the pay levels of most groups of workers. These gains meant that a majority of the working population had the means to overcome war inflation.

I FOOD PRICES AND FOOD CONSUMPTION IN WARTIME

The first question we shall address is what kinds and quantities of food working-class families purchased in wartime. The second is how much did this notional basket of consumables cost. We conclude that working-class family expenditure on food rose by about 60 per cent over the war period to a little under £2 per week.

The purchasing power of wages in wartime depended largely on fluctuations in the price of food, fuel and housing, which in the pre-war period consumed approximately 75 per cent of household budgets.[1] We shall deal with fuel and housing below, but first it is necessary to sketch the wartime history of food price movements and patterns of food consumption.

This was a controversial subject throughout the war. Many voices were raised repeatedly about increased food prices and the related phenomenon of 'profiteering'.[2] Given the inevitable failures in administration or planning, temporary food shortages appeared in numerous areas, in which considerable tension was generated. This led some housewives to take out their exasperation on shopkeepers or on farmers who were demanding an 'unfair' price.[3] Despite the introduction of a fairly comprehensive system of rationing in 1918, housewives still had to queue for hours to obtain even rationed goods. The Metropolitan Police kept detailed records on the lengthening food queues in the capital, which were clearly a disturbing and potentially explosive phenomenon. They estimated that 80,000 Londoners were queuing for meat and 30,000 for other goods in one week in late February 1918.[4]

In the previous year, public concern had reached a point where the War Cabinet appointed a committee of inquiry into industrial unrest. One of its central findings was that trouble in the factories reflected both anger at high food prices and resentment about what was seen as an unfair distribution of food.[5] When this report was discussed in Cabinet, the Minister of Labour, G. H. Roberts, told his colleagues that real wages had declined during the war. The purchasing power of the average workman, he asserted, was '10 to 15 percent lower than it was before the war, . . .'[6] This figure was derived from a straightforward comparison of the available aggregate price and wage data.

However, these findings conflict with other evidence collected at the time. In 1918, Lloyd George asked Lord Sumner to chair a committee to investigate whether or not living standards had declined during the war. Among its members were William Ashley the economist, A. L. Bowley the statistician and J. J. Mallon, a bureaucrat at the Board of Trade sympathetic to the Labour Party. This committee's report was presented in October 1918. It was based on information on family expenditure contained in 1,300 household budgets drawn up in one week of May 1918. These data showed clearly, the committee concluded, that while the war had brought about a change in the composition of diets, it had not led to a decline in overall food consumption by working-class families. More milk, potatoes, bread and flour, and oatmeal were consumed per family in 1918 than in 1914. Meat was replaced by bacon, and bland white bread by the more nutritious, though less aesthetically pleasing, brown bread. The result may have been less appetizing, starchier meals, but aside from a decline in sugar consumption, wartime diets maintained pre-war calorific levels. In sum, they found that in the summer of 1918, 'the working classes as a whole were in a position to purchase food of substantially the same nutritive value as in June 1914. Indeed, our figures indicate that the families of unskilled workmen were slightly better fed at the later date, in spite of the rising cost of food.'[7]

The major weakness of the Sumner committee report was that it had little data on families of the millions of people working in munitions factories. But the 20 memoranda issued by the Ministry of Munitions covered the population the Sumner committee missed and confirmed its findings. An 'Investigation of Workers' Food and Suggestions as to Dietary' examined the calorific value of meals in canteens of munitions factories and found it satisfactory.[8]

Of course, after the worrying successes of the German U-boat campaign of early 1917, and after a series of investigations of the causes of labour unrest which pointed clearly to the rise in food prices as a significant grievance,[9] there may have been some pressure on the government to prove that things were not really so bad after all. Certainly everyone in the government was aware that little could undermine *military* morale more quickly than reports – whether true or not – that soldiers' families faced hardships or serious shortages in food or other essential supplies.

In fact, prior to the formation of the Sumner committee, the head army censor at Calais reported that soldiers' letters reflected widespread anger about food shortages at home. This intelligence led the army to ask Lord Rhondda to send speakers to France to tell the real story. A film entitled *The Folk Back Home* was produced to raise morale, and newspaper advertisements in England asked civilians to 'Smile Across the Channel' so that soldiers would not be distracted from the tasks at hand.[10] In this context it is distinctly possible that the Sumner committee was formed precisely to provide reassurances that civilian living standards were not deteriorating after three years of war. By the time the committee's report was published, the war was almost over, but in early 1918 the military outlook was entirely different.

There is clearly a clash of evidence about wartime movements in food prices and food consumption. For this reason, it is important to try to find additional evidence to help resolve the conflict between a pessimistic view of the war's effects on living standards which arises from some contemporary comment as well as from a survey of aggregate wage and price data and an optimistic view which arises from an official study of 1,300 working-class budgets drawn up in May 1918. Fortunately, there are sufficient data about food prices and consumption patterns to test the assertion that nutritional levels in 1918 were not significantly below those registered before the outbreak of war. In 1917–18 the Ministry of Food collected a variety of data on food prices, and – what is of more importance for our purposes – on patterns of food consumption by working-class families. Some (but not all) of these data were mashalled in a Cabinet paper submitted by Lord Rhondda, the Food Controller, to the Cabinet on 2 January 1918.[11] Other statistics appeared in the published monthly reports of his Ministry.

In a nutshell, these data show that the optimists were right, but not quite as emphatically as the Sumner committee was to argue. But before presenting the relevant data, it is important to note that, in some respects, the Ministry of Food statistics are seriously deficient. Expenditure on flour is reported but not that on bread; data on items of minor importance, such as cheese and fish, are reported, but not those for tea, vegetables, or condiments. In addition, no information is given on the precise source of these consumption statistics, and it is therefore impossible to tell whether they reflect the behaviour of a representative sample of the population. In one case – that of sugar – the level of expenditure seems unacceptably high. If the figure of 3.77 lbs sugar consumption per week in March–May 1918 were accurate, it would mean that an average family (usually defined as 4.57 persons or units of consumption) purchased about 13 ounces of sugar per person per week. The problem is that this is well above the maximum allowance of 8 ounces of sugar per person permitted under rationing regulations. In all other cases, though, the data on quantities of food purchased by working-class families per week appear to be within realistic limits, and do not differ drastically from much of the evidence in the Sumner committee report. There are clear variations in price estimates, but given the nature of war conditions this is not surprising. These statistics therefore can serve as a useful check on the validity of the assertions of other official inquiries as to the adequacy of nutritional standards in the last year of the war.

The Ministry of Food estimates are represented in Tables 7.1–7.4, and describe food consumption in three-month moving averages between October 1917 and May 1918, which is to say, in the eight months prior to the period covered by the Sumner committee report. The use of moving averages gives a better indication of trends in expenditure on food, and is less likely to

TABLE 7.1. BRITISH WORKING-CLASS FAMILIES' AVERAGE WEEKLY FOOD CONSUMPTION, 1908–13 AND 1917–18

Commodities (lbs)	1908–13	1917 Oct.–Dec.	Nov.1917– Jan. 1918	Dec. 1917 Feb. 1918	1918 Jan.–March	1918 Feb.–April	1918 March–May
Beef	4.32	4.47	3.80	3.82	3.40	3.55	3.66
Mutton	2.18	1.39	1.19	1.04	0.96	0.89	0.90
Bacon	1.38	0.93	0.80	0.75	0.84	1.50	2.03
Flour	26.24	26.24	26.39	26.40	26.62	26.65	26.34
Sugar	5.31	3.95	4.01	3.73	3.46	3.43	3.77
Milk (pts)	9.91	8.92	8.92	8.92	8.92	8.92	8.92
Potatoes	16.92	16.92	16.92	16.92	16.92	16.92	16.92
Margarine	0.39	0.88	0.95	0.95	0.93	0.81	0.74
Butter	1.55	0.62	0.41	0.41	0.53	0.63	0.86
Cheese	0.83	0.42	0.22	0.22	0.36	0.30	0.41
Fish	1.50	0.75	0.75	0.75	0.75	0.75	0.75

SOURCE: MAF 60/112, Ministry of Food, Monthly Office Reports, May 1918, p. 11.

TABLE 7.2. AN INDEX OF AVERAGE WEEKLY FOOD CONSUMPTION BY WORKING-CLASS FAMILIES, 1917–18 (1908–13 = 100)

Commodities (lbs)	1908–13	1917 Oct.–Dec.	Nov. 1917– Jan. 1918	Dec. 1917– Feb. 1918	1918 Jan.–March	1918 Feb–April	1918 March–May
Beef	100	103	88	88	79	82	85
Mutton	100	64	55	48	44	41	41
Bacon	100	67	58	54	61	109	147
Flour	100	100	101	101	101	102	100
Sugar	100	74	76	70	65	65	71
Milk (pts)	100	90	90	90	90	90	90
Potatoes	100	100	100	100	100	100	100
Margarine	100	226	244	244	238	208	190
Butter	100	40	26	26	34	41	55
Cheese	100	51	27	27	43	36	49
Fish	100	50	50	50	50	50	50

SOURCE: MAF 60/112, Ministry of Food, Monthly Office Reports, May 1918, p. 11.

TABLE 7.3. AVERAGE RETAIL PRICES OF SOME PRINCIPAL FOODSTUFFS, 1908–14 AND 1917–18

Commodities (lbs)	1908–14	1917 Oct.–Dec.	Nov. 1917–Jan. 1918	Dec. 1917–Feb. 1918	1918 Jan.–March	1918 Feb.–April	1918 March–May
				(Pence/lb)			
Beef	8.60	13.50	13.50	13.25	13.25	13.25	13.00
Mutton	8.10	12.75	12.75	12.75	12.75	11.75	11.75
Bacon	11.25	25.50	25.50	27.00	27.00	26.75	26.75
Flour (7 lbs)	10.40	16.00	16.00	16.00	16.00	16.00	16.00
Sugar	2.00	6.00	6.00	6.00	6.00	6.00	7.00
Milk (pts)	2.00	3.25	3.25	3.50	3.50	2.88	2.88
Potatoes (7 lbs)	4.75	7.00	7.00	6.50	6.50	6.75	6.75
Margarine	7.25	12.25	12.25	12.00	12.00	12.00	12.00
Butter	14.00	29.25	29.25	29.50	29.50	29.50	29.50
Cheese	9.00	16.75	16.75	16.75	16.75	16.75	17.00
Fish	4.50	13.00	13.00	13.00	13.00	13.00	13.00
Eggs (dozen)	13.00	45.75	45.75	50.00	50.00	45.00	43.75
Tea	18.50	37.50	35.75	35.75	35.75	35.75	32.00

SOURCES: MAF 60/562, Table 55, Average Retail Prices of Principal Articles of Consumption; A. L. Bowley, *Prices and Wages in the United Kingdom 1914–1920* (Oxford, 1921), pp. 84, 50, 42, 53, 52, 56, 55, 44; E. A. Winslow, 'Changes in food consumption among working-class families', *Economica*, II, 6 (1922), Table IV, p. 265.

TABLE 7.4. AN ESTIMATE OF THE COST OF AVERAGE WEEKLY CONSUMPTION OF SOME PRINCIPAL FOODS BY WORKING-CLASS FAMILIES, 1908–14 AND 1917–18

Commodities (lbs)	1908–14	1917 Oct.–Dec.	Nov. 1917–Jan. 1918	Dec. 1917–Feb. 1918	1918 Jan.–March	1918 Feb.–April	1918 March–May
				(Pence)			
Beef	37.2	60.3	51.3	50.6	45.1	47.0	47.6
Mutton	17.7	17.7	15.2	13.3	12.2	10.5	10.6
Bacon	15.5	23.7	20.4	20.3	22.7	40.1	54.3
Bread and flour[a]	50.5	81.5	81.5	81.5	81.5	81.5	81.5
Sugar	10.6	23.7	24.1	22.4	20.8	20.6	26.4
Milk (pts)	19.8	29.0	29.0	31.2	31.2	25.7	25.7
Potatoes	11.5	16.9	16.9	15.7	15.7	16.3	16.3
Margarine	2.8	10.8	11.6	11.4	11.2	9.7	8.9
Butter	21.7	18.1	12.0	12.1	15.6	18.6	25.4
Cheese	7.5	7.0	3.7	3.7	6.0	5.0	7.0
Fish	6.8	9.8	9.8	9.8	9.8	9.8	9.8
Eggs[a]	13.0	36.5	36.5	36.5	36.5	36.5	36.5
Tea[a]	14.5	19.0	19.0	19.0	19.0	19.0	19.0
Other foods[a]	55.5	113.5	113.5	113.5	113.5	113.5	113.5
Total weekly expenditure on food	284.6 (23/9)	467.5 (39/0)	444.5 (37/0)	441.0 (36/9)	440.8 (36/9)	453.8 (37/10)	482.5 (40/2)

[a] Prices and quantities consumed recorded in Sumner report, p. 18.

[b] Prices and quantities consumed recorded in Sumner report, p. 18, for lard, condensed milk, vegetables, fresh fruit, rice and tapioca, oatmeal, coffee, cocoa, jam, syrup, pickles, other foods and meals out.

SOURCES: MAF 60/112, Ministry of Food, Monthly Office Reports; MAF 60/562, Table 55, Average Retail Prices of Principle Articles of Consumption; A. L. Bowley, *Prices and Wages in the United Kingdom, 1914–1920* (Oxford, 1921); Sumner report, p. 18.

record entirely unrepresentative findings than were the Sumner estimates based on budgets drawn up in one week in May 1918.

Some of the conclusions of the Sumner report are not substantiated by the Ministry of Food data. Using these data, we cannot confirm that more milk, potatoes or bacon were consumed in wartime than in the immediate pre-war period (see Table 7.1). According to the Ministry of Food, working-class families consumed one pint less milk per week, about the same quantity of potatoes, and until mid 1918, about ten ounces less bacon than they had done in 1914.

In some respects, these estimates may be too low. For instance, no allowance is made for substitution of condensed milk for cows' milk. In other respects, they may be too high, in that periodic shortages in various goods, such as potatoes or eggs, made them impossible to find in particular regions. In addition, these data may not be a good indication of pre-1918 trends. It was fortunate that by mid 1918, imports of North American bacon to Britain had brought levels of consumption of that item well above pre-war levels. Furthermore, the index figures in Table 7.2 indicate some easing of pressure on the supply of butter by mid 1918; this is also reflected in the Sumner committee estimates. On the whole, it is apparent that had the Sumner committee scrutinized budgets dating from 1917 or early 1918 rather than from mid 1918, they would have reported a more austere, though adequate, food situation (Table 7.5).

The explanation of the discrepancy between these two surveys probably lies in the social situation of the families which responded to the questionnaire circulated by the Sumner committee. Fully 60 per cent of the working-class budgets submitted to it described conditions in families of skilled workers; this is well above the proportion of skilled workers in the wartime labour force. And, as the authors of the Sumner report acknowledged, levels of consumption in families of skilled workers were higher than in other working-class families.[12] Consequently, there is reason to believe that the lower estimates of food expenditure derived from Ministry of Food data provide a clearer picture of working-class nutrition in wartime than did the Sumner report.

Let us assume that the Ministry of Food estimates are a better guide to levels of food consumption in wartime than the findings of the Sumner committee. Still, this leaves open the question of the

TABLE 7.5. TWO ESTIMATES OF WEEKLY EXPENDITURE ON SOME ITEMS OF FOOD AMONG WORKING-CLASS FAMILIES IN THE PERIOD OF THE FIRST WORLD WAR

Commodities	Sumner Report 1914 (quantity)	Sumner Report 1918 (quantity)	Min of Food 1908–14 (quantity)	Min of Food 1918 (quantity)	Sumner Report 1914 (cost)	Sumner Report 1918 (cost)	Min of Food 1908–14 (cost)	Min of Food 1918 (cost)
Beef (Br)	6.80 lbs	4.40 lbs	4.32 lbs	3.66 lbs	58.5d.	82.0d.	37.2d.	47.6d.[a]
Mutton (Br)			2.18 lbs	0.90 lbs			17.7d.	10.6d.
Bacon	1.20 lbs	2.55 lbs	1.38 lbs	2.03 lbs	14.0d.	66.5d.	15.5d.	54.3d.
Bread and flour	33.5 lbs	34.5 lbs	26.24 lbs[a]	26.34 lbs[a]	50.5d.	81.5d.	30.0d.[a]	60.0d.[a]
Sugar	5.9 lbs	2.83 lbs	5.31 lbs	3.77 lbs	13.0d.	20.0d	10.6d.	26.4d.
Milk	9.2 pts	11.7 pts	9.91 pts	8.92 pts	16.5d.	35.5d.	19.8d.	25.7d.
Potatoes	15.6 lbs	20.0 lbs	16.92 lbs	16.92 lbs	11.0d.	25.0d.	11.5d.	16.3d.
Margarine	0.42 lbs	0.91 lbs	0.39 lbs	0.74 lbs	2.5d.	11.0d.	2.8d.	8.9d.
Butter	1.70 lbs	0.79 lbs	1.55 lbs	0.86 lbs	24.5d.	23.5d.	21.7d.	25.4d.
Cheese	0.84 lbs	0.41 lbs	0.83 lbs	0.41 lbs	7.5d.	8.5d.	7.5d.	7.0d.

[a] Flour only.

SOURCE: See Tables 7.4 and 7.6; MAF 60/562, Table 55, Average Retail Prices of Principal Articles of Consumption; A. L. Bowley, *Prices and Wages in the United Kingdom 1914–1920* (Oxford, 1921); Sumner report, p. 18.

cost of such expenditure. Here again, the Ministry of Food collected abundant data on food prices, which we have presented in Table 7.6. The italicized figures indicate when price controls for specific items of consumption were introduced. Multiplying the data on levels of weekly food consumption at various dates (Table 7.1) by the relevant price data (Table 7.3) yields a series of estimates of the cost of working-class expenditure on food in the last year of the war[13] (Table 7.4).

These calculations show that whereas working-class weekly expenditure on food totalled approximately 23s.9d. before the war, by late 1917 the cost of feeding a labourer's family for a week had risen by about 60 per cent to around 39s. In the following six months, the weekly food bill went down slightly, but again each family needed about 15s. more per week in income to pay for food in early 1918 than they had required in the pre-war period. Of course, this neglects the difficult question of quality shifts in wartime diets, but it does take account of changes in the composition of diets caused by wartime shortages.

One important point arises directly from these estimates. Given that the cost of working-class food expenditure had risen by 60 per cent between 1914 and 1918 and that the retail food price index had risen by over 100 per cent between August 1914 and the last three months of 1917, working-class families must have saved about 40 per cent on their wartime food bills by changing the composition of their diets.

The question of the calorific content of wartime diets is more problematic. Whenever such evidence is used, imprecision abounds, because the caloric intake of food varies widely depending on how food is cooked and on how much is consumed. But some inferences can be drawn from the available data. On the one hand, both the Ministry of Food estimates and those of the Sumner committee show a decline in the consumption of sugar. But since the data we have examined do not reveal any compensatory increases in the consumption of other foods, it might appear that the calorific equivalent of household diets in wartime was somewhat less than in the pre-war period. However, we must recall that over 6 million British men were being fed by the army, navy and RFC/RAF at this time. Consequently, the home population dropped in these years. We must note too that the decline in the birth rate also reduced the number of infants to be fed on

TABLE 7.6. AVERAGE RETAIL PRICES OF CERTAIN ARTICLES OF FOOD IN THE UNITED KINGDOM AT THE BEGINNING OF THE MONTHS SPECIFIED, 1914-18ᵃ

Month	Articles of Food						
	British beef (Thin flank)	Frozen beef (Thin flank)	British mutton (Breast)	Frozen mutton (Breast)	Bacon (Streaky)	Flour (7 lbs)	Bread (4 lbs)
Aug. 1914	7.00	5.50	7.00	4.75	13.25	12.50	6.50
Nov. 1914	7.00	5.75	7.25	5.00	12.00	11.75	6.25
Feb. 1915	7.50	6.25	7.50	5.25	12.25	14.25	7.25
May 1915	8.25	6.75	8.25	5.75	12.50	16.25	8.25
Aug. 1915	9.50	8.00	9.25	6.50	13.25	15.25	8.00
Nov. 1915	9.50	7.76	9.25	6.50	14.50	15.00	8.00
Feb. 1916	9.75	8.00	9.25	7.00	14.75	16.75	8.75
May 1916	10.75	8.75	10.75	8.25	15.25	16.75	8.75
Aug. 1916	11.75	9.50	11.50	8.75	15.50	15.50	8.25
Nov. 1916	11.50	9.25	11.50	8.75	17.00	18.50	9.50
Feb. 1917	12.75	10.25	12.50	9.50	18.00	20.25	10.25
May 1917	13.75	11.25	13.75	10.75	20.00	21.75	11.50
Aug. 1917	15.75	12.25	15.50	12.00	20.50	22.25	11.50
Nov. 1917	13.50	11.50	12.75	11.00	25.50	16.00	9.00
Feb. 1918	13.50	11.25	12.75	10.75	27.00	16.00	9.00
May 1918	13.00	12.75	11.75	11.00	26.75	16.00	9.00
Aug. 1918	13.00	12.75	11.50	11.00	26.75	16.00	9.00
Nov. 1918	15.00	14.75	13.25	11.00	27.00	16.00	9.00

| | | Articles of Food | | | | | |
Month	Tea	Sugar (Granulated)	Milk (qt)	Potatoes (7 lbs)	Margarine	Butter	Cheese (Canadian)
Aug. 1914	18.50	3.75	3.50	5.25	8.50	16.50	9.50
Nov. 1914	18.50	3.50	3.75	3.75	7.50	15.50	9.25
Feb. 1915	21.50	3.50	3.75	4.50	7.50	17.00	10.00
May 1915	22.75	3.50	3.75	4.75	7.50	16.50	11.00
Aug. 1915	23.75	3.50	3.88	6.00	7.50	17.25	11.25
Nov. 1915	27.50	4.00	4.25	4.25	7.50	19.25	11.00
Feb. 1916	27.50	4.25	4.50	4.75	8.00	19.25	12.00
May 1916	27.50	5.25	4.75	7.00	8.50	19.50	13.00
Aug. 1916	27.75	5.25	4.75	9.00	8.50	19.50	12.50
Nov. 1916	27.75	5.50	5.25	9.75	8.75	23.25	13.75
Feb. 1917	28.25	5.50	5.50	11.25	9.25	25.25	16.25
May 1917	31.25	5.50	5.50	11.75	11.25	25.00	19.25
Aug. 1917	32.25	6.00	5.50	7.25	12.00	24.75	17.25
Nov. 1917	37.50	6.00	6.50	7.00	12.25	29.25	16.75
Feb. 1918	35.75	6.00	7.00	6.50	12.00	29.50	16.75
May 1918	32.00	7.00	5.75	6.75	12.00	29.50	17.00
Aug. 1918	32.00	7.00	6.50	10.25	14.00	28.25	19.75
Nov. 1918	32.00	7.00	8.25	7.75	14.00	30.00	20.00

TABLE 7.6. (Continued)

Articles of Food

Month	Eggs (Dozen)	Lard[b]	Oatmeal[b]	Rice[b]	Coffee[b]	Condensed milk[b] (14 oz.)	Tomatoes[b]
Aug. 1914	17.75	7.00	1.75	3.00	14.00	7.50	5.50
Nov. 1914	21.25	8.00	2.50	2.50	14.00	7.00	7.00
Feb. 1915	21.00	8.00	2.50	2.50	14.00	6.50	9.00
May 1915	14.75	8.00	2.50	2.50	14.00	6.50	12.00
Aug. 1915	18.25	7.50	2.50	2.50	14.00	6.50	6.00
Nov. 1915	25.75	8.00	2.50	2.50	15.00	7.50	8.00
Feb. 1916	24.50	8.50	2.75	2.75	15.00	7.50	8.00
May 1916	17.50	10.00	2.75	2.75	18.00	8.50	8.00
Aug. 1916	22.25	10.50	2.75	2.75	18.00	8.50	7.00
Nov. 1916	34.50	12.50	3.00	2.75	*18.00*	8.50	8.00
Feb. 1917	34.25	14.50	n.a.	3.50	20.00	9.50	10.50
May 1917	25.75	*17.50*	*n.a.*	4.00	22.00	11.50	27.00
Aug. 1917	32.75	16.00	5.00	4.00	20.00	12.00	7.00
Nov. 1917	45.25	*n.a.*	5.00	*4.00*	20.00	12.00	12.00
Feb. 1918	50.00	n.a.	4.00	4.00	20.00	13.50	n.a.
May 1918	43.75	n.a.	4.50	4.00	20.00	*14.50*	42.00
Aug. 1918	57.00	20.00	4.50	4.00	20.00	14.50	15.00
Nov. 1918	74.00	20.00	4.50	4.00	22.00	14.50	21.00

[a] Prices in pence per lb. unless otherwise indicated; italics denote when price controls were first introduced
[b] London prices only

SOURCE: MAF 60/562, Tables 55–7.

family budgets in these years. For both these reasons, per capita calorific intake among civilians in 1918 was probably higher than it had been in 1914. Judging by army rations, the same was true for workingmen in uniform during the war.[14]

Again, we must bear in mind the way aggregate statistics on food prices and food expenditure tend to obscure regional or occupational variations. For example, even though the price of flour was controlled from August 1917, the price of the standard four lb loaf of bread still varied substantially within regions and between regions in the last year of the war. In January 1918, the retail price of the quartern loaf was over 10d. in Liverpool, 9d. in Nottingham, and about 8d. in Manchester. Similar contrasts existed in the North-east and in other regions.[15] What was true for bread prices, was no less true for those of other staple foods. And if local price movements were not uniform in this period, neither were household diets or patterns of food consumption. For this reason, blanket statements about changes in wartime standards of living must be treated with considerable caution.

II OTHER RETAIL PRICES AND WORKING-CLASS EXPENDITURE

It seems likely, then, that pre-war pay levels had to rise by 15s. (or around 60 per cent) to enable workers in late 1917 to buy a basket of consumables adjusted for price inflation. This takes account of skyrocketing food costs, but it does not reflect adjustments in expenditure on other essential items.

Because of rent control, there is little need to estimate adjustments in expenditure for rents and rates. This act was probably the most important measure in the defence of working-class living standards in wartime; it is arguable that without it, the war economy would have collapsed. Rate increases were passed on to tenants in the form of increased rents, but these constituted an insignificant addition to the working-class cost of living. Similarly slight increases may be attributed to fares and insurance.

Rising fuel costs probably added about 2s. to pre-war weekly expenditure, whatever the balance between the use of coal or gas for heating or lighting.[16] This was not negligible, but a much more substantial rise in the cost of living may be attributed to soaring clothing prices. Bowley estimated that by late 1917 the prices of many articles of apparel were beyond the reach of most working-class families.[17] But the difficulty was not merely that people found it hard to find clothes at the right prices; in many cases they had trouble in finding any clothes at all in the shops. Shortages were so severe that by 1918 the quantity index of expenditure on clothes was at 65 per cent of the 1900 level.[18] It is clear that many working-class families had to do without new clothes during the war, and that absolutely unavoidable expenditure here may have added 3s. or 4s. to the weekly cost of living.[19]

The only other significant shifts in the price of domestic consumable goods which we need to survey are those in the prices of tobacco and alcohol. It is very difficult to get accurate figures of weekly expenditure on these items, the purchase of which occasionally involved delicate strategies of deception. Aggregate statistics suggest that the increase of the price of a pint of beer from 3d. to 5d. and a trebling in the price of spirits were responsible for a substantial drop in the consumption of alcoholic beverages of all kinds. No doubt the introduction of licensing hours and a decline in the specific gravity of beer made their contribution to the fact that in 1918 the quantity index of purchases of alcohol was at only 50 per cent of the 1900 level.[20]

In contrast, pre-war levels of expenditure on tobacco were exceeded during the conflict, despite a 70 per cent increase in prices.[21] It is possible that the savings in disposable income made by the decline in the consumption of alcohol were simply diverted to the purchase of tobacco. In the absence of rigorous consumption statistics, it is probably best, therefore, to assume that together, changes in the price and volume of sales of these non-essential items cancelled each other out.

III WAGES, EARNINGS AND THE INCREASED COST OF LIVING IN WARTIME

We have estimated that on average working-class families needed at least an additional 15 shillings to pay for an adjusted basket of food in late 1917. We have also noted that an additional 1s.10d. per week was necessary to meet rising fuel costs, and that perhaps 4s. more per week would have to be set aside to replace worn-out clothing. Our estimates of clothing and food expenditure are lower than those in the Sumner report, which dealt with a preponderantly artisan population. But conceding the inevitable imprecision of such estimates, it is still possible to suggest that wages had to rise by 21s. or 22s. if working-class family incomes were to keep pace with wartime inflation. As we shall see below, the wages of most workers rose by at least this amount during the war.

First let us note that there is no field of quantitative history as treacherous as the study of real wages. This is as true of the 1914–18 period as it is of later or earlier years. Part of the difficulty lies in the nature of the evidence. Throughout the war, data on wage movements were published in the *Labour Gazette* by statisticians at the Board of Trade and the Ministry of Labour. There are at least two intractable problems historians face in handling this evidence. The first is incompleteness: these data can only give a very approximate indication of movements in wages as a whole. No employer was compelled to report wage adjustments; of the 10 million in employment, the data document the wages of only 4 million. We cannot simply assume that movements in one branch of a trade were followed either immediately or even at all in other branches. In addition, it is important to note the fact that most wage statistics are based on employers' records, and as such, may not have registered deductions from take-home pay or variations in pay scales which could have reduced take-home pay, on occasion, to a level below the rate for the shift, day or week. On the whole, though, we may accept wage-rate data as a reasonably accurate guide to minimum levels of pay in a war economy under conditions of full employment.[22]

The second problem concerns the partial picture we get by taking into account only money wages as data in the analysis of earnings. We must also note the variety of piece-rates, time rates, overtime rates, bonuses, incentives, and advances on pre-war standard payments registered in these years. It was this kaleidoscope of data on pay which led J. W. F. Rowe to develop the concept of 'true wage rates' or 'the current average rate of *earnings*' (my emphasis).[23] This is a better approximation of take-home pay than are nominal wage rates, but again, insufficient data exist for complete calculations of this more sophisticated measure of earnings. It is clear, therefore, that any comparison of earnings in 1914–18 with a pre-war standard will involve a substantial margin of error.

With these cautionary remarks in mind, what inferences can we draw from the available data on wages and incomes? First of all, the global statistics show a sharp contrast between the first two years of the war and the last two years. In 1914–16, wage rates moved upwards, slowly and unevenly. Taking 1914 as the standard of comparison, wage rates rose by approximately 10 per cent per year. In 1917–18, though, wage gains were much more robust, with a 30 per cent rise over the 1916 level in 1917, and a further 40 per cent rise in 1918 over 1917. By the end of the war, wage rates were roughly double the 1914 level, thanks largely to an upward surge in the second half of the war.

This general divide in the history of pay in wartime was true for most sectors of the economy. But the slender character of early wartime gains persisted later in the war in inessential trades or in those not directly producing goods for the armed forces. For example, wage rates in the cotton industry in 1917 were only 19 per cent above the 1914 level, which contrasted sharply with the 55 per cent increase registered for wages as a whole in these years. Bricklayers' and painters' earnings also rose very slowly indeed, reflecting the parlous state of the civilian building industry during the war. In contrast, the wages of agricultural workers, which were notoriously low in the pre-war period, rose very rapidly. By 1918, farm labourers were getting well above twice their pre-war wage. Similarly, unskilled workers in the engineering trades benefited from wartime demand for munitions labour (see Tables 7.7–7.8).

The fact that skilled engineers were indeed in demand but did not register equivalent gains in rates of pay brings us to the second key feature of the history of wages in the First World War: the narrowing of differentials. A useful indication of this change is provided by Rowe's computations of 'true wage rates'. His data extend to 1920, and undoubtedly reflect conditions in the post-war boom as much as during the war. But since many wartime economic controls were not lifted until 1920 or later, his calculations do enable us to see the broad effects of the war economy on relative levels of pay. For example, whereas skilled building workers' earnings rose from 38s. 11d. in 1913 to 97s. 2d. in 1920, the earnings of building labourers rose much more substantially, from 25s. 9d. per week in 1913 to over 84s. in 1920. This meant that the skill differential of pay in this trade was about 50 per cent in 1913

TABLE 7.7 AN INDEX OF COST OF LIVING AND WEEKLY WAGE MOVEMENTS AMONG SOME GROUPS OF WORKERS, 1914–18 (1984 = 100)

Date	Cost of living[a]	Wages: all workers[b]	Bricklayers (8 towns)	Bricklayers' labourers (7 towns)	Engineering fitters and turners	Engineering labourers	Shipbuilding platers	Iron and steel: South Wales[b]
1914	100	100	100	100	100	100	100	100
1915	123	111	102	104	110	n.a.	n.a.	102
1916	146	121	108	115	111	n.a	n.a	133
1917	176	155	122	134	134	154	169	148
1918	203	195	157	184	173	213	193	159

Date	Coalminers (N. Yorks and Durham) (Earnings)	Compositors (8 towns)	Railwaymen	Agricultural workers	Cotton workers (Earnings)	Trade board rates (Men)[b]	Trade board rates (Women)[b]	Dock labourers
1914	100	100	100	100	100	100	100	100
1915	112	100	110	112	103	100	100	111
1916	133	105	120	140	107	100	100	130
1917	158	120	155	189	119	125	135	150
1918	189	156	195	226	157	135	157	193

SOURCES: [a] *British Labour Statistics 1886–1968* (1971), Table 89; all other references are from A. L. Bowley, *Prices and Wages in the United Kingdom 1914–1920* (Oxford, 1921).
[b] D. Sells, *British Wage Boards* (Washington, DC, 1939), appendix B.

TABLE 7.8 FLUCTUATIONS IN THE COST OF LIVING AND IN AVERAGE WEEKLY MONEY WAGES OR EARNINGS AMONG SOME GROUPS OF WORKERS DURING THE 1914–18 WAR

Date	Cost of living[a] (1914=100)	All workers[b] (1914=100)	Bricklayers (8 towns) summer rates	Bricklayers labourers (7 towns) summer rates	Engineering fitters and turners	Engineering labourers	Shipbuilding platers	Dock labourers
1914	100	100	42/10	29/1	38/11	22/10	40/4	33/8
1915	123	111	43/9	30/2	42/10	n.a.	n.a.	37/6
1916	146	121	46/2	33/7	43/2	n.a.	n.a.	43/9
1917	176	155	52/2	39/0	52/2	35/2	68/2	50/3
1918	203	195	67/5	53/7	67/4	48/8	77/10	64/11

Date	Coalminers (N. Yorks. and Durham) Earnings	Compositors (8 towns)	Railwaymen	Agricultural workers	Cotton workers (Earnings)	Trade board rates (Men)[b]	Trade board rates (Women)[b]
1914	32/0	36/9	26/6	16/10	20/0	25/4	13/4
1915	35/9	36/10	29/2	18/10	20/7	25/4	13/4
1916	42/7	38/8	31/10	23/6	22/0	25/4	13/4
1917	50/5	44/0	41/1	31/9	25/7	31/6	17/6
1918	60/5	54/4	51/8	38/0	28/7	34/1	20/11

SOURCES: [a] *British Labour Statistics Historical Abstract 1886–1968* (1971); all other references are from: A. L. Bowley, *Prices and Wages in the United Kingdom 1914–1920* (Oxford, 1921).
[b] Sells, *British Wage Boards* (Washington, DC, 1939), appendix B.

but only 15 per cent in 1920. In engineering, the decline over the period 1913–20 was similarly striking. The 75 per cent skill differential in pay enjoyed by engineering turners over labourers in 1913 was reduced to 38 per cent in 1920. The same occurred among railway workers, although apparently not in the cotton trades (see Table 7.9).

This narrowing of the pay differential of skill among manual workers meant that the greatest gains in real wages were registered by those who had been most substantially underpaid in the pre-war period. As we can see in Table 7.10, the earnings of skilled bricklayers and railway engine drivers did not keep pace with price inflation over the war period. In contrast, unskilled workers in these trades, who were able to earn a bit over £1 per week in 1913, could command over three times that level of pay in 1920. This was sufficient to increase their real purchasing power by about one-quarter in the space of seven years. As is also indicated in Table 7.10, the earnings of semi-skilled workers enabled them to keep pace with the cost of living, but (with the exception of cotton workers and putters and fillers in coal-mining) their gains in real terms were more modest than those of the unskilled grades.

A brief scrutiny of data on pay shows three features of the war economy of relevance to our study: first, in aggregate terms, wages doubled during the war; secondly, most of this increase in earnings occurred only in the later parts of the war; and thirdly, in both absolute and relative terms, the greatest gains were registered by workers who had been poorly paid in the pre-war period.

It is time to return to the initial question posed at the opening of this section. Did workers' pay levels rise sufficiently to enable them to defend or even to enhance their standard of living? The answer appears to be yes, in most cases. If we return to the data in Table 7.8, we can see that most occupational groups did register at least the 22s. increase we have calculated as the minimum needed to meet rising costs in wartime. But we can also see that for workers outside the mainstream of the war economy, 1914–18 was a period of declining real incomes. Building workers, textile workers, and printing trades workers all found that their earnings could not keep pace with the rise in the price of food and fuel. On the other hand, engineering workers, railwaymen, coalminers and agricultural workers all registered gains in wage rates in the period 1914–17/18 above the level needed to match the rise in food prices.

TABLE 7.9. WEEKLY EARNINGS AMONG SOME MANUAL WORKERS, 1886–1926

1. Skilled Grades

Date	Bricklayers	Coalgetters	Cotton spinners	Engineering turners	Railway engine drivers
1886	31/1	24/6	32/6	29/9	39/7
1913	38/11	50/4	41/5	38/2	42/11
1920	97/2	135/6	129/1	98/9	103/0
1926	70/10	78/10	76/8	61/9	88/1

2. Semi-skilled Grades

Date	Painters	Coalmining putters and fillers	Cotton grinders	Engineering machinemen	Railway guards
1886	28/8	20/8	21/2	22/3	27/6
1913	34/7	36/10	29/5	30/7	30/9
1920	96/3	106/10	95/8	88/7	84/6
1926	70/10	99/3	56/10	52/3	66/5

3. Unskilled Grades

Date	Building labourers	Coalmining labourers	Cotton weavers (Women)	Engineering labourers	Railway goods porters
1886	19/4	18/0	18/0	17/11	20/0
1913	25/9	33/0	21/11	21/10	22/1
1920	84/4	99/3	72/6	71/6	72/11
1926	54/7	53/2	43/6	40/2	49/1

SOURCE: J. W. F. Rowe, *Wages in Practice and Theory* (1928), p. 42.

So far all our calculations have dealt with weekly wages of one wage-earner rather than with family incomes. We shall note below that it is likely that family incomes increased more rapidly than wages during the war. But at this stage it is possible to draw two inferences from the above estimates. The first is that even though our estimates of working-class food expenditure in 1917–18 are lower than those of the Sumner committee report, we have confirmed their central observation that working-class nutritional levels were maintained or improved during the war. Secondly, given the evidence of rapidly rising earnings among low-paid and unskilled workers, it is also likely that these people and their

TABLE 7.10. AN INDEX OF REAL WAGES OF SOME MANUAL WORKERS 1886–1926
(1913 = 100)

1. *Skilled Grades*

Date	Bricklayers	Coalgetters	Cotton spinners	Engineering turners	Railway engine drivers
1886	80	63	79	77	93
1913	100	100	100	100	100
1920	94	110	118	118	91
1926	104	97	106	106	117

2. *Semi-skilled Grades*

Date	Painters	Coalmining putters and fillers	Cotton grinders	Engineering machinemen	Railway guards
1886	83	72	72	73	89
1913	100	100	100	100	100
1920	105	123	118	109	104
1926	117	96	96	98	123

3. *Unskilled Grades*

Date	Building labourers	Coalmining labourers	Cotton weavers (Women)	Engineering labourers	Railway goods porters
1886	75	72	82	82	91
1913	100	100	100	100	100
1920	124	123	125	120	125
1926	121	99	112	125	127

SOURCE: J. W. F. Rowe, *Wages in Practice and Theory* (1928), p. 48.

families had more money during the war and spent more of it on food than they had ever done before.

IV WARTIME AUSTERITY AND THE ESCAPE FROM POVERTY

These simple calculations suggest that, while civilians had to make do with old clothes and spiralling food and fuel costs, most people were able to meet the wartime increase in the cost of necessities, and many did much better than that. There are a number of additional reasons why it is likely that most labouring people experienced the war period as a paradoxical one: bringing both severe shortages and increased earnings and increased levels of expenditure.

The first is that all calculations of real wages in pre-war Britain suffer from the intractable difficulty of accounting for unemployment, bye-employment, casual employment, and underemployment. Students of the 1914–18 period have no such difficulty. Unemployment virtually disappeared by the mid years of the war. Hence the levels of pay we have discussed are probably an accurate guide to earnings. Second, it is abundantly clear that the war drew workers from low-paid to better-paid jobs. Indeed contemporaries saw what Table 7.8 illustrates, that is, if you could get out of a trade not tied to the war economy, and find a job in a munitions works, your earnings would go up substantially. This was especially so in factories working on a piece-rate or payment by results system. Third, all the above computations have left aside the question of overtime. But the most rigorous study of labour conditions in the war has estimated that on average male war workers put in about 10 hours overtime, and females about $7\frac{1}{2}$ hours of overtime a week.[24] The wage rates we have examined were calculated for a work week normally between 49 and 52 hours; hence male workers took in on a regular basis earnings at least 20 per cent above the weekly wage. Women's war earnings were similarly inflated by overtime pay for work that was no doubt stressful and monotonous, but which gave many of them a wage they could not command before the war.[25] Fourth, many young women and boys who, under normal conditions, might not have joined the industrial labour force at that time were recruited into munitions factories or became substitutes for white-collar workers who were in uniform. The consequent increase in the number of full-time and relatively well-paid wage-earners in many working-class households was bound to raise family incomes well above the levels indicated by examining wage rates alone.

Fifth, we should note that the wartime labour market operated in another way which reinforced the trend towards increased working-class incomes, especially for poorly-paid workers. We have noted that the low-paid, unskilled grades to some extent narrowed the gap between their earnings and those of skilled workers. One reason for this was the practice of across the board flat-rate war bonuses, which tended to add a greater percentage to low wages than to higher wages. The establishment of a minimum wage in agriculture undoubtedly raised traditionally low rural wage levels substantially. In other cases, war bonuses for the low-paid were higher than for the better paid, which reduced differentials further still.[26]

Two other wartime developments helped increase levels of consumption in particular among poorly-paid and poorly-nourished workers. The first was rationing. By 1918 the following items were subject to rationing regulations: sugar, butter and margarine, lard, butcher's meat, bacon and ham, jam and (in some regions) tea and cheese.[27] The search for rationed goods was a time-consuming and exasperating one, but it is still true that for many people who were grossly underpaid in the pre-war period, good wages and rationing meant that they were able to purchase quantities of goods beyond their reach in the pre-war period.

The second reason to believe that nutritional levels rose during the war for many people whose pre-war diets were inadequate is related to the way food was distributed in working-class households prior to the war. There is considerable evidence that in working-class families male wage-earners received the lion's share of protein and other foods. This was for the common-sense reason that on their shoulders (and strength) rested the family's often precarious fortunes. The line of priority in the distribution of food seems to have been first male wage-earners, then children, then the mother.[28] With the recruitment of substantial numbers of married women into industry and commerce during the war, this arrangement changed. For the first time in many homes, women were the primary wage-earners, entitled to at least an equal share of the family's food supply. It is, of course, impossible to quantify these shifts in the way the working-class family budget was spent, but they provide additional evidence to support the view that wartime conditions enabled most families to maintain their pre-war living standards, and provided the opportunity for many to advance significantly beyond their pre-war situation. It is in this context that we can appreciate the force of Robert Roberts' remark about his native Salford that the Great War was the occasion of the 'great escape' from primary poverty. For our purposes, his vantage-point during the war was a particularly good one. As a young boy able to watch the business and listen to the gossip which flowed through his parents' corner shop in a poor working-class neighbourhood, he learned much about the social upheavals of war. 'In spite of war', he recalled,

> slum grocers managed to get hold of different and better varieties of foodstuffs of a kind sold before only in middle-class shops, and the once deprived began to savour strange delights. This brought the usual charge of 'extravagance' from their social superiors. 'But why shouldn't folk eat their fancy?' my mother said. 'They work for what they get.'
>
> One of our customers, wife of a former foundry labourer, both making big money now on munitions, airily inquired one Christmas time as to when we were going to stock 'summat worth chewin'.
>
> 'Such as what?' asked my father, sour-faced.
>
> 'Tins o'lobster!' she suggested, 'or them big jars o' pickled gherkins!.'
>
> Furious, the old man damned her from the shop. 'Before the war', he fumed, 'that one was grateful for a bit o' bread and scrape!'

Such were some of the unintended consequences of war.[29]

V   WELFARE PROVISION AND FAMILY INCOME IN WARTIME

Working-class households benefited during the war not only from labour scarcity and from changes in the sexual and the skill composition of the labour force, but also from various kinds of subsidies and social provision. Some had been initiated in the pre-war period; others appeared during the conflict itself. Together they helped protect the living standards of a substantial part of the population.

Three types of payment were directly related to war service. First, separation allowances for the families of men on active service were graduated according to family size. As of October 1917, for instance, the wife of a soldier with one child under age 14 received 23s. per week; if she had four young children, she received 40s. 6d. As we have seen, these payments would cover perhaps half the costs of weekly family expenditure. Secondly, widows' pensions were graduated, this time according to rank. The widow of an army private received a flat-rate payment of 13s. 9d. per week; a junior officer's widow got about £2 per week, together with one-third of that sum for each child, payable until the age of 18 for a son and until 21 for a daughter. The widows of men of higher ranks received more, but their situation was far removed from that of the mass of the population. Thirdly, disability pensions were paid to men according to the degree of impairment of their capacity to support themselves and their family. We shall discuss such awards in chapter 8, but from early on in the war, they did help men recovering from war wounds to get a start in trying to pick up the threads of their lives again.[30]

In addition, five forms of pre-war benefits were extended during the conflict. The first was health insurance. All those in the armed forces were automatically included in the scheme and their wives therefore received maternity benefit on giving birth. For a working woman, insured in her own right, maternity benefit was doubled. Such women were also eligible for sickness benefit, which substantial numbers of them claimed during the war.

Secondly, we have already noted the beneficial effects of the provision of industrial canteens, a pre-war development which took on much greater significance after 1914. By 1916–17, subsidized meals for day-shift workers promoted industrial efficiency, and also increased the money available for the purchase of food and other household necessities for the rest of the family.

Thirdly, the provision of meals for children of school age, initiated in 1908, was extended to cover the whole calendar year. Expenditure increased rapidly, despite the fact that fewer children were found to be in a necessitous state after 1914. For instance, in Leeds, about 130,000 meals were provided for needy children in the year ending 31 July 1914. Three years later, the total provided was 39,000, and in the summer of 1918, it was down to 6,000.[31] There was also a substantial rise in expenditure for school meals in Scotland during the war. In 1912–13, £7 million was spent on school meals; in 1917–18 the sum spent was £29 million, and a year later, the total reached £52.2 million.[32]

Fourthly, old age pensions, instituted in 1908, gave some modest but real support for many people during the war. And although the sums involved were very low, it should be remembered that this payment did not preclude paid work for the elderly. The benefit was paid whether or not the recipient was in employment, and given the shortage of labour during the war, it was inevitable that many pensioners were still in active work.

Finally, relief for war-related distress was available during the war. The Prince of Wales Relief Fund was set up to help servicemen's families and those out of work due to the dislocation of trade in 1914. But within a few months it became clear that relief was not necessary for the vast majority of workers. The same was true with respect to the Poor Law, as we can see by examining the statistics of the decline in pauperism after 1914. Just to take one example, the rate of those seeking relief under the Poor Law in Leeds in July 1914 was 126 per 10,000 population. In June 1918, the figure had dropped to 81.[33] Relatively few workers were in need of such help in this period, but such provision was still available as a charge on the community as a whole.

VI   HOUSING IN WARTIME

Whatever improvements occurred with respect to wages and earnings, or social provision, no similar progress occurred during the war in the field of housing reform. The fact that four years were lost in repairing old and dilapidated housing as well as in providing new accommodation helped crystallize a new commitment to housing reform. But whatever the fruits of this aspect of reconstruction in the long run, they were non-existent during the war itself.

In the pre-war period, the annual rate of increase of the nation's housing stock was approximately 84,000 houses per year. Between 1911 and 1918, only 238,000 houses were built, or about 34,000 per year. Since the total of new families formed in that period was 848,000, and since the dissolution of households through old age or death was probably matched by a roughly equal and opposite increase in household formation through migration and fragmentation, we can conclude that there was a clear shortage of over 600,000 houses at the end of the war.[34]

The reasons for the housing shortage were straightforward. Between 1914 and 1918, the costs of building doubled, the rate of interest rose by one-third, and building labourers found better-paid employment in munitions industries or were drafted into the army. In addition, enforcement of rent control after 1915 eliminated any economic incentive for speculative builders to provide housing for the working class. And many of the same obstacles to the construction of new housing also applied to the maintenance and repair of the existing housing stock.[35] Given the massive influx of new workers into urban centres where munitions works were located, overcrowding was bound to worsen during the war.

At the outbreak of the war the Housing (No. 2) Act of 1914 was passed, empowering the Local Government Board and the Board of Agriculture to spend up to £4 million on housing. The underlying purpose was to mitigate anticipated unemployment in the autumn of that year. When the problem of joblessness gave way to the problem of labour scarcity, this measure simply faded away. Instead, the Ministry of Munitions became the major government housing contractor, spending over £4.3 million between 1915 and 1918 to provide hostels, cottages and houses for munitions workers. But the bulk of the industrial labour force had to find lodgings in the private market, or else put up with pre-war accommodation.[36] One example will suffice to illustrate the problem. The Ministry of Munitions provided over 12,000 rooms for workers at Greenwich and Woolwich in 1915–16, but over the same period a total of only 30 houses were built in all of London.[37]

By the end of the war, all indicators pointed to worsening housing conditions. The proportion of uninhabited houses to 1,000 inhabited houses dropped substantially. This suggested that many houses uninhabited in 1914 (because they were virtually uninhabitable) had been occupied in the succeeding four years.[38] The action of local authorities in condemning insanitary housing was severely curtailed during the war, since little could be done to enforce their orders in this period. As T. Eustace Hill, the Medical Officer of Health for County Durham, told a 1919 conference of district sanitary authorities, the result inevitably was an increase in overcrowding and an increase in the population living in lodgings that were clearly insanitary.[39]

VII CONCLUSION

There seems little doubt that the recrudescence of mortality due to respiratory diseases in wartime Britain was aided and abetted by the deterioration in its housing stock between 1914 and 1918. In addition, the concentration of a large working population in munitions factories working a 10–14 hour day entailed similar costs in ill health and lower case-recovery rates of those unfortunate enough to have contracted tuberculosis, either before or during the war.

But overall, such evidence of war conditions leading to impaired health is overshadowed by many indications of the positive effects of the mobilization of the industrial population after 1914. We have demonstrated that while food supplies were reduced, diets were maintained and, in some cases, actually improved in wartime. This was in part a function of the levelling up of low wages and a shift from work traditionally poorly paid to better-paid jobs. It was also a reflection of wartime welfare policy, social subsidies, and of the redistribution of income and food within the working-class family.

In Britain during the First World War, underpaid and underemployed labourers were transformed within a few months of the outbreak of hostilities into full working partners in the war effort. The only way war-related production could have been expanded rapidly at a time of mass voluntary enlistment was by attracting low-paid workers to munitions factories by the promise of higher rates of pay, and this is precisely what the Ministry of War, and later the Ministry of Munitions, succeeded in doing. Furthermore, when a real challenge to working-class living standards arose in the form of increased rents in early 1915, the government acted with great haste to freeze rents at the pre-war level. What changed in wartime was both an enhancement of the market position of most grades of manual labour as well as a strengthening of the legal and moral entitlement of workers to exchange their labour for a living wage.[40]

This is why even though *aggregate* food supply declined during the war, nutritional levels rose. Successive governments acceded to inflationary wage adjustments precisely because they knew that the success of the war economy depended on the ability of the mass of the population to command food. The result was a levelling up of wages which, taken together with an adjustment of diets and a redistribution of food within the working-class family, meant rising standards of living, especially for those worst off in the pre-war period.

Clearly British food policy in wartime was not an unblemished achievement. But as the tension of those difficult years began to fade, many contemporaries came to see that, on balance, real gains had been made during the war. The historians of the Clyde valley during the war noted that 'the population of the area was, during the actual war years, more capable of maintaining a fair standard of comfort than in the pre-war period'.[41] A survey of rural labour conditions in Scotland also reported that real wages in this sector had risen, with particular gains registered by women workers and unmarried men.[42] Many MOHs noted a decline in the more blatant signs of malnutrition among the urban populations of England and Wales.[43] And the drop in indictments and convictions for theft and other offences as well as a decline in vagrancy and recourse to Poor Law relief seemed to others to point in the same direction: primary poverty among the urban and rural poor was an unexpected casualty of the war.[44]

This brief moment in enhanced purchasing power for industrial and agricultural workers did not survive the end of the post-war boom in 1920. But we should not underestimate the significance of these wartime developments, either for the social history of Britain or for the history of the war itself. In this context it is possible only to suggest that if German workers in 1917–18 had commanded the real incomes of their British counterparts, and if their families had been able to maintain the nutritional levels we have described above, the outcome of the war may well have been reversed. Clearly a full-scale comparison with German conditions would be necessary to establish this claim, but the available literature seems to show that it was precisely on the level of defending civilian living standards that the German war economy failed.[45] The consequences were clear: better health among British civilians; much greater deprivation, stress, and despair as well as deteriorating standards of health among a German population which paid the price British civilians never had to pay for their country's war effort.[46]

PART III   THE LEGACY OF THE GREAT WAR

8. The Demographic Aftermath of the First World War

IN the first two parts of this book, we have described the immediate impact of the First World War on the British population as a function of two separate, though overlapping, processes: military participation resulting in appallingly high casualties, on the one hand; and the creation of a successful war economy, leading to rising standards of living and declining mortality rates among most parts of the civilian population, on the other.

This emphasis on mortality fluctuations in wartime is inevitable, given the very nature of the enterprise of war. But the subject of the demographic effects of the 1914–18 conflict is not exhausted by an analysis of death rates among soldiers and civilians. For this reason, we review in this chapter trends in vital statistics in the period surrounding the war and present evidence of more indirect, though important, repercussions of the conflict on migration and nuptiality.

Even when this is done, though, the question remains as to whether the demographic developments we have described were an outcome of war or simply of the passage of time. In our discussion of mortality trends in chapters 3–4, we have argued that in some respects the war experience did leave a clear imprint on the demographic history of this country. Similarly, we present in this chapter evidence that the war brought about a clear break in the history of international migration, and through this change, significantly affected patterns of nuptiality in Britain. But in other areas, such as in the decline of fertility and related changes in the age structure of the population, it is clear that pre-war trends survived the war intact. In this context, we argue that there was a built-in momentum in the population history of Britain of sufficient strength to explain why even an upheaval of the magnitude of the Great War did not significantly deflect some demographic trends in motion long before the outbreak of hostilities.

On balance, war losses overshadow all other aspects of the demographic impact of war. The slaughter of nearly three-quarters of a million men was undoubtedly a demographic event of historical importance, but its significance lies more in the realm of the social and cultural than in the statistical and demographic.

As we suggested in the introduction to this book, population history in recent years has added to its traditional emphasis on the biological and the quantitative an awareness of the need to explore the cultural and qualitative dimensions of demographic events. This is of particular importance in a study of the effects of the First World War, for it would be absurd to limit discussion of the consequences of war-related mortality to the purely statistical questions of what difference such losses made to the structure of the labour force or to reproductive behaviour after the war. Anyone who does this is bound to miss the most profound impact of the human costs of the Great War, which was on the minds of the survivors. For this reason we have divided the last part of this book into two chapters. The first surveys the short-term and longer-term demographic repercussions of the conflict. It is followed by a concluding account of the collective memory of the slaughter, which unmistakably has cast a long shadow over British society in the years since 1918.

I   VITAL STATISTICS IN THE PERIOD OF THE FIRST WORLD WAR

A   Marriage Rates

Let us begin with nuptiality. There were three phases in the history of marriage in Britain during the 1914–18 conflict (Tables 8.1 and 8.2). The first was a surge in the marriage rate between March 1915 and March 1916. In 1914, the marriage rate in England and Wales was 15.9 per 1,000. A year later, the figure had risen sharply to 19.4 per 1,000, which was the highest figure on record. The marriage boom began only when the illusion that the war would be

TABLE 8.1. SOME VITAL STATISTICS IN THE PERIOD OF THE FIRST WORLD WAR,
ENGLAND AND WALES, 1910–22

Year	Mid-year population (000s)[a]	Marriages	Births	Deaths (Civilians only)	Natural increase	Net outward migration
1910	35,792	267,721	896,962	483,247	413,715	207,416
1911	36,136	274,943	881,138	527,810	353,328	241,151
1912	36,327	283,834	872,737	486,939	385,798	241,734
1913	36,574	286,583	881,890	504,975	376,915	203,611
1914	36,967	294,401	879,096	516,742	362,354	−108,688
1915	35,284	360,885	814,914	562,253	252,661	− 36,147
1916	34,642	279,846	785,520	508,217	277,303	1,832
1917	34,197	258,855	668,346	498,922	169,424	13,298
1918	34,624	287,163	662,661	611,861	50,800	14,850
1919	35,427	369,411	692,438	504,203	188,235	152,642
1920	37,247	379,982	958,782	466,130	492,652	167,781
1921	37,932	320,852	848,814	458,629	390,185	125,139
1922	38,205	299,524	780,124	486,780	293,344	100,946

[a] Civilian population only in 1915–18

SOURCES: *Registrar-General's Statistical Review of England and Wales, 1932*,
Tables C, D, R.

a short one had been dispelled. But it is important to note as well
that this trend was especially marked at a time when military
recruitment was still centred on the unmarried male population.
Married men were obliged to come forward for military service
only from mid 1916. It is probably unfair to suggest that marriage
was a form of draft evasion in this period, although some men may
have seen it that way. It is more likely that the upward trend in
marriages described a subtler tendency for people of all ages to
marry while they still had the chance. The Registrar-General of
England and Wales estimated that 200,000 people married in the
first phase of the war 'who in the ordinary course of events would
not have been married'. Many of these people knew that their
marriages were likely to end abruptly, but this did not dissuade
them from going ahead anyway. As in the Second World War, and
in other war situations elsewhere, the basic unit of survival in
wartime seems to have been two.

One additional feature of wartime nuptiality is of interest. The
greatest increases in marriage rates were registered in rural counties of England and Wales. This is odd, given the massive

TABLE 8.2. SOME DEMOGRAPHIC INDICATORS IN THE PERIOD OF THE FIRST WORLD
WAR, ENGLAND AND WALES, 1910–22

Year	Marriage rate	Birth rate	General fertility rate[a]	Death rate (Civilians only)	Natural increase
1910	15.0	25.1	100.7	13.5	11.6
1911	15.2	24.4	98.0	14.6	9.8
1912	15.6	24.0	96.6	13.4	10.6
1913	15.7	24.1	97.1	13.8	10.3
1914	15.9	23.8	96.2	14.0	9.8
1915	19.4	21.8	88.8	15.7	6.1
1916	14.9	21.0	85.2	14.3	6.7
1917	13.8	17.8	72.1	14.2	3.6
1918	15.3	17.7	71.1	17.3	0.4
1919	19.8	18.5	73.9	14.0	4.5
1920	20.2	25.5	101.7	12.4	13.1
1921	16.9	22.4	89.7	12.1	10.3
1922	15.7	20.4	82.1	12.8	7.6

[a] Births per 1,000 women aged 15–44.

SOURCES: *Registrar-General's Statistical Review of England and Wales, 1932*,
Tables C, D, R,
M.S. Teitelbaum, *The British Fertility Decline* (Princeton, 1984),
Table 4.A.

out-migration of rural inhabitants to staff munitions industries or
the service sector. What seems to have happened is that women
who left the land for work in wartime found husbands in the towns
and cities, but still found it desirable to marry at home. More
rural marriages, therefore, meant more rural ceremonies rather
than a real return to the land in this period.[1]

The second phase of wartime nuptiality extended from 1916 to
1918. It constituted a sharp fall in the marriage rate from the peak
of 19.4 per 1,000 in 1915 to the then lowest statistic on record –
13.8 marriages per 1,000 population – and reflects both the
mobilization of manpower and the growing casualty lists. If we
compare the 1916–18 figures not with that of 1915, but rather with
the immediate pre-war period, we can see that the decline in
nuptiality in the latter years of the war was modest, varying at a
level 10 per cent or so below the pre-war level.

The third phase of nuptiality in this period was the post-war
marriage boom, which extended from 1919 to 1921. The marriage

rate in this period was fully 30 per cent above the pre-war level, reaching 20.2 per 1,000 in 1920, when military demobilization was complete. In 1919, the most substantial rise occurred among widowers, whose remarriage rates at ages 20–45 rose by about 50 per cent. A year later, when the bulk of the army had been demobilized, bachelors registered the greatest increases in marriage rates. Previously unmarried men aged 35–45 married at a rate two-thirds above that of the pre-war period. For all bachelors, the rise was on the order of 35 per cent.[2]

It is important to note, that the post-war surge in marriages was short-lived. By the mid 1920s the marriage rate was almost identical to that of 1910–13. By the end of the decade, though, the pre-war marriage rate had been surpassed. We shall return to this subject below.

B   Birth Rates

Fluctuations in the birth rate were more severe than were variations in the marriage rate during the First World War. From a level of approximately 24 births per 1,000 population in 1910–13, the birth rate dropped 10 per cent in each of the first two years of the war. By 1917, the birth rate had descended to 17.8 per 1,000, which was the lowest on record, only to fall still further to 17.7 in the last year of the war. In aggregate terms, this meant a decline in the number of registered births from around 880,000 per year before the war to a low of 660,000 in 1918. Within this latter total, fully 6 per cent of all births were illegitimate, compared to 3 per cent before 1914. But given the decline in the overall birth rate, we should not make too much of these statistics.

Even allowing for the secular decline in fertility, it is still possible to estimate a wartime deficit of around 600,000 births in England and Wales and 70,000 in Scotland. To some observers, this meant that war losses represented only half the loss of life attributable to the war. It is this kind of reasoning which in part lay behind the surge of interest in infant health we surveyed in chapter 6.[3]

During the war itself, the seasonality of births was a function of military tactics. Eight months after the major battles there occurred small increases in the birth rate, followed by sharp decreases nine or ten months after the beginnings of the battles of

TABLE 8.3. AN INDEX OF SOME DEMOGRAPHIC INDICATORS IN THE PERIOD OF THE
FIRST WORLD WAR, ENGLAND AND WALES, 1910–22 (1910–13 = 100)

Year	Marriage rate	Birth rate	General fertility rate[a]	Death rate (Civilians only)	Natural increase
1910–13	100	100	100	100	100
1914	103	98	98	101	93
1915	126	89	91	114	58
1916	97	86	87	103	63
1917	90	73	73	103	34
1918	100	73	72	125	4
1919	129	76	75	101	43
1920	131	105	104	90	124
1921	110	92	91	88	97
1922	102	84	84	93	72

[a] Births per 1,000 women aged 15–44.

SOURCES: *Registrar-General's Statistical Review of England and Wales, 1932*,
         Tables C, D, R.;
         M. S. Teitelbaum, *The British Fertility Decline* (Princeton, 1984),
         Table 4.A.

the Somme or Passchendaele. The structure of army leave determined such movements in fertility in the course of the conflict.

As we can see in Table 8.3, the post-war baby boom was really a
'boomlet', reflecting the recovery of deferred births rather than a
change in strategies of family formation. The peak birth rate of
1920 was only 4 per cent above that of the pre-war period. In the
early 1920s, the trend in the birth rate, which had been a subject of
concern for 50 years, resumed its downward path. We shall return
to this point below.

C Death Rates and Natural Increase

We have already surveyed movements in mortality rates among
soldiers and civilians in wartime Britain (see chapters 3–4). Suffice
it to say that since fertility fell more rapidly than mortality during
the war, natural increase (births over deaths) was bound to drop
substantially. From a pre-war level of around 10 per 1,000 (or 1
per cent) natural increase was almost nil in 1918.

After the influenza epidemic of 1918–19, the secular decline of
mortality was resumed. By 1925, death rates were about 12 per
cent below pre-war levels. But the decline in the birth rate was

more rapid still, thus depressing rates of natural increase in the later 1920s well below pre-war levels. Of course, by then the interwar depression was well under way, complicating efforts to disentangle the effects of war from the effects of other economic and social changes.

D   Migration

We can see a much sharper break in the demographic history of Britain in the period of the First World War when we turn to the subject of migration. The war closed an extraordinary chapter in the history of European migration, which had drawn over 30 million people westward and overseas. In the British case, this meant the end of a period of substantial out-migration primarily to extra-European ports. In the years before 1914, the net annual loss of population due to out-migration was 200,000 or more. During the war, the pull of patriotism among expatriates and the call of enlistment, conscription, and full employment among the home populations put a stop to the population drain. After the war, a more modest outflow resumed, which is a point to which we shall return below. This subject brings us immediately to the theme of demographic discontinuities in this period of British history.

II   DISCONTINUITIES

Now that we have provided a rough sketch of the movement of vital statistics in the period of the First World War, it is time to address the question as to whether in demographic terms the war was a temporary upheaval, or whether its repercussions were longer lived.

A   The War and Marriage Patterns

First let us consider the institution of marriage. It is a commonplace that the slaughter of young men of marriageable age during the First World War deprived a generation of young women of marriage partners. Aged spinsters still point to the Great War as a catastrophe which sealed their fate, and no doubt in many cases they were right. What is more surprising, though, in a survey of nuptiality in the war period and in the interwar years is how relatively little evidence there is of an increase in celibacy in Britain. In the short term, some changes can be identified, but on the whole the marriage market was much less disturbed in Britain than in France or elsewhere on the Continent.

Indeed, the war's effects on British marriage patterns appear to have been precisely in the opposite direction. As we shall note below, the impact of war may have been to increase the popularity of marriage and to reinforce a trend towards more universal marriage at younger ages.

1   War Losses and the Age Structure of Marriage

We have noted in chapter 3 that roughly three-quarters of the men who died or were killed in the war were under age 30 and unmarried. It is logical to assume that some adjustment in marriage patterns would take place in the aftermath of the war, as a glance at the predictable and precipitate rise in the male/female sex-ratio in the age groups 20–24 and 25–29 will show. This was as true for Britain as it was for France or Germany. In 1919, there were only three German men to four German women at the prime marriageable ages of 25–29, a fact undoubtedly attributable to war losses. A similar imbalance of the order of four men to five women can be observed in the cases of France and Britain.[4]

What is most surprising about the *British* data is that celibacy rates did not rise in the post-war period. The proportion of women married at ages 25–34 is remarkably stable in the war decade in both England and Wales and Scotland. How can we account for the apparent success of British women in finding marriage partners despite the carnage of war?

In this context, it may be useful to shift our attention to France for a moment. As in so many other areas of population history, the great French demographer Louis Henry has pointed the way to a possible answer to this question. In the French case, compensation for war losses came from three sources. First, a surge of male immigration after the war augmented the pool of potential marriage partners for Frenchwomen. Secondly, surviving bachelors, widowers and divorced men married or remarried at rates well above those of the pre-war period. Thirdly, Frenchwomen started to marry men the same age as they were or younger, since the older men they would have married on the basis of pre-war patterns of nuptiality were dead. This third compensatory mechanism accounted for well over 50 per cent of the adjustment in marriage choices which lay behind the strategy Frenchwomen adopted to avoid celibacy in the aftermath of the First World War.[5]

We shall discuss the subjects of migration below, but at this point let us consider the relevance of Henry's finding to our study. We have already noted the surge in remarriages in 1919, which preceded the return to England of the bulk of the army. This seems distinctly similar to what occurred in France. But there was little similarity between the two countries with respect to the age structure of marriage in this period. In the British case, an increase in celibacy was avoided without the need for a decline in the age difference between spouses. Using age-at-marriage matrices published annually in reports of the Registrar-General of England and Wales, we have calculated the average age difference of all marriages at ages 15–49 over the period 1914–20 and 1926. Most earlier and later data for England and Wales and for Scotland are insufficiently complete to permit the construction of a longer time-series.

As is indicated in Table 8.4, the results show that the phenomenon Henry detected for France did not occur in England. In 1914 the average age difference between spouses was about two years. During the war it rose slightly, reflecting the absence of younger men in the civilian population, but by 1919 the figure dropped to 2.2 years, and then settled at 2.1 years in the post-war period. When we survey the evidence concerning specific age cohorts, the overall picture of stability in the war period is the same. Younger women who traditionally had married substantially older men continued to do so after the war; older women who, after the age of 40, had tended to marry men slightly younger than they were, also replicated this pattern in 1919 and 1920.

Two sources of the contrast between British and French behaviour may be identified. Firstly, French war losses were substantially higher than the British. The figure of 700,000 British war dead (or 15 per cent of the male population aged 15–29 in 1911) seems to have been below the 'critical mass' needed to explode pre-war patterns of nuptiality. The loss of 1.5 million Frenchmen (fully 33 per cent of the male population aged 15–29 in 1911) was sufficient to undermine 'normal' strategies of nuptiality.

TABLE 8.4. AVERAGE AGE DIFFERENCE BETWEEN MARRIAGE PARTNERS AT AGES 15–49 IN ENGLAND AND WALES, IN 1914–20 AND 1926[a]

Age	Wives								Husbands							
	1914	1915	1916	1917	1918	1919	1920	1926	1914	1915	1916	1917	1918	1919	1920	1926
15	10.0	7.8	9.2	6.9	9.8	6.9	6.9	6.4	–	–	–	–	–	–	–	–
16	5.4	6.6	6.7	6.0	6.2	6.4	6.0	5.4	-1.5	-2.6	-3.1	-2.4	-3.3	-2.5	-2.2	-2.1
17	4.8	5.2	5.2	5.4	4.9	5.0	4.8	4.7	-1.7	-2.0	-1.8	-2.0	-2.1	-2.0	-2.0	-1.5
18	4.1	4.1	4.4	4.4	4.4	4.4	4.2	4.1	-0.9	-0.7	-1.2	-1.4	-1.5	-1.4	-1.3	-1.0
19	3.6	3.8	4.0	4.0	4.0	3.8	3.7	3.7	-0.5	-0.7	-0.8	-0.8	-1.0	-0.9	-0.8	-0.5
20	3.3	3.5	3.7	3.7	3.7	3.6	3.4	3.4	-0.2	-0.4	-0.5	-0.5	-0.6	-0.5	-0.5	-0.2
21	3.0	3.0	3.2	3.3	3.3	3.2	3.0	3.0	0.0	-0.1	-0.2	-0.2	-0.3	-0.2	-0.2	0.0
22	2.8	2.7	2.9	3.1	3.0	2.9	2.7	2.7	0.3	0.1	0.2	0.1	0.1	0.1	0.2	0.4
23	2.4	2.4	2.6	2.7	2.7	2.7	2.4	2.4	0.5	0.4	0.5	0.5	0.5	0.5	0.5	0.7
24	2.2	2.1	2.3	2.4	2.4	2.5	2.2	2.2	0.7	0.7	0.8	0.8	0.8	0.8	0.8	0.9
25	1.9	1.7	2.0	2.2	2.2	2.3	2.0	1.9	1.0	1.0	1.1	1.2	1.1	1.1	1.1	1.2
26	1.5	1.5	1.8	2.0	1.9	2.1	1.7	1.6	1.4	1.4	1.5	1.6	1.6	1.5	1.5	1.5
27	1.3	1.2	1.6	1.8	1.8	1.9	1.5	1.4	1.8	1.8	1.9	2.0	2.0	1.9	1.9	1.9
28	1.1	1.0	1.4	1.6	1.6	1.7	1.4	1.5	2.1	2.1	2.2	2.4	2.5	2.2	2.2	2.4
29	1.0	0.9	1.4	1.6	1.5	1.6	1.2	1.0	2.5	2.5	2.7	2.7	2.8	2.6	2.6	2.7
30	0.8	0.8	1.4	1.5	1.6	1.5	1.1	1.1	2.8	2.8	3.0	3.2	3.2	3.0	3.0	3.2
31	0.7	0.6	1.2	1.5	1.5	1.5	1.0	1.1	3.2	3.2	3.4	3.5	3.6	3.3	3.4	3.6
32	0.5	0.5	1.1	1.5	1.6	1.2	0.8	1.0	3.8	3.6	3.8	4.1	4.2	3.9	3.8	4.0
33	0.7	0.3	1.1	1.4	1.5	1.1	0.8	0.9	3.8	3.8	4.1	4.5	4.6	4.1	4.1	4.4
34	0.2	-0.1	0.8	1.1	1.2	0.9	0.3	0.6	4.4	4.2	4.4	4.8	4.8	4.5	4.6	4.9

35	0.0	−0.1	0.7	1.0	1.3	0.9	0.5	0.6	4.7	4.6	4.7	5.2	5.4	5.0	5.0	5.3
36	−0.2	0.0	0.5	0.7	1.0	0.6	0.5	0.4	5.1	4.8	5.2	5.6	5.7	5.2	5.3	5.6
37	−0.3	−0.3	0.2	0.8	0.8	0.5	0.3	0.2	5.3	5.1	5.3	6.0	6.0	5.3	5.6	5.8
38	−0.3	−0.6	0.0	0.6	0.7	−0.5	−0.1	0.0	5.7	5.3	5.5	6.0	6.2	5.7	6.1	6.5
39	−0.1	−1.0	−0.1	0.4	0.4	−1.0	−0.3	0.0	5.5	5.4	5.8	6.1	6.5	5.7	6.1	6.5
40	−1.4	−1.2	−0.6	−0.2	0.3	−1.0	−0.6	−0.7	6.0	6.0	6.2	6.7	7.0	6.2	6.8	7.3
41	−1.3	−1.5	−0.6	−0.4	0.2	−1.2	−0.7	−0.8	6.7	6.0	6.4	6.7	7.0	6.6	6.9	7.2
42	−2.0	−1.8	−1.2	−0.9	−0.3	−1.4	−1.5	−1.3	7.3	6.6	6.8	7.7	7.6	6.9	7.1	7.8
43	−1.9	−1.9	−0.9	−0.6	−0.4	−1.9	−1.4	−1.6	7.5	6.8	7.1	8.1	8.1	7.1	7.5	7.9
44	−2.3	−3.0	−1.9	−1.5	−0.8	−2.2	−1.9	−1.6	7.8	7.3	7.8	8.3	8.2	8.0	8.2	8.1
45	−3.1	−3.3	−2.6	−2.4	−1.6	−2.7	−2.5	−2.5	8.8	8.3	8.1	8.9	8.7	8.6	8.5	8.7
46	−4.0	−4.0	−3.4	−2.6	−2.1	−3.4	−2.6	−2.5	8.7	8.1	8.8	9.5	9.0	8.8	9.2	9.4
47	−3.7	−4.0	−3.8	−3.0	−2.7	−3.5	−3.4	−3.5	9.7	8.7	9.1	9.6	9.7	9.3	9.6	9.5
48	−5.1	−5.0	−4.4	−4.0	−3.2	−4.2	−4.1	−3.9	10.1	9.0	9.7	10.0	10.2	10.4	10.1	10.3
49	−5.3	−5.1	−5.0	−4.7	−4.1	−5.2	−4.5	−4.9	9.8	9.7	10.1	10.8	10.6	10.9	10.6	10.8
15–49	2.0	1.9	2.2	2.4	2.4	2.2	2.1	2.1	2.2	1.9	2.0	2.4	2.4	2.2	2.1	2.1

a. + = husbands older;
 − = wives older.

SOURCES: *Registrar-General's Annual Report for England and Wales*, 1914–1920, 1926, Table on Ages of Persons Married in 1914–1920, 1926.

Second, we must note the sharp divergence between the pre-war age structure of marriage in France and in Britain. In the pre-1914 period, roughly 55 per cent of all Frenchwomen chose marriage partners aged between 5 and 15 years older than themselves. In Britain only 35 per cent did so. It is this substantial age difference which was reduced sharply after the war. What occurred in France as a result of the war had already happened in this country prior to 1914. British women were already prepared to marry men of roughly the same age, or (after age 35 or so) men younger than they were, and they continued to do so throughout the period surrounding the war.

Another source of the distinction between British and French nuptiality in this period may lie in the contrasting social composition of casualties in the two countries. The French agrarian labour force and the British white-collar labour force both suffered disproportionately high casualties.[6] In the French case, an adjustment in notions of the appropriate age difference between marriage partners helped to keep celibacy rates down. In the British case, it seems more likely that a change in middle-class notions of the appropriate social distance between marriage partners may have achieved the same end.

There are a number of indications that in Britain marriage across geographical and social lines increased after 1914. The sheer physical mobility of the population increased the pool of potential marriage partners available to women during and after the war. We have noted above the tendency for marriage rates in wartime to rise in rural areas, indicating that women recruited into war industry or commerce in urban areas still returned home to be married during the war. The same phenomenon is reflected in data on the increasing geographical distance between the homes of brides and grooms in rural West Sussex during the war.[7]

The war may have also reduced the social distance between potential marriage partners. Because of the much higher death rates among middle-class men and their social superiors who served in the war, many middle-class women may have had to change their ideas of who was a socially acceptable marriage partner in order to find a husband. For some of them, loyalty to pre-war social prejudices meant spinsterhood. This they avoided by 'cohort raiding' across social divisions just as Frenchwomen avoided it by 'cohort raiding' across age divisions.

2   War and the Popularity of Marriage

While the age structure of marriage in Britain was unaffected by the war, in other respects it is apparent that the war decade was a period of discontinuity in the history of nuptiality in Britain. As John Hajnal has shown, one of the most striking features of the history of marriage in Britain between 1900 and 1939 was the increasing popularity of marriage. Using nuptiality tables (which are like life tables in that they describe the risk not of dying at any age but of marrying at any age, given the age-specific marriage rates of a population), Hajnal reached the following conclusions. Under the nuptiality conditions that obtained before the First World War, roughly 13 per cent of all males and 19 per cent of all females never married.[8] In the interwar years, celibacy declined substantially. By 1938, the figures had dropped to 7 per cent for males and 10 per cent for females who remained unmarried throughout their child-bearing years. The years surrounding the 1914–18 war constitute a clear break from earlier trends, in which the proportion of the population which never married had increased between 1881 and 1911.[9]

The war decade also separates two phases of the history of English nuptiality in a second and related way. Between 1881 and 1911 the average age of first marriage for women rose from 25.3 to 26.3 years. Thereafter, the average age of first marriage for women declined, reaching 25.7 in 1931. This was slightly higher than the figure registered for 1851.[10] There was less variation in the average age at marriage for men throughout this period.[11] The inescapable conclusion is that a greater proportion of the British population were marrying after the war than before it, and that they were doing so at younger ages in the 1920s and 1930s than in the preceding decades.

These changes can be illustrated in another way. An index of fertility-related trends has been derived from the experience of a Protestant sect, the Hutterites, whose fertility schedule is the highest on record. The behaviour of Hutterites married in the period 1921–30 thus serves as a convenient benchmark for purposes of comparison over time and space.[12] We shall refer to these indices with respect to marital fertility below, but in this context, it is useful to employ the index I(m), which uses Hutterite data to establish a standard of female nuptiality in a community with very high proportions married. I(m) may be defined as 'a weighted

TABLE 8.5. AN INDEX OF PROPORTIONS MARRIED [I (m)] FOR SOME EUROPEAN COUNTRIES, 1881–1931

Year	England and Wales	Scotland	Belgium[a]	France	Germany[b]	Italy
1881	0.501	0.438	0.435	0.538	0.501	0.549
1891	0.477	0.420	0.436	0.540	0.497	0.549
1901	0.476	0.425	0.479	0.543	0.513	0.549
1911	0.479	0.428	0.517	0.591	0.524	0.534
1921	0.489	0.433	0.501	0.534	–	0.495
1931	0.503	0.441	0.602	0.613	0.583	0.513

[a] Data for 1880, 1890, 1900, 1910, 1920, 1930.
[b] Data for 1880, 1890, 1900, 1910, and 1939.
SOURCE: M. S. Teitelbaum, *The British Fertility Decline* (1984), Table 5.4.

average of the proportion married, in which the weights are the fertility rates of the standard fertility of Hutterite married women in the years 1921–30'.[13] This index shows a similar reversal of direction in the period surrounding the First World War. Whereas I(m) for England and Wales had declined from 0.501 in 1881 to 0.479 in 1911, it rose thereafter to 0.489 in 1921 and 0.503 in 1931. The same pre-war downward slope and post-war upward slope can be discerned in the Scottish data.[14]

Table 8.5 presents data on I(m) for other combatant countries in the period surrounding the war. What these statistics demonstrate is that there is no uniform pattern of change in European nuptiality in the period of the Great War. In the cases of France and Belgium, I(m) rose from 1881–1911, fell in the war decade, and then continued its pre-war upward trend. In Italy, I(m) was unchanged between 1881 and 1901, fell slightly in both 1911 and 1921 and then rose in the post-war years. Unfortunately, the absence of data on Germany in 1920 precludes direct comparison, but it is clear that in Germany I(m) was rising well before the war. Since France and Italy both experienced combat on their own soil, and since the toll of war deaths was greater among Continental combatants than in Britain, we should not be too surprised by the contrast between a rise in I(m) over the war decade for Britain and a decline over the same period for France and Italy.

In Britain the growing propensity to marry was a striking feature of the demographic history of interwar Britain. But it is important to note the exceptional position of those age cohorts particularly decimated by war losses. The men who suffered the heaviest casualties during the war were born between 1892 and 1900 and were aged between 14 and 22 in 1914. This cohort was substantially smaller than those of younger or older men, born in the late 1880s or after 1900, who were too old or too young to have born the brunt of war losses. Consequently, the supply of marriageable women available to this reduced cohort was relatively abundant. Celibacy rates for what we may term the male war generation were therefore relatively low, a fact which we can see in the 1930s, when this age group was aged 30–39. As these men aged, they were replaced in the 30–39 age group by men 'relative to whose number the supply of marriageable women was not so plentiful'. Thus the proportions married in these male age groups – and only in these age groups – declined slightly during the 1930s. Not surprisingly, exactly the opposite pattern may be discerned with respect to women born between 1894 and 1902, from which most of the male war generation would choose their wives. But this is a feature of the ageing of a decimated cohort rather than a characteristic of the population as a whole.[15]

The aggregate trend is much clearer: in 1911, about 24 per cent of all women in England and Wales aged 20–24 were married; ten years later, the figure had risen to 27.4 per cent, and had reached 34.4 per cent by 1939. Similar evidence of earlier and more universal marriage may be detected for the male population over this period as well.[16] This seems to indicate a growing preference for what demographers call 'neo-Malthusian' restraints, related to contraceptive practice, as opposed to older 'Malthusian' restraints on population growth, related to the age at marriage.

3 War and the Divorce Rate
It is an intriguing feature of the war period that it occasioned not only a decrease in celibacy rates but also an increase in recourse to divorce. A glance at the statistics will show that the number of petitions filed for dissolution or nullity and the divorce rate soared during the 1914–18 war. In 1913 approximately 1,000 petitions were filed for divorce in England and Wales, yielding a divorce rate of about 2 per 10,000 married women aged 15–49. Six years later, at the end of the war, over 5,000 petitions were filed, increasing the divorce rate to 9 per 10,000 women. While these numbers are still relatively low, it is still true that the war years

mark a divide in the history of divorce which indicates its growing social acceptance.

There were three reasons why this occurred. The first is administrative: changes in legal aid or poor persons' procedure in 1914 made it possible for many working people to afford divorce proceedings. The second is also related to cost: higher incomes among working-class men and women also gave them sufficient funds to contemplate the material costs of divorce and of an independent life without their spouses. The third is a function of the wartime marriage boom noted above. It must have been the case that many hasty and disastrously inappropriate unions were consecrated in the rush to the altar in 1915. When these men came home from the army, many married people must have realized the mistake they had made. For some veterans, their wives' adultery was more than a soldier's cliché; hence the increase in husbands' petitions for divorce at the end of the war. But for whatever reason, it is clear that more people were both getting into and out of marriages after the First World War than before 1914.[17]

4   Domesticity and the Upheaval of War
It is not so easy, however, to account for fluctuations in overall nuptiality in this period. For this question requires us to confront the classic conundrum embedded in all writing on the consequences of the Great War. Were these changes caused by the war or did they merely coincide with it?

There are five lines of inquiry that may provide clues to the answer. Four are related to domestic events; the fifth, which we shall discuss below, is related to international migration. Let us deal initially with internal British developments. The first concerns the war experience itself. It is possible that the wartime and post-war 'marriage boom' set a pattern for a society which came to place a higher value on domesticity in the midst of international chaos. If families were seen as some kind of 'haven in a heartless world',[18] then it is possible that the slaughter of so many young men led their contemporaries in greater numbers to accept both the burdens and the benefits of family life. Certainly the thrust of much pro-natalist propaganda which we noted in chapter 6 was in precisely this direction.

A second possibility is that celibacy declined because of the demobilization of the war economy and the onset of the interwar depression. On the whole, female workers new to industrial employment went home after the Armistice. And given the rise in long-term unemployment after mid 1920, most could not have returned to their jobs even if they had wanted to do so. Especially in working-class households, marriage in the interwar years was the only way out of the uncomfortable position of unemployed female dependence on limited family resources.

Thirdly, by opening up new areas of white-collar work for women, the war helped to reduce the proportion of the female labour force in domestic service. After 1914, the wider opportunities, better pay and less demanding duties of office or factory work compared to a life in service increasingly drew women away from what had been traditionally a late-marrying occupation.

A fourth possibility is that the marriage rate increased with the extension of social provision. A marriage certificate was of considerable economic value during and after the war. For example, women who were married to insured workers and were themselves employed during the war received a double maternity benefit upon delivery of their children. They would also have had little trouble qualifying for separation allowances or other war-related payments.

One bizarre example from the post-war period may illustrate this point. Private A. Loosemore won the Victoria Cross for conspicuous bravery during combat in the Ypres salient in 1917. His record was remarkable, even given the high standards of the time. During the episode for which he was decorated, he was severely wounded. He returned to England, married his childhood sweetheart, but unfortunately died of war wounds three years after the Armistice. When his widow applied for a pension, she was shocked to learn that she was ineligible. The reasoning was astounding, yet irrefutable. The Ministry of Pensions held that had Loosemore married his girlfriend in 1914, and then had gone on to bravery and death, she would have been entitled to a pension. But they had married after he had been wounded, and therefore the applicant had made a contract with a damaged bridegroom, in full knowledge of the state of his health. The state would live up to its obligation to support those who had been dependants before the war, but it would not accept the claims of those who waited a bit too long before sealing the marriage bond. Administrative rulings of such appalling insensitivity made it apparent that delaying marriage had its costs in the period of the First World War.[19]

The main reason why these suggestions must remain tentative is that they apply just as forcefully to European populations, some of which registered rises in celibacy in contrast to the British case. While it would be foolish to ignore the factors discussed above, it is probably best to place greater emphasis on the one aspect of demographic history indisputably changed by the war – international migration.

B International Migration and the War

The years immediately prior to the outbreak of the First World War were years of heavy out-migration from the British Isles. In the years 1911–14, migration between Britain and extra-European destinations produced a net loss to Britain of over 1 million people. To a certain extent, immigration from European ports compensated for this exodus, but the flow of traffic was still overwhelmingly one-way – out of the British Isles. For example, in 1913, there was a net gain of 120,000 immigrants from Europe, but a net loss of 329,000 emigrants to extra-European destinations. The net loss of population due to all international migratory flows in 1911–13 varied between 200,000 and 240,000 people (Table 8.6).

Between 1914 and 1918, the flow of out-migration was reduced to a trickle. This was in part a reflection of the zeal of expatriates, who rushed back to the motherland to join in the fight. In 1914, immigrants exceeded emigrants by over 100,000 people, a clear reversal of pre-war trends. Over the next four years, migratory flows were small and virtually cancelled each other out. For example, in 1916 a net loss of 7,000 emigrants to Europe was offset by a net gain of 5,000 immigrants from extra-European ports.

After 1918, out-migration resumed, but this time as a small stream rather than the flood which characterized the pre-war period. The net loss of population due to out-migration was about half that of the years before 1914 (see Table 8.1).[20]

Let us assume for a moment that the war did not take place and that the balance of out-migration registered in 1911–13 was maintained in the following five years. Of course, this is an unlikely proposition, given that migration is a cyclical phenomenon. But solely for the purposes of argument, let us posit a steady state of out-migration. This counterfactual exercise suggests that, in the

TABLE 8.6. NET MIGRATION FROM THE UNITED KINGDOM, 1911–21 (THOUSANDS)

Year	To and from Europe			Extra European		
	Inward	Outward	Net inward	Inward	Outward	Net inward
1911	1,115	1,083	32	350	623	−273
1912	1,150	1,075	75	341	657	−316
1913	1,310	1,184	126	373	702	−329
1914	1,054	854	200	360	451	−91
1915	447	432	15	147	127	20
1916	212	219	−7	99	94	5
1917	182	202	−20	34	28	6
1918	171	189	−18	26	23	3
1919	425	570	−145	194	202	−8
1920	725	739	−14	284	438	−154
1921	861	836	25	228	378	−150

SOURCE: N. H. Carrier and J. R. Jeffery, *External Migration. A Study of the Available Statistics 1815–1950* (1953), General Register Office Studies in Medical and Population Subjects no. 6, Table B(1).

absence of war, the net loss of population due to emigration might have been about 1 million people. In chapter 3, we estimated that male mortality in wartime exceeded 'normal' mortality by about 637,000 (see pp. 81–2). It is clear, therefore, that population loss through out-migration in the pre-war period was substantially greater than population loss through military combat between 1914 and 1918.

Pre-war out-migration had a direct bearing on nuptiality because of the peculiar sex-ratio and age structure of migrants. It is extremely difficult to speak of the 'typical' migrant in Edwardian Britain, but if there was such a person, he was male, unmarried, and between the ages of 18 and 30. As we can see in Table 8.7, about half of all male emigrants were in this prime marriageable age group.

These data show a clear discontinuity between the age structures of international migrants before and after the war. After 1918, a smaller proportion of both male and female emigrants was in the 18–30 age group, and a much larger proportion was in the post-30s cohorts. For example, the over-30s constituted about 29 per cent of male emigrants and 32 per cent of female emigrants in 1912–13.

TABLE 8.7. AGE STRUCTURE OF MIGRANTS, ENGLAND AND WALES, 1912–29:
PROPORTION OF MIGRANTS IN SELECTED AGE GROUPS

Age group	1912–13	1920	1921–3	1924–9	1912–13	1920	1921–3	1924–9
	Male emigrants				*Male immigrants*			
All	10,000	10,000	10,000	10,000	10,000	10,000	10,000	10,000
Under 12	1,762	1,749	1,511	1,506	1,384	2,126	1,925	1,798
12–17	613	626	804	1,203	180	337	354	381
18–20			765	908			316	386
21–25	4,720	3,929	1,851	1,912	3,844	2,254	972	1,245
26–30			1,497	1,414			1,246	1,405
31–45	2,293	2,688	2,557	2,123	3,319	3,341	3,147	2,796
46+	611	1,009	1,015	933	1,273	1,942	2,040	1,990
	Female emigrants				*Female immigrants*			
All	10,000	10,000	10,000	10,000	10,000	10,000	10,000	10,000
Under 12	2,124	1,605	1,716	1,714	2,021	2,094	1,846	1,732
12–17	589	547	584	669	338	404	406	411
18–20			445	497			262	280
21–25	4,043	3,798	1,365	1,342	3,409	2,328	920	847
26–30			1,628	1,636			1,403	1,424
31–45	2,465	2,839	2,902	2,777	2,936	3,340	3,157	3,155
46+	779	1,210	1,361	1,365	1,296	1,833	2,006	2,150

SOURCE: N. H. Carrier and J. R. Jeffery, *External Migration, A Study of the Available Statistics 1815–1950* (1953), General Register Office Studies in Medical and Population Subjects no. 6.

By 1920 about 37 per cent of all male emigrants and 40 per cent of all female emigrants were in this age group. Immigrants to Britain were also on average older after the war than before it.

This change in the age structure of migration is one important reason why the concentration of British war losses in the prime marriageable age groups under age 30 did not undermine British marriage patterns. During the war out-migration virtually ceased, and after the Armistice the revival of migration drew fewer young unmarried men out of the British population.

As the 1920s went on, the flow of migrants was reduced in part due to political developments. Before the war, British migrants left this country for many destinations, but the attraction of the United States was unsurpassed. Brinley Thomas has described the links between the United States and Britain before 1914 as forming a kind of Atlantic economy. Rhythms of capital movements and migratory flows in Britain were intimately tied to American economic development.[21] After the First World War, many of those ties were loosened, and some were broken. American immigration controls were introduced from 1921, but they were not fully effective until the late 1920s. Such restrictions did give British immigrants precedence over those from eastern or southern Europe, but it was apparent at the time that the heyday of mass migration to the United States was at an end.

There was some shift in destination among those determined to leave Britain in any case; some of the American decrease became increases for Australia, Canada and New Zealand. By 1926, about half of the outward balance of extra-European migration of British citizens was accounted for by settlement in Australia, versus only about 25 per cent to the Antipodes in the pre-war years. Many of these newcomers benefited from the British government's Free Passage Scheme, designed to help ex-soldiers and their families get a new start abroad. Further assistance came in the form of the Empire Settlement Act of 1922, which authorized up to £3.5 million expenditure per year to help populate the overseas dominions. However, the hopes of a revival of emigration were short-lived, as the economic instability of the interwar years limited the absorptive capacity of the economies of receiver states.[22]

It is of course futile to try to explain trends in nuptiality by reference to any one phenomenon. We know too little about the workings of local marriage markets and about the effects of internal migration on nuptiality to do more than suggest tentative conclusions. In addition, there were two wartime developments which complicate this discussion considerably. The first is the influenza epidemic. As we have noted above, its age incidence was highly unusual (see p. 121). Case-fatality rates were highest among the 15–35 age group, thus reducing both the male and female populations at prime marriageable ages. The second was the Irish rebellion, leading in 1922 to independence for the Irish Free State, made up of all but six counties of Ireland. What are euphemistically known as the 'troubles' surrounding Irish politics in this period were bound to have an effect on the substantial (but unquantifiable) population flows across the Irish sea. The relatively free movement of Irishmen and women to and from Britain complicates population estimates to this day and provides another reason for caution in an account of migration in the period under review.

With these qualifications in mind, two inferences may be drawn from the evidence presented here. First, after 1914 a greater proportion of the British population remained in this country than had done so in the pre-war period. And secondly, those younger age groups which had been substantially reduced by out-migration before the war were less depleted in the 1920s. In consequence, the population with a 'high risk' of marriage increased after the war, thus accounting in part for the rise in nuptiality in the interwar years.

III CONTINUITIES

When we turn from nuptiality and migration to questions of fertility and mortality in Britain in the period of the First World War, we see the continuation of pre-war trends rather than any major discontinuities. On the one hand, the decline in fertility was uninterrupted by the war. On the other hand, as we have already remarked, the fact that mortality rates continued to decline in wartime is evidence of the strength of Britain's wartime economy as a whole, and of the benefits it offered in particular to the poorest sections of the population. Those gains were not reversed in the post-war years.

A Fertility Trends

We have noted above the utility of an index of nuptiality derived from the experience of the Hutterites in the period 1921–30. Demographers have also derived from data on this sect a number of indices of fertility, which permit a comparison of the flow of births in any given population with that registered by a community with the highest fertility on record. Using these indices, it is apparent that the First World War made little impression on the decline of fertility in Britain. Overall fertility [I (f)] declined by about 10 per cent in each decade from 1901 to 1931. Overall fertility is composed of marital and extra-marital fertility, fluctuations of which can also be compared to the Hutterite standard. Thus, while illegitimate fertility [I (h)] dropped only slightly in both 1901–10 and in the war decade, marital fertility [I (g)] fell by the same rate in 1911–20 as in 1901–10 or 1921–30[23] (see Table 8.8).

TABLE 8.8. AN INDEX OF OVERALL FERTILITY, MARITAL FERTILITY, AND
EXTRA-MARITAL FERTILITY IN ENGLAND AND WALES AND SCOTLAND, 1901–31

| Year | England & Wales | | | Scotland | | |
	Overall fertility [I(f)]	Marital fertility [I(g)]	Extra-marital fertility [I(h)]	Overall fertility [I(f)]	Marital fertility [I(g)]	Extra-marital fertility [I(h)]
1901	0.273	0.553	0.021	0.288	0.632	0.033
1911	0.234	0.467	0.019	0.260	0.565	0.031
1921	0.193	0.375	0.018	0.224	0.480	0.028
1931	0.154	0.292	0.014	0.193	0.404	0.024

SOURCE: Teitelbaum, *The British Fertility Decline*, Tables 4.3, 6.1, 6.8.

It is apparent that the increase in nuptiality described above did not yield an increase in fertility in the period surrounding the war. While proportionately more men and women were prepared to marry after the war than before it, they did so at a time when recourse to contraception was becoming more universal. It is possible that the distribution of rubber sheaths among soldiers in the First World War, as a protection against venereal disease, helped popularize contraception among some men. The wartime increase in female employment, which required substantial internal migration, may have exposed more women to currents of opinion or propaganda favourable to contraception. But whatever the source, it is clear that more couples were using contraceptives after the war than before it. In a survey conducted for the Royal Commission on Population after the Second World War, Lewis-Faning found that while 16 per cent of women married before 1910 said they used birth control during their married life, fully 41 per cent of those married in 1910–19 and 59 per cent of those married in 1920–4 did so.[24] These trends may have been accelerated by wartime developments, but their origins lie well before 1914. Greater recourse to contraception among the unmarried also explains why the illegitimate birth rate, which rose during the war, continued its downward trend in the interwar years.

B Mortality Trends

Despite the onset of the interwar depression in 1920, the post-war history of mortality in Britain is largely one of the perpetuation of pre-war trends. Life expectancy at birth for men increased from 49 in 1911 to 56 years in 1921, and this gain was roughly the same as that in the preceding and succeeding decades. That this was so is somewhat surprising, given the extremely high unemployment rates of this period and the undoubted deprivation that long-term joblessness inflicted on the working population.

Demographic change is never a simple reflex of economic change. It is therefore impossible to reduce the decline of mortality to a function of the trade cycle in this or in any other period. Still, there are several ways in which we can link changes in material conditions to the persistence of mortality decline. The first is that war-related extensions of social provision were not dismantled after the Armistice. The most important of these measures was unemployment insurance, extended to all workers in munitions production during the war, and to virtually the entire workforce in 1920. Many other measures, such as rent control, health insurance and the belated appearance of council housing, all helped blunt the force of the interwar trade cycle.

The second is that while wage levels dropped substantially after the war, so did prices, and in particular food prices. For many of those who kept their jobs, the interwar years were a period of stable or rising real wages in Britain. This was especially so for unskilled workers, who benefited most from the levelling up of low wages in the war years.

This was why Bowley and Hogg came to an affirmative answer to the question posed in the title of their 1925 study *Has Poverty Diminished*? They surveyed conditions in five towns, the inhabitants of which had formed the object of a pre-war study of poverty, and found that the number whose income was insufficient to keep them above a conventional poverty line had diminished by half over the war decade. One-third of the improvement was attributable to declining fertility rates, which meant more food per family member. But two-thirds of the change was due to a rise in the wages of the worst-paid, and they noted 'It has needed a war to do it, . . .'[25]

In this context, it is important to note that the wartime gains in real wages and nutritional levels which we outlined in chapter 7 probably had a shadow effect on survival rates in the post-war decades. In other words, better nutrition among women and children in wartime helped increase their resistance to diseases contracted in later years. The unplanned wartime improvements in living standards which were particularly important among the families of unskilled workers meant higher recovery rates and lower mortality rates in the subsequent generation. And this lesson was not lost on those who ran the war economy of 1939–45. It is therefore clear that the two periods in this century were, ironically enough, occasions for major improvements in the health and well-being of the civilian population.[26]

IV PENSIONERS, WIDOWS AND A 'BURNT-OUT GENERATION'?

There is one other area in which the question of the long-term effects of the war on mortality rates was posed in later years. It was over the question as to whether ex-servicemen – both those injured and those unscathed by combat – constituted a 'burnt-out generation' subject to higher mortality rates than those who did not see active service in the 1914–18 war.

But before addressing this question, let us survey briefly the statistics on the proportion of the population in receipt of war pensions. The first claimants on the state were the families of the men who died in the war. By March 1919, approximately 190,000 widows' pensions and 10,000 orphans' pensions had been granted. In total, benefits were provided to approximately 350,000 children whose fathers had died in the war (see Table 8.9).

A substantially larger population of about 1.2 million men – or about one-quarter of the total who served in the war – were entitled to disability pensions. Two-thirds of these pensions were granted to men whose disability was deemed to be minor, such as the loss of fingers or toes, which constituted a rating of 30 per cent disablement or less. A much smaller number – about 40,000 – received pensions on the basis of their total or near-total disability. This was defined as including those who suffered the loss of two limbs, both eyes, both feet, or who were totally paralysed, permanently bedridden, suffering from severe facial disfigurement, lunacy, or incurable disease. As we can see in Table 8.10, officers were disproportionately represented in the higher disablement classes.

While the single largest category of causes of disability was wounds and amputations, the data in Table 8.11 show that disease

TABLE 8.9. PENSIONS GRANTED TO DEPENDANTS OF BRITISH MEN WHO DIED ON
ACTIVE SERVICE IN THE FIRST WORLD WAR

Family status of widow	Pensions granted:			Total children
	to 31.3.17	to 31.3.18	to 31.3.19	
Childless	13,033	14,587	16,896	–
One child	18,560	16,698	18,717	53,975
Two children	14,354	11,998	12,680	78,064
Three children	9,875	7,460	7,511	74,538
Four children	6,295	4,377	4,328	60,000
Five children	3,556	2,467	2,189	41,060
Six children or more	2,596	1,729	1,391	36,969
Total	68,269	59,316	63,712	344,606

Total widows' pensions granted to 31.3.19	192,678[a]		
Pensions granted to orphans to 31.3.19	10,605	Total children whose fathers died at war	355,211
Total married soldiers who died during the war	203,283	As % of all who died at war	28.1
Total bachelors who died	519,502		

[a] Includes: 338 pensions to separated wives and 1,403 temporary pensions.

SOURCE: Ministry of Pensions, *Second Annual Report, PP 1920, XIV, Cmd 19.*

accounted for a majority of pensionable disabilities. A soldier who contracted tuberculosis or malaria on active service could not be sure when he would suffer a recrudescence of his condition. It is reasonable to suggest that the afflictions some ex-soldiers bore shortened their lives either directly or indirectly by reducing their resistance to other endemic diseases.

In the 1930s the British Legion tried to stir up public interest in this question. In 1936, the Legion appointed a committee to investigate the problems of those they saw as prematurely aged ex-servicemen. Two years later, this committee asked the Prime Minister to consider broadening pensions benefits for veterans to cover those suffering from 'latent results of service', whether or not they had been wounded or disabled by illness while on active service. The Government Actuary advised Chamberlain that it was impossible to compare rigorously the morbidity and mortality experience of men who served in the 1914–18 war and men who

275

TABLE 8.10 PENSIONS GRANTED TO BRITISH MEN SUFFERING FROM WAR DISABILITIES AS OF MARCH 1921, ACCORDING TO DEGREE OF DISABILITY

Category	% Disablement	Injury	Officers	Ranks	Total
I.	100	Loss of two limbs; leg and eye; both feet; total paralysis; lunacy; permanently bedridden; severe facial disfigurement; incurable disease	3,400	33,000	36,400
II.	90	Amputation of arm	50	3,000	3,050
III.	80	Amputation of leg; facial disfigurement; loss of speech	1,000	20,000	21,000
IV.	70	Partial leg or arm amputation (severe)	1,100	29,000	30,100
V.	60	Partial leg or arm amputation (moderately severe)	1,900	49,000	50,900
VI.	50	Partial leg or arm amputation (less severe)	3,800	98,000	101,800
VII.	40	Loss of fingers or toes, or right thumb	4,450	126,000	130,450
VIII.	30	Loss of fingers or toes (less severe), or thumb of left hand	8,950	238,000	246,950
IX.	20	Loss of two fingers or toes	12,800	554,000	566,800
		All categories	37,450	1,150,000	1,187,450

SOURCE: *International Labour Organization, Studies and Reports, Series E, No.4, Compensation for War Disabilities in Great Britain and the United States* (Geneva, 1921), appendix 4.

TABLE 8.11. CAUSES OF DISABILITY AMONG BRITISH FIRST WORLD WAR PENSIONERS

Disability	Number of cases	% of all disabilities
1. Wounds and amputations	324,722	38.0
2. Tuberculosis	65,370	7.6
3. Respiratory diseases	55,383	6.5
4. Organic diseases of the heart	31,502	3.7
5. Functional diseases of the heart	44,855	5.2
6. Neurasthenia	58,402	6.8
7. Malaria	44,749	5.2
8. Rheumatism	33,908	4.0
9. Ear diseases	23,772	2.7
10. Psychoses	13,030	1.5
11. Dysentery	8,025	0.9
12. Nephritis	15,837	1.8
13. Other causes	135,933	15.9
All disabilities	855,488	100.0
of which	80,000	died of war-related conditions or diseases
	229,034	remained seriously disabled (categories I-VII above 30% disablement in 1929.

SOURCE: T. J. Mitchell and G.M. Smith, *Medical Services: Casualties and Medical Statistics of the Great War* (1931), p. 349.

did not. Consequently, the Chamberlain government declined to set up an official inquiry to examine the question as to whether ex-servicemen who were not disabled during the war nonetheless showed an increased propensity to ill-health, premature ageing and early death.[27]

In political terms, there the question rested. But it does raise an issue of relevance to the demographic history of the war. It is, of course, impossible to be precise about the effects of military service on the future health of men who served without contracting illness or receiving a wound. Even among the 1.5 million men who had been ill or wounded in uniform, it was terribly difficult in many instances to say whether the disability in question was war-related or not. Many widows suffered from an adverse decision by the Ministry of Pensions that their husbands had 'died of a disability of which a continuous medical history has not been shown from the termination of active service in the war, and which cannot be certified as attributable to or aggravated by such service'.[28]

This viewpoint no doubt made legal and financial sense to the Ministry concerned, but was it the truth? We shall probably never know, for it is impossible to prove that the men who served had on average a lower life expectancy than those who did not serve. Still, there is at least one set of data which provides evidence consistent with the view that long-term military service had costs which the Ministry of Pensions never recognized.

Let us briefly examine data on the sex ratio of mortality over the years 1896–1948. In nearly every age group, female mortality rates declined more rapidly than male mortality rates in the first half of the twentieth century. The age group in which the differential grew most substantially over this period was aged 45–75 in 1948. These men had been aged 15–45 during the war period, and formed the bulk of the survivors of the war. All we can do is to raise the possibility that war service may have been related to the widening of the sex difference of mortality in these particular age groups. Of course, other behavioural factors – such as smoking and the consumption of alcoholic beverages – are undoubtedly reflected in this phenomenon. Furthermore, the appearance of prontosil and other sulfa drugs by the late 1940s helped improve women's health in particular by reducing maternal mortality in a spectacular fashion. It is apparent therefore, that no strong inferences from these data may be drawn. Still, it would be foolish to neglect completely the question of the lingering aftermath of military service in the life history of the male cohort that went to war in 1914–18 (see Table 8.12).[29]

One example may suffice to illustrate this point. H. Roberts was a gunner in the Royal Field Artillery. He contracted sandfly fever in India and was invalided out of the army. Six years later, in 1924, he died of pulmonary embolism, at the age of 34. The trainer of Oldham Athletic Football Club testified that Roberts was one of the fittest amateurs who had played with the team before the war. His employer certified that he had been a robust man in 1914, but was prone to illness after 1918. His widow's request for a pension was denied.[30] To his family, Roberts was a casualty of the war, and who can swear that they were wrong?

This one instance brings us squarely to the limitations of the

TABLE 8.12. THE SEX-RATIO OF MORTALITY IN ENGLAND AND WALES, 1896–1900 AND 1948 (MALE AGE-SPECIFIC DEATH RATES DIVIDED BY FEMALE AGE-SPECIFIC DEATH RATES)

Age group	1896–1900	1948
0–4	1.18	1.28
5–9	0.99	1.42
10–14	0.97	1.16
15–19	1.07	1.16
20–24	1.18	0.99
25–34	1.15	1.06
35–44	1.22	1.29
45–54	1.29	1.55
55–64	1.24	1.77
65–74	1.17	1.53
75–84	1.13	1.28
85+	1.09	1.15

SOURCE: P. Stocks, 'Fifty years of progress as shown by vital statistics', *British Medical Journal* (1950), I, 54.

statistical analysis of the impact of war on British society. No history of the 1914–18 conflict is complete without reference to the demographic phenomena we have discussed in the course of this book. But the careful evaluation of demographic evidence, while essential, does not unravel the full effect of war losses or illuminate the unique space the Great War has occupied in modern British social history. The cultural outcome of these demographic events may have been their most lasting legacy. To see the force of this claim, we must turn to the memory of war which survivors carried with them in the years after the Armistice. It is this issue which we address in the next and final chapter.

9. Demographic History, Cultural History and Memories of War

I DEMOGRAPHIC HISTORY AND CULTURAL HISTORY: THE CASE OF THE FIRST WORLD WAR

So far, this book has approached the demographic history of Britain in the First World War mainly from the viewpoint of the quantitative historian. We have tried to measure war-related change, whenever measurement was possible, in order to provide a rigorous and precise account of important facets of the impact of the First World War on British society. The result has been to deepen our understanding of the war experience in the following ways.

First, both demographic and economic data support the view that social inequality in Britain was reduced during the war, primarily on account of the demands of the war economy. We have shown that there was an overall improvement in life expectancy for civilians after 1914. This benefited all classes. But what also changed was the relative position both of the working class vis-à-vis other classes, and of the poorest sections of the working class vis-à-vis the rest of the working-class population. The general rule was that the worse off a section of society was before 1914, the greater were its gains in life expectancy in wartime.

The demographic evidence to support these arguments is of four kinds. First, the use of life tables derived from the mortality experience of a substantial part of the working-class population indicated that for men lucky enough to stay out of the trenches, life expectancy in wartime was actually greater than that which they would have enjoyed had there been no war. Secondly, we

279

have shown that the gap between the mortality levels of poorly-paid and better-paid occupational groups was reduced during the war decade. Thirdly, we have demonstrated that within the overall pattern of mortality decline, nutrition-related diseases declined most during the war. Fourthly, we have noted that infant and maternal mortality rates declined sharply during the war, and that these gains were especially marked in overcrowded urban centres where the mass of the unskilled and semi-skilled labour force and their families lived.

Once the demographic picture relating to civilian health was complete, we turned to explanations for these wartime developments. Our main conclusion was that while medical intervention and health administration helped prevent a deterioration in public health during the war, the gains in life expectancy registered during the war occurred primarily because of an improvement in nutritional standards of the working class, and especially of the poorest strata within it.

Our analysis of wages, prices and food consumption showed how this happened, despite an overall decline in aggregate food supply. The evidence we presented pointed to an increase in the earnings of working-class families, and thereby of their nutritional levels, during the war. It was certainly one of the ironies of the war that during a period of food shortage, what remained to the nation was distributed much more equitably in wartime than had been the case before 1914. In part this was made possible by an increase in home agricultural output and by limited but effective controls on consumption. But such measures would not have been successful had there not also been a sharp increase in family incomes, such that for most working people, earnings kept pace with or out-stripped price rises.

This was one of the most important achievements of the British war economy. It contrasts sharply with the performance of the German war economy, which could not manage as efficiently as the British to distribute goods and resources as between civilian and military requirements. Herein lies one of the reasons why Britain and her Allies won the war.

It is true that there were many people whose fortunes were adversely affected by the war, but those at the bottom of the social scale, who had had the least to lose, were not among them. Income gains, we have noted, were greatest, both absolutely and relatively, among the poorest-paid and least skilled. In the post-war period, mass unemployment reduced but did not wipe out much of what had been achieved during the war. This was in part because of the permanent extension of some wartime social provision, in particular, unemployment insurance, which helped protect working-class families from the full effects of the depression. Wage differentials widened, but rural and urban poverty of the kind endemic in pre-1914 Britain never recurred.

In contrast, both during and after the war, many wealthy families were severely hit by a decline in real incomes derived from rent. In addition, many civil servants and retired people, who lived on fixed incomes or savings, were impoverished by war inflation. Skilled workers and men in some clerical jobs also did not do well, and in certain cases, suffered a decline in real income. In sum, we can conclude that the First World War reduced the economic and demographic distance between classes and between strata within classes. One of the entirely unanticipated effects of the 1914–18 war was, therefore, to compress the class structure of early twentieth-century Britain.

There was, of course, an entirely different side to the demographic history of the war – that related to military participation and war losses. Here our central argument is that there was an unequal distribution of war losses within the British population. In general, the higher up in the social scale a man was, the greater were his chances of becoming a casualty of the Great War. This was for three reasons. First, enlistment rates were higher among the middle and upper classes than among working-class men. Secondly, more working-class men failed to pass the medical tests for military service, or passed them as fit only for home duty. Their physical disabilities probably saved the lives of thousands of such men. Thirdly, casualties suffered by the educated and propertied classes were proportionately greater than those suffered by the working class for two simple reasons: (i) the officer corps was recruited until almost the end of the war from the sons of the middle and upper classes; and (ii) casualty rates among officers were roughly double those of the men they led. In statistical terms, there was a 'Lost Generation' of the better off, in the sense that the more privileged payed a proportionately higher human price for the war than did the less privileged.

The true 'Lost Generation', though, was that of the nation as a whole. For every officer killed, twenty men of lower ranks fell during the war. And since individual families did not experience war losses in proportional terms, we must not lose sight of the fact that British war losses – like the British army and the British nation – were made up of a majority of working-class people. They bore the brunt of the bloodiest war this nation has ever fought.

So far we have remained in the realm of the quantitative. But there is an important sense in which to stop here is unsatisfactory, for to do so is to risk giving the impression that the history of the war can be written in the form of a desiccated retrospective cost-benefit analysis. Costs and benefits there certainly were, but their historical meaning cannot be determined by statistical analysis and inference alone.

We have explored two – and only two – facets of the war experience: war losses and civilian health. But the significance of these features of the Great War is not simply a quantitative question. It requires attention to the way contemporaries reacted to them and remembered them. To complete this study, we must therefore go beyond the quantitative realm to take account of memories and perceptions of the impact of war. In effect, my claim is that no demographic history of the Great War is complete without an account of the cultural significance of the demographic events we have explored.

It is apparent, though, that to do so we must enter a very different terrain from that we have surveyed in the first two sections of this book. We cannot use the same methods, or present arguments in the same way, for cultural history is not a field where we can prove or disprove competing assertions or explanations. Hence the following discussion is of necessity exploratory and tentative.

Furthermore, to do justice to the cultural legacy of the Great War would require at least a book in itself. But as we noted in the introduction, demographic historians have become increasingly aware of the cultural dimensions of their subject, and it is hoped that our study will reinforce this trend. Some scholars have sought the sources of demographic events, such as fertility movements, in marriage patterns, contraceptive practices or other aspects of cultural life.[1] Our aim is different. It is simply to indicate some of the ways that demographic events of the magnitude of the Great War left a lasting impression on the cultural history of this country.

The cultural legacy of the war on the home front has been ably examined by Professor Marwick and Dr Waites. In different ways they have shown that popular attitudes to class changed as a result of the wartime escape from subsistence standards of living. The outcome was a decline in the deferential acceptance of poverty and powerlessness as fate or as natural and therefore unalterable circumstances. The war exploded these notions, and thereby tended to reduce servility while increasing the expectations, hopes and aspirations of ordinary people.[2]

The cultural historian must attend to such developments, but in an overall account of the aftermath of the war they must take a subordinate position to the more harrowing legacy of the conflict. For in the decades which have elapsed since 1918, to remember the war experience has been first and foremost to reflect on the soldiers' war, and thereby on the terrible price British soldiers and sailors paid for victory.

In this chapter we explore the ways in which some of the survivors, both during the conflict and long after the Armistice, remembered 'their' war and the men who fell in it. To this end, we shall refer mainly to a rich and varied source, namely soldiers' writings about the war. This is not to diminish the significance of civilian responses to the slaughter: on the contrary. It is rather to suggest that in their re-creations of the war, many soldier-writers raised an issue of central importance in the cultural history of this period. It is the belief developed over time, that the millions of men who saw combat constituted a race apart, indelibly imprinted with and differentiated by the direct experience of a war of unprecedented carnage. Whether this judgment is valid or not is impossible to say, but that many of the men who fought felt that it was true is an incontrovertible fact.

To explore this theme, we confront a mountain of material, written for different purposes and by different talents, which threatens to bury anyone who tries to sift through it. It may be useful to identify, within the large body of reminiscences, reflections, self-justification, verse and fiction of the period since 1914, three kinds of writing which re-created the soldiers' war: (i) popular literature written by civilians and for civilians who wanted to add their voices in support of the men in uniform; (ii) trench journalism written during the war by soldiers and for those who served with them; and (iii) what may be termed 'war literature' –

a body of soldiers' poetry and a new genre of fictionalized memoir or autobiographical fiction of great power and appeal. This was produced by a number of servicemen both during and after the war, and constitutes an enduring part of the war's cultural legacy. In this chapter, we begin with a brief discussion of what popular literature and trench journalism can tell us about the separate world of the soldier, before turning to the evidence contained in some of the novels and verse of the war.

But before we start, a few comments are in order on the question of the representativeness of these sources. There is no way to prove that the beliefs of the men who wrote were representative of the men who did not. On the one hand, the authors of much writing about the war certainly occupied a very narrow position within British society and used a very different language from the men in uniform whom they led. Many soldiers who went through the same campaigns, either as officers or in the ranks, either never had the same reactions as these soldier-writers or managed to repress or consign to oblivion the emotions and responses which soldier-writers captured. On the other hand, we do know that the fact of memory was not peculiar to these writers: the various commemoration services, local and national, civilian and military, the graves and the wreaths are with us still. All we can say with full confidence, therefore, is that this evidence forms an important part of the cultural legacy of the Great War, and that these writings are indispensable guides to how some contemporaries tried to come to terms with the slaughter.

Indeed we can probably go further and argue that such approximations of truth as later generations have gleaned about the soldiers' war arise largely from the extraordinary literary record left by a group of soldier-writers, poets and novelists who served mainly on the Western Front between 1914 and 1918. Since this body of literature is itself one of the most poignant legacies of the conflict, and since it has served as the point of entry into the mental landscape of war for millions who have grown up in succeeding generations, no history of the aftermath of the Great War is complete which fails to take account of this evidence.

II POPULAR LITERATURE AND TRENCH
JOURNALISM

The literary reconstruction of the soldiers' war started long before
the guns were silenced in 1918. Beginning early in the war and
continuing throughout the interwar years, civilian writers produced an avalanche of reportage, propaganda, and patriotic por-
traits of the war efforts of individuals, military units, and communities.[3] Much of this writing was an attempt to bridge the
gap between those who had joined up and those who had stayed at
home. These ventures may have succeeded in boosting civilian
morale and in saluting the virtues of resolution and sacrifice
essential for victory. But they failed in their primary purpose, for
the literature of celebration and civilian commemoration unwittingly highlighted and to some extent deepened the divide between
soldiers and non-combatants.

The stark contrast between civilian accounts of 'Our Men at the
Front' and the quite different private language and humour of the
soldiers themselves may be seen by comparing journals produced
for sale in Britain with the hundreds of trench newspapers of a few
pages and a few issues which appeared during the war.[4] These
papers sprang up without official encouragement or sponsorship,
and it is clear that they appealed to many who cocked an eyebrow
at civilian versions of what the war was like. Consider the image of
war projected by one civilian war paper distributed in Britain and
North America, the *War Illustrated*. Its editor, J. A. Hammerton,
made sure that it was full of stirring stuff about the men at the
Front. The drawing on the cover of the issue of 28 April 1918 is of
'British Cavalry Charging the Oncoming Germans in the Great
Battle in the Somme Area'. In the time-honoured (and totally
outdated) tradition of the Bengal Lancers, British horsemen are
shown 'Getting In With the Point' of their lances, thus scattering a
cluster of terrified Germans[5] (see Fig. 9.1). The articles which
followed were all hortatory and full of the rhetoric of war as
adventure.

What some soldiers made of this journal, which began appearing in 1915, and more importantly, what they made of the sentiments behind it, may be surmised by comparing it with one of the
most enduring trench newspapers, the *New Church Times*, which
started its life as the *Wipers Times* in 1915. In Fig. 9.2, we find the

FIG. 9.1   A civilian's view of the war
SOURCE: *War Illustrated*, 29 April 1918

following two notices which appeared prominently in the issue of 1 May 1916. The hand of the ex-public-schoolboy turned subaltern is apparent here, as it is in the light-hearted and irreverent tone of the articles and verses published in it. Many dealt effectively with the limitations of civilian journalism about the war. A series of spoofs on 'How to Win the War' by 'Belary Helloc' sent up the tactic of frontal assault applauded by those far removed from the battlefield. It was also a subtle way of veiling criticism of the General Staff approach to offensive warfare under a cloak of sarcasm supposedly directed against ignorant civilians. Consider these two extracts from the thoughts of 'Belary Helloc'. To win the war, he urged, the army had to

FIG. 9.2 A soldier's view of the war
SOURCE: *New Church Times*, 1 May 1916

Take things like this. The line held on all fronts is 1,500 miles (circa). This is 2,640,000 yards. Now we must get that number of our troops and allot one yard per man. Give each man a bomb, and at a given signal let them all go over and each to account for his own particular opponent. This would account for 2,000,000 of the enemy (that is giving the generous allowance of 640,000 failures), besides putting him to much inconvenience. Each time the enemy brings up reinforcements and reestablishes his line then repeat the performance. I think I may safely say that, after the tenth or eleventh attack, the enemy would be ready to consider the advisability of making terms rather than continue the war.

Helloc's uncanny recapitulation of the logic of staff thinking about the war and of the unreality of the assumptions of those at home who wanted one more big push may be seen in the following passage in an earlier issue of the same trench paper. On 26 February 1916, readers of the *Wipers Times* were entertained by this Hellocian calculation:

In this article I wish to show plainly that under existing conditions, everything points to a speedy disintegration of the enemy. We will take first of all the effect of war on the male population of Germany. Firstly let us take our figures 12,000,000 as the total fighting population of Germany. Of these 8,000,000 are killed or being killed, hence we have 4,000,000 remaining. Of these 1,000,000 are non-combatants, being in the Navy. Of the 3,000,000 remaining, we can write off 2,500,000 as temperamentally unsuitable for fighting, owing to obesity and other ailments engendered by a gross mode of living. This leaves us 500,000 as the full strength. Of these 497,240 are known to be suffering from incurable diseases, of the remaining 600, 584 are Generals and Staff. Thus we find that there are 16 men on the Western Front. This number I maintain is not enough to give them even a fair chance of resisting four more big pushes, and hence the collapse of the Western Campaign.

The extent to which life imitated art in the Great War may be seen in the 'original' form of this argument, in a document probably written by the Chief of the Imperial General Staff, General Robertson, to the Minister of War, Lord Kitchener, in the spring of 1916, which presented the military situation in the Western Front in precisely these terms.[6] It is unlikely that the anonymous writer of the *Wipers Times* was privy to these discussions; what he caught was the insane logic of the frontal attack philosophy, which cost the lives of tens of thousands of men. Only a few months later, the Battle of the Somme began on 1 July 1916, and these journalistic jests turned into truth.

It was a truth which many soldiers felt that only those who had been there could really understand. In the later phases of the war, and after the Armistice, soldiers renewed what they took to be a unique bond of experience. On Armistice Day, in reunions, in casual encounters or in ex-servicemen's clubs, men would return to *their* war, with a degree of accuracy which varied with time and temperament. The vagaries of memory mattered less than the retrieval of moments charged with emotion, excitement and the flavour of military companionship. On these occasions, sarcasm of the kind expressed in the *Wipers Times* against those who were not there could come out and further underline the distinction between those who went to war and those who stayed at home.

III   WAR LITERATURE

In contrast to the more ephemeral writing described above, war literature can be understood on many levels of varying degrees of depth. The first and most obvious level on which to perceive the writings of soldier-poets and novelists of the Great War, apparent in even the most cursory reading, is in terms of their mission to expose the ugliness of war. Again we confront the message that soldiers and civilians spoke entirely different languages about the war.

A   The Literature of Warning

Most soldier-writers believed that the ugliness of war had been concealed beneath a patina of civilian ignorance, lies and distortions. Just as the artist Paul Nash wanted to use his work to 'help rob war of the last shred of glory the last shine of glamour' and to become 'a messenger who brings back word from the men who are fighting to those who want the war to go on forever',[7] so poets took on the task of exploding the cruel patriotic myths of the nobility of armed struggle. Charles Hamilton Sorley, who was killed in October 1915 at the age of 20, set the terms of the indictment in a sonnet written shortly before his death:

> When you see millions of the mouthless dead
> Across your dreams in pale battalions go,
> Say not soft things as other men have said . . . .[8]

We should note that this was a turning away from his own and others' earlier verse celebrating the men who volunteered for war, and from what he had called 'the music of their going'.[9] The cacophony of battle had stilled the voice of innocence among the troops, but many continued to believe that among civilians, deception and self-deception frequently took longer to die, if they died at all. This caused in many soldiers the bitterness which we have seen in the sarcasm of the *Wipers Times*, and which has been captured in Siegfried Sassoon's 'Blighters':

> The house is crammed: tier beyond tier they grin
> And cackle at the Show, while prancing ranks
> Of harlots shrill the chorus, drunk with din;
> 'We're sure the Kaiser loves our dear old Tanks.'
>
> 'I'd like to see a Tank come down the stalls'
> Lurching to rag-time tunes, or 'Home, sweet Home',
> And there'd be no more jokes in Music-Halls
> To mock the riddled corpses round Bapaume.[10]

Music-hall gaiety, Fleet-Street bluster, bellicose sermons, and military propaganda so clouded the atmosphere of wartime Britain that soldier-writers made it their business to clear the air by telling the truth about the war, 'I mean the truth untold/ The pity of war, the pity war distilled',[11] in Wilfred Owen's phrase.

When Sassoon published a collection of verse in 1918, its title *Counter-attack* was meant to convey the anger he and other soldiers felt about civilian ignorance of the reality of war. As the 1920s wore on, a new generation grew up with even less direct knowledge of what the war had been like. In one respect, it was to warn this as yet unknowing world about the casual slaughters and false judgments of the war on the Western Front that a second fusillade of war writing was let loose.[12] Its purpose was, in Henry Williamson's words, to 'try to tear the Truth out of the past so that all men shall see plainly',[13] and thereby to disrupt mental preparation for a new war, especially among the young. After watching a few hundred schoolchildren cheering at a patriotic film on the war, Williamson wrote:

> The children, I know, are but the mirrors of the mental attitudes of their parents, of their school and religious teachers; but surely, after the bitter waste and agony of the Lost Generation, it is time that these people should begin to know 'what they do'.[14]

B   The Soldiers' War: Separation and Bereavement

On one level then it was, as Edmund Blunden put it, 'to convey the monstrous and complex circumstances of destruction' that 'the great unveilings of war as it was'[15] were written in the late 1920s and early 1930s. But concentration on this level of the soldier writers' intent obscures two other levels of the meaning of war writing. These had more to do with the aftermath of war than with the war itself. It is perhaps best to understand most of the war literature published in the interwar years less as a literature of warning, than first as a literature of separation and bereavement, and secondly as a literature of the guilt of the survivor.

Many of those who wrote about the war felt that their task was to describe the indescribable. The unexpected duration and mechanized nature of the war on the Western Front, and the horrifying toll of human lives devoured in the machinery of warfare, were sufficient to justify the view of many soldier-writers that what they saw and what they knew were beyond anything in living memory and, indeed, were virtually beyond comprehension. Traditional forms of language seemed unsuited to transmit the images of surreal nightmare that Verdun, the Somme and Passchendaele provide in abundance. Perhaps no language was fitted to that task, especially when cultural codes of literary decorum precluded unexpurgated accounts of profanity and horror.[16] As it was, most British writers of the war generation could only try to wrest to new uses the Georgian language which was the only one they had; and thereby, to turn its Arcadian-pastoral modes into bitter irony. By straining the Georgian modes to their utmost, and beyond, they created something that, however technically flawed, was a powerful testimony to the experience of those who fought in the war and a moving memorial to their dead comrades.

This act of remembrance was, indeed, their primary purpose. But it was one which civilians could not share. This was because the war itself had a fascination for many soldiers who were under no illusions as to its character. It is this ambivalence towards a war of staggering carnage which made their being bereaved so difficult and so full of shifting emotions, which made it difficult for some ex-soldiers even to talk about the war with people who weren't there. In nearly all war literature, disgust at the meaninglessness of death in the trenches was accompanied by profound affection for the men who fell, as well as for those who managed to survive. As Robert Graves put it in his poem 'Two Fusiliers':

> Show me the two so closely bound
> As we, by the wet bond of blood,
> By friendship, blossoming from mud,
> By death: we faced him, and we found
> Beauty in Death,
> In dead men breath.[17]

Such sentiments did not in any sense constitute an indictment of war which can be termed pacifist, a point that applies with equal force to trench journalism. With a few exceptions, what mattered to the men who fought in the Great War was not whether that war, or indeed any war, was just or justifiable. What gripped their imagination was rather the camaraderie of the trenches and the courage and sheer tenacity in the art of survival of the men with whom they served. This was as true of officers like Graves or Sassoon as of men who served in the ranks like the poet Ivor Gurney or the Australian writer Frederic Manning, author of *Her Privates We* (1930).

It is probably true that nearly all of these writers hated the war. But what is most important in appreciating their attitude and their art is that they saw the war as a unique moment, which those who did not serve could never really know. Guy Chapman, author of *A Passionate Prodigality* (1933), described how, despite the fear that accompanied frontline duty, there grew in his heart 'a compelling fascination' with combat.

> I do not think I exaggerate: for in that fascination lies War's power. Once you have lain in her arms you can admit no other mistress. You may loathe, you may execrate, but you cannot deny her . . . . Every writer of imagination who has set down in honesty his experience has confessed it. Even those who hate her most are prisoners to her spell. They rise from her embraces, pillaged, soiled, it may be ashamed: but they are still hers.[18]

Chapman here expressed the central view, found in trench journalism as well, that soldier-writers during and after the war created a literature about other soldiers and largely for other soldiers, who were the only ones who could really understand what they had to say. This is what Ivor Gurney meant when he described his war poems to a friend: 'Old ladies wont [sic] like them, but soldiers may . . . .'[19]

This is the first of the two central themes stated in war literature I want to emphasize. Much of the poetry and prose of the 1914–18 war was written in order to recapture the process by which the soldiers who served during the Great War became a race apart. For example, Charles Carrington, a survivor of the Somme and Passchendaele, and author of *A Subaltern's War* (1929), believed that all who served in the war bore with pride an indelible mark visible only to those who shared it. In 1968 he wrote:

> We are still an initiate generation, possessing a secret that can never be communicated . . . . Twenty million of us, of whom perhaps 2,000,000 are still alive, shared the experience with one another but with no one else, and are what we are because, in that war, we were soldiers. There are many such dedicated societies in the world, but no other, so far as I know, which comprises a whole age-group of the able-bodied men, while excluding other age groups and the other sex.[20]

Siegfried Sassoon's first experience of this special kind of alienation was his profound discomfort in the company of civilians during the war. Similarly the central figure of Ford Madox Ford's *Parade's End* (1924–7) had 'some of the slight nausea that in those days you felt at contact with the civilian who knew none of your thoughts, phrases, or preoccupations'.[21]

Not only did most war writers excoriate blind enthusiasm for a war which most civilians would never see, but as Sassoon put it, non-combatants simply could not know the ways in which over the years 'The Front . . . could lay its hands on our hearts'. This was the real burden of the war generation: they felt they were men 'carrying something in our heads which belonged to us alone, and to those we had left behind us in the battle'.[22] Sassoon spoke for many others when he wrote that 'the man who really endured the War at its worst was everlastingly differentiated from everyone except his fellow soldiers'.[23] They shared the belief that in a sense none of them had ever really returned from France and Flanders.[24]

Guy Chapman ended his war memoir by describing his reasons for volunteering for the Allied Army of Occupation in February 1919, rather than returning home to civilian life:

> Isn't there a fairy tale about two countries held together by a hair, and when that broke, they fled apart? England had vanished over the horizon of the mind. I did not want to see it.[25]

This remark encapsulates some of the unrepresentativeness of these writings. Almost all ordinary soldiers very much did want to see England, and presented the British army with its only real threat of mutiny when, at the end of the war, demobilization was delayed. Many men who served in the trenches had, as we have already remarked, the necessary and merciful gift of forgetfulness, despite (or even because of) their feelings of alienation. But in later years, ex-soldiers frequently returned to this sense of separation which war writers recaptured. Some German and Austrian war literature also reflects the soldiers' pervasive feeling of marginality, of separation from a civilian world to which it seemed impossible to return. Of course defeat and revolution in these countries precludes direct comparison with English conditions, and the fact that some war novels in Germany were commissioned by ex-servicemen's organizations further complicates any attempt to discuss European war literature as a single entity.[26] Nevertheless, many ex-servicemen in a number of countries came to feel the loneliness of those whose only free communion is with the dead, or with other ex-soldiers.

Many soldiers who were to become writers had experienced the first months of the war as a great adventure, or as a release from the mechanical and shabby commercialism of pre-war life. In this they shared the general reaction to the early phase of the war. But soon enough many came to see that they were trapped in a machine much more powerful than the one they had thought to escape by going off to war.[27] Their sense of new-found freedom is certainly reflected in war literature. But the freedom of which they wrote was described as that of the wanderer in all too many cases, of men who had lost many ties to civilian life and felt doomed never completely to recover them or to forge new ones in their place. The war had given a form to their lives – one that had made it virtually impossible for some ex-soldiers to reintegrate into peacetime society.[28] This is why Gertrude Stein referred to the déclassé writers of post-war Paris, as the 'Lost Generation'.

But we are dealing with a phenomenon of a more general kind, since the sense that many veterans had, of being trapped between the battlefront and the home front long after the war had ended, troubled not only many of their lives, but also the lives of those who tried to live with them. Vera Brittain, the author of *Testament of Youth* (1933), lost her brother, her fiancé, and nearly all her childhood male friends in the war; she also served in France in a Voluntary Aid Detachment as a nurse to hideously wounded men. She believed that the conflict had erected 'a barrier of indescribable experience . . . between the men at the front and the women who loved them' which could never be surmounted. This 'tragic, profound freemasonry' united the men, but kept them in a separate sphere.[29] The French writer, Henri Massis, a Catholic mystic and follower of Barrès and Bergson, concurred. Writing in 1968, he described the Great War as 'the home of our youth', which survivors were destined to carry on their backs for the rest of their lives. For some this was a burden; for others a comfort; for all, an unavoidable fate:

> We were born of the war, the war was immediately upon us, and in truth we have never done anything else . . . . After an armistice of some years, war led us back up there, to those regions we never departed, which guard our deepest secrets, where we have left our souls with the bodies of our friends.[30]

This image of the fallen brings us squarely to the second defining feature of this aspect of soldiers' writing about the war: the resurrection of the dead. The companionship of the dead had a very material meaning to the men who manned the seemingly endless line of trenches dug between the Flemish coast of the English Channel and the Swiss frontier. For the earthworks they built were repeatedly churned into a morass by three years of artillery fire – and contained the remains of well over 1 million men. To this day bits of soldiers' bones can be seen by anyone who walks in the brush of Verdun. During the war, the stench of decomposition still clung to the bones. Some of the corpses managed to retain a certain degree of dignity; others soon putrified into 'ghastly dolls', as Sassoon called them,[31] or broke up into the detritus of warfare which soldiers stepped on, tripped over, tossed away, or reassembled into the protective walls of another trench. Almost all war writers spoke of this contact, or contamination through contact, with the dead. Wilfred Owen wrote of 'the distortion of the dead, whose unburiable bodies sit outside the dug-outs all day, all night, the most execrable sights on earth. In poetry we call them the most glorious. But we sit with them all day, all night . . . and a week later come back and find them still sitting there in motionless groups.'[32] The hero of Frederic Manning's novel *Her Privates We* recalled the image of:

> the unburied dead with whom one lived, he might say, cheek by jowl, Briton and Hun impartially confounded, festering, fly-blown corruption, the pasture of rats, blackening in the heat, swollen with distended bellies, or shrivelling away with their mouldering rags: and even when night covered them, one vented in the wind the stench of death.[33]

The Western Front was not the only theatre of operations that had the appearance of a mass open grave. One of the earliest war novels, A. P. Herbert's *Secret Battle* (1919), recounted that in Gallipoli 'there was a hideous fascination about the things, so that after a few hours a man came to know the bodies in his bay with a sickening intimacy' made worse by the fact that: 'All of them were alive with flies . . .'[34] In France and Flanders, some of the eeriest encounters between the living and the dead were in muddy or waterlogged shell holes, where survivors of an attack crawled to await dawn or rescue. Charles Carrington spoke of his love for the dead German who was his sole companion in one corner of the front throughout one such nocturnal vigil.[35]

Like Carrington, other soldiers sought relief from (and perhaps unintentionally reinforced) the horror of confronting the dead without aid of ritual or decent burial, by imagining that the corpses retained some semblance of life. Perhaps this made them seem less dead, or even not dead at all. Sassoon passed a line of 50 dead British soldiers who had served in different units, but who 'were beyond regimental rivalry now – their fingers mingled in blood-stained bunches, as though acknowledging the companionship of death'.[36] In Ford's *Parade's End* we learn that the central character had caught his foot between two hands: 'Sticking up out of the frozen ground . . . As it might be in prayer . . . like this.'[37] Arthur Graeme West, another poet killed in the war, wrote this poem shortly before his own death. It is a description of a night patrol and of what he had found during it:

> They lay, all clothed
> Each in some new and piteous attitude
> That we well marked to guide us back: as he
> Outside our wire, that lay on his back and crossed
> His legs Crusader-wise: I smiled at that,
> And thought on Elia and his Temple Church.
> From him, at quarter left, lay a small corpse,
> Down in a hollow, huddled as in bed,
> That one of us put his hands on unawares.
> Next was a bunch of half a dozen men
> All blown to bits, an archipelago
> Of corrupt fragments.[38]

Edmund Blunden in *Undertones of War* (1929), recorded seeing one dead Scottish soldier who was:

> kneeling, facing east, so that one could scarcely credit death in him; he was seen at some little distance from the usual tracks, and no one had much time in Thiepval just then for sight-seeing or burying. Death could not kneel so, I thought, and approaching I ascertained with a sudden shrivelling of spirit that Death could and did.[39]

Others shared Blunden's sense of living with the dead, a fate that was made unendurable for those who knew much about the men whose torn bodies were frequently rotting just out of reach. It was perhaps only natural that such moments would lead Blunden to reflect that for many years to come he would be 'going over the ground again'. Indeed he would continue to do so until the time 'when it shall be the simplest thing to take in your hands the hands' of dead companions 'in whose recaptured gentleness no sign of death's astonishment or time's separation shall be imaginable'.[40]

Guy Chapman notes how frequently soldiers scavenged the remains of the dead for whatever items could be extracted from them.[41] This was normal in wartime, and especially natural in the terrible conditions under which soldiers lived in the Ypres salient when Chapman served. What was virtually unprecedented was the dismemberment and arbitrary scattering of remains which so often made traditional (or any) burial impossible. This fact may help to account for the importance of rituals like Armistice Day – or indeed the ritual writing of war memoirs. Such rituals both perpetuated the living ex-soldiers' relationship with their dead companions and constituted the funeral ceremonies that those dead never had.

But these collective rituals were insufficient to prevent survivors from carrying with them the memory of the dead. One such was Hugh Dalton; before the war he had been up at Cambridge, where he was a friend of Rupert Brooke, who died early in 1915. After the war, in 1921, Dalton returned to the Italian countryside where he had served a few years earlier as a British soldier, and noted in his diary:

> In the night a very vivid dream, in which Rupert came and talked to me in some house where I was living . . . . Rupert and I both knew that he was dead, killed in the war, but the conversation was quite matter-of-fact. In the course of it I said, 'What good things have been published lately in your shop?' (meaning in the way of literature) and he told me two books, the names of which I forget and added, 'But Shaw's last book isn't worth reading . . .' I had a photograph of him in my room and he said, 'I see you have a picture of me here', and it apparently had written below it some lines by one Cook: 'And we turned our thumbs down on them'.

Dalton further remembered that Brooke had touched him; it 'felt quite corporeal, but I had a shrinking feeling, which prevented me from voluntarily touching him'. They agreed to dine in a restaurant, parted, and Dalton got lost *en route*. 'But at last', he reports, 'I stumbled in and found it pretty full. Most of those who were sitting there were young men, who smiled rather sarcastically and knowingly at me as I came in'. Dalton found his wife Ruth at the restaurant; she asked:

> 'Isn't Rupert coming?' I said, 'No, he's gone'. Then she smiled too and said, 'What, has the expedition for Constantinople

started so early?' Then I woke. I had remembered the day before the story of the Greek who had written on the cross on Rupert's grave in Skyros, that he died in the war to free Constantinople from the Turks.[42]

The unnerving image of being visited by the dead disturbed the sleep of many others. Wilfred Owen's brother Harold recounted a visit by his dead brother, who 'did not speak but only smiled his most gentle smile'.[43] One of the heroes of Mottram's *The Spanish Farm Trilogy* (1924–7) could not shake off the image of one casualty of war, a 'Corporal, his face out of sight, as if in the midst of a hearty laugh. It needed only a glance, however, to see that there was no head on his shoulders.' Only after years did 'his recurrent nightmare of the Headless Man' begin to fade out.[44]

In some instances, this sense that the dead had the power to return to haunt the living and to join what the Welsh poet L. Wyn Griffiths called 'this company of ghosts about my heart'[45] was reinforced by cases of real return. In *Memoirs of an Infantry Officer*, Sassoon described how he believed the reports about the death of a friend, David Cromlech. (This name was a disguise, the real David Cromlech was Robert Graves.) Then, almost before he had had time to grieve, Sassoon received a cable announcing that Cromlech had 'risen again' and was recuperating in a London hospital. Graves' own account of the bizarre coincidence by which his 21st birthday was also the 'official date of my death' adds a comic touch to this theme.[46] The chaos of war was bound to yield such jarring reversals. Of course, they often worked the other way around: reports of survival turned out to be only temporary reprieves from news of death.

Those unable to repress the haunting images of the dead were bound to suffer from what Charles Carrington called the '1916 fixation'. 'I could not escape from the comradeship of the trenches', he wrote. They had become 'a mental internment camp, or should I say a soldiers' home'. He believed that he 'might as well have been in Chelsea Hospital' for the rest of his life.[47] The central character of Ford's *Parade's End* brooded over 'the blackness that descends on you when you think of your dead . . . . As if joined to your own identity by a black cord.' Back at home, he revisited the battlefield in his sleep and would shout out half-remembered phrases of enemies and comrades.[48] Similarly, Robert

Graves recorded, long after the end of the war, that: 'Shells used to come bursting on my bed at midnight . . .; strangers in daytime would assume the faces of friends who had been killed.'[49] Vera Brittain too dreamt of the dead. This was part of the pain of survival after a war which meant 'the wholesale annihilation of my masculine contemporaries'. For many years 'there was no way of escaping' the echoes of the guns of France. Her 'accursed generation . . . had to listen and look whether it wanted to do so or not'. What was worse was the sense of being 'condemned to live to the end of my days in a world without confidence and security . . . in which life would seem threatened perpetually by death, and happiness appear a house without duration, built upon the shifting sands of chance.' Her world was that of a 'haphazard survivor from another life, without a place in society'.[50]

C The Aftermath of War and the Guilt of the Survivor

Vera Brittain's remarks show how difficult it is to sustain the claim, advanced by many soldiers, that the memory of war was entirely different for those who had fought and for those who had not seen combat. Of course, as a nurse, Vera Brittain had seen the ugly face of the war in a way that most non-combatants fortunately never did. But her writing raises another important aspect of the cultural aftermath of the Great War. It is that much war literature, which has been read by millions who have wanted to find out about 'what it was really like', was in effect less about the war period than about the difficulty of living with the memory of war long after the Armistice. Here again, we must note that this problem simply did not exist for thousands of veterans; we see again the danger of generalizing from war literature to the experience and recollection of all ex-soldiers. But for some the war and the havoc it had wrought seemed to dominate their lives.

It may be useful at this point tentatively to borrow a set of concepts derived from an aspect of the history of the Second World War in order to explore this theme. The problem of the guilt of the survivor has received considerable attention in the fields of social psychiatry and psychology since Dachau and Hiroshima, for instance, in Robert Jay Lifton's *Death in Life. Survivors of Hiroshima* (1968). I do not want to equate the fate of those soldiers who went willingly to war (though without knowing the kind of war they were volunteering for, with that of the civilians who perished in the camps or cities without any choice as to their fate. Still, the anguish of many survivors of the 1914–18 war in a sense prefigured the terrible lingering aftermath of the Second World War.

What was experienced both by those who had been trapped in the shadow of the first atomic bomb and by many veterans of the trenches was what Lifton called the 'death imprint': 'the psychological sense that death was not only everywhere, but was bizarre, unnatural, indecent, absurd'.[51] The very grotesqueness of mass death was a fact from which many could not escape; and this fact led to the second key feature of their condition: 'the survivor's struggle with guilt'.[52]

For many soldiers in the 1914–18 war, this took a number of forms which appear repeatedly in war literature: guilt at the act of killing,[53] guilt about having sent men on missions from which they did not return,[54] guilt about not having granted leave to men subsequently killed,[55] guilt about the very fact of survival in a war in which the dead were only rarely put to rest. Manning's hero Bourne 'wondered why the dead should be a reproach to the living'.[56] Richard Aldington's war novel *Death of a Hero* (1929) provides the semblance of an answer. 'I hold a brief for the war generation', he wrote and, in the name of the fallen, launched into a withering embittered attack on the shallow and hypocritical world of the lesser men who had outlived them. Again and again he returned to the point that the survivors were the ones to be pitied. The real question for him was:

> What right have I to live? Is it five million, is it ten million, is it twenty million? What does the exact count matter? There they are and we are responsible. Tortures of hell, we are responsible. When I meet an unmaimed man of my generation, I want to shout at him: 'How did you escape? How did you dodge it? What dirty trick did you play? Why are you not dead, trickster?' It is dreadful to have outlived your life, to have shirked your fate, to have overspent your welcome . . . . You the war dead, I think you died in vain. I think you died for nothing for a blast of wind, a blather, a humbug, a newspaper stunt, a politician's ramp. But at least you died. You did not reject the sharp, sweet shock of bullets, the sudden smashing of the shell-burst, the

insinuating agony of poison gas. You got rid of it all. You chose the better path.[57]

The tension described in this intemperate and nearly incoherent passage describes the danger faced by those who could not forget – the danger of breaking under the unbearable strain of surviving, like Ivor Gurney. Before the war, he had suffered from periodic bouts of mental instability, but it may be speculated that it was his three years' active service as a private with the Gloucesters, during which time he was gassed and wounded, that led to his incarceration in a series of mental hospitals for the rest of his life. As early as October 1917, he told a friend that the war perhaps 'wasn't bad, but my brain was really getting stuck over there'.[58] Gurney was one of the thousands whom Wilfred Owen's poem 'Mental Cases' described as 'men whose minds the Dead have ravished'.[59]

Herein lies the similarity between the dreams that plagued Sassoon, Graves, Dalton, Brittain and Aldington, and the haunted state of mind which Lifton found among the *hibakusha*, the survivors of Hiroshima. He summarized their troubled internal logic in these words:

> I almost died; I should have died; I did die, or at least I am not really alive; or if I am alive, it is impure of me to be so; and anything I do which affirms life is also impure and an insult to the dead, who alone are pure.

Such a state of mind is nearly intolerable, because it is infused with a burden of guilt which makes life a type of walking death, or which requires total identification with the dead who continue to live inside the survivor.[60]

Ten years after the Armistice, Henry Williamson, then in the process of writing his war memoir *The Patriot's Progress* (1930), went back to Flanders to retrace the steps he took as a soldier. He noted in the preface to his diary: 'I must return to my old comrades of the Great War – to the brown, the treeless, the flat and grave-set plain of Flanders – to the rolling, heat miraged downlands of the Somme – for I am dead with them, and they live in me again.'[61] Little of this sentiment can be found in the memoir itself, the writing of which may have helped to dispel it or diminish its hold over Williamson's mind. For Wyn Griffith, remembering the war in poetry and prose was a kind of 'surgical operation' after which he felt 'purged of the pain of war'.[62] The opening paragraphs of Chapman's *A Passionate Prodigality* describe the lingering feeling that 'the war, the forms and colours of that experience, possessed a part of my senses. My life was involved with the lives of other men, a few living, some dead. It is only now that I can separate myself from them.'[63] It is that attempt to balance his memories of the war and of the men who died in it which is at the heart of Chapman's war writing. Vera Brittain's memoirs were likewise created out of an 'urgent need for reconciliation with the past'.[64]

That act of remembrance was conducted in different ways and with different voices, some ironic, some literal. Perhaps this point can be made most clearly in reference to one of the most famous of war novels, Robert Graves' *Goodbye to All That* (1929). To Bernard Bergonzi, Graves' writing is an example of the search for 'emotional liberation' through the writing of war fiction.[65] But Graves introduces a different mode of handling the memories of the war from that discussed above, and his particular genre of black humour and trench comedy deserves to be recognized as a distinctive form of war literature. But were its origins and intentions really so different from those of his fellow soldier-writers? The central problem in answering this question is that, as Paul Fussell has pointed out, Graves was 'a joker, a manic illusionist', who deliberately tried to mislead his readers into believing that his book was a history. Graves' own claim in *Goodbye to All That* was that 'in 1916, when on leave in England after being wounded, I began an account of my first few months in France. Having stupidly written it as a novel, I have now to re-translate it into history.'[66] As Fussell shows, it is anything but a 'documentary transcription of the actual'; and Graves himself admitted this in later years:

The memoirs of a man who went through some of the worst experiences of trench warfare are not truthful if they do not contain a high proportion of falsities. High explosive barrages will make a temporary liar or visionary of anyone; the old trench mind is at work in all over-estimation of casualties, 'unnecessary' dwelling on horrors, mixing of dates and confusion between rumours and scenes actually witnessed.[67]

It is my contention that the 'old trench mind' is present in all kinds of soldiers' writings about the war, whether it is the sad poetry of Wilfred Owen, the experimental epic of Ford Madox Ford or the sardonic chronicles of Robert Graves. Each in his own way expressed complex feelings of separation from those who did not fight and bereavement for those who did but who never came back. To a greater or lesser degree, they all confronted the problem of the sheer arbitrariness of death which left them alive while their comrades perished. On occasion this chance outcome was a subject which touched feelings of guilt which other survivors of war in this century have known.[68] Of course, many men who served did not share these concerns; they were the lucky ones. But to deny that the reactions to survival revealed in war literature did take place is not only pointless but also risks obscuring some of the central ways in which the conflict was remembered by many of the men who fought in the Great War.

The soldier-writers' task was a difficult one: that of trying to find a way to glorify those who died in war without glorifying war itself.[69] And here we must attend to what is old in war literature as much as to what is new. It is true that there was no easy way in which soldier-writers could recreate trench warfare in the manner traditionally used to describe combat among professional soldiers in set-piece battles, after which the dead on both sides (who were by and large in one piece) were buried and the issue was resolved. War had changed, and as Paul Fussell has shown, the fictional language in which the war experience was recaptured changed as well. Graves, Sassoon, Blunden and others did develop a complex style of memoir as fiction, which Fussell describes as the creation of a new ironic mode of writing.[70] But we must distinguish between style and content in war literature, for however innovatively ironic in tone, these writings dealt centrally with an ancient set of questions related to the aftermath of war. Here we are indeed in a very old environment, for the theme of the ex-soldier returning home has engaged the imagination at least since the *Odyssey*. Soldiers' writings of the Great War may have inaugurated a new chapter in literary history, but they were also a rereading (with new emphases and in new forms) of old texts concerning the terrible problem of trying to live with the memory of war.

IV CONCLUSION

In any account of the impact of the Great War, there are limits beyond which a historian cannot go. Who can quarrel with the deep belief held by many ex-soldiers that only those who had been through battle could really understand the full meaning of war? This applies as much to historians as to non-combatants alive at the time.

There was an unbridgeable existential divide in the experience of war. However, as we have tried to demonstrate in this book, there were other, less terrifying 'meanings' of war to which a historian must attend. Among them is the paradox that because of armed conflict, this country became a healthier place in which to live. But that phenomenon, however important in the long-term social history of this country, was bound to be eclipsed by the memory of the human costs of the conflict.

In this respect, the legacy of the 1914–18 war was ecumenical. War losses touched virtually every household in Britain, and nearly every family was diminished by the death in combat of a father, a son, a brother, a cousin, or a friend. Four years of bloodletting had created a bond of bereavement which transcended distinctions of class or caste, for what mattered was not that the war had destroyed potential leaders or poets, but that it had cut a swathe through an entire generation.

Given that the individuality of death had been buried under literally millions of corpses, it was inevitable that new rites of collective mourning would flourish after 1918. In later years this took the form of public ceremonies and private séances, of great unveilings in Whitehall or of obscure meetings in small villages, in quiet meditation on Armistice Day, and in the publication of soldiers' memoirs. In all these gestures, the survivors of the war provided compelling testimony of their efforts to come to terms with the memory of the fallen.[71]

This oft-repeated act of commemoration has become a distinctive part of British culture. To wear a poppy in November or to glance at a war memorial in a church, chapel or school, is to look back on an extraordinary moment in British history, when this country joined the rest of Europe in embarking on a new era of warfare. That era is with us still, a fact which makes remembering the 'Lost Generation' more than a matter of purely historical significance.

Statistical Appendix

ESTIMATES OF WAR-RELATED DEATHS IN ENGLAND AND WALES, 1914–1918, USING DIFFERENT LIFE TABLES

The abridged life tables, reflecting the mortality experience of the working-class population insured by the Prudential Life Assurance Company and published in the *Journal of the Institute of Actuaries* in 1918 (Table A-1) permit us to estimate the level and age-structure of male mortality in England and Wales had there been no war in 1914. Two alternative approaches were adopted initially. The first was to assume that the life table mortality rates (qx) for 1913 remained constant throughout the subsequent five years.[1] This was the basis of Estimate A. The second was to assume that in the absence of war the pre-war rate of mortality decline would have continued unabated. This was the basis of Estimate B.

In both estimates, abridged life tables for 1913–18 were constructed on the basis of the qx values given in Table A-1. Mid-year populations at ages 16–60 for 1912–18 were calculated by multiplying the 1911 male census population of England and Wales by survival ratios derived from the Prudential life table for 1913. Once age-specific death rates (Mx) were derived from mortality rates, through the equation $Mx = 2qx/(2 - qx)$, we obtained the age structure of deaths by multiplying Mx for each year and age by the appropriate mid-year populations. The results may be found in tables A-2 and A-3, which describe two hypothetical estimates of male mortality in England and Wales for the years 1914–18.

In Estimate A, we assumed that qx rates for 1914–18 were identical to those of 1913. It is essential, therefore, to note that the hypothetical age structure of male mortality in Estimate A is not strictly speaking a full or realistic counterfactual picture of what would have happened had there been no war. Such a picture

TABLE A-1 RATES OF MORTALITY AMONG MALE INDUSTRIAL POLICYHOLDERS IN THE PRUDENTIAL ASSURANCE COMPANY, 1913, 1915, 1916, 1917

Age	English Life No. 8	1913	Prudential experience 1915	1916	1917
16	0.00259	0.00290	0.00467	0.00404	0.00374
17	0.00279	0.00317	0.00790	0.00840	0.00483
18	0.00302	0.00379	0.01386	0.01856	0.01283
19	0.00326	0.00372	0.01845	0.03201	0.03834
20	0.00348	0.00397	0.02008	0.03731	0.04742
21	0.00366	0.00386	0.01838	0.03772	0.04559
22	0.00378	0.00386	0.01695	0.03460	0.04394
23	0.00386	0.00377	0.01665	0.03124	0.04063
24	0.00392	0.00399	0.01534	0.02805	0.03769
25	0.00400	0.00441	0.01376	0.02572	0.03507
26	0.00411	0.00442	0.01340	0.02379	0.03248
27	0.00425	0.00451	0.01311	0.02192	0.03014
28	0.00440	0.00475	0.01199	0.02098	0.02886
29	0.00458	0.00532	0.01246	0.02001	0.02794
30	0.00478	0.00499	0.01168	0.01915	0.02601
31	0.00502	0.00562	0.01182	0.01773	0.02501
32	0.00528	0.00520	0.01177	0.01675	0.02304
33	0.00558	0.00605	0.01225	0.01576	0.02265
34	0.00590	0.00594	0.01145	0.01565	0.02194
35	0.00624	0.00642	0.01118	0.01488	0.02097
36	0.00659	0.00667	0.01087	0.01440	0.01977
37	0.00695	0.00714	0.01069	0.01369	0.01816
38	0.00731	0.00742	0.01065	0.01286	0.01744
39	0.00769	0.00811	0.01130	0.01216	0.01588
40	0.00811	0.00798	0.01119	0.01152	0.01452
41	0.00858	0.00902	0.01094	0.01140	0.01286
42	0.00909	0.00908	0.01137	0.01099	0.01159
43	0.00964	0.01005	0.01123	0.01065	0.01111
44	0.01024	0.01063	0.01169	0.01173	0.01043
45	0.01089	0.01121	0.01258	0.01130	0.01154
46	0.01158	0.01184	0.01288	0.01253	0.01236
47	0.01231	0.01308	0.01438	0.01233	0.01205
48	0.01308	0.01391	0.01469	0.01316	0.01290
49	0.01391	0.01520	0.01660	0.01479	0.01427
50	0.01482	0.01609	0.01781	0.01551	0.01413
51	0.01586	0.01717	0.01831	0.01643	0.01533
52	0.01701	0.01877	0.01873	0.01710	0.01637
53	0.01827	0.01861	0.02107	0.01898	0.01854
54	0.01963	0.02269	0.02255	0.02008	0.01987
55	0.02111	0.02423	0.02372	0.02234	0.02283
56	0.02272	0.02637	0.02642	0.02397	0.02318
57	0.02444	0.02852	0.02869	0.02629	0.02558
58	0.02629	0.02991	0.03191	0.02786	0.02731
59	0.02827	0.03307	0.03559	0.03075	0.02996
60	0.03042	0.03462	0.03802	0.03268	0.03291

SOURCE: J. Burn, 'Industrial Mortality in 1915–1917', *Journal of the Institute of Actuaries*, LI (1918), 69–71.

TABLE A-2 ESTIMATES OF MALE MORTALITY, ENGLAND AND WALES, AT AGES 16-60

Age	Prudential hypothetical Estimate A: (1) using constant mortality rates	Prudential hypothetical Estimate B: (2) using declining mortality rates	Actual working-class war-estimate (3)	War-related deaths Estimate A (4) (3) - (1)	Estimate A: percent increase (+) or decrease (−) due to war (4)/(1)	War-related deaths Estimate B (5) (3) - (2)	Estimate B: percent increase (+) or decrease (−) due to war (5)/(2)
16	5,072	4,793	6,934	1,862	36.72	2,141	44.67
17	5,490	5,183	10,739	5,249	95.61	5,556	107.20
18	6,499	6,164	22,560	16,061	247.14	16,396	266.00
19	6,276	5,981	46,438	40,162	639.91	40,457	676.43
20	6,606	6,301	53,659	47,053	712.22	47,358	751.59
21	6,371	6,036	50,479	44,108	692.30	44,443	736.30
22	6,283	5,883	46,912	40,629	646.65	41,029	697.42
23	6,028	5,570	43,157	37,129	615.94	37,587	674.81
24	6,257	5,766	39,225	32,968	526.91	33,459	580.28
25	6,781	6,273	35,664	28,883	425.97	29,391	468.53
26	6,634	6,130	32,508	25,874	390.01	26,378	430.31
27	6,654	6,135	30,594	23,940	359.76	24,459	398.68
28	6,926	6,343	28,137	21,211	306.25	21,794	343.59
29	7,711	7,044	27,459	19,748	256.08	20,415	289.82
30	7,172	6,414	25,638	18,466	257.47	19,224	299.72
31	8,059	7,226	24,761	16,702	207.24	17,535	242.67
32	7,404	6,523	23,132	15,728	212.42	16,609	254.62
33	8,704	7,799	23,056	14,352	164.88	15,257	195.63

34	8,319	7,417	22,014	13,695	164.63	14,597	196.80
35	8,963	8,055	21,231	12,268	136.87	13,176	163.58
36	9,061	8,162	19,929	10,868	119.94	11,767	144.17
37	9,548	8,635	18,486	8,938	93.61	9,851	114.08
38	9,603	8,708	17,226	7,623	79.39	8,518	97.82
39	10,505	9,584	16,621	6,116	58.22	7,037	73.42
40	9,960	9,057	15,205	5,245	52.66	6,148	67.88
41	11,284	10,377	14,415	3,131	27.75	4,038	38.91
42	11,054	10,152	13,496	2,442	22.09	3,344	32.94
43	12,176	11,266	13,178	1,002	8.23	1,912	16.97
44	12,194	11,286	12,673	479	3.93	1,387	12.29
45	12,733	11,798	13,273	540	4.24	1,475	12.50
46	12,656	11,741	13,323	667	5.27	1,582	13.47
47	13,404	12,468	13,114	−290	−2.16	646	5.18
48	13,422	12,513	13,065	−357	−2.66	552	4.41
49	14,406	13,447	14,345	−61	−0.42	898	6.68
50	14,433	13,493	14,030	−403	−2.79	537	3.98
51	15,225	14,278	14,698	−527	−3.46	420	2.94
52	16,248	15,294	15,101	−1,147	−7.06	−193	−1.26
53	15,895	14,952	16,540	645	4.06	1,588	10.62
54	18,385	17,448	16,985	−1,400	−7.61	−463	−2.65
55	18,945	18,011	18,053	−892	−4.71	42	0.23
56	19,244	18,357	17,904	−1,340	−6.96	−453	−2.47
57	19,803	18,943	18,680	−1,123	−5.67	−263	−1.39
58	18,905	18,125	18,369	−536	−2.84	244	1.35
59	20,486	19,698	19,872	−614	−3.00	174	0.88
60	19,959	19,206	19,906	−53	−0.26	700	3.64
Total	497,743	464,035	1,012,784	515,041	103.48	548,749	118.26

TABLE A-3 ESTIMATES OF MALE MORTALITY, ENGLAND AND WALES, 1914–18, AT AGES 16–60, BY AGE COHORT

Age group	Prudential hypothetical Estimate A: using constant mortality rates (1)	Prudential hypothetical Estimate B: using declining mortality rates (2)	Actual working-class war estimate (3)	War-related deaths Estimate A (4) (3)-(1)	War-related deaths Estimate B (5) (3)-(2)	Estimate A: percent increase (+) or decrease (−) due to war (4)/(1)	Estimate B: percent increase (+) or decrease (−) due to war (5)/(2)
16–19	23,337	22,121	86,671	63,334	64,550	271.40	291.80
20–24	31,545	29,556	233,432	201,887	203,876	639.99	689.80
25–29	34,706	31,925	154,362	119,656	122,437	344.76	383.51
30–34	39,658	35,379	118,601	78,943	83,222	199.05	235.23
35–39	47,680	43,144	93,493	45,813	50,349	96.09	116.70
40–44	56,668	52,138	68,967	12,299	16,829	21.70	32.28
45–49	66,621	61,967	67,120	499	5,153	0.75	8.32
50–54	80,186	75,465	77,354	−2,832	1,889	−3.53	2.50
55–60	117,342	112,340	112,784	−4,558	444	−3.88	0.40
Total	497,743	464,035	1,012,784	515,041	548,749	103.48	118.26

SOURCE: See Table A-1.

would require us to base our analysis on the assumption of a downward progression of working-class mortality rates rather than on the 1913 rates held constant for a growing population.

This we have done in Estimate B. We have derived the annual rate of mortality decline in pre-war England and Wales from the difference between qx values in English Life Table 7, covering the years 1901–10, and English Life Table 8, which refer to 1910–12. We assumed that the hypothetical slope of mortality decline in 1914–18 for the whole population was the same as for the Prudential working-class population, and that the hypothetical decline in the absence of war would have been linear. We therefore reduced qx values after 1913 by the age-specific annual rate of decline registered in the pre-war decade. The result is a demographically plausible set of counterfactual life table mortality rates for 1914–18. Mx rates were then calculated and applied to the appropriate mid-year populations. In this way we obtained the estimates of total male deaths listed as Estimate B of Tables A-2 and A.3.

A third estimate was made to identify actual mortality patterns during the war years. Again, the 1911 male census population was 'aged' to 1913 on the basis of 1913 survival ratios. Then mid-year populations for 1914–18 were obtained by the use of survival ratios in Prudential abridged life tables constructed for 1913–17. Two additional assumptions were necessary to cope with the absence of data for 1914 and 1918. Since seven months of 1914 passed peacefully, qx rates for 1914 were calculated as an amalgam of 1913 and 1915 qx rates in appropriate proportions. And *faute de mieux*, 1918 qx rates were deemed to be identical to those of 1917. The age structure of actual deaths in 1914–18 (column 3 of tables A-2 and A-3) is the product of Mx for each year and each age, and the appropriate mid-year populations.

The difference between the totals of actual deaths in the war period and the totals of hypothetical deaths in Estimates A and B yielded two approximations of the age structure and dimensions of war-related mortality. Since Estimate B was based on the assumption of continuing mortality decline in the years 1914–18, whereas Estimate A assumed a steady state, it was inevitable that the totals of war-related deaths using Estimate B would be greater than those using Estimate A. But as we can see in Tables A-2 and A-3, the difference is not very substantial. Actual wartime mortality at ages 16–60 exceeded Estimate A by 515,000 and Estimate B by

TABLE A-4   AGE STRUCTURE OF WAR-RELATED DEATHS, 1914–18

Age group	War-related deaths: Estimate A	War-related deaths: Estimate B	Estimate A: percent WRD in each cohort	Estimate B: percent WRD in each cohort
16–19	63,334	64,550	12.30	11.76
20–24	201,887	203,876	39.20	37.15
25–29	119,656	122,437	23.23	22.31
30–34	78,943	83,222	15.33	15.17
35–39	45,813	50,349	8.90	9.18
40–44	12,299	16,829	2.39	3.07
45–49	499	5,153	0.10	0.94
50–54	–2,832	1,889	–0.55	0.34
55–60	–4,558	444	–0.88	0.08

549,000. To adopt the 'unrealistic' assumption of constant mortality over the war period leads, therefore, to an underestimate of war-related deaths of approximately 6.6 per cent.

When we turn to the question of the age structure of male mortality, the difference between the two estimates is even less substantial. As we can see in Table A-4, there is hardly any difference between the distribution of war-related deaths by age cohort between ages 16 and 45. After age 45, there is some variance. Whereas totals of war-related deaths turn negative in both estimates in 1916–18, this occurs after age 46 in Estimate A and after age 49 in Estimate B. As the quinquennial totals in Table A-3 indicate, the phenomenon of negative war-related mortality is much more striking in Estimate A than in Estimate B. However, the key point to notice is that the finding of negative war-related mortality at certain ages was registered whether or not we assume a decline in male mortality rates in the counterfactual case.

Despite the fact that the differences between Estimates A and B are relatively small, we have used the results of the more 'realistic' counterfactual B in the text. This is not only on grounds of plausibility. It is also that in quantitative history, it is conventional for scholars facing a choice between alternative assumptions to adopt the one less congenial to their overall argument. In this case, the finding of negative war-related mortality is more robust in

Estimate A. Thus to use Estimate B enables us both to be more rigorous and to avoid the temptation to choose evidence favourable to one of the central hypotheses of this book, namely that civilian survival rates improved in wartime.

Notes

(All works published in London unless otherwise noted)

INTRODUCTION

1. The man commissioned to write these books was Dr A. W. J. MacFadden, Senior Medical Officer of the Ministry of Health in the interwar years. What became of the books is a mystery.
2. M. Huber, *La Population de la France pendant la guerre* (Paris, 1931); M. Meerwarth *et al.*, *Die Einwirkung des Krieges auf Bevölkerungsbewegung und Lebenshaltung in Deutschland* (Stuttgart, 1932).
3. See the discussion in chapter 9.
4. P. Fussell, *The Great War and Modern Memory* (Oxford, 1975). See also J. Keegan, *The Face of Battle* (1976) and E. J. Leed, *No Man's Land. Combat and Identity in World War I* (Cambridge, 1979).
5. J. Hinton, *The First Shop Stewards' Movement* (1973); R. McKibbin, *The Evolution of the Labour Party, 1910–1924* (Oxford, 1974).
6. *Census of England and Wales, 1921. General Report with Appendices*, Table 2, p. 14; see also D. Glass, *Population Policies and Movements in Europe* (1940), pp. 2, 416.
7. The literature on this subject is vast. See R. Fogel, *Railroads and American Economic Growth* (Baltimore, 1966); S. Fenoaltea, 'The discipline and they', *Journal of European History*, III (1973), 729–46; P. O'Brien, *The New Economic History of the Railways* (1979); and P. Lee, *The Quantitative Approach to Economic History* (1979), ch. 6.
8. M. M. Postan, 'Some Social consequences of the Hundred Years' War', *Economic History Review*, XII (1942), 1–12.
9. R. Schofield and E. A. Wrigley, *The Population History of England 1541–1871* (1981).
10. Prof. G. Steiner of the University of Geneva has drawn to my attention a marvellous satire by Karl Kraus on the danger of such statistical obfuscations of the reality of war. See Kraus, *The Last Days of Mankind*, abridged and edited by F. Ungar (New York, 1974), Act IV, Scene VII.

1 STRATEGIC DEMOGRAPHY

1. C. E. Pollock, 'Comparison of recruiting statistics in Germany for the year 1906', *Journal of the Royal Army Medical Corps*, XIV (1910), 465; J. A. Balck,

'Recruiting in the German Army', *Jnl Roy. Army Med. Corps*, xv (1910), 567–73.

2. J. C. Hunter, 'The problem of the French birth rate on the eve of World War I', *French Historical Studies*, II (1962), 490–503.

3. For a fuller discussion, see R. Tomlinson, 'The Politics of *Dénatalité* in the French Third Republic, 1880–1940', Cambridge PhD. 1983; and J. M. Winter and M. S. Teitelbaum, *The Fear of Population Decline* (New York, 1985).

4. R. Soloway, *Birth Control and the Population Question in England, 1879–1930* (Chapel Hill, North Carolina, 1982).

5. As cited in J. M. Winter, 'The decline of mortality in Britain, 1870–1950', in T. Barker and M. Drake (eds), *Population and Society* (1982), p. 80.

6. See P. Thompson, *The Edwardians* (1979), ch. 1.

7. *United Nations Demographic Yearbook, 1976* (New York, 1976), Table 21.

8. See B. Gilbert, *The Evolution of National Insurance in Great Britain* (1966); G. Searle, *The Quest for National Efficiency* (Oxford, 1971); Searle, *Eugenics and Politics in Britain 1900–1914* (Leyden 1979).

9. For the report: PP 1903, xxx, Cd 1507; for the evidence: PP 1903, xxx, Cd 1903. All references to the evidence are cited as PTS.

10. For the report: PP 1904, xxii, Cd 2175; for the evidence, PP 1904, xxii, Cd 2110; for the appendices: PP 1904, xxii, Cd 2186. All references to the evidence are cited as PDC.

11. PTS, qq 474, 479.

12. PTS, qq 5713, 5755. See also G. Stedman Jones, *Outcast London* (1971), ch. 6.

13. PTS, q 7223.

14. PTS, q 6899.

15. PTS, qq 6983, 6986, 6987.

16. PTS, qq 7081, 7116, 7138.

17. PTS, q 13831.

18. PDC, qq 2432, 2447.

19. PDC, q 11007.

20. PDC, qq 12243-4.

21. PDC, q 3336 and q 9518, for examples.

22. PDC, q 435.

23. PDC, q 556.

24. PDC, q 3126.

25. PDC, q 2110.

26. PDC, qq 6745–6, 6766a, 6772.

27. Report, p. 46. I am grateful to Dr Helen Brock and Dr Tim Cole for their advice on current medical and nutritionists' views on this question.

28. PDC, q 3257.

29. PDC, q 3371.

30. PTS, q 7272.

31. Scottish report, appendix VI, no. 8; and PDC, qq 3656–62, 6090, 8524, 9409, 10022, 10356, 11137.

32. See Sir John Gorst's statement in Parliament, in *Hansard's Parliamentary Debates* (Hansard), 4th ser., vol. 141, 14 Feb. 1905, col. 145.

33. Col. Onslow, who was a member of the Interdepartmental Committee and an Inspector of Naval Recruiting, insisted repeatedly on this distinction. See PDC, qq 166 *et seq.*

34. PDC, qq 171, 435, 2188, 4040, 11003; PTS, q 8295.

35. Scottish report, app. IX.

36. PDC, q 987.

37. PDC, qq 10226, 10277.

38. PTS, qq 154–5.
39. PDC, qq 5039, 5265, 5350.
40. PDC, qq 1916, 1919, 1936.
41. PDC, q 11790.
42. PDC, q 11017.
43. *Reports on the Papers and Discussion at the Cambridge Meeting of the British Association, 1904, and on the Alleged Physical Deterioration of the People and the Utility of an Anthropometric Survey* (1905), p. 26.
44. F. Galton, *Hereditary Genius* (1889).
45. J. M. Winter, 'Britain's "lost generation" of the First World War; *Population Studies*, XXXI (1977), 449–66.

2 MANPOWER AND MILITARY SERVICE, 1914–1918

1. H. M. D. Parker, *Manpower* (1956), ch. 1, for a convenient summary.
2. *General Annual Report of the British Army 1913–1919*, PP 1921, XX, Cmd 1193.
3. M. Middlebrook, *The First Day of the Somme* (1971), pp. 3–4.
4. Public Record Office, London, Kitchener Papers, PRO 30/57/73, Gascoyne to Kitchener, 24 Sept. 1914.
5. Public Record Office, London, Cabinet Papers, CAB 25/95, Enlistment for the Regular Army and Territorial Forces.
6. Kitchener Papers, PRO 30/57/73, Derby to Kitchener, 29 Nov. 1914.
7. Imperial War Museum, Manuscript Collection, Account of Lt H. V. Drinkwater, DS/Misc/54. (Soldier's diaries or memoirs are listed under the author's name, and usually give the highest rank he reached in the army. These documents are hereafter referred to as IWM.)
8. IWM, Account of G. Shilton, 79/17/1.
9. IWM, Account of Col. C. B. Arnold, 81/30/1.
10. IWM, Account of H. J. Haywood, 77/155/1.
11. IWM, Accounts of Maj. W. G. Bailey, 74/127/1, and G. Shilton.
12. IWM, Account of Maj. C. H. Emerson, P/115.
13. IWM, Account of T. A. Jennings, 79/17/1; Kitchener Papers, PRO 30/57/73, Locally-raised Units.
14. IWM, Account of Capt. J. Garvie, 79/5/1.
15. IWM, Account of H. J. Haywood, 77/155/1.
16. Kitchener Papers, PRO 30/57/73, List of Locally-raised Units.
17. F. Kemster and H. C. E. Westropp, *Manchester City Battalions of the 90th and 91st Infantry Brigades Book of Honour* (Manchester, 1917), p. XII.
18. Kemster and Westropp, *Manchester City Battalions*, p. xii.
19. *Report of the Board of Trade on the State of Employment in the United Kingdom in October 1914*, PP 1914–16 XXIV, Cmd 7703, pp. 28–39. (This document formed part of a series of similar enquiries, all of which are referred to hereafter as 'Employment statistics'.)
20. P. E. Dewey, 'Military recruiting and the British labour force during the First World War', *Historical Journal*, XXVII (1984), 199–223.
21. Employment statistics, Feb. 1915, p. 11.
22. W. Jett Lauck, 'Coal mining', *British Industrial Experience during the War*, Pt V, p. 1170. United States Congress (56th), 1917, Document No. 114.
23. Lauck, 'Manufacturing industries', *British Industrial Experience*, Pt III, p. 946. On early enlistment among miners, see *Report of the Departmental Committee*

Appointed to Enquire into Conditions Prevailing in the Coal Mining Industry Due to the War, PP 1914–16, XXVIII, Cmd 7939.

24. R. Page Arnot, *Miners: Years of Struggle* (1960), p. 160.

25. Employment statistics, Oct. 1914, pp. 28–39.

26. *2nd General Report of the Departmental Committee Appointed to Enquire into the Conditions Prevailing in the Coal Mining Industry due to the War*, PP 1914–16, XXVIII, Cd 8147, p. 307.

27. Employment statistics, Feb. 1915, PP 1914–16, XXI, Cmd 7580, pp. 16–17.

28. Employment statistics, Feb. 1915, pp. 16–17.

29. Employment statistics, Dec. 1914, PP 1914–16, XXIV, Cmd 7755, p. 9.

30. Employment statistics, Dec. 1914, p. 10.

31. Employment statistics, Feb. 1915, p. 15.

32. Public Record Office, London, Reconstruction Papers, RECON 1/832, Report on Employment in April 1916, p. 20. Some bias may have been introduced into these statistics by their concentration on the experience of larger firms. I am grateful to Dr David Fitzpatrick of Trinity College, Dublin for his comments on this and other points.

33. Reconstruction Papers, RECON 1/832, Report on Employment in April 1916, p. 20.

34. E. J. W. Disbrow, *History of the Volunteer Movement in Cheshire 1914–1920* (Stockport, 1920), p. 12a.

35. *Ministry of Reconstruction, 2nd, 3rd, 4th, and 5th Interim Reports of the (Civil) War Workers Committee*, PP 1918, XIV, Cd 9120, p. 655.

36. Cabinet Papers, CAB 25/95, Enlistment for the Regular Army and Territorial Forces.

37. Ministry of National Service Papers, NATS 1/400, Statistical Tables on Enlistment.

38. R. S. Churchill, *Lord Derby. 'King of Lancashire'* (1959), pp. 201–8.

39. Ministry of National Service Papers, NATS 1/400, Statistical Tables on Enlistment.

40. W. K. Hancock and M. M. Gowing, *British War Economy 1939–45* (1965), ch. 1.

41. P. Guinn, *British Strategy and Politics 1914–1918* (1965), chs 4–6.

42. C. Wrigley, *Lloyd George and the British Labour Movement* (Brighton, 1976).

43. Cabinet Papers, CAB 24/28, GT 1481, A. C. Geddes, The Theory and Practice of Recruiting, 22 July 1917.

44. CAB 24/28, GT 2295, A. C. Geddes, Recruiting Position. The Problems and Prospects, 13 Oct. 1917.

45. CAB 24/28, GT 2295.

46. CAB 24/28 GT 2295; *History of the Ministry of Munitions,*, vol. VI, pt II, *The Control of Industrial Manpower 1917–18* (1923), p. 41.

47. CAB 24/52, GT 4618, A. C. Geddes, Maintenance of the Army in France, 22 May 1918.

48. *Statistics of the Military Effort of the British Empire during the Great War* (1922), pp. 707, 713.

49. I. O. Andrews, *Economic Effects of the War upon Women and Children in Great Britain* (New York, 1918), pp. 182–3.

50. A. W. Kirkaldy (ed.), *British Labour Replacement and Conciliation 1914–21* (1921), Table 1, p. 3.

51. Ministry of National Service Papers NATS 1/14/M156. Report upon the Medical Department of the Ministry of National Service, pp. 12–13.

52. *Special Report from the Select Committee on the Military Service (Review of*

Exemptions) Act 1917. PP 1917–18, III, 327, appendix I. (Hereafter referred to as 'Shortt committee')

53. Shortt committee, q. 1171.
54. Shortt committee, appendix I.
55. Shortt committee, qq 1208 ff.
56. Shortt committee, qq 832, 938, 1056.
57. Shortt committee, q 1646.
58. Shortt committee, q 4741.
59. 'National service ministry', *British Medical Journal* (1917), II, 487–8; NATS 1/12/M43, Payment for part-time medical services.
60. NATS 1/13/M87, General Directions, MNSR 24, pp. 43ff.
61. NATS 1/14/12/M26, Medical Grades and Categories.
62. *Report upon the Physical Examination of Men of Military Age by National Service Medical Boards from November 1st, 1917–October 31st. 1918*, PP 1919, XXVI, Cmd 504, pp. 48, 49, 64. (Hereafter referred to as Medical Report.)
63. NATS 1/12/M49, Report of the Inspector of Medical Boards, Yorkshire and East Midlands Region. See also NATS 1/13/M53, R. Owen to Galloway, 6 March 1918, on Reading.
64. *Hansard*, 1918, vol. 107, 27 June 1918, col. 1262.
65. *Hansard*, 27 June 1918, cols. 1283–4.
66. *Hansard*, 27 June 1918, cols. 1285–7.
67. *Hansard*, 27 June 1918, col. 1306.
68. *Hansard*, 27 June 1918, col. 1308.
69. *Hansard*, 27 June 1918, col. 1305.
70. *Hansard*, 1918, vol. 107,18 June 1918, cols 301ff.
71. NATS 1/15/M2/658, RAF Complaints re: enlistment of Unfit Men.
72. 'Medical notes in Parliament', *BMJ* (1918), I, p. 732.
73. *Hansard*, 1919, vol. 122, 9 Dec. 1919, cols 1169–70.
74. *Hansard*, 9 Dec. 1919, col. 1175.
75. Medical Report, p. 9.
76. Medical Report, p. 66.
77. Medical Report, p. 7.
78. Medical Report, p. 23.
79. Medical Report, p. 105.
80. Medical Report, p. 17.
81. Medical Report, p. 18.
82. Medical Report, p. 138.
83. Medical Report, p. 17.
84. Medical Report, p. 17.
85. For a full discussion of some of the biases and problems inherent in this evidence, see J. M. Winter, 'Military fitness and public health in Britain in the First World War', *Journal of Contemporary History*, XV (1980), 211–44.
86. Medical Report, p. 24.

3 THE LOST GENERATION

1. For a list of 33 such estimates, see Table 3.1 from J. M. Winter, 'Some aspects of the demographic consequences of the First World War in Britain', *Population Studies*, XXX (1976), 540.
2. Winter, 'Some aspects', p. 539.

3. See O. Morgenstern, *On the Accuracy of Economic Observations* (1960), ch. 10 in particular.

4. Winter, 'Some aspects', p. 541.

5. C. von Clausewitz, *On War*, trans., J. J. Graham (3 vols, 1911), I, p. 250.

6. For example, see Public Record Office, Ministry of Air Papers, AIR 1/14/15/1/57, for German estimates prepared in 1922 on the subject of relative losses on the Western Front.

7. *Synopsis of British Air Effort during the War*, PP 1919, XXXIII, Cmd 100.

8. *Statement of the First Lord of the Admiralty Explanatory of the Naval Estimates 1919–1920*, PP 1919, XXXIII, Cmd 451.

9. T. J. Mitchell and G. M. Smith, *Medical Services: Casualties and Medical Statistics of the Great War* (1931).

10. *Statistics of the Military Effort of the British Empire during the Great War* (1922).

11. *Hansard*, vol. 141, 4 May 1921, cols 1033–4.

12. *General Annual Report of the British Army 1913–1919*, PP 1921, XX, Cmd 1193.

13. H. Newbolt, *History of the Great War. Naval Operations* (1931), vols 4–5.

14. H. A. Jones, *History of the Great War. The War in the Air* (1931), vols 2–6.

15. I am grateful for the help of the staff of the Imperial War Museum on this point.

16. The records of the Ministry of Air at the Public Record Office do not provide much help here. See AIR 1/681/21/13/2211, 2248, and 2252 for the documentation on which the published figures were based.

17. L. Hersch, 'La mortalité causée par la guerre mondiale', *Metron*, V (1925), 89–133; B. Urlanis, *Wars and Population* (Moscow, 1971), p. 210.

18. Hersch, 'La mortalité', p. 131.

19. Major Greenwood, 'British loss of life in the wars of 1794–1815 and 1914–1918', *Journal of the Royal Statistical Society*, CV, 1 (1942), 1–11.

20. W. B. Hodge, 'On the mortality arising from military operations', *Assurance Magazine and Journal of the Institute of Actuaries* (1857–8), 80–90, 151–74, 201–17, 275–85.

21. Greenwood, 'British loss of life', p. 7.

22. These data may be found in Huber, *La Population*; and in Meerwarth *et al.*, *Die Einwirkung*.

23. W. F. Mellor (ed.), *Medical History of the Second World War. Casualties and Medical Statistics* (1972).

24. J. Burn, 'Industrial mortality in 1915–1917', *Journal of the Institute of Actuaries*, LI, (1918) 69–71.

25. R. W. Barnard (ed.), *A Century of Service: the Story of the Prudential, 1848–1948* (1948), pp. 13, 16.

26. Barnard, *A Century*, p. 78; and *Report of the Departmental Committee on the Encouragement of the Life Insurance System of the Post Office, with the Evidence*, PP 1908, XXV, (312), pp. 275ff.

27. Private communication from R. D. Clarke of the Prudential Assurance Company to the author, 25 Feb. 1975.

28. J. Benson, 'English coal miners' trade union accident funds 1850–1900', *Econ. Hist. Rev.*, 2nd ser., XXVIII (1975), 403.

29. Burn, 'Industrial mortality', p. 69.

30. See the Appendix and G. W. Barclay, *Techniques of Population Analysis* (New York, 1958), for the procedure used in this exercise.

31. *Decennial Supplement to the Annual Report of the Registrar-General of England and Wales, 1911–20* (1933), vol. II, Table 2.

32. For a full discussion of the reliability of these estimates, see Winter 'Aspects of the demographic consequences', pp. 539–51.

33. *Statistics of the Military Effort*, pp. 707, 713. See Public Record Office, Board of Trade Papers, BT 13/80/E/33741/16, for a list showing the full definition of each occupational group in the demobilization lists.

34. *Statistics of the Military Effort*, p. 713.

35. R. A. R. Redmayne, *The British Coal Mining Industry during the War* (Oxford, 1923), p. 54.

36. *General Annual Report of the British Army*, pt IV.

37. *General Annual Report of the British Army*, pt IV.

38. There is an acute juxtaposition of a picture of a real trench at the front and a 'model' trench surveyed by staff officers, in Paul Fussell, *The Great War and Modern Memory* (1975), p. 54.

39. N. N. Golovine, *The Russian Army in the World War* (Oxford, 1931), p. 83.

40. Lt-Col. Larcher, 'Données statistiques sur les forces françaises 1914–1918', *Revue militaire française* (1934), 558–9.

41. A. Vagts, 'Battle and other combat casualties in the Second World War', *Journal of Politics*, VII (1945), 284.

42. G. Bodard, *Losses of Life in Modern Wars* (Oxford, 1916), p. 18.

43. L. A. Clutterbuck (ed.), *The Bond of Sacrifice* (1915), n.p.

44. J. E. Mackenzie (ed.),*University of Edinburgh Roll of Honour 1914–1919* (Edinburgh, 1921).

45. *Statistics of the Military Effort*, p. 235.

46. See Table 3.8.

47. *The Regimental Roll of Honour and War Record of the Artists' Rifles* (1922).

48. *Artists' Rifles*, pp. xi–xii.

49. R. Graves, *Goodbye to All That* (1929), p. 133.

50. R. H. Mottram, *The Spanish Farm Trilogy* (1924–7), p. 387.

51. Larcher, 'Données statistiques', pp. 558–9.

52. Larcher, 'Données statistiques', p. 559.

53. J. M. Winter, 'Balliol's 'Lost Generation' of the First World War', *Balliol College Record* (1975), pp. 10–14.

54. Winter, 'Balliol', p. 11.

55. *British Universities and the War: A Record and its Meaning* (1919), pp. 22, 26, 32; G. V. Carey (ed.), *The War List of the University of Cambridge* (Cambridge, 1920); E. S. Craig and W. M. Gibson (eds), *Oxford University Roll of Service* (Oxford, 1920).

56. *The University of Liverpool Calendar 1918–19* (Liverpool, 1918), p. 197.

57. *The Mermaid Guild of Graduates Supplement* (Birmingham, 1917). No figures exist for the entire war period.

58. Clutterbuck (ed.), *The Bond of Sacrifice*, for biographies of officers killed in 1914.

59. *British Universities and the War*, p. xiii.

60. A. H. H. Maclean, *Public Schools and the Great War 1914–19* (n.d.), pp. 17–18.

61. R. C. Sherriff, 'The English public schools in the war', in G. A. Panichas (ed.), *Promise of Greatness* (1968), p. 134.

62. C. F. Kernot, *British Public Schools War Memorials* (1927), p. 136.

63. E. W. Moss-Blundell, *The House of Commons Book of Remembrance 1914–1918* (1931).

64. H. A. Doubleday and Lord Howard de Walden, *The Complete Peerage* (8 vols, 1932), VIII, appendix F by Major E. Martin and H. A. Doubleday.

65. C. F. G. Masterman, *England after the War: A Study* (1922), pp. 31–2.

66. T. H. Hollingsworth, 'A Demographic study of the British ducal families', in D. V. Glass and D. E. C. Eversley (eds), *Population in History* (1965), p. 359.

4 CIVILIAN HEALTH IN WARTIME BRITAIN

1. L. Hersch, 'La Mortalité causée par la guerre mondiale', *Metron*, VII (1927), 3.

2. W. Waller, *War and the Family* (New York, 1940), p. 19.

3. R. W. B. Ellis, 'Social change and child health', *Pediatrics*, xx (1955), 1042.

4. J. Ibarolla, *Les incidences des deux conflits mondiaux sur l'évolution démographique française* (Paris, 1964), p. 161. The reference is to D. Villey, *Leçons de démographie* (Paris, 1957).

5. L. Hersch, 'Demographic effects of modern warfare', in N. Angell (ed.), *What Would Be the Character of a New War?* (1933), p. 233; M. Greenwood, 'British loss of life in the Wars of 1794–1815 and 1914–18', p. 6, settles on 281,000 excess civilian deaths in Britain. This figure was drawn from Dumas and Vedel-Petersen, *Losses of Life*, pp. 133ff.

6. F. Notestein *et al.*, *The Future Population of Europe and the Soviet Union* (Geneva, 1944), p. 75. They added 67,000 to correct for the reduction of infant deaths due to the decline in the birth rate, to the figure of 402,000 for excess civilian deaths over age one, to yield a grand total of 469,000 excess civilian deaths. Thanks are due to Professor Ansley Coale for trying to find the original calculations, which alas have disappeared.

7. B. Abel-Smith, *The Hospitals, 1850–1948* (1964), p. 280.

8. J. C. Drummond and A. Wilbraham, *The Englishman's Food* (1957), p. 529.

9. For a full discussion, see J. M. Winter, 'Aspects of the impact of the First World War on infant mortality in Britain', *Journal of European Economic History*, XI (1982), 713–38.

10. The literature on this subject is huge. See for instance, P. Temin (ed.), *The New Economic History* (1973); P. O'Brien, *The New Economic History of the Railways* (1979); J. Fenoaltea, 'The Discipline and They: notes on counterfactual methodology and the 'new' economic history', *Jnl Eur. Econ. Hist.*, III (1973), 729–46; P. McClelland, *Causal Explanation and Model Building in History, Economics, and the New Economic History* (1975).

11. J. M. Winter, *Socialism and the Challenge of War* (1974), ch. 7.

12. *Mortality of Men in Certain Occupations in the Years 1910, 1911, and 1912. Supplement to the 75th Report of the Registrar General of England and Wales*, Pt IV (1923); *Occupational Mortality, Decennial Supplement to the Annual Report of the Registrar-General of England and Wales, 1911–20*, pt II (1933).

13. The only substantive difference between them is in terms of age limits: for the 1900–12 period, it is 25–65; for 1921–3, it is 20–65.

14. L. I. Dublin, *The Mortality Experience of the Working Population, 1911–16* (New York, 1921).

15. S. H. Preston, N. Keyfitz, R. Schoen, *Causes of Death. Life Tables for National Populations* (New York, 1972), p. 6.

16. Preston, *Mortality Patterns in National Populations* (1976), ch. 4.

17. *Report on the Mortality from Influenza in England and Wales, during the Epidemic of 1918–19. Supplement to the 83rd Report of the Registrar-General of England and Wales*. PP 1920, x, Cmd 760.

18. L. Hersch, 'La Guerre et la grippe', *Bibliothèque universelle de Génève* (1924), pp. 709–11.

19. A. W. Crosby, *Epidemic and Peace, 1918* (1976).

20. Thanks are due to Dr Michael Teitelbaum of the Alfred Sloan Foundation for advice on this point.

21. Preston, *Mortality*, p. 20.

22. See A. Omran, 'The Epidemiological transition: a theory of the epidemiology of population change', *Milbank Memorial Fund Quarterly*, XLIX (1971), 509–38, as cited in S. Kunitz, 'Speculations on the European mortality decline', *Econ. Hist. Rev.*, 2nd ser., XXXVI (1983), 350.

23. *Decennial Supplement, 1911–20*, p. cxxxviii.

24. I am grateful to Lord Adrian of Pembroke College, Cambridge for advice on this point. See *Decennial Supplement, 1911–20*, p. lxxxvii; and *Registrar-General's Statistical Review of England and Wales for 1921*, Table 5.

25. *Decennial Supplement, 1911–20*, pp. xcix, cxxiv.

26. C. Dyhouse, 'Working-class mothers and infant mortality in England and Wales, 1895–1914', *Journal of Social History*, XII (1978).

27. *Decennial Supplement, 1911–20*, p. xciii.

28. K. Faber, 'Tuberculosis and nutrition', *Acta Tuberculosea Scandinavica* (1938), 287–335.

29. E. Collis and M. Greenwood, *The Health of the Industrial Worker* (1921), pp. 132–3.

30. *Report of the Committee on Tuberculosis in War-time*. Medical Research Council Special Report Series No. 246 (1942), p. 34.

31. R. and T. Dubos, *The White Plague. Tuberculosis, Man and Society* (1953).

32. *Decennial Supplement, 1911–20*, pp. xcii–xciii; *Registrar-General's Statistical Review for England and Wales*, 1935–8.

33. Department of Health and Social Security Library, Sir George Newman Diaries, 10 Oct. 1915.

34. Hersch, 'Mortalité', (1927), p. 11.

35. Hersch, 'Mortalité', (1927), p. 11.

36. These remarks are based on the full statistical tables presented in J. M. Winter, 'Infant mortality in Britain during the First World War', SSRC Report HR/5071 (1980).

37. Wallis Taylor, 'The Changing pattern of mortality in England and Wales. I. Infant mortality', *British Journal of Preventive and Social Medicine* VIII (1954), 3.

38. J. B. Hardy, 'Fetal consequences of viral infection in pregnancy', *Archives of Otolaryngology*, XCVIII (1973), 218–27.

39. *78th Report of the Registrar-General for England and Wales for 1915*, PP 1917–18, v, Cmd 8484; *61st Report of the Registrar-General for Scotland*, PP 1916, VI, Cmd 8339; N. Scrimshaw, C. Taylor, and J. Gordon, *Interactions of Nutrition and Infection* (Geneva, 1968), p. 245.

40. E. W. Hope, *Report on the Physical Welfare of Mothers and Children* (Dunfermline, 1917), vol. 1; W. Leslie Mackenzie, *Scottish Mothers and Children* (Dunfermline, 1917); Newsholme's report may be found in PP 1917–18, XVI, Cd 8496.

41. P. L. McKinlay, 'Some statistical aspects of infant mortality', *Journal of Hygiene*, XXVIII (1929), 394–417; N. Scrimshaw, C. Taylor and J. Gordon, 'Interactions of nutrition and infection', *American Journal of the Medical Sciences* (1959), 363–403; P. Newberne and G. Williams, 'Nutritional influences on the course of infection', in H. Dunlop and H. Moon (eds), *Resistance to Infectious Disease* (Saskatoon, 1970); L. Mata and R. Wyatt, 'Host resistance to infection', *American Journal of Clinical Nutrition* (1971), 976–86; W. Akroyd, 'Nutrition and mortality in infancy', *American Journal of Clinical Nutrition* (1971), 480–7; W. Page Falk, L. Mata and G. Edsall, 'Effects of malnutrition on the immune response in humans: a review', *Tropical Diseases Bulletin* (1975), 89–103.

5   MEDICAL CARE IN WARTIME

1. E. M. Little, *History of the British Medical Association 1832–1932* (1932), p. 238. J. R. Currie, *The Mustering of Medical Services in Scotland 1914–1919* (Edinburgh, 1922). p. 117.
2. Currie, *Mustering*, p. 17.
3. Currie, *Mustering*, p. 5.
4. British Medical Association Archives, Papers of the Central Medical War Committee, Minutes, 30 July 1915. (Hereafter referred to as CMWC)
5. F. Honigsbaum, *The Division in British Medicine* (1979), p. 326, and A. Cox, *Among the Doctors* (1950), pp. 109–23.
6. CMWC minutes, 30 July 1915.
7. CMWC minutes, 4 Aug. 1915.
8. CMWC minutes, 15 Sept. 1915.
9. CMWC minutes, 20 Sept. 1914, for the first discussion of this matter.
10. *Royal Commission on National. Health Insurance, Appendices and Index* PP 1926, xiv, Cmd 2596 Appendix I, Section 8, p. 10.
11. CMWC minutes, 15 Oct. 1915.
12. CMWC minutes, 25 Oct. 1915.
13. CMWC minutes, 10 Nov. 1915, 15 Nov. 1915.
14. CMWC minutes, 15 Nov. 1915. Memorandum on Recruitment of Medical Officers for the Army and Navy as Affecting the Medical Services of the Civilian Population.
15. CMWC minutes, 19 Nov. 1915.
16. CMWC minutes, 24 Nov. 1915.
17. CMWC minutes, 6 Dec. 1915.
18. CMWC minutes, 23 Dec. 1915.
19. CMWC minutes, 31 Dec. 1915.
20. CMWC minutes, 31 Dec. 1915.
21. CMWC minutes, 22 Dec. 1915.
22. CMWC minutes, 7 April 1916.
23. CMWC minutes, 23 June 1916.
24. CMWC minutes, 12 May 1916 and 19 May 1916.
25. CMWC minutes, 1 Dec. 1916 for a survey of the year's events.
26. CMWC minutes, 1 Dec. 1916.
27. CMWC minutes, 1 Dec. 1916.
28. CMWC minutes, 15 Dec. 1916 and 19 Jan. 1917.
29. CMWC minutes, 19 Jan. 1917.
30. CMWC minutes, 26 Feb. 1917 and 11 April 1917.
31. Currie, *Mustering*, p. 111; CMWC minutes, 27 April 1917.
32. Currie, *Mustering*, pp. 112–13.
33. CMWC minutes, 5 April 1917.
34. Currie, *Mustering*, pp. 116–17.
35. CMWC minutes, 25 May 1917.
36. CMWC minutes, 14 June 1917.
37. CMWC minutes, 21 June 1917.
38. CMWC minutes, 1 Aug. 1917.
39. NATS 1/720, Keogh to Geddes, 1 Sept. 1917.
40. NATS 1/720, Memorandum on the Relation of the Ministry of National Service to the Central Medical War Committee.
41. NATS 1/854, Report of the Commission on Medical Establishments in France, 20 Dec. 1917.

42. NATS 1/720, Memorandum on the Relation of the Ministry of National Service to the Central War Committee.

43. NATS 1/720, Meeting of the Ministry of National Service, Central Medical War Committee, and Scottish Medical Services Emergency Committee, minutes, 1 Dec. 1917.

44. NATS 1/740, Morant to Geddes, 22 Dec. 1917.

45. NATS 1/740, Galloway to Morant, 22 Dec. 1917; CMWC minutes, 29 Dec. 1917.

46. MH 7/9, Geddes Memorandum on War Office Demands for Medical Practitioners, 1918; NATS 1/13/M83 for War Office calculations arriving at the figure of 500.

47. MH 7/9, Morant Memorandum, 'The Question of Further Withdrawals of Doctors from Civilian Medical Practice for Recruitment of the Army Medical Services', 5 March 1918.

48. CMWC minutes, 22 March 1918.

49. 'The Employment of alien doctors at hospitals', The Hospital, LXII (26 May 1917), 144; 'An Indian on the staff', The Hospital, LXII (26 May 1917), 144.

50. CMWC minutes, 12 Oct. 1917.

51. CMWC minutes, 12 Sept. 1917. See also NATS 1/814 on shortages of medical students.

52. CMWC minutes, 20 Nov. 1917.

53. CMWC minutes, 11 Jan. 1918.

54. NATS 1/711, Committee of Reference Memorandum on Shortage of Medical Students and Medical Men on Whole-time Military Service.

55. CMWC minutes, 17 Jan. 1917.

56. CMWC minutes, 4 July 1916, 'Scheme for the Care of Practices'.

57. NATS 1/14/M132, Glasgow Medical Services.

58. CMWC minutes, 16 July 1918.

59. NATS 1/760, Hallett to Galloway, 29 April 1918.

60. CMWC minutes, 11 Feb. 1916 for one of many statements of this scheme drawn up by Harman.

61. CMWC minutes, 26 Jan. 1917, 'Notes on Mobilization'; see also Little, BMA, p. 429.

62. Currie, Mustering, p. 148.

63. CMWC minutes, 18 June 1918.

64. CMWC minutes, 21 May 1918.

65. CMWC minutes, 11 June 1918.

66. NATS 1/839, 'RAMC Requirements for Medical Men 1918–19', L. A. Boyd to War Office, 19 July 1918.

67. British Medical Association Archives, Medico-Political Committee minutes, 6 Nov. 1914. (Hereafter referred to as MPC)

68. MPC, 6 Nov. 1914.

69. MPC, 8 Jan. 1915.

70. MPC, 18 Feb. 1915.

71. MPC, 9 Dec. 1915.

72. MPC, 25 May 1916, 14 June 1916, 11 Oct. 1915.

73. MPC, 11 Oct. 1916.

74. MPC, 6 July 1917, 3 Oct. 1917.

75. MPC, 31 Jan. 1917.

76. Scottish Record Office, Edinburgh, Carnegie Papers, HH 281/65/14.

77. MPC, 14 Sept. 1917, 5 March 1918.

78. MPC, 3 April 1918.

79. MPC, 15 Aug. 1916.

80. R. Earwicker, 'Miners' medical services before the First World War: the South Wales coalfield', *Llafur*, III (1981), 39–52.
81. MPC, 27 March 1917.
82. MPC, 6 June 1917.
83. Preston *et al.*, *Causes of Death*, p. 35.
84. NATS 1/812, Dean Hacker to Galloway, 11 Dec. 1917.

6 HEALTH ADMINISTRATION IN WARTIME

1. G. F. McLeary, *The Maternity and Child Welfare Movement* (1935). A. Oakley's *The Captured Womb* (Oxford, 1984), was published too late for inclusion in this study.
2. On the different milieux in which these discussions took place, see R. Tomlinson, 'The Politics of *Dénatalité* during the French Third Republic, 1890–1940', Cambridge PhD (1983).
3. See M. S. Teitelbaum and J. M. Winter, *The Fear of Population Decline* (New York, 1985), ch. 2.
4. On the Cooperative Women's Guild and this issue, see M. Llewellyn-Davies (ed.), *Maternity* (1915).
5. Population Investigation Committee and Royal College of Obstetrics and Gynaecology, *Maternity* (1948), and J. M. Winter, 'Unemployment, nutrition and infant mortality in Britain 1920–1950', in J. M. Winter (ed.), *The Working Class in Modern British History* (Cambridge, 1983).
6. See M.-M. Huss, 'Propaganda and pro-natalism in wartime France', in R. Wall and J. M. Winter (eds), *The Upheaval of War: Family, Work, and Welfare in Europe 1914–1918* (Cambridge, 1986).
7. R. M. Titmuss, 'War and social policy', in *Essays on 'the Welfare State* (1958), pp. 75–87.
8. McCleary, *Maternity*, p. 16.
9. McCleary, *Maternity*, p. 18n.
10. McCleary, *Maternity*, pp. 19–20.
11. 'Baby Week', *Daily Telegraph*, 3 July 1917.
12. 'Baby Week', *The Times*, 3 July 1917.
13. 'Bishop and the Babies', *Daily Telegraph*, 2 July 1917.
14. 'National Baby Week', *Daily Telegraph*, 28 May 1917. Dr A. E. Harris, Medical Officer of Health for Islington, was disturbed by this remark. He noted that the *Daily Telegraph* leader 'may express the military point of view, which, though a practical one, is, nevertheless, a very poor reason in a Christian country'. *61st Annual Report on the Health and Sanitary Condition of the Metropolitan Borough of Islington* (1917), p. 11.
15. J. Cossar Ewart, 'The saving of child life', *Nineteenth Century and After*, LXXXII (1917), 119.
16. See Teitelbaum and Winter, *Fear*, ch. 2.
17. PP. 1914–16, xxv,Cd 8153. *44th Report of the Local Government Board for 1914–15*, appendix to pt 1: LGB Circular no. 1 on Maternity and Child Health.
18. *Ibid.* For later developments, see in subsequent reports of the Chief Medical Officer of the LGB, LGB Circular no. 3 on 'Notification of Births (Extension) Act 1915. Circular Letter to County Councils and Sanitary Authorities', 29 July 1915. LGB Circular no. 4 on 'Regulations under which Grant will be Paid by the Local Government Board to Maternity Centres during the Year ending 31st March 1916', 7 July 1916.
19. M. Bell, 'Review of reports on war work in England, France, and Germany

with special reference to the care of women during pregnancy and labor', *American Journal of Obstetrics*, LXXXVII (1918), 475.

20. Bell, 'Review', p. 475. This is confirmed by the Welfare Advisory Committee of the Ministry of Munitions. See also PRO, MUN 5/346/140.

21. McCleary, *Maternity*, p. 20; and for the 1918 regulations, dated 9 August 1918, see MH 53/51.

22. E. W. Hope, *Report on the Physical Welfare of Mothers and Children. England and Wales. Volume I* (Dunfermline, 1917), epitomes of local reports, Middlesbrough.

23. *Local Government Board. Maternity and Child Welfare. Report on Provision made by Public Health Authorities and Voluntary Agencies in England and Wales* (1917). This was an occasional paper rather than a command paper. For a full discussion and tabulation of local variations in maternal and infant welfare work in this period, see J. M. Winter, 'Aspects of the impact of the First World War on infant mortality in Britain', *Journal of European Economic History*, XI, 3 (1982), 713–38.

24. Hope, *Physical Welfare*, epitomes of local reports, Wandsworth.

25. *Mothers' Welcome. Metropolitan Borough of Wandsworth, Wandsworth and Putney Centres. First Annual Report, 1915–16* (1916), pp. 3–5.

26. MH 55/543. Newsholme to Lane-Claypon, 13 Aug. 1914.

27. MH 55/543. Lane-Claypon to Newsholme, 15 Aug. 1914.

28. A copy may be found in MH 55/543.

29. MH 48/168. Islington Borough Council to Harris, 15 Dec. 1915.

30. MH 48/168. Long to Islington Borough Council, 12 June 1916.

31. MH 48/163. Copy of *Daily Telegraph* article of 17 June 1916; Islington Borough Council to LGB, 17 June 1916.

32. MH 48/163. Islington Borough Council to LGB, 7 Sept. 1916.

33. MH 48/161. Minute of Newsholme, 4 Sept. 1911.

34. MH 48/161. Copy of 'Save the Babies', *South London Press*, 30 June 1916.

35. MH 48/161. Copy of 'Camberwell Nonconformity', *Medical Officer*, 27 Jan. 1917.

36. MH 48/23. LGB to Clerk, Cornwall County Council. 4 Oct. 1915; Boscawen to LGB, 16 Oct. 1915.

37. MH 48/23, for extensive correspondence on this point.

38. MH 48/42. Copy of *Durham County Advertiser* of 11 March 1911.

39. All references are to remarks reported in the epitomes of local reports in Hope, *Physical Welfare*, vol. 1.

40. MH 55/542, Papers on Carnegie Trust. See also, Scottish Record Office, GD/281/63/1-10, on the same project.

41. PP 1917–18, XXV Cmd 2020. *Return of Grants by the Local Government Board in 1916–17 to the 27 London Boroughs and the City of Westminster, and to the Cities of Birmingham, Manchester, Liverpool, Leeds and Bradford, in Aid of Municipal and Voluntary Infant Welfare Centres, with the Names of the Institutions*.

42. *History of the Ministry of Munitions*, vol. V, pt III, *Welfare: the Control of Working Conditions*, p. 1. (All reference to this multi-volume history are referred to hereafter as HMM.)

43. Ministry of Munitions, *Health of the Munitions Worker Handbook* (1917).

44. HMM, V, pt III, p. 2.

45. HMM, V, pt III, p. 5.

46. HMM, V, pt III, p. 68

47. For instance, see A. Livingstone-Learmouth and B.M. Cunningham, 'Observations on the effects of tri-nitro-toluene on women workers', *Lancet*, 12 Aug. 1916, 261–4.

48. Ministry of Munitions, *Handbook*, p. 115.
49. MUN 5/346/140.
50. E. Matthias, 'Getting more from workers by giving them more', *System*, XXIII, 5 (1918), 308–14.
51. R. R. Hyde, 'Making the factory boy efficient', *System*, XXXI (1916), 3–10.
52. HMM, V, pt III, p. 47.
53. MUN 5/93/346/142, for remarks made at a welfare conference at Oxford in 1918.
54. LAB 2/50/17, Memorandum on Day Nurseries, 23 July 1917, by Dr Scurfield. I have been unable to identify this commentator.
55. LAB 2/50/17, G. M. Duckworth on Day Nurseries Grants, 24 July 1916.
56. LAB 2/50/17, G. M. Duckworth memorandum of 25 July 1916.
57. LAB 2/50/17, Duckworth to Treasury, 9 April 1918.
58. On this problem, see the hesitations in the Ministry of Health response to a proposed International Labour Organization Maternity Convention on the payment of pregnant women to leave the labour force for a fixed period before and after delivery, in MH 55/228.
59. National Insurance Act of 1911 (1 & 2 Geo. 5. Ch. 55).
60. N. Whiteside, 'Welfare legislation and the unions during the First World War', *Historical Journal*, XXIII, 4 (1980), 862.
61. MH 62/94, Payment to Doctors, Memorandum of Chief Actuary, A. W. Watson, 11 Feb. 1918.
62. PIN 2/40, Subcommittee of Advisory Committee of the NHIC, 13 July 1915.
63. PIN 2/40, Cornwall memorandum to War Cabinet, 31 Oct. 1917.
64. J. Turner, 'State purchase of the liquor trade in the First World War', *Hist. Jnl*, XXIII, 3 (1980), 589–615.
65. T. N. Carver, *Government Control of the Liquor Business in Great Britain and the United States* (New York, 1919), p. 119.
66. J. M. Winter, 'Some aspects of the demographic consequences of the First World War in Britain', *Pop. Stud.*, XXX (1976), 539–52.
67. M. E. Rose, 'The Success of social reform? The Central Control Board (Liquor Traffic) 1915–21', in M. R. D. Foot (ed.), *War and Society* (1973), p. 76.
68. M. Scharlieb, 'The Relation of alcohol and alcoholism to maternal and child welfare', *British Journal of Inebriety* (1919), p. 95.
69. HMM, vol. V, pt IV: *The Provision of Canteens in War Factories*, p. 19.
70. M. A. Crowther, *The Workhouse System* (1982).
71. On VD, see the discussion in J. M. Winter, 'Military fitness and public health', p. 499.
72. See E. Miller (ed.), *Neuroses of War* (1944).
73. E. L. Collis and M. Greenwood, *The Health of the Industrial Worker* (1921), ch. 6.
74. G. Jessel, 'Tuberculosis and the war', *Public Health*, XXXI, 11 (1918), 124–6.
75. E. L. Collis, 'Discussion on the incidence of industrial tuberculosis', *Proceedings of the Royal Society of Medicine*, XI, 2 (1918), 133–41 and subsequent papers.

7 STANDARDS OF LIVING AND STANDARDS OF HEALTH

1. *Report of the Committee Appointed to Enquire into and Report upon (i) the Actual Increase since June 1914, in the Cost of Living to the Working Classes and (ii)*

Any Counter-balancing Factors (Apart from Increase of Wages) which May have Arisen under War Conditions, PP 1918, VII, Cd 8980, p. 7. (Hereafter referred to as the Summer report.)

2. A. Mor O'Brien, 'Patriotism on trial: the strike of the South Wales miners, July 1915, *Welsh History Review*, XXX (1984), 76–104. For an evaluation of 'profiteering', see J. S. Boswell and B. R. Johns, 'Patriots or profiteers? British businessmen and the First World War', *Journal of European Economic History*, XI (1982), 432–45.

3. A. J. Coles, 'The moral economy of the crowd: some twentieth century food riots', *Journal of British Studies*, XVIII (1978), 157–76.

4. PRO MAF 60/243, Rationing food queues; and MAF 60/562, Table 84, Estimates of number of people in food queues in Metropolitan Police District, 1918.

5. *Inquiry into Industrial Unrest*, PP 1917–18, XV, Cd 8662–9, 8696.

6. PRO CAB 24/30, GT 2465, 'Wages and Prices', 29 Oct. 1917.

7. Sumner report, p. 9.

8. PP 1917–18, XVI, Cd 8511, Ministry of Munitions, Health of Munitions Workers Committee, *Interim Report. Industrial Efficiency and Fatigue*, Oct. 1916.

9. *Inquiry into Industrial Unrest*, PP 1917–18, XV, Cd 8662–9, 8696.

10. PRO MAF 60/243, The effect of food queues at home on men at the front, 16 April 1918.

11. PRO MAF 60/104, Memorandum on Food since 1914, 2 Jan. 1918. For evidence found in other, more limited, contemporary surveys, see M. Ferguson, 'The family budgets and dietaries of forty labouring class families in Glasgow in wartime', *Proceedings of the Royal Society of Edinburgh*, XXXVII (1917), 117–36; F. Wood, 'The increase in the cost of food for different classes of society since the outbreak of the war', *Jnl Roy. Stat. Soc.*, LXXIX (1916), 501–8; M. S. Pembrey, 'The Restricted supply of food; its relation to health and efficiency', *Journal of the Royal Sanitary Institute*, XXXVIII (1917), 59–70; and Viscount Dunluce and M. Greenwood, 'An inquiry into the composition of dietaries, with special reference to the dietaries of munitions workers', Medical Research Council, *Special Report Series*, no. 13 (1918).

12. Sumner report, p. 12.

13. In the cases of tea, eggs, bread and flour, and an assortment of other minor foods, we have used the more complete data in the Sumner report. See Table 7.5.

14. See the list of rations for men serving in the army and navy in PRO MAF 60/562, Table 78.

15. PRO 30/68, Anderson Papers, retail and wholesale bread prices, 1917-18.

16. Sumner report, p. 7. This was true for all grades of workers submitting budgets to the Sumner committee.

17. A. L. Bowley, *Prices and Wages in the United Kingdom 1914–1920* (Oxford, 1921), pp. 97ff.

18. A. R. Prest, *Consumer Expenditure in the United Kingdom 1900–1919* (Cambridge, 1954), p. 123.

19. Bowley, *Prices and Wages*, pp. 63–6.

20. Prest, *Consumer Expenditure*, p. 75.

21. Prest, *Consumer Expenditure*, p. 89.

22. See A. L. Bowley's comments in the discussion of J. E. Allen, 'Some changes in the distribution of the national income during the war', *Journal of the Royal Statistical Society*, LXXXIII (1920), 86–126.

23. J. W. F. Rowe, *Wages in Theory and Practice* (1928), p. 3.

24. N. B. Dearle, *The Labor Cost of the World War to Great Britain 1914–1922* (New Haven, Conn., 1940), p. 73.

25. D. M. Barton, 'The course of women's wages', *Jnl Roy. Stat. Soc.*, LXXXII (1919), 508–53.

26. A. L. Bowley, *Prices and Wages in the United Kingdom 1914–1920* (Oxford, 1921), pp. 97ff.

27. W. Beveridge, *British Food Control* (Oxford, 1928), ch. x.

28. L. Oren, 'The welfare of women in labouring families in England 1850–1950', L. Banner and L. Hartmann (eds), *Clio's Consciousness Raised* (1974), pp. 50–102.

29. R. Roberts, *The Classic Slum* (Harmondsworth, 1966), ch. 9.

30. M. Barlow, *War Pensions, Gratuities, Allowances, Treatment and Training for Officers, Non-commissioned Officers and Men* (1918).

31. V. J. Purton, 'An investigation of the living standards of the working class in Leeds and Norwich in the First World War', Diploma in Historical Studies dissertation, Cambridge, 1983, p. 61.

32. Scottish Record Office, Edinburgh, SRO HH 4/2, Memorandum on the feeding of school children, 29 Nov. 1922.

33. Purton, 'Investigation', p. 60.

34. M. Bowley, *Housing and the State 1919–1944* (1945).

35. M. Swenarton, *Homes Fit for Heroes* (1981), p. 52.

36. Swenarton, *Homes*, p. 51.

37. F. E. Fremantle, *The Housing of the Nation* (1927).

38. Fremantle, *Housing*, p. 29.

39. Durham County Record Office, Transcript of Conference on the Housing of the Working Classes, 2 May 1919. For a comparison of overcrowding in the country as a whole in 1911 and 1921, see *Census of England and Wales, 1921*, vol. II, General Tables, Table 27.

40. See the interesting remarks on the weakness of arguments relating nutritional levels primarily to aggregate food supply, in A. Sen, *Poverty and Famines* (Oxford, 1981).

41. W. R. Scott and J. Cunnison, *The Industries of the Clyde Valley during the War* (Oxford, 1924), p. 170.

42. D. T. Jones *et al.*, *Rural Scotland during the War* (1926), ch. 2.

43. See the epitomes of local reports in E. W. Hope, *Report on the Physical Welfare of Mothers and Children* (Dunfermline, 1917).

44. F. Mannheim, *War and Crime* (1927); 'Pauperism during the war', *Labour Gazette*, March 1920, p. 122.

45. See J. Lee, 'Administrators and agriculture: some aspects of German agricultural policy in the First World War', in J. M. Winter (ed.), *War and Economic Development* (Cambridge, 1975); and Kocka, *German Society at War* (Leamington Spa, 1985), ch. 2.

46. See both P. E. Dewey, 'Food consumption in the United Kingdom 1914–1918', and R. Spree, 'Nutrition and mortality in wartime Germany', in Wall and Winter (eds), *The Upheaval of War*.

8   THE DEMOGRAPHIC AFTERMATH OF THE FIRST WORLD WAR

1. For an overview written during the war, see B. Mallet, 'Vital statistics as affected by the war', *Journal of the Royal Statistical Society*, LXXXI (1918), 1–36. On wartime movements in marriage rates, see the *78th Annual Report of the Registrar-General of England and Wales for 1915*, PP 1917–18, V, Cd 8484, p. xi; *81st Annual Report of the Registrar-General of England and Wales for 1918*, PP 1920, X, Cmd 608, p. xxi.

2. *The Registrar-General's Decennial Supplement. England and Wales 1921. Part III. Estimates of Population. Statistics of Marriages, Births and Deaths 1911–1920* (1933), pp. xvi–xxiii.

3. F. Notestein *et al.*, *The Future Population of Europe and the Soviet Union* (Geneva, 1944), p. 75.

4. L. Hersch, 'Demographic effects of modern warfare', in N. Angell *et al.*, *What Would be the Character of a New War?* (1933), pp. 55–6.

5. L. Henry, 'Perturbations de la nuptialité résultant de la guerre 1914–1918', *Population*, XXI (1966), 272–332.

6. See G. Cadoux, 'Nos pertes de guerre, Leur réparations et nos dettes de guerre', *Journal de la société de statistique de Paris*, LXV (1925), 326; and chapter 3 above.

7. M. Beard, 'The Impact of the First World War on Agricultural Society in West Sussex', Cambridge, M Litt., 1984.

8. J. Hajnal, 'Aspects of recent trends in marriage in England and Wales', *Population Studies*, I (1947), Table 2.

9. Hajnal, 'Marriage', Table 1.

10. M. S. Teitelbaum, *The British Fertility Decline: Demographic Transition in the Crucible of the Industrial Revolution* (Princeton, 1984), p. 100.

11. Hajnal, 'Marriage', Table 5.

12. See A. J. Coale, 'The decline of fertility in Europe from the French Revolution to World War II', in S. J. Behrman *et al.*, *Fertility and Family Planning: A World View* (Ann Arbor, 1969), pp. 3–24.

13. Teitelbaum, *British Fertility Decline*, p. 101.

14. Teitelbaum, *British Fertility Decline*, p. 101.

15. Hajnal, 'Marriage', pp. 81n, 85.

16. Hajnal, 'Marriage', Table 1.

17. G. Rowntree and N. H. Carrier, 'The resort to divorce in England and Wales, 1858–1957', *Population Studies*, XI (1958), 188–233. See also O. McGregor, *Divorce in England* (1957).

18. C. Lasch, *Haven in a Heartless World: the Family Besieged* (1977).

19. PRO, PIN26/18, for the correspondence on this case. There are numerous similar examples in the Ministry of Pensions' Medical Disablement Files, soon to be deposited at the PRO.

20. N. B. Dearle, *The Labor Cost of the World War to Great Britain 1914–1922* (New Haven, Conn., 1940), ch. IX.

21. B. Thomas, *Migration and Economic Development: A Study of Great Britain and the Atlantic Economy* (Cambridge, 1973); and his bibliographic survey, *International Migration and Economic Development* (Paris, 1961).

22. N. H. Carrier and J. R. Jeffery, *External Migration, A Study of the Available Statistics 1815–1950* (1953), General Register Office Studies in Medical and Population Subjects no. 6, pp. 24–5, 34–7.

23. Teitelbaum, *The British Fertility Decline*, Tables 4.2., 6.2, 6.8.

24. D. Glass and D. Grebenik, *The Trend and Pattern of Fertility in Great Britain. A Report on the Family Census of 1946.* Papers of the Royal Commission on Population, vol. VI, pt 1, p. 253.

25. A. L. Bowley and M. H. Hogg, *Has Poverty Diminished? A Sequel to 'Livelihood and Poverty'* (1925), pp. 16–23.

26. See J. M. Winter, 'Unemployment, nutrition, and infant mortality in Britain, 1920–1950', in J. M. Winter (ed.), *The Working Class in Modern British History* (Cambridge, 1983), for a full discussion of this theme.

27. *Copy of Reports Made to the Prime Minister by the British Legion Regarding the Condition of Ex-service Men and of His Reply.* PP 1937–8, X, Cmd 5738.

28. This formula can be found in numerous files in the Ministry of Pensions, Medical Disablement Files.

29. P. Stocks, 'Fifty years of progress as shown by vital statistics', *British Medical Journal* (1950), I, 54.

30. Ministry of Pensions, Medical Disablement Files.

9 DEMOGRAPHIC HISTORY, CULTURAL HISTORY AND MEMORIES OF WAR

1. See Wrigley and Schofield's *Population History of England 1541–1871* (1981); A. J. Coale, 'The Decline of fertility in Western Europe since the French Revolution', in Behrman (ed), *Fertility and Family Planning* (Ann Arbor, 1965), and the numerous volumes in the Princeton series on European fertility decline.

2. A. Marwick, *The Deluge* (1966); B. Waites, 'The impact of the First World War on class and status in England, 1910–20', PhD, Open University, 1983.

3. See the Cambridge War Collection in the Cambridge University Library for hundreds of examples of each of these categories.

4. For a full examination of trench journalism, see the forthcoming Cambridge Phd dissertation of John Fuller.

5. *War Illustrated*, 20 April 1918.

6. Kitchener Papers, PRO 30/57/74, unsigned memorandum, 'A Note on the resources of the Allies and of the enemy, and their effect on the duration of the war', 31 March 1916. I am grateful for the advice of Trevor Wilson of the University of Adelaide in identifying Robertson as the likely author of this document.

7. C. C. Abbott and A. Bertram (eds), *Poet and Painter, Being the Correspondence between Gordon Bottomley and Paul Nash 1910–1944* (1955), p. 99; F. Nash, *Outline* (1949), p. 203.

8. I. M. Parsons, *Men Who March Away* (1965), p. 163. (Hereafter cited as Parsons).

9. Parsons, p. 35.

10. Parsons, p. 90.

11. Parsons, p. 91.

12. H. Read, 'The failure of the war books', in *A Coat of Many Colours* (1945), pp. 72–6.

13. H. Williamson, *The Wet Flanders Plain* (1929), p. 18.

14. Williamson, *Flanders Plain*, p. 19.

15. E. Blunden, in a 1964 introduction to F. Manning, *Her Privates We* (pb. ed., 1967), p. 10.

16. P. Fussell, *The Great War and Modern Memory* (Oxford, 1975), p. 334.

17. Parsons, p. 168.

18. G. Chapman, *A Passionate Prodigality* (1933), p. 277.

19. R. K. R. Thornton (ed.), *Ivor Gurney. War Letters* (Ashington, 1983), p. 130.

20. V. A. Panichas (ed.), *Promise of Greatness* (1968), p. 157. (Hereafter cited as Panichas.)

21. F. M. Ford, *Parade's End* (Harmondsworth, 1982), p. 181.

22. S. Sassoon, *Memoirs of an Infantry Officer* (1930), p. 171; see also R. Graves, *Goodbye to All That* (1929), pp. 188, 196.

23. Sassoon, *Memoirs of an Infantry Officer*, p. 205.

24. Sassoon, *Sherston's Progress* (1936), p. 165.

25. Chapman, *Passionate*, p. 346.

26. See H. Klein (ed.), *The First World War in Fiction* (1973) and K. Vondung (ed.), *Kriegserlebnis* (Gottingen, 1979). I am grateful for the advice of Professor Volker Berghahn of the University of Warwick on this point.

27. See M. Ferro, *The Great War 1914–1918* (1973), pp. 3–8.

28. E Leed, *No Man's Land. Combat and Identity in World War One* (Cambridge, 1979). On war as a machine, see Manning, *Her Privates We*, p. 74 and *passim*. The ribald undertone of the title can be understood in this context.

29. Panichas, p. 374.

30. Panichas, p. 284.

31. Sassoon, *Memoirs of an Infantry Officer*, p. 59.

32. As cited in J. Stallworthy, *Wilfred Owen* (1974), p. 159.

33. Manning, *Her Privates We*, p. 20.

34. A. P. Herbert, *The Secret Battle* (1919), p. 63.

35. Panichas, p. 164.

36. Sassoon, *Memoirs of an Infantry Officer*, p. 148.

37. Ford, *Parade's End*, p. 434.

38. As cited in E. Blunden, *War Poets 1914–1918* (1959), p. 22.

39. E. Blunden, *Undertones of War* (1928), p. 114. See also Chapman, *Passionate*, p. 126.

40. Blunden, *Undertones*, p. 12.

41. Chapman, *Passionate*, pp. 64, 265.

42. British Library of Political and Economic Science, Dalton Papers, Dalton Diaries, 5 Sept. 1921.

43. Stallworthy, *Owen*, p. 287.

44. R. H. Mottram, *The Spanish Farm Trilogy* (1927), pp. 575–6, 781.

45. Panichas, p. 286.

46. Sassoon, *Memoirs of an Infantry Officer*, p. 94; Graves, *Goodbye*, pp. 182–4.

47. C. Carrington, *Soldiers from the Wars Returning* (1965), pp. 252–3.

48. Ford, *Parade's End*, pp. 356, 813.

49. Graves, *Goodbye*, p. 235.

50. V. Brittain, *Testament of Youth* (1933), pp. 168, 366, 469–70, 579.

51. R. J. Lifton, *Death in Life. The Survivors of Hiroshima* (1968), p. 481.

52. Lifton, *Death in Life*, p. 489.

53. R. H. Tawney, 'The Attack', in *The Attack and other papers* (1953), pp. 1–11.

54. Panichas, p. 163.

55. Ford, *Parade's End*, pp. 355–6, 484, 561.

56. F. Manning, *Her Privates We* (1929), p. 273.

57. R. Aldington, *Death of a Hero* (1929), pp. 155, 201.

58. See Thornton's introduction to *Ivor Gurney. War Letters* and Gurney's letter to Marion Scott, 4 Oct. 1917, p. 215.

59. Parsons, p. 140.

60. Lifton, *Death in Life*, p. 500.

61. Williamson, *Flanders Plain*, p. 19.

62. Panichas, p. 290.

63. Chapman, *Passionate*, p. 3. Indeed the title of his book bears learned witness to the personal meaning of bereavement. He took it from a passage in Sir Thomas Browne's *Urn Burial* (1658) which reads: 'to drink of the ashes of dead relations, a passionate prodigality. He that hath the ashes of his friend hath an everlasting treasure:' The reference is to the myth in which Artemis's craving to be one with her dead husband, Mausolus, led her to drink his ashes. Browne rejected this as an excess and pointed to the need for a via media, a mid-point between extremes of bereavement. See C. Sayle (ed.), *The Works of Sir Thomas Browne* (Edinburgh,

1929), iii, pp. 132–3. I am grateful for advice on this point from Dr Howard Erskine-Hill of Pembroke College, Cambridge.

64. Panichas, p. 379.

65. B. Bergonzi, *Heroes' Twilight* (1965), p. 68.

66. Graves, *Goodbye*, p. 79.

67. As cited in Fussell, *The Great War*, p. 203.

68. See J. Glenn Gray, *The Warriors* (New York, 1960).

69. I owe this formulation to Prof. George Mosse of the University of Wisconsin. See his article in Vondung (ed.), *Kriegserlebnis*.

70. Fussell, *The Great War*, passim.

71. D. Cannadine, 'War and death, grief and mourning in modern Britain', in J. Whaley (ed.), *Mirrors of Mortality* (1982), pp. 187–242.

STATISTICAL APPENDIX

1. This was the basis of the calculations initially reported in 'Some aspects of the demographic consequences of the First World War in Britain', *Population Studies*, xxx (1976), 539–52. As will be apparent from the text, we have adopted other assumptions here. In addition, we have corrected some computational errors in the original estimation of hypothetical mortality levels had there been no war.

Bibliography

I MANUSCRIPT SOURCES

1 Public Record Office, Kew

Admiralty papers (ADM)
Anderson papers (PRO 30)
Board of Education papers (ED)
Board of Trade papers (BT)
Cabinet papers (CAB)
Government Actuary's papers (ACT)
Kitchener papers (PRO 30)
Ministry of Agriculture and Fisheries papers (MAF)
Ministry of Air papers (AIR)
Ministry of Health papers (MH)
Ministry of Labour papers (LAB2)
Ministry of Munitions papers (MUN)
Ministry of National Service papers (NATS)
Ministry of Pensions papers (PIN)
Ministry of Reconstruction papers (RECO)
Privy Council Original Correspondence (PC)
Treasury Papers (T)
Home Office papers (HO)
War Office papers (WO)

2 Scottish Record Office, Edinburgh

Carnegie United Kingdom Trust papers (LGD)
Development Department papers (DD)
Education Department papers (ED)
Home and Health Department papers (HH)
Steel Maitland papers (GD)

3 National Library of Wales, Aberystwyth

D. A. Thomas (Lord Rhondda) papers
Lloyd George papers
Medical Officer of Health Reports
Monmouthshire Training Centre for Midwives papers

4   Local Record Offices:

For a full set of references to holdings in these archives, see J. M. Winter, 'The impact of the First World War on infant and maternal health in Britain', SSRC grant HR/5091, final report. The following indicates where records relevant to the subject of civilian health in wartime have been found. It is not a complete list of such archives, but rather a list of those searched in the course of research.

A   Lancashire, Cheshire, and Yorkshire

Chester Record Office, The Castle, Chester
Lancashire County Record Office, Preston
Leeds Archives Department, Sheepscar, Chapeltown Road, Leeds
Leeds City Reference Library
Manchester Borough Archive, Manchester Central Library
Preston County Borough Archive, Preston Central Library
Warrington Borough Archive, Warrington Central Library
Wigan Borough Records, Leigh Town Hall

B   East Anglia

Norwich and Norfolk Local Sources Library
Norwich and Norfolk Record Office
Cambridge Record Office, Cambridge
Cambridge City Library, Cambridgeshire Collection
Huntingdon Record Office

C   London

Greater London Council Record Office and History Library

D   North-east England

Darlington Library
Durham County Record Office
Gateshead Library
Tyne and Wear Record Office, Newcastle

E   Wales

Cardiff Central Library, Reference Department
Dyfed Record Office, Haverfordwest
Glamorgan Archive Service, Cardiff
Gwent Record Office, Cwmbran
Merthyr Tydfil Health Centre and Carnegie Library
Swansea Central Library, Reference Department
Swansea Guildhall (The Brangwyn Hall)

5   Imperial War Museum, London, Archives and Library

6   Private papers

Addison papers, Bodleian Library, Oxford
Baldwin papers, Cambridge University Library

Beveridge papers, British Library of Political and Economic Science (BLPES)
British Medical Association archives, BMA, London
Dalton papers (BLPES)
Eugenics Society papers, Wellcome Institute, London
Fawcett Library, City of London Polytechnic
Lloyd George papers, House of Lords Library
Sir James Marchant papers, British Library, London
Newman papers, Department of Health and Social Security Library, London
Newman papers, Hereford and Worcester Record Office
Newsholme Files, London School of Hygiene and Tropical Medicine
Passfield papers (BLPES)
Ponsonby papers, Bodleian Library, Oxford
Royal Society papers, Royal Society, London
Society of Medical Officers of Health papers, Wellcome Unit for the History of
   Medicine, Oxford
Gertrude Tuckwell Collection, Trades Union Congress Library, London
Webb Reconstruction papers, BLPES

II PARLIAMENTARY PAPERS

(The following are Parliamentary Papers cited in the text in addition to the annual
reports of the Registrars-General of England and Wales and of Scotland, of the
Chief Medical Officer of the Local Government Board, and Census reports, which
are listed in section III below.)

PP 1903, xxx, Cd 1507, 1508: *Reports and Papers of the Royal Commission on
   Physical Training in Scotland*
PP 1904, xxxii, Cd 2175, 2210, 2186: *Report and Papers of the Interdepartmental
   Committee on Physical Deterioration*
PP 1908, xxv, 312: *Report of the Departmental Committee on the Encouragement of
   the Life Insurance System of the Post Office*
PP 1914–16, xxi, Cmd 7580: *Report of the Board of Trade on the State of
   Employment in the United Kingdom in February 1915*
PP 1914–16, xxiv, Cmd 7703: *Report of the Board of Trade on the State of
   Employment in the United Kingdom in 1914*
PP 1914–16, xxiv, Cmd 7755: *Report of the Board of Trade on the State of
   Employment in the United Kingdom in December 1914*
PP 1914–16, xxviii, Cmd 7939: *Report of the Departmental Committee Appointed to
   Enquire into Conditions Prevailing in the Coal Mining Industry due to the War*
PP 1914–16, xxviii, Cd 8147: *2nd General Report of the Departmental Committee
   Appointed to Enquire into Conditions Prevailing in the Coal Mining Industry due
   to the War*
PP 1914–16, xxxv, Cd 8111, 8154: *Increase in Rents in Scottish Industrial Districts*
PP 1914–16, xxxix, Cd 8149: *Earl of Derby's Report on Recruiting*
PP 1914–16, xxxix, Cd 8168: *Report on Recruiting in Ireland*
PP 1916, xvii, Cd 8390: *Men of Military Age in Ireland*
PP 1917–18, iii, 327: *Special Report from the Select Committee on the Military
   Service (Review of Exemptions) Act 1917*
PP 1917–18, xv, Cd 8662–9 and xv, Cd 8696: *Industrial Unrest: Reports of Inquiry*
PP 1917–18, xvi, Cd 8511: *Ministry of Munitions. Health of Munitions Workers
   Committee. Interim Report. Industrial Efficiency and Fatigue*
PP 1917–18, xxv, Cmd 2020: *Return of Grants by the Local Government Board in*

1916–17 to the 27 London Boroughs and the City of Westminster, and to the Cities of Birmingham, Manchester, Liverpool, Leeds, and Bradford, in Aid of Municipal and Voluntary Infant Welfare Centres, with the Names of the Institutions

PP 1918, VII, Cd 8980: *Report of the Committee Appointed to Enquire into and Report upon: (i) the Actual Increase since June 1914, in the Cost of Living to the Working Classes and (ii) Any Counter-balancing Factors (Apart from Increase in Wages) which May Have Arisen under War Conditions*

PP 1918, XIV, Cd 9120: *Ministry of Reconstruction, 2nd, 3rd, 4th, and 5th Interim Reports of the (Civil) War Workers Committee*

PP 1919, XXVI, Cmd 504: *Report upon the Physical Examination of Men of Military Age by National Service Medical Boards from November 1st, 1917–October 31st 1918*

PP 1919, XXXIII, Cmd 100: *Synopsis of the British Air Effort during the War*

PP 1919, XXXIII, Cmd 451: *Statement of the First Lord of the Admiralty Explanatory of the Naval Estimates 1919–1920*

PP 1920, XIV, Cmd 39: *Ministry of Pensions. Second Annual Report*

PP 1921, XX, Cmd 1193: *General Annual Report of the British Army 1913–1919*

PP 1926, XIV, Cmd 2596: *Royal Commission on National Health Insurance, Appendices and Index*

PP 1937–8, X, Cmd 5738: *Copy of Reports Made to the Prime Minister by the British Legion regarding the Condition of Ex-servicemen and of his Reply*

III   VITAL STATISTICS, HEALTH AND CENSUS REPORTS

1   Census Reports

A   England and Wales:

1. *Census of England and Wales, 1901, General, Report:* PP 1904, CVIII, Cd 2174

2. *Census of England and Wales, 1911, Preliminary Report:* PP 1911, LXXI, Cd 5705

3. *Census of England and Wales, 1921, Preliminary Report:* PP 1921, XVI, Cmd 1485, *General Report with Appendices* (1927).

B   Scotland:

1. *Census of Scotland, 1901, Preliminary Report:* PP 1901, XC, Cd 644

2. *Census of Scotland, 1911, Preliminary Report:* PP 1911, LXXI, Cd 5700

3. *Census of Scotland, 1921, Preliminary Report:* PP 1921, XVI, Cmd 1473

2   Central Midwives Board, Annual Reports:

A   England and Wales

For 1914–15: PP 1914–16, XXVII, Cd 8142
    1915–16: PP 1916, XIII, Cd 8408
    1916–17: PP 1917–18, XVI, Cd 8906
    1917–18: PP 1919, XXV, Cmd 17

B   *Scotland:*

> 1916–17: PP 1917–18, xvi, Cd 8616
> 1917–18: PP 1918, xii, Cd 9116
> 1918–19: PP 1919, xxv, Cmd 332

3   *Local Government Board, Annual Reports:*

A   *England and Wales*: (Reports of the Chief Medical Officer)

> For 1911–12: PP 1912–13, xxxvi, Cd 6341
> 1912–13: PP 1914, xxxvii, Cd 7181
> 1913–14: PP 1914, xxxix, Cd 7612
> 1914–15: PP 1914–16, xxv, Cd 8153
> 1915–16: PP 1916, xiii, Cd 8423
> 1916–17: PP 1917–18, xvi, Cd 8767
> 1917–18: PP 1918, xi, Cd 9169
> 1918–19: PP 1919, xxiv, Cmd 462

B   *Scotland*: (Annual Reports)

> For 1911: PP 1912–13, xxxvii, Cd 6192
> 1912: PP 1913, xxxiii, Cd 6720
> 1913: PP 1914, xi, Cd 7327
> 1914: PP 1914–16, xxvi, Cd 8041
> 1915: PP 1916, xiii, Cd 8273
> 1916: PP 1917–18, xvi, Cd 8517
> 1917: PP 1918, xi, Cd 9020
> 1918: PP 1919, xxv, Cmd 230
> 1919: PP 1920, xxi, Cmd 824

C   *Supplements and Special Reports*:

> 1. *Infant and Child Mortality*, PP 1910, xxxix, Cd 5263
> 2. *Infant and Child Mortality*, PP 1913, xxxii, Cd 6909
> 3. *Infant Mortality in Lancashire*, PP 1914, xxxix, Cd 7511
> 4. *Report on Maternal Mortality in Connection with Childrearing and its Relation to Infant Mortality*, PP 1914–16, xxv, Cd 8085
> 5. *Supplement on Child Mortality at Ages 0-5*, PP 1917–18, xvi, Cd 8496
> 6. *Maternity and Child Welfare. Report on Provision made by Public Authorities and Voluntary Agencies in England and Wales* (1917).

4   *Registrar-General, Annual Reports and Supplements*

(After 1919, these reports are not published as Parliamentary Papers, but may be found listed annually as the *Registrar-General's Statistical Review*.)

A   *England and Wales*:

> For 1911: PP 1912–13, xiii, Cd 6578
> 1912: PP 1913, xvii, Cd 7028
> 1913: PP 1914–16, ix, Cd 7780
> 1914: PP 1916, v, Cd 8206
> 1915: PP 1917–18, v, Cd 8484
> 1916: PP 1917–18, vi, Cd 8869

1917: PP 1919, x, Cmd 40
1918: PP 1920, x, Cmd 608
1919: PP 1920, xi, Cmd 1017

B   Scotland:

For 1911: PP 1912–13, xiv, Cd 6143
1912: PP 1913, xv, Cd 6843
1913: PP 1914–16, x, Cd 7893
1914: PP 1914–16, xi, Cd 8160
1915: PP 1916, vi, Cd 8339
1916: PP 1918, vi, Cd 9014
1917: PP 1919, x, Cmd 287
1918: PP 1920, xii, Cmd 655
1919: PP 1920, xii, Cmd 980

C   Supplements:

A. *Supplement to the 75th Annual Report of the Registrar-General of England and Wales, Part IV, Mortality of Men in Certain Occupations in the Three Years 1910, 1911 and 1912* (1923)
B. *Report (Supplementary to the Annual Report) on the Mortality from Influenza in Scotland during the Epidemic of 1918–19* PP 1919, x, Cmd 282
C. *Supplement to the 83rd Annual Report of the Registrar-General of England and Wales, Report on the Mortality from Influenza in England and Wales, during the Epidemic of 1918–19.* PP 1920, x, Cmd 760
D. *Decennial Supplement to the Annual Report of the Registrar-General of England and Wales, 1911–20* (1927, 1933)

IV   CONTEMPORARY NEWSPAPERS AND PERIODICALS

American Journal of Obstetrics
Board of Trade and Labour Gazette
British Journal of Inebriety
British Medical Journal
Daily Telegraph
Eugenics Review
Hansard's Parliamentary Debates
The Hospital
Journal of Hygiene
Journal of Mental Science
Journal of State Medicine
Journal of the Institute of Actuaries
Journal of the Royal Army Medical Corps
Journal of the Royal Sanitary Institute
Journal of the Royal Statistical Society
Journal of Tropical Medicine
Lancet
Medical Officer
Metron
Nineteenth Century and After
The Practitioner

Proceedings of the Royal Society of Edinburgh
Proceedings of the Royal Society of Medicine
Public Health
System
The Times
War Illustrated
Wipers Times

V DISSERTATIONS

1. M. Beard, The Impact of the First World War on Agricultural Society in West Sussex, Cambridge MLitt, 1985
2. J. Donneson, The Development of the Profession of Midwife in England from 1750 to 1902, London PhD, 1974
3. D. Dwork, The History of the Infant Welfare Movement in England, 1898–1918, London PhD, 1984
4. J. Fuller, Morale in British Forces during the First World War, Cambridge PhD. 1986.
5. J. Gillespie, Economic and Political Change in the East End of London during the 1920s, Cambridge PhD, 1983
6. V. Purton, An Investigation of the Living Standards of the Working Class in Leeds and Norwich in the First World War, Cambridge Diploma in Historical Studies, 1983
7. S. Szreter, The Decline of Marital Fertility in England and Wales, *C* 1870–1914, Cambridge PhD, 1984
8. R. Tomlinson, The Politics of *Dénatalité* during the French Third Republic, 1890–1940, Cambridge PhD, 1983
9. B. Waites, The Impact of the First World War on Class and Status in England, Open University PhD, 1983

VI BOOKS AND ARTICLES

(All works published in London unless otherwise indicated)

Abbot, C. C. and Bertram, A. (eds), *Poet and Painter, Being the Correspondence between Gordon Bottomley and Paul Nash 1910–1944* (1955)
Abel-Smith, B., *The Hospitals 1800–1948* (1955)
Akroyd, W., 'Nutrition and mortality in infancy', *American Journal of Clinical Nutrition*, xx (1971), 480–7
Aldington, R., *Death of a Hero* (1929)
Allardyce, M. D. (ed.), *University of Aberdeen Roll of Service in the Great War 1914–1919* (Aberdeen, 1920)
Allen, F. J., 'The coming race', *Public Health*, xxix (1915), 26–36
Allen, J. E., 'Some changes in the distribution of the national income during the war', *Journal of the Royal Statistical Society*, Lxxxiii (1920), 86–126
Andrews, I. O., *Economic Effects of the War upon Women and Children in Great Britain* (New York, 1918)
Arnot, R. P., *Miners: Years of Struggle* (1960)
Bailey, T. R., 'War and national welfare', *Public Health*, xxx (1916), 52–61
Balck, J. A., 'Recruiting in the German Army', *Journal of the Royal Army Medical Corps*, xv (1910), 567–73

Barclay, G. W., *Techniques of Population Analysis* (New York, 1958)

Barker, T. and Drake, M. (eds), *Population and Society* (1982)

Barlow, M., *War Pensions, Gratuities, Allowances, Treatment and Training for Officers, Non-commissioned Officers and Men* (1918)

Barnard, R. W. (ed.), *A Century of Service: the Story of the Prudential, 1848–1948* (1948)

Barnett, C., 'A military historian's view of the Great War', *Essays by Divers Hands*, n.s. XXXVI (1970), 1–18

Barton, D. M., 'The course of women's wages', *Jnl Roy. Stat. Soc.*, LXXXII (1919), 508–53

Behrman, S. J. *et al.*, *Fertility and Family Planning* (Ann Arbor, 1969)

Bell, M., 'Review of reports on war work in England, France, and Germany with special reference to the care of women during pregnancy and labor', *American Journal of Obstetrics*, LXXXVII (1918), 445–75

Benson, J., 'English coal miners' trade union accident funds 1850–1900', *Economic History Review*, 2nd ser., XXVIII (1975), 390–410

Bergonzi, B., *Heroes' Twilight* (1965)

Beveridge, W., *British Food Control* (Oxford, 1928)

Blunden, E., *Undertones of War* (1929)

Blunden, E., *War Poets 1914–1918* (1959)

Boag, H., 'Human capital and the cost of the war', *Journal of the Royal Statistical Society*, LXXIX (1916), 7–17

Bodard, G., *Losses of Life in Modern Wars* (Oxford, 1916)

Bogart, E. L., *Direct and Indirect Costs of the Great War* (1920)

Booth, C., *Life and Labour of the People of London* (1903)

Boswell, J. S. and Johns, B. R., 'Patriots or profiteers? British businessmen and the First World War', *Journal of European Economic History*, XI (1982), 423–45

Bourgeois-Pichat, J., 'La mesure de la mortalité infantile', *Population*, VI (1951), 233–48 and 459–80

Bowley, A. L., *Prices and Wages in the United Kingdom 1914–1920* (Oxford, 1921).

Bowley, A. L. and Hogg, M. H., *Has Poverty Diminished? A Sequel to 'Livelihood and Poverty'* (1925)

Bowley, M., *Housing and the State 1919–1944* (1945)

British Industrial Experience during the War, US Congress (56th) Sessional Paper (Washington, 1917)

British Labour Statistics, 1886–1968 (1971)

British Universities and the War: A Record and its Meaning (1919)

Brittain, V., *Testament of Youth* (1933)

Bryce, Lord, 'Facts and questions before us', *Hibbert Journal*, XIV(1915), 70–80

Burns, J., 'Industrial mortality in 1915–1917', *Journal of the Institute of Actuaries*, LI (1918), 69–71

Cadoux, G., 'Nos pertes de guerre, leur réparations et nos dettes de guerre', *Journal de la Société de Statistique de Paris*, LXV (1925), 326–33

Campbell, H., 'War neuroses', *The Practitioner*, XCVI (1916), 501–9

Campbell, M., 'Death rate from diseases of the heart: 1876–1959', *British Medical Journal* (1963), II, 528–35.

Campbell, J., *Maternity Services* (1935)

Cannadine, D., 'War and death, grief and mourning in modern Britain', in J. Whaley (ed.), *Mirrors of Mortality* (1982), pp. 187–242

Carey, G. V. (ed.), *The War List of the University of Cambridge* (Cambridge, 1920)

Carrier, N. H. and Jeffery, J. R., *External Migration. A Study of the Available Statistics 1815–1950*. General Register Office Studies in Medical and Population Subjects no. 6 (1953)

Carrington, C., *Soldiers from the Wars Returning* (1965)

Carver, T. N., *Government Control of the Liquor Business in Great Britain and the United States* (New York, 1919)

Chapman, G., *A Passionate Prodigality* (1933)

Chapman, G. (ed.), *Vain Glory* (1960)

Checkland, O. and Lamb, M. (eds), *Health Care as Social History. The Glasgow Case* (Aberdeen, 1981)

Churchill, R. S., *Lord Derby. 'King of Lancashire'* (1959)

Clausewitz, C. von, *On War*, trans. J. J. Graham (1911)

Clutterbuck, L. A. (ed.), *The Bond of Sacrifice* (1915)

Coles, A. J., 'The moral economy of the crowd: some twentieth century food riots', *Journal of British Studies*, XVIII (1978), 157–76

Collis, E., 'Discussion on the incidence of industrial tuberculosis', *Proceedings of the Royal Society of Medicine*, XI (1918), 133–41

Collis, E., 'The protection of the health of munitions workers', *Journal of State Medicine*, XXV (1917), 203–13

Collis, E. and Greenwood, M., *The Health of the Industrial Worker* (1921)

Cox, A., *Among the Doctors* (1950)

Cox, P. R., *Demography* (Cambridge, 1970)

Craig, E. S. and Gibson, W. M. (eds), *Oxford University Roll of Service* (Oxford, 1920)

Crosby, A. W., *Epidemic and Peace, 1918* (1976)

Crowther, M. A., *The Workhouse System, 1830–1929* (1982)

Cruttwell, C. M. R. F., *A History of the Great War, 1914–18* (1936)

Currie, J. R., *The Mustering of Medical Services in Scotland 1914–1919* (Edinburgh, 1922)

Darling, C., *Inner Templars who Volunteered and Served in the Great War* (1924)

Darwin, L., 'On the statistical enquiries needed after the war in connection with eugenics', *Journal of the Royal Statistical Society*, LXXIX (1916), 159–75

Dearle, N. B., *The Labor Cost of the World War to Great Britain 1914–1922* (New Haven, Conn, 1940)

Dembrey, M., 'The Restricted supply of food: its relation to health and hygiene', *Journal of the Royal Sanitary Institute*, XXXVIII (1917), 61–70

Dewey, P., 'Food consumption in the United Kingdom, 1914–1918', in Winter and Walls (eds), *The Upheaval of War* (Cambridge, 1986)

Dewey, P., 'Military recruiting and the British labour force during the First World War', *Historical Journal*, XXXVII, (1984), 199–223

Disbrow, E. J. W., *History of the Volunteer Movement in Cheshire 1914–1920* (Stockport, 1920)

Doubleday, H. A. and de Walden, Lord Howard, *The Complete Peerage*, 8 vols (1932)

Drummond, J. C. and Wilbraham, A., *The Englishman's Food* (1957)

Dublin, L. I., *The Mortality Experience of the Working Population 1911–16* (New York, 1921)

Dubos, R. and T., *The White Plague. Tuberculosis, Man and Society* (1953)

Dudfield, R., 'Still-births in relation to infantile mortality', *Journal of the Royal Statistical Society*, LXXVI (1912), 1–27

Dumas, S. and Vedel-Petersen, P. O., *Losses of Life Caused by War* (Oxford, 1923)

Duncan, L. C., 'The comparative mortality of disease and battle casualties in the historic wars of the world', *Journal of the Military Service Institution of the United States*, LIV (1914), 142–77

Dunlop, H. and Moon, H. (eds), *Resistance to Infectious Disease* (Saskatoon, 1970)

Dunluce, Viscount and Greenwood, M., 'An inquiry into the composition of the dietaries of munitions workers', *Medical Research Council Special Report Series*, no. 13 (1918)

Dyhouse, C., 'Working-class mothers and infant mortality in England, 1895–1914', *Journal of Social History*, XII (1978), 248–67

Earwicker, R., 'Miners' medical services before the First World War: the South Wales coalfield', *Llafur*, III (1981), 39–52

Edmonds, J. E., *A Short History of the World War* (1951)

Ellis, F. P., and Rowlands, A., 'The health of the Navy in two world wars', *Journal of the Royal Naval Medical Service*, LII (1966), 1–20

Ellis, R. W. B., 'Social change and child health', *Pediatrics*, XX (1955), 1040–50

Ewert, J. Cossar, 'The Saving of child life', *Nineteenth Century and After*, LXXXII (1917), 117–20

Faber, K., 'Tuberculosis and nutrition', *Acta Tuberculosea Scandinavica*, XII (1938), 287–335

Falk, W. P., Mata, L. and Edsall, G., 'Effects of malnutrition on the immune response in humans: a review', *Tropical Diseases Bulletin*, XX (1975), 89–103

Fenoaltea, S., 'The discipline and they: Notes on counterfactual methodology and the 'new' economic theory history', *Journal of European Economic History*, III (1973), 729–46

Ferguson, M., 'The family budgets and dietaries of forty labouring class families in Glasgow in wartime', *Proceedings of the Royal Society of Edinburgh*, XXVII (1917), 117–36

Ferro, M., *The Great War 1914–1918*, trans. N. Stone (1973)

Fogel, R., *Railroads and American Economic Growth* (Baltimore, 1966)

Foot, M. R. D. (ed.), *War and Society* (1973)

Ford, F. M., *Parade's End* (Harmondsworth, 1982)

Fremantle, F. E., *The Housing of the Nation* (1927)

Fussell, P., *The Great War and Modern Memory* (Oxford, 1975)

Galton, F., *Hereditary Genius* (1889)

Gilbert, B., *British Social Policy 1914–1939* (1970)

Gilbert, B., *The Evolution of National Insurance in Great Britain* (1966)

Glass, D., *Population Policies and Movements in Europe* (1940)

Glass, D. and Grebenik, E., *The Trend and Pattern of Fertility in Great Britain* (1954)

Golovine, N. N., *The Russian Army in the World War* (Oxford, 1931)

Graves, R., *Goodbye to All That* (1929)

Gray, J. Glenn, *The Warriors* (New York, 1960)

Greenwood, M., 'British loss of life in the wars of 1794–1815 and 1914–1918', *Journal of the Royal Statistical Society*, CV (1942), 1–11

Guinn, P., *British Strategy and Politics 1914–1918* (1965)

Hardy, J. B., 'Fetal consequences of viral infection in pregnancy', *Archives of Otolaryngology*, XCVIII (1973), 218–27

Hajnal, J., 'Aspects of recent trends in marriage in England and Wales', *Population Studies*, I (1947), 72–98

Hancock, W. K. and Gowing, M. M., *British War Economy 1939–45* (1965)

Henry, L, 'Perturbations de la nuptialité résultant de la guerre 1914–1918', *Population*, XXI (1966), 272–332

Herbert, A. P., *The Secret Battle* (1919)

Hersch, L., 'Demographic effects of modern warfare', in N. Angell *et al.*, *What Would Be the Character of a New War?* (1933)

Hersch, L., 'La guerre et la grippe', *Bibliothèque universelle de Génève*, I (1924), 709–11

Hersch, L., 'La mortalité causée par la guerre mondiale', *Metron*, V (1925), 89–133; VII (1927), 3–83

Hersch, L., *Pauvreté et mortalité selon les principales causes de décès d' après les statistiques de la ville de Paris* (Rome, 1932)

Hinton, J., *The First Shop Stewards' Movement* (1973)

History of the Ministry of Munitions, 12 vols (1923)

Hodge, W. B., 'On the mortality arising from military operations', *Assurance Magazine and Journal of the Institute of Actuaries* (1857–8), 80–90, 151–74, 201–17, 275–85

Hollingsworth, T. H., 'A demographic study of the British ducal families', in Glass, D. and Eversley, D.E.C. (eds), *Population in History* (1965)

Honigsbaum, F., *The Division in British Medicine* (1979)

Honigsbaum, F., *The Struggle for the Ministry of Health 1914–1919*, London School of Economics Department of Social Administration Occasional Paper no. 37 (1972)

Hope, E. W., *Report on the Physical Welfare of Mothers and Children* (Dunfermline, 1917)

Huber, M., *La population de la France pendant la guerre* (Paris, 1931)

Hunter, J. C., 'The Problem of the French birth rate on the eve of World War I', *French Historical Studies*, II (1962), 490–503

Huss, M.-M., 'Propaganda and pro-natalism in wartime France', in R. Wall and J. M. Winter (eds), *The Upheaval of War: Family, Work, and Welfare in Europe 1914–1918* (Cambridge, 1985)

Hyde, R. R., 'Making the factory boy efficient', *System*, XXX (1916), 3–10

Ibarolla, J., *Les incidences des deux conflits mondiaux sur l'évolution démographique française* (Paris, 1964)

International Labour Organization, *Compensation for War Disabilities in Great Britain and the United States* Studies and Reports, Series E, no. 4 (Geneva, 1921)

Ireland's Memorial Record 1914–18 (Dublin, 1923)

Jessel, G., 'Tuberculosis and the war', *Public Health*, XXXI (1918), 124–6

Jones, D. T. *et al.*, *Rural Scotland during the War* (1926)

Jones, H. A., *History of the Great War. The War in the Air* (1931)

Kayne, G. G., *The Control of Tuberculosis in England. Past and Present (1937)*

Keay, J., 'War and the burden of insanity', *Journal of Mental Science*, LXIV (1918), 320–30

Keegan, J., *The Face of Battle* (1976)

Kemster, F., and Westropp, H. C. E., *Manchester City Battalions of the 90th and 91st Infantry Brigades Book of Honour* (Manchester, 1917)

Kernot, C. F., *British Public Schools War Memorials* (1927)

Kirkaldy, A. W. (ed.), *British Labour Replacement and Conciliation 1914–21* (1921)

Klein, H. (ed.), *The First World War in Fiction* (1973)

Kocka, J., *German Society at War*, trans. B. Weinberger (Leamington Spa, 1985)

Kraus, K., *The Last Days of Mankind* (New York, 1974)

Kunitz, S., 'Speculations on the European mortality decline', *Economic History Review*, 2nd ser., XXXVI (1983), 345–70

Lane-Claypon, J., *The Child Welfare Movement* (1920)

Larcher, Lt Col., 'Données statistiques sur les forces françaises 1914–1918,' *Revue militaire française* (1934) 198–223, 351–63, and 558–9

Lasch, C., *Haven in a Heartless World: the Family Besieged* (1977)

Lee, J., 'Administrators and agriculture: some aspects of German agricultural policy in the First World War', in J. M. Winter (ed.), *War and Economic Development* (Cambridge, 1975)

Lee, P., *The Quantitative Approach to Economic History* (1979)

Leed, E. J., *No Man's Land. Combat and Identity in World War I* (Cambridge, 1979)

Lewis, J., *The Politics of Motherhood* (1980)

Lifton, R. J., *Death in Life. The Survivors of Hiroshima* (1968)

Little, E. M., *History of the British Medical Association 1832–1932* (1932)

Livingstone-Learmouth, A. and Cunningham, B. M., 'Observations on the effects of tri-nitro-toluene on women workers', *Lancet*, CLXI (1916), II, 261–4.

Llewellyn-Davies, M. (ed.), *Maternity* (1915)

McGregor, O., *Divorce in England* (1957)

Mackenzie, J. E. (ed.), *University of Edinburgh Roll of Honour 1914–1919* (Edinburgh, 1921)

MacKenzie, W. L., *Scottish Mothers and Children* (Dunfermline, 1917)

McKibbin, R., *The Evolution of the Labour Party, 1910–1924* (Oxford, 1974)

McKinlay, P. L., 'Some statistical aspects of infant mortality', *Journal of Hygiene*, XXVIII (1929), 394–417

Maclean, A. H. H., *Public Schools and the Great War* (n.d.)

McClelland, P. D., *Causal Explanation and Model Building in History, Economics, and the New Economic History* (1975)

McLeary, G. F., *The Maternity and Child Welfare Movement* (1935)

Mallet, B., 'Vital statistics as affected by the war', *Journal of the Royal Statistical Society*, LXXXI (1918), 1–36

Manchester University Roll of Service (Manchester, 1922)

Mannheim, F., *War and Crime* (1927)

Manning, F., *Her Privates We* (1967)

Marwick, A., *Britain in the Century of Total War* (1968)

Marwick, A., *The Deluge* (1966)

Marwick, A., *War and Social Change in the Twentieth Century* (1974)

Masterman, C. F. G., *England after the War: a Study* (1922)

Mata, L. and Wyatt, R., 'Host resistance to infection', *American Journal of Clinical Nutrition*, XX (1971), 976–86

Matthias, E., 'Getting more from workers by giving them more', *System*, XXIII (1918), 308–14

May, O., 'The prevention of venereal diseases in the Army', *The Practitioner*, XCVI (1916), 482–90

Medical Research Council, *Report of the Committee on Tuberculosis in Wartime* (1942)

Meerwarth, M. *et al.*, *Die Eienwirkung des Krieges auf Bevölkerungsbewegung und Lebenshaltung in Deutschland* (Stuttgart, 1932)

Mellor, W. F. (ed.), *Medical History of the Second World War. Casualties and Medical Statistics* (1972)

Members of the University of Glasgow and the University Contingent of the Officers' Training Corps who Served in the Forces of the Crown 1914–1919 (Glasgow, 1922)

The Mermaid Guild of Graduates Supplement (Birmingham, 1917)

Middlebrook, M., *The First Day of the Somme* (1971)

'Military effort of the British Empire', *Round Table*, IX (1919), 1–9

Miller, E. *(ed.), The Neuroses of War* (1944)

Mitchell, T. J. and Smith, G. M., *Medical Services: Casualties and Medical Statistics of the Great War* (1931)

Morgenstern, O., *On the Accuracy of Economic Observations* (1960)

Morris, J. N. and Heady, J. A., 'Social and biological factors in infant mortality. V. Mortality in relation to the father's occupation 1911–1950', *Lancet* (1955), I 554–9

Moss-Blundell, E. W., *The House of Commons Book of Remembrance 1914–1918* (1931)

Mottram, R. H., *The Spanish Farm Trilogy* (1924–7)

Nash, P., *Outline* (1949)

National Register of the United Kingdom and the Isle of the Man. State of Population on 19 September 1939 (1944)

The National University of Ireland. War List. Roll of Honour (Dublin, 1919)

Newberne, P. and Williams, G., 'Nutritional influences on the course of infection', in Dunlop, H., and Moon, H. (eds), *Resistance to Infectious Disease* (Saskatoon, 1970)

Newbolt, H., *History of the Great War. Naval Operations* (1931)

Newsholme, A., *International Studies on the Relation between the Private and Official Practice of Medicine with Special Reference to the Prevention of Disease*, vol. 3, *England and Wales, Scotland, Ireland* (1931)

Notestein, F. *et al.*, *The Future Population of Europe and the Soviet Union* (Geneva, 1944)

Oakley, A., *The Captured Womb* (Oxford, 1984)

O'Brien, A. Mor, 'Patriotism on trial: the strike of the South Wales miners, July 1915', *Welsh History Review*, XXX (1984), 76–104

O'Brien, P., *The New Economic History of the Railways* (1979)

Office of Health Economics, *The Venereal Diseases* (1963)

Omran, A., 'The epidemiological transition: a theory of the epidemiology of population change', *Milbank Memorial Fund Quarterly*, XLIX (1971), 509–38

Oren, L., 'The welfare of women in labouring families in England, 1850–1950', in L. Banner and L. Hartmann (eds), *Clio's Consciousness Raised* (1974), 50–102

Osler, W., *Bacilli and Bullets* (Oxford, 1914)

Palmer, M., *Life-saving in Wartime* (1916)

Panichas, G. A. (ed.), *Promise of Greatness* (1968)

Parker, H. M. D., *Manpower* (1956)

Parsons, I. M., *Men who March Away* (1965)

Pembrey, M. S., 'The restricted supply of food: its relation to health and efficiency', *Journal of the Royal Sanitary Institute*, XXXV (1917), 59–70

'Les pertes des nations belligérantes au cours de la grande guerre', *Archives de la grande guerre* (1921), 1–10

Pollock, C. E., 'Comparison of recruiting statistics in Germany for the year 1906', *Journal of the Royal Army Medical Corps*, XIV (1910), 465

Poock, Monsignor, 'Certain influences affecting the national rate of population', *Transactions of the Manchester Statistical Society*, (1917–18), 31–58

Population Investigation Committee and the Royal College of Obstetricians and Gynaecologists, *Maternity* (1948)

Portway, D., *Militant Don* (1964)

Postan, M. M., 'Some social consequences of the Hundred Years' War', *Economic History Review*, XII (1942), 1–12

Prest, A. R., *Consumer Expenditure in the United Kingdom, 1900–1919* (Cambridge, 1954)

Preston, S., *Mortality Patterns in National Populations* (1976)

Preston, S., Keyfitz, N. and Schoen, R., *Causes of Death. Life Tables for National Populations* (New York, 1972)

Read, H., *A Coat of Many Colours* (1945)

Redmayne, R. A. R., *The British Coal Mining Industry during the War* (Oxford, 1923)

The Regimental Roll of Honour and War Record of the Artists' Rifles (1922)

Register of the Associates and Old Students of the Royal School of Mines (1935)

Register of the Students of the City and Guilds of London College 1884–1934 (1936)

Renouvin, P., *La crise européenne et la première guerre mondiale* (Paris, 1962)

Reports on the Papers and Discussion at the Cambridge Meeting of the British

Association, 1904, and on the Alleged Physical Deterioration of the People and the Utility of an Anthropometric Survey (1905)

Roberts, R., *The Classic Slum* (Harmondsworth, 1966)

Robertson, T. B., 'A comparison of the weights at birth of British infants born in the British Isles, the United States, and Australia', *University of California Publications in Physiology*, IV (1915), 207–10

Rose, M. E., 'The success of social reform? The Central Control Board (Liquor Traffic) 1915–21', in M.R.D. Foot (ed.), *War and Society* (1973)

Rowe, J. W. F., *Wages in Theory and Practice* (1928)

Rowntree, S., *Poverty. A Study in Town Life (1901)*

Rowntree, G. and Carrier, N., 'The resort to divorce in England and Wales, 1858–1957', *Population Studies*, XI (1958), 188–233

Royal Statistical Society, 'Report of special committee on infantile mortality', *Journal of the Royal Statistical Society*, LXXVI (1912), 27–87

The Royal Technical College, Glasgow, Sacrifice and Service in the Great War (Glasgow, 1921)

Saleeby, C., 'The longest price of war', *Proceedings of the Manchester Statistical Society*, CXI (1914–15), 1–12

Saleeby, C., *War and Waste* (Manchester, 1914)

Sassoon, S., *Memoirs of an Infantry Officer* (1930)

Sassoon, S., *Sherston's Progress* (1936)

Sayle, C. (ed.), *The Works of Sir Thomas Browne* (Edinburgh, 1929)

Scharlieb, M., 'The nation's children and our duty towards them', *Nineteenth Century and After*, CXXII (1917), 1277–89

Scharlieb, M., 'The relation of alcohol and alcoholism to maternal and child welfare', *British Journal of Inebriety*, XI (1919), 80–95

Scharlieb, M., 'A terrible census', *Nineteenth Century and After*, LXXXVIII (1920), 128–35

Scharlieb, M., *The Welfare of the Expectant Mother* (1919)

Scott, W. R. and Cunnison, J., *The Industries of the Clyde Valley during the War* (Oxford, 1924)

Scrimshaw, N., Taylor, C. and Gordon, J., *Interactions of Nutrition and Infection* (Geneva, 1968)

Scrimshaw, N., Taylor, C. and Gordon, J., 'Interactions of nutrition and infection', *American Journal of the Medical Sciences*, LX (1959), 363–403

Searle, G., *Eugenics and Politics in Britain 1900–1914* (Leyden, 1979)

Searle, G., *The Quest for National Efficiency* (Oxford, 1971)

Sells, D., *British Wage Boards* (Washington, DC, 1939)

Sen, A., *Poverty and Famines* (Oxford, 1981)

Singer, J. D. and Small, M., *The Wages of War 1815–1965. A Statistical Handbook* (New York, 1972)

Soloway, R. A., *Birth Control and the Population Question in England 1877–1930* (Chapel Hill, NC, 1982)

Stallworthy, J., *Wilfred Owen* (1974)

Statistics of the Military Effort of the British Empire during the Great War (1922)

Stevenson, T. H. C., 'The social distribution of mortality from different causes in England and Wales, 1910–12', *Biometrika*, XV (1923), 382–400

Stocks, P., 'Fifty years of progress as shown by vital statistics', *British Medical Journal* (1950), I, 50–4

Swenarton, M., *Homes Fit for Heroes* (1981)

Tawney, R. H., *The Attack and Other Papers* (1953)

Taylor, W., 'The changing pattern of mortality in England and Wales. I. Infant mortality', *British Journal of Preventive and Social Medicine*, VIII (1954), 1–19

Teitelbaum, M. S., *The British Fertility Decline* (Princeton, 1984)
Teitelbaum, M. S. and Winter, J. M., *The Fear of Population Decline* (New York, 1985)
Temin, P. (ed.), *The New Economic History* (1973)
Thomas, B., *International Migration and Economic Development* (Paris, 1961)
Thomas, B., *Migration and Economic Development. A Study of Great Britain and the Atlantic Economy* (Cambridge, 1973)
Thompson, P., *The Edwardians* (1979)
Thomson, A. Landsborough, *Half a Century of Medical Research.* Volume Two: *The Programme of the Medical Research Council* (UK) (1965)
Thornton, R. K.R. (ed.), *Ivor Gurney. War Letters* (Ashington, 1983)
The Times Diary and Index of the War (1920)
Titmuss, R., *Essays on 'the Welfare State'* (1958)
Turner, J., 'State purchase of the liquor trade in the First World War', *Historical Journal*, XXIII (1980), 589–615
United Nations Demographic Yearbook, 1976 (New York, 1976)
University of St Andrews Roll of Honour and Roll of Service 1914–1919 for King and Country (Edinburgh, 1920)
University of Bristol Annual Report of Council to Court, 1917 (Bristol, 1917)
University of Dublin, Trinity College. War List (Dublin, 1922)
University of Durham Roll of Service (Durham, 1922)
University of Liverpool Calendar 1918–19 (Liverpool, 1918)
University of Liverpool Roll of Service in the Great War 1914–1919 (Liverpool, 1921)
University of Wales Roll of Service 1914–1918 (Bangor, 1921)
Urlanis, B., *Wars and Population* (Moscow, 1971)
Vagts, A., 'Battle and other combat casualties in the Second World War', *Journal of Politics*, VII (1945), 280–95
Villey, D., *Leçons de démographie* (Paris, 1957)
Vondung, K. (ed.), *Kriegserlebnis* (Gottingen, 1979)
Wall, R. and Winter, J. M. (eds), *The Upheaval of War: Family, Work and Welfare in Europe, 1914–1918* (Cambridge, 1986)
Waller, W., *War and the Family* (New York, 1940)
Waller, W., *War and the Family* (New York, 1940)
Waller, W. (ed.), *War in the Twentieth Century* (New York, 1940)
The War Book of Gray's Inn (1921)
Whitaker's Almanac, 1919 (1919)
Whiteside, N., 'Welfare legislation and the unions during the First World War', *Historical Journal*, XXIII (1980), 857–74
Williamson, H., *Patriot's Progress* (1930)
Williamson, H., *The Wet Flanders Plain* (1929)
Winslow, E. A., 'Changes in food consumption among working-class families', *Economica*, II (1922), 250–66
Winter, J. M., 'Aspects of the impact of the First World War on infant mortality in Britain', *Journal of European Economic History*, XI (1982), 713–38
Winter, J. M., 'Balliol's "Lost Generation" of the First World War', *Balliol College Record* (1975), 10–14
Winter, J. M., 'Britain's "Lost Generation" of the First World War', *Population Studies*, XXXI (1977), 449–66
Winter, J. M., 'The decline of mortality in Britain, 1870–1950', in Barker, T. and Drake, M. (eds), *Population and Society* (1982)
Winter, J. M., 'The impact of the First World War on civilian health in Britain', *Economic History Review*, 2nd ser., XXX (1977), 489–504

Winter, J. M., *Infant Mortality in Britain during the First World War*, SSRC Report HR 5071 (1980)

Winter, J. M., 'Military fitness and public health in Britain in the First World War', *Journal of Contemporary History*, xv (1980), 211–44

Winter, J. M., *Socialism and the Challenge of War* (1974)

Winter, J. M., 'Some aspects of the demographic consequences of the First World War in Britain', *Population Studies*, xxx (1976) 539–52

Winter, J. M., 'Unemployment, nutrition and infant mortality in Britain, 1920–1950', in J.M. Winter (ed.), *The Working Class in Modern British History* (Cambridge, 1983)

Winter, J. M., (ed.), *War and Economic Development* (Cambridge, 1975)

Winter, J. M., (ed.), *The Working Class in Modern British History* (Cambridge, 1983)

Women's Co-operative Guild, *Memorandum on the National Care of Maternity* (1918)

Women's Co-operative Guild, *A Rural Maternity and Infant Centre in the Making* (n.p., n.d.)

Wood, F., 'The increase in the cost of food for different classes of society since the outbreak of war', *Journal of the Royal Statistical Society*, LXXIX (1916), 501–8

Woodward, E. L., *Short Journey* (1942)

Wright, Q., *A Study of War* (Chicago, 1942)

Wrigley, C., *Lloyd George and the British Labour Movement* (Brighton, 1976)

Wrigley, E. A. and Schofield, R., *The Population History of England 1541–1871* (1981)

Index